The transformation of Europe since the Second World War is nothing short of staggering. The continent that tore itself apart, then built a physical and ideological barrier through its heart before knocking it all down, may not be ready to embrace Churchill's vision of a 'United States of Europe', but 28 of its nations are members of a single trading market and 17 have so far signed up to a single currency. Such startling political developments, along with the rise of budget airlines, have opened up the continent to travel as never before. Since the 1990s it has been possible to fly from London to Naples on Friday, see the best of the city and fly back in time for Sunday dinner. You can gaze in awe at Picasso's *Guernica* in Madrid one weekend and climb to the top of Norman Foster's Reichstag in Berlin the next. Some feared that such ease of access, combined with the inexorable advance of globalization, would result in an identikit Europe in which national characteristics and idiosyncrasies were lost forever. However, Europe in the 21st century remains wonderfully and startlingly diverse. It is a continent that encompasses the geothermal activity of Reykjavik and the sun-kissed languor of Nice, the Nordic cool of Copenhagen and the cultural intensity of Istanbul. Athens or Amsterdam? Vienna or Venice? Each has its own appeal, whether it's world-class museums, delicious food, cheap booze or stunning architecture. What's more, the recent global economic crisis means that, for many of these cities, the money generated from tourism is more important than ever. The 34 cities listed in this book are all worth at least a weekend of anyone's time, so, go on – give yourself a break.

About the book

From the Acropolis in Athens to Bilbao's Guggenheim Museum, we've highlighted the best of Europe's heritage, old and new, artistic and technological. We have taken the strain out of choosing where to sleep, where to eat and what to do by selecting the very top hotels and restaurants in different price ranges, the best bars, clubs and entertainment venues, and the pick of the sights. On the opening page of each city you'll find handy star ratings that give an immediate idea of the city's stongest and weakest points (1 star = lowest, 5 stars = highest) in six categories: Arts and culture, Eating, Nightlife, Shopping, Sightseeing and Value for money. The highest-scoring cities in each category are shown opposite. So whatever you want from your city break, this guide will point you in the right direction.

Hotel price codes
€€€ Expensive, over €200
€€ Mid-range, €100-200
€ Cheap, under €100
Prices are for a double room in high season.

Restaurant price codes
€€€ Expensive, over €200
€€ Mid-range, €20-40
€ Cheap, under €20
Prices are for a two-course meal without drinks or service.

European City Breaks

C70217470/

Contents

Star cities

★ Arts and culture

★ Eating

★ Nightlife

Berlin p46; Budapest p84; Florence p138; London p166.

Cities that have an outstanding reputation for all-round cultural excellence, with vibrant art, literature, theatre and music scenes.

Brussels p74; Istanbul p148; London p166; Paris p220.

Cities that have a thriving culinary scene and a number of world-class restaurants.

Athens p16; Barcelona p26; Berlin p46; Lisbon p158; London p166; Madrid p178; Valencia p294.

The ultimate places to party after dark.

★ Sightseeing

★ Shopping

★ Value for money

Florence p138; Istanbul p148; London p166; Paris p220; Rome p266; Venice p302.

The places to go for world famous sights: museums, monuments, castles, towers, Ferris wheels, etc.

Barcelona p26; Istanbul p148; London p166; Milan p196; Paris p220.

Cities with outstanding and varied retail therapy opportunities.

Lisbon p158; Naples p202.

The best places to go if you are on a tight budget.

Ratings

Art and culture ☆☆☆☆☆
Eating ☆☆☆
Nightlife ☆☆☆☆
Shopping ☆☆☆
Sightseeing ☆☆☆☆
Value for money ☆☆☆
Overall city rating ☆☆☆

Amsterdam

Amsterdam shouldn't really exist. The city was dragged out of marshy bogs, dried and carved into the place we know today. It was an unconventional start, and one which seems to have set the tone for things to come. Today, despite something of a conservative Dutch backlash, Amsterdam remains Europe's most non-conformist city. Locals shun the car and choose instead to career around on bicycles. Prostitution is both legal and public, and this is the only city in the world where you can peruse a cannabis menu and smoke a joint in a coffeeshop. The Netherlands was also the first country to legalize marriage between gay couples. Alongside these progressive ways are, conversely, some of Europe's greatest traditional attractions. The Rijksmuseum and Van Gogh Museum hold two of the finest art collections in the world, while smaller museums, such as the Anne Frank House or Rembrandthuis, provide a real insight into the city's past. The city's future direction seems less certain. Its 'anything goes' attitude is under threat from the government's new hard line on soft drugs, which has seen a fall in the number of coffeeshops, and the main political parties are distancing themselves from the city's tradition of multiculturalism. Is Amsterdam becoming less tolerant, more like the rest of Europe? It somehow seems unlikely in this engaging, liberal oddball of a city.

Canal reflections.

At a glance

Amsterdam's old centre is hemmed in by the Ij River and Centraal Station to the north, and spreads south in a web of medieval streets and canals. The main arteries are Damrak and Rokin, busy thoroughfares which split the centre into the **Nieuwe Zijde** (New Side), to the west of Dam Square, and the **Oude Zijde** (Old Side) to the east.

The red-light district, **De Wallen**, lies on the Old Side and is a predictably seedy grid of streets, though not without its charm. Beyond here are the **Nieuwmarkt** and **Plantage** districts, home to Amsterdam's biggest flea market and Rembrandt's house. To the north is the **Oostelijk Havengebied**, extensively renovated docklands holding some impressively adventurous architecture.

West of Damrak, Nieuwe Zijde is Amsterdam's main shopping area and leads to the **Grachtengordel**, the four major canals that ring the old centre. South of the Grachtengordel is the **Museumplein** (Museum Quarter), full of grand old buildings, including – most famously – the enormous, neo-Gothic Rijksmuseum.

24 hours in the city

Sip a wake-up coffee at **Café Luxembourg** before heading south to the Museumplein, where you should pop into the **Rijksmuseum** to admire its refurbishment and to ogle Rembrandt's *Nightwatch*. A few steps along Museumplein brings you to the **Van Gogh Museum**, which warrants a good few hours. Get a breath of fresh air with a boat trip along the canals of the Grachtengordel before heading to one of the pavement cafés on **Nieuwmarkt** for lunch. Afterwards, hire a bike and either head south for a snoop around the flea market on **Waterlooplein**, or west to gawp at the painted ladies of the red-light district. Then pedal over to **Anne Frank's House**. Have an early evening drink in one of the many *bruine cafés* and then cross town for contemporary Dutch cuisine in the history-soaked interior of **d'Vijff Vlieghen**. Finish off in the **Sugar Factory**, a 'multi-disciplinary night theatre' where nightclub and performance mix.

Dam Square

Tram 4, 9, 14, 16, 24 or 25. Map C2.

Known simply as the 'Dam', this broad, tourist- and pigeon-filled square lies at the core of Amsterdam's medieval centre. It was the location of the original dam across the Amstel which gave the city its name. The **Koninklijk Paleis** (Royal Palace), originally the town hall, was built between 1648 and 1665 in an imposing Dutch Classicist style. It became a royal residence when Louis Bonaparte kicked out the mayor in 1808, during the French occupation, and it is now used for state functions. Nearby is the **Nieuwe Kerk**, dating from 1408, while, in the centre of the square, is the city's war memorial, a rather stark obelisk and a popular meeting place.

De Wallen red-light district

Tram 4, 9, 14, 16, 24 or 25. Map D2.

Amsterdam's infamous red-light district covers the area to the east of Damrak and is as seedy as you'd expect. Prostitutes pose in windows; groups of beery lads barter with pimps, and touts try to entice passers-by with promises of live sex shows. But the area is also such a tourist attraction that it rarely feels threatening (at least not during the day). You'll be sharing the pavement with giggling couples and family groups wandering nonchalantly past the brothel windows. The area also has some of the city's most attractive old houses. Stroll along **Warmoesstraat** to take in the elegant façades, interspersed with sex shops and red-lit windows, and along any of the little streets branching off between **Oudezijds Voorburgwal** and **Ousezijds Achterburgwal** canals.

Two important sights in the area are, ironically, religious. Just east of Warmoesstraat is **De Oude Kerk**, *Oudekerksplein 23, Mon-Sat 1100-1700, Sun 1300-1700,* Amsterdam's oldest church, an attractive Gothic structure with a beautiful tower, dating from the 14th century. A few steps north is **Ons' Lieve Heer op Solder** (Our Lord in The Attic), *Oudezijds Voorburgwal 40, T020 624 6604, www. opsolder.nl, Mon-Sat 1000-1700, Sun 1300-1700, €8,*

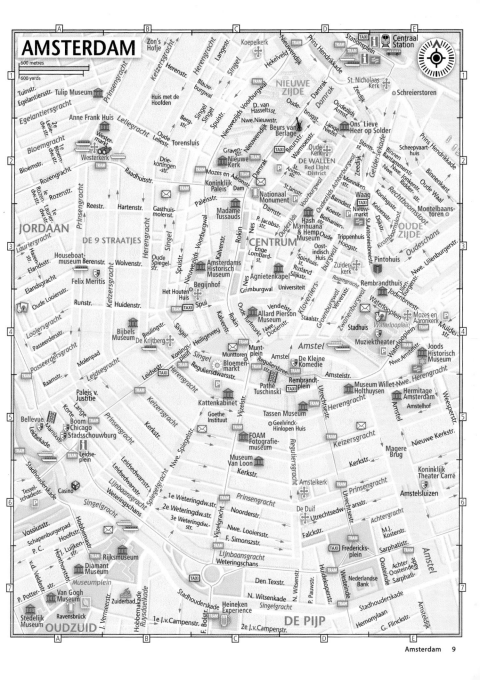

Up in smoke

Thank heavens for Bob Marley. Without Bob and the Rastafarian flag – green, gold and red stripes – tourists would have a tough time spotting a coffeeshop in Amsterdam. That's 'coffeeshop', not coffeehouse. The difference, of course, is that the former is permitted to sell cannabis, although it's illegal to advertise this fact. Hence all the Rasta paraphernalia: a sure-fire way to tell tourists that they've come to the right (or wrong) place, depending on their views. Amsterdam remains the only city in the world with such a liberal attitude towards soft drugs, attracting a fare percentage of drug tourists, much to the annoyance of many locals and politicians. The law is very clear on what it will tolerate: an individual can possess 30 g and can buy up to 5 g of cannabis at a time from a licensed purveyor. Any use of hard drugs (heroin, cocaine and ecstasy) is strictly illegal. Coffeeshops aren't permitted to sell alcohol, and there's an age limit of 18. Recent rumours about limiting tourists' access to coffeeshops have proved unfounded, and for now it seems this unique side of Amsterdam is here to stay.

second-hand clothes, old vinyl records and leather jackets. The square is lorded over by the 1986 Stadhuis and Muziektheater, designed by Willem Holzbauer and known locally as the **Stopera** (a combination of 'Stad' and 'Opera'). Although the complex was hugely controversial when it was built, the theatre now has an excellent reputation. Free concerts are held here at least once a week.

Rembrandthuis

Jodenbreestraat 4, T020 520 0400, www.rembrandthuis.nl.
Daily 1000-1800. €12.50. Metro to Nieuwmarkt, Hoogstraat exit. Tram 9 or 14. Map E4.

an ordinary townhouse with an extraordinary attic, containing the city's only surviving clandestine church. It dates from the Reformation, when public Catholic worship was outlawed.

Nieuwmarkt

Metro Nieuwmarkt. Map D3.

Once a major market for inhabitants from the nearby Jewish quarter – all but wiped out during the Nazi occupation – this broad square is today flanked by cafés and shops, leading to the city's Chinatown in Zeedijk, just to the north. The square is towered over by **De Waag**, a 15th-century fortress-like structure, once a city gate. During the week there's a small fruit and vegetable market, and, in summer, an antique market is held here every Sunday.

Waterlooplein

Tram 4, 9 or 14. Metro Waterlooplein. Map E4.

Amsterdam's oldest **flea market**, *Mon-Sat 0900-1800*, is a labyrinthine sprawl of stalls, stuffed with

This graceful house was Rembrandt's home from 1639 to 1658. He lived in the elegant rooms on the ground floor and worked in the large studio upstairs during his most successful period. Today the rooms are stocked with original fittings and period furniture. Also on display is a superb collection of his etchings – over 260 pieces.

Nieuwe Zijde

Tram 1, 2, 13 or 17. Map D1.

The New Side of the medieval centre was actually settled earlier than the Oude Zijde and today covers the area west of the Dam. It's a mixed area of uninspiring shopping and pretty side streets, leading to the Grachtengordel. Worth a look is the **Amsterdam Museum**, *Kalverstraat 92, T020 523 1822, www.amsterdammuseum.nl, daily 1000-1700 (closed public holidays), €10*, located in the old city orphanage. As well as housing some interesting paintings, the building itself, with its two courtyards and winding corridors, is fascinating.

Anne Frank House

Prinsengracht 263, T020 556 7100, www.annefrank.org.
Apr to Oct daily 0900-2100; Nov-Mar daily 0900-1900, closed Yom Kippur. €9.50.
Tram 13 or 17. Bus 21, 170, 171 or 172 to Westermarkt. Map B2.

The gripping, heart-breaking story of Anne Frank is one of the most enduring accounts of life in hiding during the Second World War. The unassuming house provides a harrowing glimpse of the claustrophobic existence behind blacked-out windows led by the Frank family and friends for two years during the Nazi occupation. The diary itself, sitting alone in a glass case, is startlingly poignant. The only survivor of the Frank family was Anne's father, Otto, who returned to the house, published the diary and helped to open the museum in 1960. The entrance is now in a modern building next door.

Opposite page: Rembrandt statue.
Above: Rijksmuseum.

Rijksmuseum

Jan Luijkenstraat 1, T020 674 7000, www.rijksmuseum.nl.
Daily 0900-1700. €15. Tram 2 or 5 to Hobbemastraat, 12 to Concertgebouw, or 6, 7 or 10 to Spiegelgracht. Map B7.

Amsterdam's enormous flagship museum displays masterpieces of Dutch art as well temporary exhibitions. The building itself, designed by Pierre Cuypers, is a striking neo-Gothic riot of towers, turrets and stained glass windows and dominates the Museum Quarter. It finally re-opened its doors in 2013 after a multi-million pound renovation. Inside, the collection is split into various sections, most famous of which is the extraordinary Dutch Golden Age collection of paintings. Other sections include sculpture, decorative arts, prints and photographs.

The museum's prize piece, Rembrandt's *Nightwatch*, is still on show; it's worth visiting for this alone. The painting was originally called *The Militia Company of Captain Frans Banning Cocq* but became known as the 'Nightwatch' as the picture darkened with grime over the years; it has since been cleaned to reveal its true daytime setting.

Van Gogh Museum

Paulus Potterstraat 7, T020 570 5200, www.vangoghmuseum.nl.
Daily May-Aug daily 0900-1800, Sep-Apr daily 0900- 1700. €15. Tram 2, 3, 5 or 12 to between Paulus Potterstraat and Van Baerlestraat. Map A7.

Travel essentials

Getting there

Schiphol Airport (www.schiphol.nl) lies 15 km southwest of the city centre. Trains run from beneath the main concourse to Centraal Station every 15 mins 0445-2400 and every hour thereafter, taking 15 mins (€3.90 single). Buses also run to the centre, including No 370 which stops in the Museum Quarter. A taxi to the centre takes around 20 mins and costs about €45. **Schiphol Travel Taxi**, T0900 8876, is a good-value shared minibus.

Centraal Station, T0900-9296, www.ns.nl, Amsterdam's main station, is right in the centre of town at the end of Damrak. There are regular international services, including a high-speed link with Brussels Midi for connections to the Eurostar. Another high-speed service, the Dutch Flyer, links Centraal Station with the Hook of Holland for ferries to and from Harwich.

Getting around

Most of the city's main sights are within easy walking distance of each other. Alternatively, make like a local and hire a bike; a list of recommended outlets is provided on the iamsterdam.com website. The average rental price for a full day is €8. The public transport system is excellent; trams are the most useful, but there are also buses and a small metro (best for outlying districts). All public transport is run by the **GVB**, www.gvb.nl, which has an information and ticket office opposite Centraal Station. Its website is also a great source of travel information. Tickets can be bought at tram stops, newsagents and on board trams and buses. A smart-card ticketing system, **OV-chipkaart**, is available, but the €7.50 fee for the card itself means that it probably isn't worth buying for short visits to the city. Alternatively, travel passes, valid on the whole network, cost €7.50, €12 or €16.50 for 24, 48 and 72 hrs. Taxis have ranks around the city but are pricey.

Tourist information

The main office is opposite Centraal Station, T0900 400 4040, www.iamsterdam.com, daily 0900-1700. There's another inside the station, Mon-Thu and Sat 0800-2000, Fri 0800-2100, Sun 0900-1700; and another on the corner of Leidseplein and Leidsestraat, daily 0900-1700. The **IAmsterdam City Card** offers unlimited travel on public transport, a free canal boat trip, and free entrance to most of the city's museums. Tickets cost €42, €52 or €62 for 1, 2, or 3 days and are available from the tourist and GVB information offices. Among the canal tours, the most useful is **Lovers Museumboat**, T020 530 1090, www.lovers.nl, a hop-on/hop-off service stopping at all major museums. Tickets cost €20 and include reduced entry to museums.

One of Amsterdam's finest museums holds the world's largest Vincent Van Gogh collection: over 200 pieces bequeathed by his art-collector brother, Theo. The modern building is split into five periods, starting with Van Gogh's dark Dutch works and evolving, via Paris and Arles in the south of France, into the extraordinarily lively and colourful palette for which he is known. Strikingly, Van Gogh's career lasted little longer than a decade but this marvellous collection does much to highlight how rich and productive those 10 years were. Highlights include *The Potato Eaters*, *Bedroom in Arles* and *Wheatfield with Crows*. Also in the museum are the artist's sketches, as well as works by his contemporaries, including close friend Paul Gauguin; Van Gogh famously cut off part of his ear lobe after an argument with his artist friend.

Joods Historisch Museum

Nieuwe Amstelstraat 1, T020 531 0310, www.jhm.nl.
Daily 1100-1700, closed Yom Kippur. €12. Metro Waterlooplein. Tram 9 or 14. Map E4.

The Jewish History Museum is housed in a series of four beautiful synagogues dating from the 17th century, linked by walkways. First opened in 1930, the museum was closed and ransacked during the Second World War, and it was not until the 1980s that it was restored and re-opened. It now houses a thorough collection depicting the history of Jewish life in the Netherlands, highlighting the enormous contribution Jews made to the development of Amsterdam over the centuries.

Where to stay

Amsterdam's status as a hip city-break destination means that its plentiful hotel beds don't often come cheap; moreover, most places get booked up, particularly in late spring (tulip season) and summer, so it's always essential to book ahead. Avoid the hotel touts who hang around Centraal Station.

Amstel InterContinental €€€
Professor Tulpplein 1, T020 622 6060, www.amsterdam. intercontinental.com.
The city's grande dame towers on the bank of the Amstel and attracts an impressive list of rock stars and royalty. It's a classically large, elegant hotel, with posh rooms complete with Dutch wallpaper and huge beds. The Michelin-starred La Rive restaurant is highly acclaimed.

The Dylan €€€
Keizersgracht 384, T020 530 2010, www.dylanamsterdam.com.
Style guru Anouchka Hempel designed this small hotel (formerly Blakes). Rooms are individually themed, all centred on a courtyard, and there is an excellent fusion restaurant downstairs.

Ambassade €€€-€€
Herengracht 341, T020 555 0222, www.ambassade-hotel.nl.
Ten 17th-century canalside houses make up this hotel in a lovely spot on Herengracht. This is one for bibliophiles: John Le Carré, Umberto Eco and Salman Rushdie have all stayed here (check out the signed copies in the library). Rooms are traditional and plush; those in the eaves are the most appealing.

Seven Bridges €€€-€€
Reguliersgracht 31, T020 623 1329, www.sevenbridgeshotel.nl.
Set in a 300-year-old house, this hotel is quiet, with rooms overlooking either the canal and the famous Seven Bridges or a small garden. Breakfast is served in your room. Book months in advance.

Lloyd €€€-€
Oostelijke Handelskade 34, T020 561 3636, www.lloydhotel.nl.
In an experiment, architects and designers joined forces to create the world's first 1-5 star hotel. The result is stunning, with an eclectic range of features and styles that successfully combine modern and vintage to offer something for everyone, whatever their taste.

Canal House €€
Keizersgracht 148, T020 622 5182, www.canalhouse.nl.
Canal House is impeccably styled with sleek, contemporary grey and purple fabrics and a touch of humour in the contemporary art. The location on the Keizersgracht canal is peaceful.

Amistad Hotel €
Kerkstraat 42, T020 624 8074, www.amistad.nl.
Run by husband-and-husband team, Johan and Joost, the Amistad is one of the most popular gay hotels in town. Simple, colourful rooms come with or without en suite bathrooms and have wooden floors and bright artwork. There's an internet lounge in the reception area.

Amstel InterContinental.

Restaurants

Traditional Dutch fare isn't the lightest of cuisines: expect hearty meat-and-potato dishes, thick pancakes oozing all sorts of fillings, and hefty *broodjes* (sandwiches) stacked with meat, cheeses or fish. Having said that, chefs across the city are also wallowing in an orgy of fusion cuisine, which often puts French or Asian slants on Dutch dishes. Holland's colonial heritage also means lots of Indonesian flavours, and the city's multicultural population ensures plenty of Chinese, Thai, Italian and Japanese restaurants to choose from.

Breakfast

De Bakkerswinkel €
Warmoesstraat 69, T020 489 8000.
Breakfast, lunch and tea only. Bustling, airy deli/café, completely renovated in 2013, serving excellent brunches, sandwiches and fat slices of quiche.

Winkel €
Noordermarkt 43, T020 623 0223.
Big breakfasts and legendary apple cake at this lively Jewish Quarter café. Be prepared to queue on Mon and Sat (market days).

Lunch

Café Luxembourg €
Spui 24, T020 620 6264.
Elegant café with a long marble bar and equally long menu, including favourites like split pea soup, salmon burgers and *kroketten* (croquettes).

Newspapers and a slow pace in the morning; more frenetic at lunch and dinner.

Pannekoekhuis Upstairs €
Grimburgwal 2, T020 626 5603.
Students flock to this tiny pancake house dolling out good-value servings of filled sweet and savoury pancakes. Service can be slow.

Singel 404 €
Singel 404, T020 428 0154.
A lunch-time institution in Amsterdam. Singel 404 is renowned for serving the city's best sandwiches, so attracts the locals in their droves. An impressive range of breads are available with a multitude of filling options. Should keep you going for an afternoon of sightseeing.

Dinner

Blauw aan de Wal €€€
Achterburgwal 99, T020 330 2257.
This is a real find, hidden away down an alley in the heart of the red-light district. Chic Mediterranean cuisine is the order of the day. Old wooden floors, bare brick walls and a pretty courtyard make it all rather romantic.

Christophe €€€
Leliegracht 46, T020 625 0807, www.restaurantchristophe.nl.
Tue-Sat dinner.
Classic restaurant in a quiet canal-side location. The

atmosphere is discreet and elegant (jackets are required) and the food is a sumptuous feast of French-inspired contemporary cooking. Reservations are essential.

d'Vijff Vlieghen €€
Spuistraat 294-302, T020 530 4060, www.thefiveflies.com.
Dinner only.
You won't have this place to yourself, but it's worth braving the tour groups for the food. The menu is top-notch Dutch, served in a lovely string of 17th-century houses filled with antiques and Delft tiles. Look out for the Rembrandt etchings on the walls.

Kantjil en de Tijger €€
Spuistraat 291-293, T020 620 0994, www.kantjil.nl.
Refreshingly free of the usual oriental decor, this large, chic space serves *rijsttafel* (rice table): an array of up to 20 Indonesian dishes. Arrive with an appetite. The spicy coconut prawns are good, too.

Moeders €€
Rozengracht 251, T020 618 1884, www.moeders.com.
Dozens of portraits and photographs of mothers (*moeders*) gaze down from the walls, keeping an eye on the traditional Dutch menu of hearty meals served in charming surroundings.

Getto €
Warmoesstraat 51, T020 421 5151.
**Tue-Sun dinner only,
closed Mon.**
Not your average burger joint but worth a visit for the experience. The Diva burgers on offer are all named after one of the venue's drag queen acts. Very chilled and relaxed, with a warm welcome for everyone.

Nightlife

The tourist office website, www.iamsterdam.com, has a wealth of information on what's going on around the city, covering everything from live music and events to exhibitions and museums. Amsterdam has a huge gay and lesbian scene – many call it the gay capital of Europe – with countless gay-friendly hotels, bars and clubs. These are mostly focused on the area around Reguliersdwarsstraat.

Bars and coffeeshops
Don't be put off by the term *bruine cafés* (brown cafés); these ubiquitous café-bars are the cosy mainstay of Amsterdam's nightlife and get their name because smoke has stained the walls with nicotine over the years. Lovely. Nevertheless, these friendly pubs, found all over the old centre and along the canals, are a great place to meet locals and try Dutch beer. Note that you are not allowed to smoke (anything) in these and other bars. For legal cannabis, head to a 'coffeeshop', again found throughout the centre and identified by the leaf motif or Rasta flag in the window (see page 10). These generally have menus selling various types of cannabis. Take it easy, especially with hash cakes and cookies, which can pack a powerful punch.

For a chilled-out bar scene, often with DJs and dancing late into the night, try out some of the newer lounge bars around Nieuwezijds Voorburgwal, as well as the more traditional nightlife spots around Rembrandtplein and Leidseplein.

Clubs and live music
The club scene isn't as cutting edge as you might hope, although there are some good places in the centre. The **Nachttheater Sugar Factory**, *Lijnbaansgracht 238, www.sugarfactory.nl*, combines a wide range of late-night performances with a left-field club. **Bitterzoet**, *Spuistraat 2, www.bitterzoet.com*, serves up some funk and soul for a more laid-back clubbing experience and is a refreshing break from the city's many techno-fuelled club nights.

De Wallen red-light district.

Ratings

Art and culture ☆☆☆☆☆
Eating ☆☆☆☆
Nightlife ☆☆☆☆☆
Shopping ☆☆☆
Sightseeing ☆☆☆☆☆
Value for money ☆☆☆
Overall city rating ☆☆☆☆

Athens

In preparation for the 2004 Olympics, Athens was spruced up, refined and beautified, bringing it into the 21st century with gusto. Ancient monuments were restored, neoclassical façades repainted, billboards and neon lighting torn down, the metro extended, tramlines added, pedestrian zones paved and trees planted. Since then, of course, it has experienced the crippling effects of the economic downturn. The Greek government accepted two multi-billion-euro bailouts from the European Union and the International Monetary Fund to avoid total bankruptcy on the condition that it implemented stringent austerity measures: hence, the highly publicized demonstrations, the surge in unemployment and the gradual breakdown of social services. In such testing economic times, the money generated from tourism is more important than ever. What's more, Athens has not lost its visitor appeal: far from it. This is a city where countless layers of history sit concrete-upon-brick-upon-stone, and, although it's under serious pressure to westernize, you'll still find a curious juxtaposition of Western European, Balkan and Middle Eastern cultures, all of which are reflected in the food, the music and the architecture. This is also the city that, back in its ancient heyday, invented hedonism; even now, the city seems able to shrug off its cares to ensure that Athens nightlife is still beautiful, extravagant and inexhaustible.

Reflection of Mount Lycabettus.

At a glance

Take the **Acropolis** as your main point of reference. If you are on a short stay, you'll probably be based in **Plaka**, Athens' oldest residential neighbourhood, skirting the Acropolis' northern and eastern slopes. The northern limit of Plaka is marked by **Ermou** (the main shopping street), which runs east–west from **Syntagma** (home to the Greek Parliament) to **Monastiraki**, best known for its Sunday morning flea market and its metro station, then proceeds to smart residential **Thissio** and **Gazi**. On the far side of Ermou lies Psirri and, northeast of Syntagma, the rocky mound of **Mount Lycabettus** (Lycabettus Hill) rises above the well-to-do area of **Kolonaki**. Gazi and Psirri deserve a special mention: both former industrial zones, they have recently been transformed into night-time districts filled with happening bars, restaurants, clubs and art galleries.

Another welcome addition to Athens is the new **Archaeological Promenade**, a 4-km paved, lamp-lit walkway that now links the city's ancient sites. Starting from the new Akropolis metro station, Dionissiou Areopagitou curves around the south side of the Acropolis to join Apostolou Pavlou, which then runs alongside the Ancient Agora to bring you to Thissio. From here Adrianou runs east to Plaka, while Ermou runs west past **Kerameikos** (ancient Athens' cemetery) towards Gazi.

Acropolis

Acropolis Hill, Plaka, T210 321 0219, odysseus.culture.gr.
Summer daily 0800-2000; winter daily 0830-1500. €12 (this ticket also gives free entry to the Ancient Agora, Roman Forum, Theatre of Dionysus, Kerameikos and the Temple of Olympian Zeus and is valid for 4 days). Metro Akropolis or Monastiraki. Map B5.

Most stunning at night, when it rises above the modern city bathed in golden floodlights, the Acropolis is a rocky mound crowned by three ancient temples, symbolizing the birth of Athens and indeed of Western civilization. Today it receives some three million visitors per year and is also the biggest selling point for hotel rooms and restaurant terraces claiming to glimpse its magic.

The largest and most revered temple is the fifth-century BC **Parthenon**, built entirely from marble. Supported by 46 Doric columns, it was originally intended as a sanctuary for Athena and housed a giant gold and ivory statue of the goddess. The other most important buildings are the Propylaia, the Erechtheion and the temple of Athena Nike.

Acropolis Museum

Dionysiou Areopagitou 15, Plaka, T210 900 0900, www.theacropolismuseum.gr.
Apr-Oct Tue-Thu and Sat-Sun 0800-2000, Fri 0800-2200; Nov-Mar Tue-Thu 0900-1700, Fri 0900-2200, Sat-Sun 0900-2000. €5. Map B5.

Designed by Swiss architect Bernard Tschumi, the museum combines glass, steel and concrete, creating light and airy spaces for the display of archaic and classical statues and other finds from the Acropolis site. The top floor is devoted to the marble frieze that once ran around the Parthenon. Around half the bas-reliefs are originals, while the rest, made up of crude white plaster copies, mark the pieces that were taken by Lord Elgin, British Ambassador to Athens, in 1816 and sold to the British Museum. This poignant presentation is intended as a message to London that it is time the

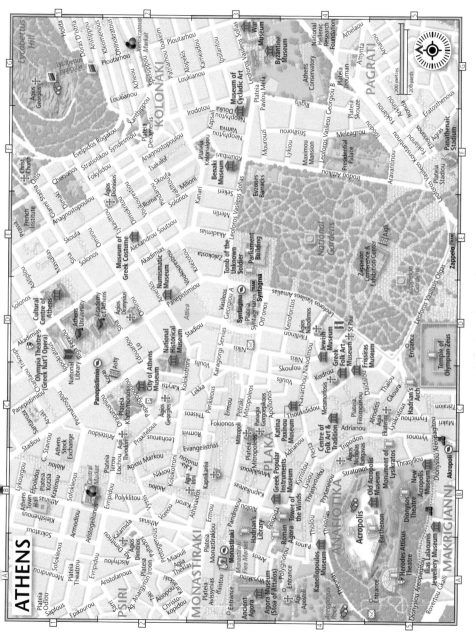

ATHENS

Around the city

controversial Elgin Marbles (Greeks prefer to call them the Parthenon Marbles) were returned to their homeland. There's an excellent café-restaurant on the second floor (see Restaurants, page 24).

Plaka

Metro Acropolis or Monastiraki. Map A3.

Built into the hillside below the Acropolis, Plaka is Athens' oldest residential quarter. Touristy but undeniably charming, it's made up of cobbled alleys lined with pastel-coloured neoclassical mansions dating from the late 19th century. (During this period Greece was trying to re-establish its cultural identity after liberation from the Ottoman Turks.) The only really old buildings remaining here are Byzantine churches. Particularly notable is the 12th-century **Little Mitropolis**, *daily 0700-1300*, standing next to the far less attractive 19th-century **cathedral**, and the residential area of **Anafiotika**, a cluster of whitewashed Cycladic-style houses built by settlers from the island of Anafi. Besides the countless souvenir shops and tavernas, look out for the museums of **Greek Popular Musical**

Below: Plaka.
Opposite page: Tower of the Winds, Agora .

Instruments, *Diogenous 1-3, www.instruments-museum.gr, Tue and Thu-Sun 1000-1400, Wed 1200-1800, free*, and **Greek Folk Art**, *Kidathineon 17, www.melt.gr, Tue-Sun 0800-1500.*

Ancient Agora

Andrianou 24, Monastiraki, T210 321 0185, odysseus.culture.gr.
Apr-Oct daily 0800-1900; Nov-Mar daily 0800-1500. €4. Metro Monastiraki. Map A3.

Today, Agora is a romantic wilderness of coarse grazing land and olive trees, strewn with fallen columns and crowned by an ancient temple. During the Golden Age, however, this was Athens' main marketplace, as well as the city's political, administrative and cultural heart. It was here that Socrates and St Paul made their public speeches and where democracy was born, although now you'll need some imagination to interpret it as such.

The buildings that remain recognisably intact are the remarkably well-preserved fifth-century BC **Temple of Haephaistos**, the **Tower of the Winds** and the **Stoa of Attalos**, a two-storey structure from the second century BC that originally functioned as a trading centre but today houses the **Agora Museum**, displaying ancient finds from the site.

Central Market

Sofokleous and Evripidou.
Mon-Sat 0900-1500. Metro Monastiraki or Omonia. Map B1.

Modern-day Athenians shop within the halls of the vast covered market, an iron and glass structure erected in 1870. A veritable feast for the eyes, it is here that you will find stalls trading in seasonal Mediterranean fruit and vegetables, dried figs, nuts, olives and spices. In the seafood section are glittering silver-scaled fish and copious quantities of octopus and squid displayed upon mounds of freshly ground ice, while the meat section (definitely not for the squeamish) is populated by blood-splattered butchers hacking at carcasses on tree trunks that improvize as chopping boards.

National Archaeological Museum

Patission 44, Omonia, T210 821 7717,
www.namuseum.gr.
Apr-Oct Mon 1300-2000, Tue-Sat 0800-2000 and
Sun 0800-1500; Nov-Mar Mon 1300-2000 and
Tue-Sun 0800-1500. €7. Metro Victoria.

Holding one of the world's finest collections of
ancient Greek art, this museum is a must-see.
The light and airy marble-floored exhibition spaces
show off elegant classical sculpture to maximum
effect. It's vast so don't try to see everything, but
be sure to catch the subtly coloured 16th-century
BC **Thira Frescoes**, found buried below lava
following a volcanic explosion on the island of
Santorini, and the **Mycenaen Collection**, a hoard
of gold jewellery and weaponry dating from the
16th to the 11th centuries BC.

Benaki Museum

Vassilissis Sofias and Koumbari 1, Kolonaki,
T210 367 1000, www.benaki.gr.
Wed and Fri 0900-1700, Thu and Sat 0900- 2400,
Sun 0900-1500. € 7 (free Thu). Metro Syntagma.
Map F3.

Born in Alexandria, Egypt, in 1873, Antonios Benakis
was an avid art collector who gave this neoclassical
house and his entire art collection to the Greek
state before his death in 1954. A journey through
the history of Greek art from 3000 BC up to the
20th century, exhibits include sculpture, ceramics,
jewellery, paintings, furniture and costumes, laid
out in chronological order. Top attractions include
a hoard of second-century BC golden filigree
jewellery inlaid with precious stones, known as the
Thessaly Treasure, two early paintings by El Greco,
and the reconstruction of two wooden-panelled
living rooms from an Ottoman-inspired house in
northern Greece from the 1750s.

Byzantine Museum

Vassilissis Sofias 22, Kolonaki, T213 213 9572,
www.byzantinemuseum.gr.
Apr-Oct Tue-Sun 0900-1800; Nov-Mar Tue-Sun
0800-1500. €4. Metro Evangelismos. Map G3.

Hidden below the courtyard of an Italianate villa,
this open-plan, split-level, underground exhibition
space opened in 2004. Pieces are displayed in
chronological order, following the development

Festivals

Each summer, from June to the end of September, the **Hellenic Festival** stages open-air theatre, opera, classical music and dance at the ancient **Odeon of Herodes Atticus**, plus rock concerts at the hilltop **Lycabettus Theatre**. A stunning venue, the second-century Odeon is carved into rocks on the southern slope of the Acropolis. The 28-m façade serves as a backdrop to the stage, and the semi-circular auditorium, with a radius of 38 m, can seat an audience of 5000. The building was commissioned by the Roman consul, Herodes Atticus, in memory of his wife Regilla. The modern festival dates back to 1955; legendary figures that have graced its stage include Maria Callas, Margot Fonteyn and Rudolph Nureyev. More recent performers include Demis Roussos, Philip Glass and the Vienna Philharmonic Orchestra.

Performances commence at 2100 (Jun-Aug) and 2030 (Sep). Advance booking begins three weeks prior to each performance; see www.greekfestival.gr for programme details and online ticket sales. Tickets are also available from the **Hellenic Festival Box Office**, 39 Panepistimiou (in the arcade), T210-327 2000 (credit card only), Mon-Fri 0900-1700 and Sat 0900-1500, and from the Odeon itself: **Odeon of Herodes Atticus**, Dionysiou Areopagitou, daily 0900-1400 and 1800-2100.

of the Byzantine Empire from the advent of Christianity (when many pagan symbols were absorbed by the creed) up to the fall of Constantinople in 1453. The exhibition starts with stone carvings, sculpture and mosaics taken from early basilicas. It then continues with icons depicting sultry eyed saints against golden backgrounds, frescoes illustrating biblical events and minutely detailed silver and gold jewellery and ecclesiastical artefacts.

Mount Lycabettus (Lycabettus Hill)

Metro Evangelismos. Map G1.

Athens' highest vantage point at 295 m, Lycabettus affords panoramic views of the city, the mountains and the sea. A network of footpaths leads up through pinewoods and lush vegetation to the summit. If the hike is too steep, take a taxi or catch the **funicular** from *Ploutarchou St in Kolonaki, every 30 mins daily 0900-0300*, for a two-minute whizz through a cliff-side tunnel. The peak is capped by the tiny white **Church of St George** and a series of terraces hosting the

Orizontes restaurant and a café. Carved into the rocks on the north-facing slope, the open-air **Lycabettus Theatre** stages summer concerts. Recent performers have included Placebo and Groove Armada.

Technopolis

Pireos 100, Gazi, T210 346 1589.
Hours vary depending on exhibitions. Free. Metro Kerameikos.

Technopolis (Art City) occupies the former city gasworks. A multi-purpose arts complex, the disused gas tanks and brick outbuildings have been converted to provide a series of spaces for exhibitions, concerts (Florence and the Machine, Friendly Fires and Shantel have played here) and theatre, while the towering brick chimneys are lit red at night and remain the symbol of new art in an urban environment.

Where to stay

Syntagma is where you'll find grand expensive hotels, the Greek Parliament and lots of traffic. For romance and easy sightseeing, opt for Plaka. For nightlife and a gritty downtown ambience, try Monastiraki and Psirri. Avoid Syngrou: it's functional and impersonal and aimed primarily at business travellers. Omonia is seedy and not very pretty.

Electra Palace €€€
Nikodimou 18, Plaka, T210 337 0000, www.electra hotels.gr.
The EP's yellow-and-white neoclassical façade, complete with wrought-iron balconies, was added during renovation for the Olympics. It's now Plaka's most stylish hotel. Some rooms have an Acropolis view. There's a small spa, plus an outdoor infinity pool and summer restaurant on the roof.

Fresh €€€
Sophocleous 26 and Klisthenous, Psirri, T210 524 8511, www.freshhotel.gr.
Close to the gritty Central Market, the look at this designer hotel is minimalist, with fresh flowers, lounge music, and vivid orange, green and pink details adding to the fun. There's a summer rooftop bar with a pool and sundeck, and nouvelle Greek cuisine served in the ground floor restaurant.

New Hotel €€€
Filellinon 16, Syntagma, T210 327 3200, www.yeshotls.gr.
After years of standing derelict, this 1950s building opened as New Hotel in summer 2011 and quickly became a member of Design Hotels. Redesigned by the Campana brothers from Brazil, its 79 rooms feature funky recycled furniture, while facilities include an all-day café-restaurant and a wellness centre.

Ochre & Brown €€€
Leokoriou 7, Psirri, T210 331 2940, www.oandbhotel.com.
This small boutique hotel has just 22 rooms and suites with stylish minimalist decor. It lies midway between the Acropolis and the Gazi nightlife district, both of which are within walking distance. It serves an excellent cooked-to-order breakfast, and is noted for its young friendly staff and personalized service.

Athens Center Square €€
15 Aristogitonos Street & Athinas, Monastiraki, T210 322 2706, www.athenscentersquarehotel.gr.
This 3-star hotel stands on a pedestrian-only square, overlooking the Central Market, just a couple of mins from Monastiraki metro station. It opened in summer 2009 and the 54 rooms have wooden floors, flatscreen TVs and free Wi-Fi; each storey is colour-themed.

Hotel Plaka €€
Kapnikareas 7, Plaka, T210 322 2096, www.plakahotel.gr.
Renovated in early 2010, this smart and discreet hotel lies in a side street between Monastiraki and Syntagma metro stations. The 67 rooms have pine floors, minimalist furniture and primary-coloured fabrics. There's a roof garden with a bar on summer evenings, so you can watch the sun set over the Acropolis.

Athens Backpackers €
Makri 12, Makrigianni, T201 922 4044, www.athensbackpackers.gr.
Offering both dorms and self-contained apartments, this Australian-owned hostel is clean, friendly and well managed. It lies on the edge of Plaka, close to the New Acropolis Museum, and has a summer rooftop bar with Acropolis views. The same people run the nearby **Athens Studios**, www.athensstudios.gr.

EP16 €
Epikourou 16, Psirri, T698 508 3556, www.ep16.com.
Ideal for couples or families, EP16 is a 1930s building housing 5 stylish self-catering apartments with wooden floors and retro design furniture, plus a shared roof terrace. The welcoming owners give guests a quick orientation tour of Psirri, plus Greek mobile phones to avoid roaming costs.

Restaurants

Plaka is fine for lunch, but to really tap into Athenian nightlife dine in Monastiraki, Psirri or Gazi, where funky new eateries breathe life into standard Greek taverna fare and stay open well beyond midnight.

Breakfast

Acropolis Museum Café-Restaurant €
15 Dionysiou Areopagitou, T210 900 0915, www.the acropolismuseum.gr.
With stunning Acropolis views, this museum café serves a generous traditional Greek breakfast, Tue-Sun till noon. Expect dishes such as Greek yoghurt with thyme honey, and *strapatsada* (scrambled eggs with fresh tomato). Note that you can access the café without buying a ticket for the museum itself.

Hip Café €
Mitropoleos 26 & Petraki 3, Syntagma, T213 015 4698.
For breakfast in the city centre, Hip has a pastel-coloured interior with Eames chairs and Saarinen

tables, and a menu including freshly squeezed juice, eggs benedict and frothy cappuccino. There's also fast free Wi-Fi.

Lunch

To Kouti €€
Adrianou 23, Monastiraki, T210 321 3229.
Playful salads, meat and seafood dishes, seasoned with spices and aromatic herbs, are guaranteed to make your tastebuds sing. Great for dinner with an Acropolis view, or lunch after a trip to Monastiraki's Sun flea market.

O Platanos €
Diogenous 4, Plaka, T210 322 0666.
One of the oldest and most hidden tavernas in Plaka, O Platanos dates back to 1932. Homely meat-and-vegetable casseroles – such as lamb with aubergine and veal with spinach – are served at tables on a bougainvillea-covered terrace, in the shade of an old plane tree, after which the restaurant is named.

Dinner

Funky Gourmet €€€
Paramithias 13 & Salaminos, Gazi, T210 524 2727, www.funkygourmet.com.
In a neo-classical building with a glass rooftop extension, this Michelin-starred restaurant serves beautifully presented creative Mediterranean cuisine. To try a selection of the chef's

outstanding specialities, opt for a degustation menu. Reservations essential.

Café Avissinia €€
Platia Avissinia, Monastiraki, T201 321 7047, www.avissinia.gr.
Closed Mon.
On a small square where antiques shops restore wooden furniture, this old-fashioned bistro serves Greek dishes with flavours from Anatolia. There's regular live music, plus a romantic roof terrace with stunning views onto the floodlit Acropolis.

Melilotos €
Kalamiotou 19, Syntagma, T210 322 2458, www.melilotos.gr.
Centrally located, just a 5-min walk from Syntagma Square, this informal eatery opened in 2011 and scored instant success with locals. The menu changes daily, depending on available fresh produce; the chef's favourite ingredients include lentils, chickpeas, leeks, chicken and salmon. No credit cards.

Skoufias €
Vasilaiou tou Megalou 50, Gazi, T210 341 2252.
Excellent value for money and a great starting point for a night in Gazi, this boho-chic eatery serves Cretan-inspired modern taverna fare. Both inside and out, you get mismatched wooden tables and chairs, coloured ceramics and a handwritten menu that changes daily.

Nightlife

Ask Athenians what they think their city does better than any other European capital and they will probably tell you about the nightlife. All year round Monastiraki, Psirri and Gazi are buzzing.

In Monastiraki, **A for Athens**, *Miaouli 2-4, www.aforathens.com*, is a rooftop cocktail bar with DJ music and stunning views of the Acropolis floodlit at night. It gets incredibly crowded after midnight at weekends, when you may have to queue for the lift up to the top floor. Nearby, **TAF**, *Normanou 5, www.theart foundation.gr*, is a bar-gallery, with semi-derelict outbuildings hosting art and photography exhibitions and installations, and a lovely courtyard garden with mellow lighting and chill-out music for drinks.

Up the road, between Monastiraki and Syntagma, arty **Booze**, *Kolokotroni 57, www.boozecooperativa.com*, occupies 3 levels in a restored neoclassical building. On the ground floor there are 2 bars staging occasional contemporary exhibitions, while up top there's alternative music, another bar and plenty of space to dance.

In Plaka, **Brettos**, *Kidathineon 41, www.brettosplaka.com*, is a cosy bar attached to a family distillery dating from 1909. Come here to try the fruit-flavoured spirits in the warm glow of the back-lit coloured bottles that line the floor-to-ceiling shelves.

Travel essentials

Getting there
Athens International Airport (Eleftherios Venizelos), T210 353 0000, www.aia.gr, lies 27 km northeast of the city. There are several frequent express bus services to the city centre (journey time 40 mins, €5); a ticket allows for same-day unlimited travel on the city's public transport. Alternatively, take the train to Larissis Station (every 30 mins, 0550-2250, €8). A taxi will cost you €35 (daytime fixed rate).

Getting around
Most of the main attractions lie within walking distance of one another in the city centre, parts of which are paved and pedestrian only. A 1-day pass for all forms of public transport (bus, metro and tram) costs €4. **Buses** are cheap and frequent but often crowded (single €1.40). There are 3 **metro** lines (€1.40), the main nodal points being Monastiraki, Syntagma and Omonia. On the blue line, some trains run all the way from Monastiraki and Syntagma to the airport. The green line is especially useful for reaching the port at Piraeus. Two **tram** lines connect Syntagma in the city centre to the coast and are ideal for reaching beaches in the Glyfada area. For further information contact OASA (Athens Public Transport Organization), T185, www.oasa.gr. Athens' **taxis** are among the cheapest in Europe, and Athenian taxi drivers among the most erratic. Taxis are no luxury – everyone takes them, and it is quite normal to share a ride with other passengers going in a similar direction.

Tourist information
Greek National Tourism Organisation (GNTO) has a new walk-in visitor centre at Dionysiou Areopagitou 18-20 (opposite the Acropolis Museum), T210 331 0716, Mon-Fri 0900-1900, Sat-Sun 1000-1600; also at the airport, T210 353 0448, Mon-Fri 0800-1900, Sat-Sun 1000-1600. Head office is at Tsocha 7, Ambelokipi, T210 870 7000, www.visitgreece.gr.

In summer, many of the big clubs in the centre are closed as they move out to the coastal strip from Kalamaki to Varkiza. The most memorable seaside summer club has to be **Island**, 27 km southeast of the city centre at Varkiza, *www.island clubrestaurant.gr*, which has a minimalist white wooden deck hosting waterside music and cocktails around sunset. There's also a restaurant serving creative Mediterranean cuisine and sushi.

Ratings

Art and culture ★☆☆☆
Eating ★★★★
Nightlife ★★★★★
Shopping ★★★★★
Sightseeing ★★★★
Value for money ★★
Overall city rating ★★★★★

Barcelona

Barcelona dips its toes in the Mediterranean and basks in year-round sunshine. Its skyline is indelibly marked by the visionary architect Antoni Gaudí, whose delirious buildings – resembling dragons, cliffs or gingerbread houses – seem to have magically erupted across the city. At its heart lie the ancient passages, gargoyles and ghostly spires of the old Gothic city, apparently untouched by modernity. Forget flamenco, sangría and other stock Spanish clichés, Barcelona is the proud capital of the ancient kingdom of Catalunya, with a distinct language and its own customs and traditions. These are staunchly preserved and exuberantly celebrated, with fire-spitting dragons, demons and giants.

Barcelona put itself on the map with the 1992 Olympics, which was the focus of a massive city-wide transformation. Its extraordinary collection of Modernista monuments were restored, and the seafront was entirely remodelled to become a glossy playground packed with beaches, marinas, and slick new hotels and apartment complexes. The transformation has continued apace, with a slew of celebrity starchitects from Richard Rogers to Jean Nouvel creating eye-catching new buildings which keep the city firmly in the spotlight. Add the fantastic and varied nightlife, discerning cuisine, a nose for the latest and best in fashion and design, and a population bent on having a good time, and it's not surprising that Barcelona has become one of the most visited cities in Europe.

Dragon spine, Casa Batlló.

Around the city

Les Rambles

Metro Plaça de Catalunya/Liceu, E3/D5.

The best introduction to Barcelona is a stroll down Les Rambles, the mile-long promenade that meanders down from Plaça de Catalunya to the port. It may look like one street but it is made up of five separate *rambles*, each with its own name and characteristics. Together they present an oddly appealing mixture of the picturesque and the tacky: street entertainers, fast-food outlets, crumbling theatres, whimsical Modernista mansions and pretty turn-of-the-century kiosks overflowing with flowers. It's at its best early in the morning and on Sunday afternoons.

Halfway down is **La Boqueria**, the city's irresistible market, with its wrought-iron roof and

At a glance

Finding your way around the Catalan capital isn't difficult. The Old City (Ciutat Vella) is at its heart, divided by **Les Rambles** (Las Ramblas in Castilian), the city's famous tree-lined promenade, which meanders from Plaça de Catalunya down to the port. To the east of the Rambles is the shadowy, medieval maze of the **Barri Gòtic** – the Gothic Quarter – with the flamboyant cathedral at its centre. This has been the heart of the city since Roman times and still buzzes day and night. East of the Barri Gòtic is **El Born**, another medieval district, which has become the coolest neighbourhood in a city famed for its addiction to fashion. Packed with über-chic boutiques, designer stores and the trendiest restaurants, bars and clubs, it rubs shoulders with **Sant Pere**, still charmingly old-fashioned but rapidly rising in the style stakes. West of the Rambles, **El Raval** spreads south to the raffish old theatre district of Parallel. Once a notorious red-light district, the Raval was given a massive clean-up and the glossy Museum of Contemporary Art in the 1990s and now has hip galleries, clothes stores and bohemian bars.

When the city burst out of its medieval walls in the 19th century, the rich commissioned new mansions in the airy grid of the **Eixample** (meaning extension in Catalan). Gaudí and his Modernista colleagues had a ball, leaving a spectacular legacy which now comprises one of the greatest concentrations of art nouveau architecture in the world. Beyond Eixample is **Gràcia**, once independent from the city and still with a relaxed vibe of its own. On the outskirts is **Park Güell**, Gaudí's fairytale extravaganza with magical views over the city.

To the west of the centre, overlooking the sea, is **Montjuïc Hill**, from where you can enjoy panoramic views of the city. The Olympics left their mark here with a string of excellent sporting facilities. Close by is the Fundació Miró, dedicated to the Catalan master and, at the bottom of the hill, is MNAC.

The regenerated waterfront stretches northeast from the Columbus monument at the foot of the Rambles. **Port Vell**'s warehouses hold restaurants, museums and an entertainment complex, while the **Port Olímpic** is crammed with bars and seafood restaurants and flanked by sandy beaches. Beyond it lies **Diagonal Mar**, a new neighbourhood of towering hotels, office buildings and apartment blocks, with a marina and two new beaches. In contrast, the traditional dock-workers' neighbourhood of **Barceloneta** is more atmospheric, with tiny tapas bars tucked away in its depths. The city's outskirts are home to parks, funfairs and museums: the best views are from **Tibidabo**, Barcelona's funfair mountain and highest peak, reached by a rickety tram and funicular.

24 hours in the city

Get a feel for the city by strolling down the **Rambles**, with a stop at **La Boquería** market on the way to take in the sights, sounds and smells. Alternatively, have a coffee at **Café de l'Òpera** and watch the world go by. Then dive into the chaotic maze of the **Barri Gòtic**, where you'll find the Gothic cathedral (take the lift to the roof for fantastic views) and plenty of great shops, bars and restaurants. If you prefer something a bit edgier, head across the Rambles to **El Raval**, home to the excellent Museum of Contemporary Art (**MACBA**), and lots of vintage clothes stores and galleries. Have lunch on the terrace at **Plaça dels Àngels** and afterwards explore the elegant **Passeig de Gràcia**, home to the city's most emblematic Modernista buildings, including Gaudí's **Casa Batlló** and **La Pedrera**. An alternative would be to visit the extraordinary **Sagrada Família**. In the late afternoon head to the seafront for a stroll and a dip. In the evening, check out the fashionable bars and clubs of **El Born**, or take in a game at the legendary **Camp Nou** stadium – if you can get tickets.

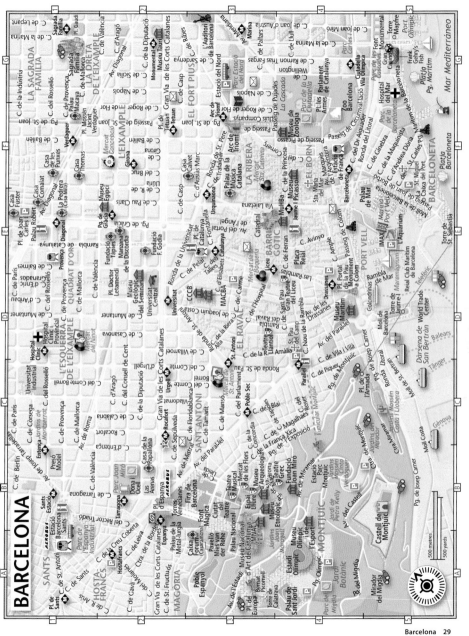

BARCELONA

Around the city

Modernista sign. Inside are piles of gleaming fruit, vegetables, fish and other local specialities, plus a liberal sprinkling of tiny bars for coffee or cava. Nearer the port is the city's 19th-century opera house, the **Gran Teatre del Liceu**.

Barri Gòtic

Metro Liceu, E3.

The Barri Gòtic has been the hub of the city for more than 2000 years. It's one of the best-preserved Gothic quarters in Europe, a dizzy maze of palaces, squares and churches piled on top of an original Roman settlement. The area is grubby, noisy, chaotic and packed with shops, bars and clubs. The streets are just as crowded at midnight as they are at midday.

Exploring the narrow alleyways, it's impossible to miss the **Catedral de la Seu** (Plaça Nova) with its

dramatic spires and neo-Gothic façade. The cathedral dates back to the 13th century and the magnificent interior is suitably dim and hushed. A lift behind the altar swoops to the top for a bird's-eye view of huddled rooftops.

Close by, the imposing medieval façades of the **Generalitat** (Catalan Parliament) and the **Ajuntament** (City Council) face each other across the Plaça Sant Jaume. From here, shadowy passages, scattered with Roman ruins and ancient churches, lead to lovely squares such as Plaça Sant Just, Plaça Felip Neri and Plaça del Pi.

Museu d'Història de Barcelona (MuHBa)

Plaça del Rei s/n, T93 256 2100, www.museuhistoria.bcn.es. Oct-May Tue-Sat 1000-1400 and 1600-1900, Sun 1000-2000; Jun-Sep Tue-Sat 1000-1900, Sun 1000-2000. €7 (includes entry to the Museu-Monestir de Pedralbes, Museu-Casa Verdaguer and the Interpretation Centre for the Park Güell); free 1st Sat of month and Sun 1500-2000. Metro Jaume I. Map E4.

This fascinating museum reveals the history of the city layer by layer. A glass lift glides down to the subterranean excavations of Roman Barcino, revealing 2000-year-old watchtowers, baths, temples, homes and businesses, discovered less than a century ago. Towards the site of the cathedral, the Roman ruins become interspersed with the remnants of fifth-century Visigothic churches. Stairs lead up to the medieval Royal Palace and the Golden Age of the city's history. The echoing Saló de Tinell, built in 1359, is a masterpiece of Catalan Gothic.

MACBA

Plaça dels Àngels, El Raval, T93 412 0810, www.macba.cat. 25 Sep-24 Jun Mon, Wed-Fri 1100-1930, Sat 1000-2000, Sun 1000-1500; 25 Jun-24 Sep Mon, Wed-Fri 1000-2000; Jul-Aug Thu until 2400,

Left: Les Rambles.
Opposite page: MACBA.

Sun 1000-1500. €11 for permanent collection; temporary exhibitions €6. Metro Universitat. Map D3.

Richard Meiers' huge, glassy home for MACBA was built in 1995 as a symbol of the city's urban renewal. The collection is loosely structured around three periods; the 1940s and 1950s are represented by members of the Dau al Set, a loose collection of writers and artists influenced by the Surrealists and Joan Miró. Work from the 1960s and 1970s shows the impact of popular and consumer culture on art, while the 1980s and early 1990s are marked by a return to painting and traditional forms, plus good photographic pieces. Excellent temporary exhibitions focus on the latest digital and multimedia works. MACBA has a great bookshop and a café-bar in the spacious square that it shares with the **CCCB** (Centre of Contemporary Culture).

Passeig de Gràcia

Metro Passeig de Gràcia, E1/E2/E3.

At the heart of the Eixample is this glossy boulevard of chic boutiques, neoclassical office buildings and Modernista mansions. The most famous stretch is the **Mançana de la Discòrdia** ('block of discord')

Best of the rest

Camp Nou Experience
Camp Nou, www.fcbarcelona.cat. €19 including tour, €15.50 for children 6-13. Metro Collblanc.
Football paraphernalia plus a guided tour of the stadium.

CCCB
C Montalegre 5, El Raval, www.cccb.org. Closed Mon. €4.50, free 1st Wed of month, Thu 2000-2200 and Sun 1500-2000. Metro Universitat.
Hosts eclectic exhibitions on contemporary culture* not covered by MACBA.

Drassanes Reials
Av Drassanes s/n, www.mmb.cat. Daily. €6. Metro Drassanes.
Currently under refurbishment, can only see the temporary exhibitions and the restored 1920s clipper, the Santa Eulalia, moored nearby at the Port Vell.

Museu Picasso
C Montcada 15-23, El Born, www.museupicasso.bcn.es. Tue-Sun. €11 for permanent and temporary exhibitions, or €6.60 for temporary exhibitions only. Free 1st Sun of month, and every Sun from 1500. Metro Jaume I.
Very popular collection, which is dominated by early works created in Barcelona.

Santa María del Mar
Pl de Santa María del Mar, El Born, D. Metro Jaume I.
This lovely 14th-century church is one of the purest examples of Catalan Gothic.

Tibidabo
Mar-Sep only. FGC to Av Tibidabo, then Tramvia Blau, then funicular.
The mountain has a great old-fashioned funfair at its summit and breathtaking views across the city.

Zoo de Barcelona
Parc de la Ciutadella, El Born, www.zoobarcelona.com. Open daily. Metro Barceloneta. Adults €19.60, children €11.80, free under 3.
The city zoo is fantastic for kids, with everything from elephants to tigers to dolphin shows, plus a petting zoo for the littlest kids. The cramped spaces inhabited by the big cats may cause some pangs, but remodelling is underway.

Around the city

between Carrer Consell de Cent and Carrer d'Aragó, where three Modernista masterpieces nudge up against each other: **Casa Lleó i Morera**, transformed by Domènech i Montaner in 1902; **Casa Amatller** (info on guided visits at www.amatller.org), designed by Puig i Cadafalch as a polychrome fairytale castle; and **Casa Batlló**, *T93 216 03 06, www.casabatllo.cat, daily 0900-2000, €20.35*, by Antoni Gaudí. Covered with shimmering trencadís (broken tiles) and culminating in a scaly roof, it gleams like an undersea dragon. The interior is soft and undulating, like whipped ice cream.

La Pedrera

C Provença 261-265, T90 220 2138, www.lapedrera.cat.
Daily Nov-Feb 0900-1830, last admission 1800; Mar-Oct 0900-2000, last admission 1930. €16.50, temporary exhibitions usually free, audioguides €4. Metro Diagonal. Map E1.

La Pedrera, better known as La Pedrera (the Stone Quarry), rises like a cream cliff draped with wrought-iron balconies. There's a recreation of a 1911 apartment on the first floor, with many original fittings. The attic houses **L'Espai Gaudí**, a museum of the architect's life and work in the city, but the climax of a visit is the sinuous rooftop terrace, studded with chimneys, air vents and stairwells disguised as extraordinary bulbous crosses and plump *trencadí*-covered towers. Enjoy a drink and live music on the rooftop on summer weekends.

La Sagrada Família

C Mallorca 401, Eixample, T93 513 2060, www.sagradafamilia.cat.
Oct-Mar daily 0900-1800; Apr-Sep daily 0900-2000. €13.50 or €18 with guide or audioguide. Metro Sagrada Família. Map G1.

Gaudí's unfinished masterpiece, the Expiatory Temple of the Holy Family, is the most emblematic and controversial monument in Barcelona. The towers measure almost 100 m and the central spire, when finished, will soar 180 m into the sky. The temple is set for completion in 2026, the anniversary of Gaudí's death. In November 2010, the temple was consecrated by Pope Benedict XVI in the presence of the Spanish King and Queen. Although construction is a long way from complete, the nave has now been covered, an organ installed, and mass is said daily.

Gaudí designed three façades for the temple but only the Nativity façade was completed by the time of his death in 1926. The Passion façade on the other side of the church is grim and lifeless in comparison. Inside, work has begun on the construction of four huge columns to support the enormous domed roof.

There's a lift up the towers (€4.50); brave visitors can climb even higher, before descending via the vertiginous spiral staircase. Underneath, the crypt contains Gaudí's tomb and an interactive museum.

La Pedrera.

MNAC

Palau Nacional, Montjuïc, T93 622 0360,
www.mnac.cat.
Oct-Apr Tue-Sat 1000-1800, Sun 1000-1500;
May-Sep Tue-Sat 1000-2000, Sun 1000-1500.
€12, free Sat from 1500 and 1st Sun of month.
Metro Espanya. Map A3.

Housed in the dour Palau Nacional on Montjuïc
is a magnificent collection of the best of Catalan
art. The highlight is the array of spellbinding
Romanesque murals gathered from Catalan
churches and displayed on reconstructed church
interiors. The Gothic collection reflects Catalunya's
glory years from the 13th to the 15th centuries, with
rooms devoted to the three outstanding painters
of the time: Bernat Martorell, Lluís Dalmau and
Jaume Huguet. The Thyssen bequest, with roughly
a hundred masterpieces including works by
Fra Angelico, Raphael, Zurbarán and others,
has been housed here since 2004. There is also
an extensive collection of 19th-century art and
sculpture, including wonderful Modernista furniture
(including pieces by Gaudí) and objets d'art.

Below MNAC, at the top of Avenida María
Cristina, is the **Font Màgica**, *Pl de Carles Buïgas,*
Feb-Apr and Oct-Dec Fri and Sat 1900-2030; May-Sep
Thu-Sun 2100-2300, free, a fountain from 1929 that
puts on a fabulous sound and light show; it's
gloriously tacky, yet undeniably magical.

Fundació Miró

Parc de Montjuïc s/n, T93 443 9470,
fundaciomiro-bcn.org.
Oct-Jun Tue-Sat 1000-1900 (Thu until 2130),
Sun 1000-1430; Jul-Aug Tue-Sat 1000-2000
(Thu until 2130). €11 for permanent and
temporary exhibitions, €7 for temporary
exhibitions only. Metro Espanya, then bus
55 or 150, or funicular from Paral·lel. Map B4.

The fabulous Fundació Miró is set in a white,
light-drenched building by Josep Lluís Sert on
Montjuïc. It contains the most important and
comprehensive gathering of Miró's works in the

Modernisme

The great rediscovery and celebration of Catalunya's
cultural identity, known as the Renaixença
(Renaissance), began in the 1850s. Architecture,
literature, painting, sculpture, furniture, craft and
design were galvanized by the new spirit of cultural
and political optimism. This arts movement came to
be known as *Modernisme* and was partly influenced
by the international art nouveau and Jugenstil
movements. When the medieval city walls were
torn down in 1854, Ildefons Cerdà's airy grid-shaped
extension (Eixample in Catalan) was constructed,
giving the most influential architects of the day the
chance to display their originality and virtuosity.
Three names stand out: Antoni Gaudí i Cornet, Lluis
Domènech i Montaner and Josep Puig i Cadafalch.
You can choose your favourite in the Mançana de
la Discòrdia (see page 31). The list of Modernista
monuments in Barcelona is breathtakingly long;
highlights include Gaudí's Casa Batlló, La Pedrera, Park
Güell and the Sagrada Família; Montaner's Palau de la
Música Catalana; and Puig i Cadafalch's Casa Amatller.

world, from his early experiments with Cubism and
Fauvism through to his later paintings, which are
increasingly gestural and impulsive. There are
spectacular sculptures from the 1960s and 1970s;
some are displayed on the rooftop sculpture terrace.

Park Güell

C Olot 7, T902 200 302 or 934 091 831 (from abroad),
www.parcguell.cat.
Nov-Feb daily 1000-1800; Mar and Oct daily
1000-1900; Apr and Sep daily 1000-2000; May-
Aug daily 1000-2100. €8 at the gate or €7 online.
Metro Lesseps, then a (signposted) 10-min walk,
or bus 24. Off map.

The Park Güell is perhaps the most delightful of Gaudí's
visionary creations. Two fairytale pavilions guard the
entrance (one houses an exhibition on the park's
history, *T93 285 6899, same hours as the park*), from
where stairs sweep up past the famous multi-coloured
salamander, which has become one of Barcelona's
best-known and best-loved symbols. The steps
culminate in the **Sala Hipóstila**, also known as the Hall

of a Hundred Columns because of the thick Doric columns which support its undulating roof. Gaudí's talented collaborator, the architect and mosaicist Josep Maria Jujol, was given free reign to colour the vaulted ceiling with elaborate whimsy; look carefully and you'll see the designs are made of smashed china, ceramic dolls' heads, wine glasses and old bottles. Above the hall is the main square with its snaking bench, thickly encrusted with *trencadís*, like the scales of a monstrous dragon. Surrounding it are porticoes and viaducts, made from unworked stone, which hug the slopes of the hillside for more than 3 km.

Just off the main esplanade is the **Casa Museu Gaudí**, *T93 219 3811, €5.50, combined ticket with Sagrada Família available, info at www.sagrada familia.cat*, housed in the small Torre Rosa, Gaudí's home towards the end of his life.

Seafront

Metro Barceloneta/Ciutadella-Vila Olímpica. Map E4/G5.

Barcelona's seafront was the main focus of Olympic redevelopment in the early 1990s. A boardwalk runs from the foot of the Rambles to the glittering **Port Vell** (Old Port) development which includes a marina, restaurants, shopping centre, IMAX and the impressive **Aquàrium** (€20).

To the northeast is the old fishermen's neighbourhood of **Barceloneta**, a district of narrow streets and traditional seafood bars. From here the **Telèferic** (€11 single, €16.50 return) begins its vertiginous journey over the harbour to Montjuïc. Beyond is the **Port Olímpic**, marked by Frank Gehry's shimmering copper fish.

Travel essentials

Getting there
Barcelona International Airport is 12 km south of the city (flights T91 321 1000, 902 404 704, www.aena-aeropuertos.es). International airlines use the new Terminal 1 and Terminal 2 (formerly terminals A and B, now called T2A and T2B). The **airport train** (€3.80) runs from outside Terminal 2 to Estació de Sants and Passeig de Gràcia every 30 mins, 0542-2338. The **Aerobús** (take the A1 for Terminal 1, runs every 5-10 mins; A2 for Terminal 2, runs 10-20 mins; €5.90 single, €10.20 return, under 4s free, www.aerobusbcn.com) runs from Plaça de Catalunya, via the Plaça d'Espanya 0530-0030. Taxis cost up to €25 to the centre, or more after 2200 and at weekends (supplements for luggage). **Estació de Sants** (metro Sants) is the main train station, although sleeper trains to/from Paris use Estació de França (metro Barceloneta). Many trains also stop at **Passeig de Gràcia**. For timetables and prices: T902 320 320, www.renfe.es.

Getting around
The Old City and Eixample, north of Plaça de Catalunya, are easy to walk around. The Sagrada Família and Park Güell need a short bus or metro ride; Montjuïc and Tibidabo are reached by cable car, bus or funicular. Public transport is cheap and efficient; the main hub is Plaça de Catalunya. 11 **metro** lines run Mon-Thu 0500-2400, Fri 0500-0200, Sat 24 hrs, Sun 0500-2300. **Buses** run Mon-Sat 0600-2230 (less frequently Sun), and nightbuses (N) 2230-0400. Gràcia and Tibidabo are served by **FGC** train (T012, www.fgc.net). A single bus or metro ticket costs €1.40; a T-Dia (€7.25) allows unlimited journeys for 1 day; a T-10 (€9.80), which is the most useful for visitors, allows 10 trips and can be shared. For maps and information, visit the **TMB** office under Plaça Universitat (T902 075 027, www.tmb.cat). There's a taxi stand on Plaça de Catalunya, opposite the main tourist office, or call **Barnataxi**, T93 551 9368, or **Fono-Taxi**, T93 300 1100.

Tourist information
The main office is at Plaça de Catalunya, T93 385 3834 (call centre, Mon-Fri 0800-2000), daily 0900-2100. It books hotel rooms and tours and sells discount cards and maps. It also offers themed walking tours (€11-49, 10% discount if bought online). There are branches at Plaça Sant Jaume, Estació de Sants and the airport. See www.barcelonaturisme.com and www.bcn.cat. The **Barcelona Card** (€37/€47/€56/€62 for 2 to 5 days, www.barcelonacard.com) gives unlimited travel by public transport plus discounts at shops, restaurants and major museums. The hop-on/hop-off **Bus Turístic** (1 day €26, 2 days €34, www.barcelonabusturistic.cat) tours the sights every 20 mins.

Where to stay

Barcelona is one of the most popular weekend destinations in Europe and, although the number of beds has increased dramatically, you should always book as early as possible and never just turn up and hope to find somewhere to stay. Book through an agent or check out online deals at www.barcelonahotels.com and www.barcelona-online.com.

Most of the cheaper places are in the Old City (Barri Gòtic, El Born and El Raval); these are also the noisiest places to stay. The smartest (and quietest) places are generally concentrated in the Eixample. Hotels are ranked with one to five stars; pensiones have fewer facilities and are ranked with one to three stars. Note that a modest hotel may be known as a 'hostal'; this is not the same as a 'hostel', which will have dormitory accommodation.

Arts Barcelona €€€
C Marina 19-21, Vila Olímpica, T93 221 1000, www.hotelarts barcelona.com. Metro Ciutadella–Vila Olímpica.
One of the city's most glamorous hotels, the Arts occupies one of the enormous glassy towers at the entrance to the Port Olímpic. It was inaugurated in 1992 and offers 33 floors of unbridled luxury, including indoor and outdoor pools, a fine restaurant, a piano bar overlooking the hotel gardens and the sea, a sauna, a gym and a beauty centre.

Hotel W €€€
Plaça de la Rosa dels Vents 1, T93 295 2800, www.w-barcelona. com. Metro Barceloneta.
This huge sail-shaped hotel was designed by Ricardo Bofill and is a favourite with international fashionistas. Restaurants and bars include the panoramic Eclipse bar on the 26th floor, and other amenities include an infinity pool overlooking the beach and a Bliss spa.

Banys Orientals €€
C Argentería 37, El Born, T93 269 8490, www.hotelbanysorientals. com. Metro Jaume I.
A chic boutique-style hotel close to the Museu Picasso. Rooms are a little small, but are furnished with sleek modern fabrics. A nearby annexe offers larger suites for slightly more.

Room Mate Pau €€
Carrer Fontanella 7, T93 343 6300, pau.room-matehotels.com. Metro Urquinaona.
This offers contemporary minimalism at an affordable price, plus a stylish café-bar and a terrace. What's more, it's just a short walk from the Picasso Museum and the hip boutiques of the Born neighbourhood.

Bonic Guesthouse €€-€
C/Josep Anselm Clavé 9, Barri Gòtic, T62 605 3434, www.bonic-barcelona.com.
Perfectly located just off the Rambla, with just 6 stylishly decorated rooms, this sweet little guesthouse is run by charming hosts. Thoughtful extras include free tea and coffee, dressing gowns in each room, and free Wi-Fi. The rooms share 3 spotless bathrooms.

ANBA €
Ronda de Sant Pere 27, T93 299 1627, www.anba.es. Metro Urquinaona
This charming and luxurious B&B has just a few rooms, all exquisitely furnished with antiques. A generous buffet breakfast is served, featuring local goodies, and guests can relax in the delightful garden.

Hostalin Barcelona €
Gran Via de les Corts Catalanes 657, T93 192 5040, www.hostalin barcelona.es. Metro Tetuan.
A recently opened budget option within a short walk of the Passeig de Gràcia, this has simple but stylish guest rooms with en suite bathrooms and balconies. The friendly staff will happily offer tips on what to see and do.

Restaurants

Catalan dishes are simple and rely on fresh local ingredients. Meat and fish are often grilled or cooked slowly in the oven (*al forn*). There are some delicious vegetable dishes, like *escalivada*, a salad of roasted aubergine, peppers and onions. Rice dishes are also popular. Wash it all down with Catalan wine, sparkling cava or local Estrella beer. Breakfast is usually a milky coffee (*café amb llet/café con leche*) and a pastry. Lunch is taken seriously and eaten around 1400, when many restaurants offer a fixed-price 2-course menu including a drink. Tapas are not as much of a tradition here as in other parts of Spain, but there are plenty of old-fashioned bars near the harbour that offer fresh seafood versions. Dinner is rarely eaten before 2100 and tends to be lighter than the midday meal.

Breakfast

El Café de l'Òpera €
Les Rambles 74. Metro Liceu.
Opposite the Liceu Opera House, this is the perfect café for people-watching. Original Modernista fittings and an old-world ambience.

La Pallaresa €
C Petritxol 11, Barri Gòtic. Metro Liceu.
This is where to get your *chocolate con churros* (thick hot chocolate with fried dough strips) in the morning – locals swear it's the best *xocolatería* in the city.

Lunch

Cinc Sentits €€€
C/Aribau 58, Eixample, T93 323 9490, www.cincsentits.com. Metro Passeig de Gràcia or Universitat.
Canadian-Catalan chef Jordi Artal has been recognized with a Michelin star, but the set menus (including a €30 set lunch) at his elegant restaurant make it affordable for a splurge. Imaginative Catalan cuisine prepared with superb locally sourced produce is the key to his success. Book well in advance.

Kaiku €€
Plaça del Mar 1, T93 221 9082. Metro Barceloneta.
It's easy to pass this unassuming restaurant without giving it a second glance, but that would be a mistake: not only does it make the best rice dishes in town (try the *arròs del xef*, made with smoked rice), but daily specials might include such exotic delights as sea anemones in a light tempura. Note that it's only open at lunchtimes.

Bar Pinotxo €
Mercat de la Boquería 66-67, Les Rambles. Closed Sun. Metro Liceu.
The market's best-loved counter bar, serving excellent, freshly prepared food; try the tortilla with artichokes.

Pla dels Àngels €
C Ferlandina 23, El Raval, T93 329 4047. Metro Universitat.
This large, popular restaurant opposite MACBA has bright, modern decor and a summer terrace. It serves extremely well-priced salads, meats and pastas, plus excellent wine.

Dinner

Omm €€€
C/Rosselló 265, Eixample, T93 445 4000, www.hotelomm.es. Metro Diagonal.
A very fashionable restaurant in the über-chic Hotel Omm, this is overseen by the much lauded Roca brothers who ensure substance triumphs over style. Expect extraordinary contemporary cuisine accompanied by one of the finest wine lists in the city.

Cal Pep €€
Plaça Olles 8, El Born, T93 310 7961. Metro Barceloneta.
A classic: there's a smart brick-lined dining area at the back but it's more entertaining to perch at the bar, as Pepe dishes up tempting treats and holds court at the same time. Reservations essential.

Arc Café €
C/d'en Carabassa 19, Barri Gòtic, T93 302 5204, www.arccafe.com. Metro Drassanes or Jaume I.
A delightful little stone-walled café hidden down a narrow Gothic street, this serves delicious international food from houmous to carpaccios and from tartiflette to curry. Great home-made desserts, too.

Nightlife

To find out what's on, check the listings guide *Guía del Ocio*, *B-Guided* magazine or look out for flyers. Up-to-date information is also provided at www.bcn.es.

Bars and clubs
Barcelona is a popular stop on the international DJ circuit, with cutting-edge clubs (*discotecas*) playing the very latest tunes. Some of the best clubs can be found on **Carrer Nou de Francesc** in the Barri Gòtic and along the painfully hip **Passeig del Born** in

El Born. There are also several excellent bars in the Ciutat Vella, where you can enjoy a mellow copa on a candlelit terrace.
El Raval has a concentration of funky bohemian clubs as well as louche bars where you can sip absinthe in timeless surroundings. Bigger clubs, catering for the frenetic summer party crowd, can be found on **Montjuïc** and around the **Port Olímpic**, while gay clubs are clustered in the so-called **Gaixample**, east of Passeig del Gràcia.

Contemporary music
There are plenty of live music venues. Popular clubs like **Jamboree**, *Plaça Reial 17, Barri Gòtic*, and **Luz de Gas**, *Muntaner 246*, *Gràcia*, offer a mixed bag of musical styles. Visit **Harlem Jazz Club**, *Comtessa de Sobradiel 8, Barri Gòtic*, for the city's jazz scene. Latin and African music are also popular.
For lovers of electronica, the **Sónar**, *www.sonar.es*, summer festival of multimedia music and art is fantastic. The **BAM** festival in Sep is another great time to catch alternative sounds.

Classical music and theatre
Enjoy opera at the beautiful **Gran Teatre de Liceu**, *La Rambla 51-59, T93 485 9900, www.liceu barcelona.cat*, or a rousing performance by Orfeó Català in the stunning Modernista surroundings of the **Palau de la Música**, *C Sant Francesc de*

Shop till you drop

The designer shop **Galleries Vinçon** on the Passeig de Gràcia used to have the slogan 'I shop therefore I am' emblazoned across its packaging and this seems to be the attitude of many of the city's residents, for Barcelona has more shops per capita than anywhere else in Europe. Best buys are leather, cutting-edge fashion, homewares and local wines and food. Head to **Barri Gòtic** for quirky one-off shops, **Carrer Portaferrissa** for fashion chains, **El Raval** for vintage clothes and music and **El Born** for unusual fashion and interior design shops (on and around Passeig del Born). For international fashion, designer furnishings and art galleries head to **Passeig de Gràcia** and **Diagonal**, in Eixample.

Paula 2, Sant Pere, T93 295 7200, www.palaumusica.org. **Ciutat del Teatre** complex, *Plaça Margarida Xirgu, Montjuïc*, holds a dramatic arts museum and several performance spaces, including the celebrated **Teatre Lliure**, *T93 228 9747, www.teatrelliure.com*. In Jun and Jul, see the renowned **Festival de Barcelona Grec**, *www.barcelonafestival.com*.

Ratings

Art and culture ★★
Eating ★★★
Nightlife ★★★
Shopping ★★
Sightseeing ★★★
Value for money ★★★
Overall city rating ★★★

Belfast

After decades of turmoil played out on a global stage, Belfast finally finds itself making headlines for all the right reasons. At long last it seems to have shaken itself free from the shackles of notoriety and is fast establishing itself as a city to visit. Belfast has undergone a transformation in the past 15 years that has left it barely recognizable. The same streets that once hosted army battalions, rioters and burnt-out vehicles now play home to some of Ireland's finest restaurants, high-class hotels, a thriving café culture and a vibrant club scene. Landmark buildings have been refurbished, new arts and culture centres built, and Belfast has officially declared itself 'open for business'. It hasn't forgotten its past, but the memories are being used to spur on the momentum for change.

Albert Clocktower.

At a glance

Belfast is a great walking city with a compact centre that revolves around the **City Hall**. Its distinctive copper dome provides a valuable landmark for finding your bearings wherever you are. Head north onto Donegall Place and Royal Avenue for big brand shopping, or southwest to the Lisburn Road for home-grown boutiques and craft shops. This is also where you will find one of Belfast's main cultural areas, **Queens Quarter** (named after Queens University), whose bars, cafés and music venues are populated by the city's bright young things. The other key cultural area is the **Cathedral Quarter** in the northeast of the city, where there are plenty of arts venues, restaurants and pubs; the crowd here is a little older and a little less self-conscious. To the east lies the River Lagan and the Waterfront Hall, a modern venue overlooking the water that often hosts big-name performers from the music world and comedy circuit. A short stroll further on is the regenerated **Titanic Quarter**, birthplace of the ill-fated liner, where you'll find trendy apartment blocks, Belfast Metropolitan College, the Odyssey Arena and the multi-million pound Titanic Centre.

Top: City Hall.
Above: Palm House.

Botanic Gardens & Palm House

College Park, Botanic Av, T028 9031 4762,
www.belfastcity.gov.uk.
Park daily from 0730. Palm House Apr-Sep 1300-1700, Oct-Mar 1300-1600. Free.

First established in 1828, the gardens were declared a public park in 1895. The **Rose Garden** in full bloom is a sight to behold and often attracts misty-eyed newly weds to its borders for photo opportunities. It's also a popular haunt for students attending nearby Queens University and an excellent picnic spot for both locals and tourists. The Victorian **Palm House** nestled in the heart of the gardens is one of the earliest examples of a curvilinear cast-iron glasshouse. Designed by Charles Lanyon, the two wings were completed in 1840 by Dubliner Richard Turner, who also built the Great Palm House at Kew. Throughout the year the Gardens play host to a number of events including opera recitals and the annual Belfast Mela every August, the region's largest multi-cultural festival (www.artsekta.org.uk).

Ulster Museum

Botanic Gardens, T0845 608 0000,
www.nmni.com/um.
Tue-Sun 1000-1700. Free.

This is one of Belfast's must-do rainy day options. The museum closed in 2006 for a £17 million renovation programme and re-opened to the general public in 2009. The previously tired building has been completely re-vamped to provide additional exhibition space and to showcase old favourites, such as long-standing resident Takabuti, the Egyptian mummy, as well as an extensive collection of art by modern Irish artists from both sides of the border. There are three main zones within the museum designed around the themes of art, nature and history. Both young and old can get interactive in each zone's Discovery section, trying on costumes, creating their own works of art and unearthing ancient relics.

Linen Hall Library

17 Donegall Sq North, T028 9032 1707, www.linenhall.com.
Mon-Fri 0930-1730, Sat 0930-1600. Free, donations welcome. Map A2.

Founded in 1788, this is the oldest library in Belfast with an unparalleled collection of books on Irish and local studies that range from first editions printed in Ulster to over 250,000 titles in the Northern Ireland Political Collection. For those interested in the country's recent Troubles, this is the place to pull up a chair. The library offers free public reference use with general lending for members. It's worth checking the website for information on talks and events as the library usually attracts an illustrious range of speakers through the year. There is a café and gift shop on site.

Belfast City Hall

Donegall Pl, T028 9032 0202, www.belfastcity.gov.uk.
Mon-Thu 0830-1700, Fri 0830-1630. Free guided tours Mon-Fri 1100, 1400 and 1500, Sat 1400 and 1500. Map A3.

Having established itself as a key industrial player thanks to its thriving shipbuilding, tobacco and textile industries, Belfast was granted its city status by Queen Victoria in 1888. Some 10 years later, the first brick was laid for what was to eventually become Belfast City Hall. This magnificent building took eight years to build, finally opening its doors in August 1906. It's built in a baroque revival style, and its central copper dome (173 ft) dominates the city's skyline. The marble interior has stained glass windows that look out on to the well-groomed lawns and a collection of statues and monuments, ranging from Queen Victoria herself to Sir Edward Harland, co-founder of the city's shipbuilders Harland & Wolff and former Mayor of Belfast. A big

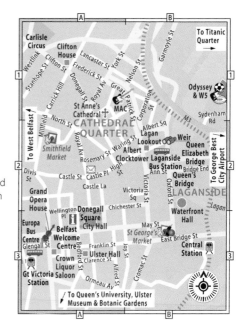

screen is now a permanent feature in the grounds, broadcasting major events from the Olympics to the Proms. In November and December the open-air Christmas Market also takes up residence, offering a wide range of food and craft stalls along with an ever-popular beer tent.

Cathedral Quarter

www.thecathedralquarter.com.

This area of the city has undergone a complete rejuvenation during the past 20 years, thanks in part to chef and restaurateur, Nick Price. He took a gamble and opened his multi-award-winning restaurant, **Nick's Warehouse**, here in 1989 when very few were tempted to venture into the area. On his retirement in 2013 the restaurant closed, but his legacy is clear to see in the neighbouring streets where you'll now find top-notch eateries and a vibrant arts scene. The Quarter takes its name from lofty **St Anne's Cathedral**, *www.belfast*

Best of the rest

Belfast Famous Black Cab Tour

T07790 955227, www.belfastblackcabtours.co.uk.
Affable taxi drivers with plenty to say take you into
both the Republican and Loyalist areas of the city
pointing out some of the places where key events
took place in Belfast's darkest days. Passengers
also get a chance to stop at the 'Peace Wall', now
decorated in graffiti, and to see some of the city's
famed political murals.

Parliament Buildings

*Ballymiscaw, Stormont, T02890 521802, www.ni
assembly.gov.uk. Tours Mon-Fri 1000 and 1500.*
Northern Ireland's Parliament Buildings are located
within Stormont Estate on the outskirts of Belfast.
The iconic white building is home to the country's
power-sharing Assembly (established after the
1998 Good Friday Agreement) and can be visited
on a guided tour. The rest of the extensive estate,
including a children's play park, fitness trails and
plenty of green space, is open daily.

cathedral.org, Mon-Sat 0800-1800, Sun 0800-1600;
it's worth checking out the interior, complete
with marble labyrinth. The newly re-developed
St Anne's Square is surrounded by eating options
(see Restaurants, opposite) and is home to the
city's latest arts venue, the **Metropolitan Arts
Centre (MAC)**, *T028 9023 5053, www.themaclive.
com, daily 1000-1900, later on performance nights*,
which provides a diverse programme of drama,
dance and music performances. There are also a
host of pubs in the neighbourhood with their own
live music nights (see Nightlife, page 45). During
the day the area is pleasant to stroll through but
it's in the evenings that it really comes alive.

Titanic Belfast

*1 Olympic Way, Queens Rd, T028 9076 6399,
www.titanicbelfast.com.*
Daily Apr-Sep 0900-1900, Oct-Mar 1000-1700.
£14.75.

Millions of pounds have been spent so far in
redeveloping the Titanic Quarter as a desirable
place to both live and visit. The jewel in its crown is
the state-of-the-art **Titanic Centre** which opened
in March 2012 to coincide with the centenary of the
ship's tragic maiden voyage. It's a breathtakingly
beautiful building made from over 3000 anodized
aluminium silver shards that shimmer in the
sunlight as it proudly points down the slipway at
the docks, just as the Titanic would have done in
1912. The design is meant to be reminiscent of the
prow of a ship but in a display of Belfast's black
humour, locals have already nicknamed it 'The
Iceberg'. The centre is built on the former site of
the shipbuilding firm Harland & Wolff, and it tells
the story of the ill-fated vessel from its conception
and design, through its build and launch to the
subsequent disaster when it tragically sank in April
1912. The exhibition also portrays the aftermath
of the sinking, the various inquiries that followed
and the many myths that are still associated with
the ship. The final gallery gives visitors a fish-eye
view of the sunken wreck beneath them. It's a
fascinating insight into one of history's most
compelling shipping disasters while also managing
to celebrate Belfast's glory days when it reigned
supreme as the world's greatest shipbuilding city.
As well as visiting the Titanic Centre, enthusiasts
can join one of the independent tours of the area;
contact **Titanic Walking Tours**, *T075 4648 9875,
www.titanicwalk.com*, or **Segway NI Titanic Tour**,
T028 9073 7171, www.segwayni.co.uk.

Titanica statue.

Where to stay

There was once a shortage of good hotels in Belfast's city centre. For decades Hasting's Europa was the only hotel of choice for the discerning traveller but now it faces stiff competition.

The Merchant €€€
16 Skipper St, T028 9023 4888, www.themerchanthotel.com.
A truly luxurious 5-star spa hotel housed in a Grade-A building in the heart of Belfast's historical Cathedral Quarter. Once the headquarters of the Ulster Bank, it boasts a spectacular dining room in the former main banking hall. A recent extension means guests can choose to stay in bedrooms and suites decorated in traditional velvets and silks or art deco.

Fitzwilliam €€€-€€
Great Victoria St, T028 9044 2080, www.fitzwilliamhotelbelfast.com.
A modern and chic hotel in an excellent location in the city centre, with the Grand Opera House on its doorstep. The hotel's award-winning restaurant, *Eat*, is definitely worth checking out, especially its affordable pre-theatre menu.

Malmaison €€
34-38 Victoria St, T084 4693 0650, www.malmaison.com.
The city's rock 'n' roll hotel is housed in a former seed warehouse with an imposing exterior, complete with gargoyles. The interior continues the gothic theme, with low lighting and red and black velvets throughout. This is the hotel of choice when pop stars arrive in town to play at the nearby Odyssey Arena. The hotel's Samson Suite (check out the purple pool table) has welcomed both Kylie and Lady GaGa during their UK tours. Hip and very funky.

Ten Square €€
10 Donegall Sq South, T028 9024 1001, www.tensquare.co.uk.
A stylish boutique hotel, located slap bang in the middle of the city centre, across from the City Hall. Downstairs the Grill Bar has live entertainment most Fri and Sat nights, ranging from salsa dancing to resident DJ sets.

Vagabonds €
9 University Rd, T028 9023 3017, www.vagabondsbelfast.com.
A top-notch hostel for urban travellers. It's clean, modern and more than a little bit funky. Handy for Queens University, the Botanic Gardens and the Ulster Museum. The city centre is only a short stroll away. Free bed linen, Wi-Fi and breakfast.

Restaurants

A culinary revolution has taken place in Belfast over the past 20 years. There are still plenty of greasy spoons serving a traditional Ulster Fry for breakfast (this will set you up for the day), but you'll now also find world-class restaurants with award-winning chefs in every corner of the city. There's a particularly high concentration on St Anne's Square in the Cathedral Quarter, including **Salt Bistro**, *T028 9023 8012*, for local seafood dishes from Dundrum mussels to Strangford crab; **The Potted Hen**, *T028 9023 4554*, for a great-value family Sunday lunch; **Coppi**, *T028 9031 1959*, for Italian-inspired small and large plates; **House of Zen**, *T028 9027 8688*, for knock-out Asian cuisine, and **4th Wall**, *T028 9027 8707*, which serves up modern Irish fare against a back drop of new Irish artwork and a soundtrack of jazz. Elsewhere, try the following:

Ox €€€
1 Oxford St, T028 9031 4 121, www.oxbelfast.com.
Tue-Sat 1200-1430 and 1800-2200.
Fine dining without pretension is how this latest addition to the Belfast restaurant scene has been described by critics. **Ox** opened in 2013 to rave reviews with a menu that takes the very best of the region's ingredients and turns them into something really quite special. Best to book ahead.

Deanes €€€-€€
*36-40 Howard St, T028 9033 1134,
www.michaeldeane.co.uk.*
Tue-Sat 1200-1500, 1730-2200.
The flagship restaurant of
local celebrity restaurateur,
Michael Deane is one of
Belfast's longest established
fine-dining experiences. A recent
refurbishment has breathed
new life into the interior, and
the tasting menu is good value
at £55 for 6 courses.

Home Popup Belfast €€
*9 Donegall Sq West, T028 9023
4946, www.homepopup.com.*
Mon 1200-1600, Tue-Thu
1200-2130, Fri-Sat 1200-1600,
1700-2200, Sun 1300-2100.
Home started its life as an
experimental pop-up restaurant
in 2011, dipping its toe into the
water to see if the punters might
like what they were serving.
They loved it. As a result, it's
here to stay having now moved
to permanent premises. The
new interior is reminiscent of
a New York warehouse with
the dishes still being homely
and feel-good. No reservations
taken for lunch sittings.

Café Conor €€-€
*11a Stranmillis Rd, T028 9066
3266, www.cafeconor.com.*
Mon-Thu 0900-2200, Fri-Sat
0900-2300, Sun 0900-2100.
Located near the Ulster Museum
is one of the city's most popular
cafés. It serves great food from
cooked breakfasts right through
to an evening bistro-style menu.

Rocket & Relish €€-€
*479-481 Lisburn Rd, T028 9066
5655, www.rocketandrelish.com.*
Mon-Thu 1130-2100, Fri-Sat
1130-2200, Sun 1300-2100.
Consistently voted by locals as
the best burger joint in town, R&R
is out of the city centre on the
bustling Lisburn Road with its
trendy shops, cafés and bars. The
char-grilled burgers come as 6 oz
or 12 oz, with an amazing array of
toppings from feta and black
olive tapenade to goat's cheese
and jalapenos. The sweet potato
chips are worth the trip alone.

Nightlife

Belfast's nightlife scene is
thriving, with new bars opening
their doors every few months.
The latest trend seems to be for
open-air courtyards and beer
gardens, complete with
industrial patio heaters and
plenty of atmosphere. For some
alfresco socializing, check out
Filthy McNasty's, *45 Dublin Rd*,
the **Hudson Bar**, *10-12 Gresham St*
(off the beaten track but worth
seeking out) and the **National
Grand Café Bar**, *High St*. For a
glam night out, kick off with a
cocktail or two at **The
Apartment**, *2 Donegall Sq West*,
which has a view over the
floodlit City Hall; the bar in the
sumptuous and extremely
decadent **Merchant Hotel**, *16
Skipper St*, or the very funky **Love
& Death Inc**, *10a Anne St*.
Alternatively, for a taste of
nostalgia, don't miss the famed
Crown Liquor Saloon, *46 Great
Victoria St*, once a great Victorian
gin palace that has been
beautifully preserved by the
National Trust with its cosy snugs
and impressive range of real ales
on tap. The city isn't teeming

Albert Bridge.

with clubbing venues, but those that it does have cater for all musical tastes. **The Stiff Kitten**, *1 Bankmore Sq, Dublin Rd*, is open until 0300 most nights and you're guaranteed to get very, very sweaty after several hours of dance music. **The Limelight**, *17 Ormeau Av, www.limelightbelfast. com*, has different areas offering DJ sets and live music, while **The Kremlin**, *96 Donegall St*, is Belfast's long-running gay club (closed Mon and Wed) with an emphasis on pop. There's live music in the Cathedral Quarter at **McHugh's**, *T028 9050 9999*, the **John Hewitt**, *T028 9023 3768*, the **Duke of York**, *T028 9024 1062*, and the **Dark Horse**, *T028 9023 7807*. **Custom House Square** hosts open-air gigs, including the annual **Belsonic** music festival in August (*www.belsonic. com*), while the **Black Box**, *www.blackboxbelfast.com*, showcases everything from cabaret to ska, folk to rock and lots more in between. Big-name rock and pop acts pack out **The Waterfront**, *www.waterfront. co.uk*, **Ulster Hall**, *www.belfastcity. gov.uk*, and the **Odyssey**, *www.odysseyarena.com*. And, for West End shows, ballet and opera performances, the splendid Victorian **Grand Opera House**, *T028 9024 1919, www.goh. co.uk*, is still going strong. Keep an eye on the venue websites as well as checking the What's On section of *www.visit-belfast.com* and *www.belfasttimes.co.uk*.

Travel essentials

Getting there
Belfast International Airport, *T94 484848, www.belfast airport.com*, is 30 km from the city centre. The Airport Express 300 operates a 24-hr bus service between the airport and the city centre departing every 15 mins during peak times and taking 35-40 mins (£7 single, £10.50 return). Belfast Airport Taxis (T94 484353) charge £30 for transfers to the city centre. **George Best City Airport**, *T028 9093 9093, www.belfastcityairport.com*, is only 6 km from the city centre. Translink (T028 9066 6630) operates a rail service from this airport to **Great Victoria Street Station**, every 20 mins Mon-Sat 0600-2300 and hourly Sun 0900-2200. The Airport Express 600 bus fare is £2.20 single and £3.30 return. Belfast City Airport Taxis charge £10 for a transfer one-way and are available outside Arrivals. **Stena Line**, *www.stenaline.co.uk*, ferry services to/from Cairnryan and Liverpool dock at West Bank Road. Translink bus 96 runs between the ferry terminal and Upper Queen St in the city centre, £1.70; there's also a shared taxi service to the centre or the train stations, £9. The Enterprise train service, www.translink.co.uk, runs between Dublin and **Belfast Central Station** daily, from £8.99 single.

Getting around
Walking is the best way to get around this compact city, but if you need to use public transport then **Metro Bus Services**, *www.translink.co.uk*, run frequently across all areas of Belfast. The Metro Day Ticket is great value at £3.70, allowing holders to travel anywhere on the Metro network for one day Mon-Sat (available at Metro kiosks in the city centre). The Belfast Visitor Pass gives unlimited rail and bus travel, plus discounts on entry to many of the city's attractions for 1, 2 or 3 consecutive days (£6.30, £10.50, £14). Buy it from the Translink website or in the Belfast Welcome Centre. A walking tour around the city with a **Blue Badge Guide**, *T028 9029 2631, www.belfast-city-walking-tours.co.uk*, is recommended.

Tourist information
For information on events, tours, hotel bookings and to purchase tickets for attractions and travel passes, head to **Belfast Welcome Centre**, currently at *47 Donegall Pl, T028 9024 6609, www.visit-belfast.com*, Jun-Sep Mon-Sat 0900-1900, Sun 1100-1600, Oct-May Mon-Sat 0900-1730, Sun 1100-1600. It is relocating to a new site opposite City Hall in summer 2014. There is also a 24-hr touch screen information point located outside the Belfast Welcome Centre and in each of the airports.

Ratings

Art and culture ☆☆☆☆☆
Eating ☆☆☆
Nightlife ☆☆☆☆
Shopping ☆☆☆
Sightseeing ☆☆☆
Value for money ☆☆☆
Overall city rating ☆☆☆☆☆

Berlin

The capital of Germany since 1999, Berlin is a city reborn – a phoenix risen from the flames of Second World War destruction and Cold War division. Arguably the hippest European capital, it attracts some of the most progressive fashionistas, artists and musicians from all over the world. The city may have needed a long period in rehab, but it is now confident enough to woo British architects, Italian designers and Polish restorers to its burgeoning multinational community. These days Babylonian mosaics, French bakeries and Norman Foster creations are comfortably integrated into the buildings of Schinkel and the operas of Wagner. Anything goes in Berlin, from illegal parties held in derelict warehouses to city beaches and an open-air swimming pool on the river Spree.

Inside the Reichstag dome.

At a glance

Mitte, former bohemian hub of East Berlin, is now the heart of the reunified capital and, along with its more conservative West Berlin neighbour, **Tiergarten**, is the focus of most visitors' attention. Here, the Brandenburger Gate and the Reichstag stand amid a rash of government buildings and sprawling acres of woodland, grass and lakes. **Friedrichstrasse** is the main artery dividing the eastern and western halves of the city. About 15 minutes' walk east lies **Museuminsel**, where you will find the city's most important museums, while **Potsdamer Platz**, south of the Brandenburg Gate, shows off Berlin's ultra-modern colours. Northeast of Mitte, **Prenzlauerberg** is a hip place to live and play, while **Friedrichshain**, east of Mitte, is less attractive but still on the up. **Kreuzberg**, south of Mitte, in former West Berlin, has a large Turkish population and, like its more chichi neighbour **Schöneberg**, remains a centre for the gay community. West of Tiergarten, **Charlottenburg**, once a showcase of capitalism, now competes with Mitte and Prenzlauerberg.

24 hours in the city

Visit the **Reichstag** first thing and climb up to the cupola for the views. Then head to the **Adlon Kempinski Hotel** for coffee, pausing to reflect at the **Brandenburg Gate**. Afterwards, head east along Unter den Linden as far as Bebelplatz (where the 1933 book burnings took place) and cross the road to spend an hour or two in the **Deutsches Historisches Museum**. Cross the river onto Museum Island and visit the outstanding **Pergamon Museum**, before having a late lunch. (Try the tasty snacks from the riverside sausage stands.) Walk through the Lustgarten, across the Schlossplatz and then cross the river again, continuing west to the **Gendarmenmarkt**, where there may be an afternoon concert in one of the cathedrals. On nearby **Friedrichstrasse**, with its stylish shops, is the museum commemorating Checkpoint Charlie. From here, following the fragment of the Wall west, it is possible to reach the futuristic-looking **Potsdamer Platz** for a spot of dinner. Later, take a tour of the über-chic bars and cafés around Mitte.

Brandenburger Tor and around

S-Bahn Unter den Linden. Map C2/3.

Built in 1791, Berlin's most famous icon has witnessed the highs and lows of German history. Left isolated by the construction of the Berlin Wall in 1961, the Brandenburg Gate became the emblematic backdrop to that epoch-altering event on 9 November 1989 when the border was opened and young people from both sides of the city rushed forward to scale the defining symbol of the Cold War.

On the east side of the gate, **Pariser Platz** has been transformed from a concrete wilderness into an elegant diplomatic and financial centre and regained its pre-war status as one of the city's most prestigious addresses. The French embassy has been rebuilt on the north side, while opposite is the **Akademie der Künste** (Academy of Arts), *Pariser Platz 4, www.adk.de*. This Günther Behnisch building houses the private archives of cultural greats such as Bertolt Brecht and Günter Grass, as well as promoting German arts through exhibitions and performances. Next to the Academy is the unmissable DZ Bank building, designed by Frank Gehry. Inside is an enormous sculpture whose twists and turns are in startling contrast to the bank's façade.

Brandenburg Gate.

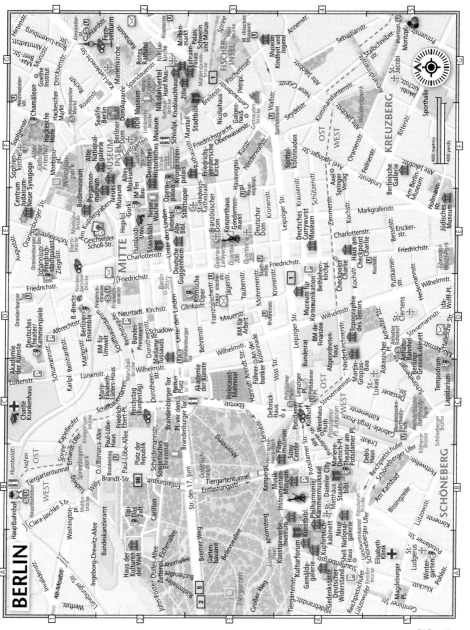

Around the city

Reichstag and around

Ebertstr.
Daily 0800-2400 (last entry 2200). Free.
S-Bahn Unter den Linden. Map C2.

The imposing late ninth-century Reichstag building has been restored to its former glory and is once again at the heart of German political life. The undoubted highlight is Norman Foster's outlandish glass dome. The views from the top are not to be missed, though the long queues certainly are (get there early or visit at night to avoid them).

The Reichstag is one of many government buildings along the Spree and backs onto the parkland of **Tiergarten**. This area has seen more redevelopment than most but, despite pressure from developers, the park's wide open spaces, lakes and woods have not been compromised. North of Tiergarten is **Hamburger Bahnhof**, *Invalidenstr 50, www.hamburgerbahnhof.de, Tue, Wed, Fri 1000-1800, Thu 1000-2000, Sat-Sun 1100-1800, €14, S-Bahn Lehrter Bahnhof.* Trains stopped running here in the 19th century, replaced in the late 1980s by challenging artworks, including pieces by Joseph Beuys.

Potsdamer Platz

S-Bahn Potsdamer Platzk. Map C4.

Once as desolate as Pariser Platz due to its proximity to the Wall, Potsdamer Platz, at the southeastern corner of Tiergarten park, is now almost a town in its own right, with skyscrapers, cinemas, embassies and museums, including the **Museum für Film und Fernsehen**, *Potsdamer Str 2, T030 300 9030, www.deutsche-kinemathek.de, Tue, Wed, Fri-Sun 1000-1800, Thu 1000-2000, €7.* Just to the west lies the **Kulturforum**, which encompasses not only the **Berlin Philharmonie** but also one of the world's most prestigious art collections at the **Gemäldegalerie**, *www.smb.spk-berlin.de, Tue, Wed, Fri-Sun 1000-1800, Thu 1000-2200, €10,* and international and German paintings from the 20th century at the **Neue Nationalgalerie**, *www.smb.spk-berlin.de, Tue, Wed, Fri 1000-1800, Thu 1000-2200, Sat, Sun 1100-1800, €8.*

Unter den Linden

S-Bahn Unter den Linden. Map D3/E2.

Unter den Linden ('Beneath the Lime Trees') runs east from the Brandenburg Gate and Pariser Platz, the trees in the centre now making a congenial pedestrian precinct between the two wide traffic lanes on either side. On the south side stands the **Russian Embassy**, an excellent example of socialist architecture but now incongruous in a Berlin eager to forget its links with the former USSR. At the eastern end of Unter den Linden is the revamped **Deutsches Historisches Museum**, *www.dhm.de, daily 1000-1800, €8, U-Bahn Französischestr,* whose permanent exhibition covers 2000 years of German history through authentic objects and multimedia displays. Temporary exhibitions are staged in a wing designed by I M Pei.

Gendarmenmarkt

U-Bahn Stadtmitte. Map E3.

If there is still a tendency to judge Germany by the worst periods of its history, a visit to Gendarmenmarkt will show the country at its most liberal. It became the centre of a French community around 1700 when Prussia gave refuge to 6000 Huguenots. On the north side, the **Französischer Dom** (French Cathedral), now

Pride

Berlin has welcomed the gay scene since the 'roaring twenties' when Marlene Dietrich and Christopher Isherwood lived and entertained around Nollendorfplatz in Schöneberg. Hitler's rise to power in 1933 and his deportation of gay people to the camps put a stop to this (outside Nollendorfplatz U-bahn station there is a plaque to commemorate the victims). But now, the city's gay and lesbian scene is more vibrant than ever. Some areas are more gay than others, but around the centre it's all quite mixed, with lots of bars and clubs catering to a gay and straight crowd. Kreuzberg has a very liberal feel to it, whereas Nollendorfplatz is more hardcore. Friedrichshain and Prenzlauerberg have quite an experimental feel to them. Christopher Street Day, www.csdberlin.de, which takes place every summer, is Berlin's most flamboyant festival. Loud and outrageous, this gay and lesbian parade was named after the New York Stonewall riots of 1969 and is not one for the faint-hearted.

home to the **Hugenottenmuseum**, *Tue-Sun 1200-1700, €2*, dates from this time, as does the similarly proportioned **Deutscher Dom**, *May-Sep Tue-Sun 1000-1900, Oct-Apr Tue-Sun 1000-1800*, on the south side. In the centre of the square, the **Konzerthaus**, or Schauspielhaus, in the centre of the square, was one of the earliest buildings designed by the prolific architect Karl Friedrich Schinkel (1781-1841).

Museuminsel

T030 2090 5577, www.smb.museum.
Fri-Wed 1000-1800, Thu 1000-2200; Alte Nationalgalerie closed Mon. One museum €8; Museuminsel €12; free 1st Sun in the month. S-Bahn Hackescher Markt. Map F2.

Museum Island is an extraordinary collection of first-rate galleries in the middle of the Spree. Recognized by UNESCO as a World Cultural Heritage Site, the complex is currently undergoing a major restoration and redevelopment project that will unite all five buildings and their disparate collections by 2015.

Right: The TV Tower, Alexanderplatz.
Opposite page: Unter den Linden.

The **Altes Museum**, *Lustgarten*, designed by Karl Friedrich Schinkel and considered his finest work, exhibits Greek, Roman and Etruscan antiquities.

The **Pergamon Museum**, *Am Kupfergraben 5*, houses one of the world's great archaeological collections, with entire complexes on display that are dramatically lit at night. The second-century BC Pergamon Altar and the Babylonian Street are the stars of the show.

The **Alte Nationalgalerie**, *Bodestrasse 1-3*, exhibits 19th-century sculptures and paintings, while the **Bode Museum**, *Monbijoubrücke*, houses the coin collection, sculpture collection and Byzantine art, together with Old Master paintings from the Gemäldegalerie.

After 70 years' closure, the **Neues Museum** finally reopened in 2009 and houses the Ancient Egyptian collection that was previously in the Altes Museum.

Alexanderplatz

S/U-Bahn Alexanderplatz. Map G1.

East of the museums, 'Alex' has, in an architectural sense, stood still for over 30 years, as a time-warped legacy of old East Berlin. In the early 1970s, the best that the town could offer was here on a vast pedestrian precinct. The 365-m-high

Best of the rest

East Side Gallery
Running along Mühlenstr to Warschauerstr, www.eastsidegallery.com. U-Bahn Warschauer Str.
One of the last remaining stretches of the Wall is decorated with street art.

Sans Souci
Apr-Oct Tue-Sun 1000-1800, No-Mar Tue-Sun 1000-1700. €8-€12. S-Bahn Potsdamer Hauptbahnhof, then bus 695.
Frederick the Great's summer pleasure palace.

The Story of Berlin
Kurfürsten-damm 207, www.story-of-berlin.de. Daily 1000-2000, last entry 1800. €12. U-bahn Uhlandstrasse, S-bahn Savignyplatz.
This brings the city's eventful past to life. Don't miss the tour of the nuclear shelter, a sealed-off underground town.

East Side Gallery.

Fernsehturm (TV tower), *www.tv-turm.de, Mar-Oct daily 0900-2400, Nov-Feb daily 1000-2400, €12.50,* completed the image of a modern town centre. The **Weltzeituhr** (World Clock) has always been a convenient meeting point, although when it was built in 1969, it was seen by some East Berliners as a cruel reminder of all the places they could not visit.

Charlottenberg

S/U-Bahn Zoologischer Garten, U-Bahn Richard-Wagner or Sophie-Charlotte Platz, off map.

Charlottenburg has lost much of its cachet since reunification but still boasts many of the institutions that made West Berlin famous. First among these is the iconic **Gedächtniskirche** (Memorial Church), *Breitscheidplatz, daily 0900-1900 for the church, daily tours in English at 1315, 1400 and 1500, €4,* built shortly after the death of Kaiser Wilhelm in 1888 and largely destroyed by an air raid in 1943.

Lavish **Schloss Charlottenburg** (Charlottenburg Palace), *T030 320 911, www.schloss charlottenburg.de, Apr-Oct Tue-Sun 1000-1800, Nov-Mar Tue-Sun 1000-1700, €10,* is a one-stop shop for two centuries of German architecture. It was built as a summer residence for Queen Charlotte (1669-1705) by her husband Friedrich I (1657-1713) and was expanded into its present baroque and rococo form in 1701 when Friedrich crowned himself King of Prussia.

A few kilometres northwest is **Olympiastadion**, which underwent a multi-million renovation for the 2006 World Cup.

Kreuzberg

U-Bahn Hallesches Tor, Koch Str, Kottbusser Tor.

Once a haven of alternative living – before everyone moved to Prenzlauerberg – Kreuzberg is now home to a large Turkish community and to some of Berlin's most disturbing sights. Nazi crimes are detailed at the open-air **Topographie des Terrors**, *Niederkirchnerstr, www.topographie.de, daily 1000-2000, free* (Map D4), while the **Haus am Checkpoint Charlie**, *Friedrichstr 43-45, www. mauermuseum.de, daily 0900-2200, €12.50* (Map E4), documents East Berliners' desperate efforts to cross the border. The powerful, innovative **Jüdisches Museum**, *Lindenstr 9-14, www.jmberlin. de, Mon 1000-2200, Tue-Sun 1000-2000, €7* (Map E5), shows 2000 years of German-Jewish history, with a harrowing section on the Holocaust.

Where to stay

Berlin has a good selection of accommodation. Its more upmarket hotels are often large, modern affairs at the forefront of contemporary design. There are also many traditional pensions, particularly on and around the Kurfürstendamm in Tiergarten and Charlottenburg. Mitte and Prenzlauerberg have some first-rate arty and individual hotels.

Hotel Adlon Kempinski €€€
Unter den Linden 77, T030 22610, www.kempinski.com.
U-Bahn Brandenburger Tor
Beside the Brandenburg Gate, the Adlon is not discreet but that doesn't seem to deter a regular turnover of celebrities. They follow in hallowed footsteps: Albert Einstein, Charlie Chaplin and Theodore Roosevelt all stayed here. The current building is a replica of the original – opulent and showy but also impressively stylish.

Hotel de Rome €€€
Behrenstrasse 37, T030 4606 090, www.hotelderome.com.
U-Bahn Stadtmitte.
Once headquarters of the Dresden Bank, this majestic building now houses a 5-star spa hotel. Architecturally splendid with a contemporary twist, its high ceilings and original features provide guests with an insight into the regal grandeur of Old Berlin while sumptuous furnishings and the latest spa experience provide every comfort.

Cosmo Hotel Berlin Mitte €€
Spittelmarkt 13, T030 5858 2222, www.cosm-hotel.de.
U-Bahn Spittelmarkt.
An incredibly stylish and über-modern boutique hotel whose central location offers guests a fantastic base for exploring the city.

Ku'Damm 101 €€
Kurfürstendamm 101, Charlottenburg, T030 520 0550, www.kudamm101.com.
U-Bahn Adenauerplatz.
This bold hotel opened in 2003 and makes a good out-of-centre base. Its minimalist take on vaguely 1950s and 1970s themes involves curves: lots of them. Even the buffet breakfast (on the 7th floor with spectacular views) is visually striking.

Circus Hostels €
Weinbergsweg 1a, T030 2000 3939, www.circus-berlin.de.
U-Bahn Rosenthaler Platz.
This place is very popular and for good reason. It offers rooms for 2 or 4 people along with newly modernized flats. It's also in a buzzing location.

Pension Funk €
Fasanenstrasse 69, T030 8827 193, www.hotel-pensionfunk.de.
U-Bahn Spichernstrasse or Uhlandstrasse.
A beautiful house in a central location, dating back to 1895. It was home to silent movie star Asta Nielsen in the 1930s and is full of charm and original features. A very affordable option in a great spot.

Restaurants

In no other German city can you eat as well, or as internationally, as in Berlin. There are now many great restaurants and, though often pricey, they are on the whole very good value for money. As well as international cuisine, there are lots of traditional German restaurants serving generous portions of heavy but extremely tasty food.

Breakfast
Café November €
Husemannstrasse 15, T030 442 8425, www.cafe-november.de.
Mon-Fri 1000-0200, Sat-Sun 0900-0200.
U-Bahn Eberswalder Str.
An almost overwhelming selection of platters with the emphasis on traditional and hearty German fare to set you up for the day. Cosy and rustic with a very laid-back vibe.

Lunch
Borchardt €€€
Französische Str 47, T030 8188 6262, www.borchardt-restaurant.de.
Daily 1130-0000.
U-Bahn Französische Str.
Restaurant serving international cuisine and favoured by politicians and journalists. The

interior is 18th century, and the mosaics and period-style floors make this Gerndarmenmarkt institution well worth a visit. The food is also first rate. High-end dinner menu available but you'll need to book ahead.

Restauration 1900 €€
Husemannstr 1, T030 442 2494, www.restauration-1900.de. Daily from 0930 (summer) 1100-2400 (winter). U-Bahn Eberswalder Str, Senefelder Platz.
A local hang-out on Kollwitz Platz. Dishes include traditional German cuisine, such as pork knuckle and braised oxtail, but generally it has a global feel. At weekends a delicious and quite substantial brunch is served.

Konnopke Imbiss €
Schonhauser Allee 44a, www.konnopke-imbiss.de. U-Bahn Eberswalder Strasse. Mon-Fri 1000-2000, Sat 1200-2000. U-Bahn Rosa Luxemburg Platz.
Serving *Currywurst* to the locals for over 80 years. A hidden gem, off the tourist trail, tucked away under the U-bahn station. A must for an authentic Berlin fast-food experience.

Dinner
Nocti Vagus €€€
Saarbrucker Strasse 36, T030 7474 9123, www.nocyivagus.com. U-Bahn Senefelderplatz.
German cuisine with a twist. At Nocti Vagus specially trained blind and visually impaired

waiters and waitresses will serve you, in complete darkness. The idea is to truly awaken your taste buds and heighten your senses. There's also a 'dark' performance element to the evening. A truly unique experience.

Yosoy €€
Rosenthaler Str 37, T030 2839 1213, www.yosoy.de. S-Bahn Hackescher Markt, U-Bahn Weinmeisterstr. Daily from 1100.
The feeling that you're in a North African souk is all pervasive when visiting this late-night haunt, where delicious tapas are served on tiled counters. A pleasant alternative to the super-smart Mitte bars.

Burgermeister €
Oberbaumstrasse 8, www.burger-meister.de. U-bahn Schlesische Tor.
Don't let the fact that you're dining beneath train tracks and in the remains of a public toilet put you off! This is a rightly popular burger joint offering perfect pre-clubbing fodder to those heading into Kreuzberg for the night.

Nightlife

Bars and clubs
Berlin offers some of the best nightlife in Europe: laid-back, accessible and cutting edge at the same time. The further east you go, the more shabby-chic the bars tend to be; the further west, the smarter and more

elegant they become. You'll never be pushed for somewhere to go. **Mitte** has more than its fair share of suitable watering holes, with the area around Oranienburger Str being particularly popular with tourists. For something a bit more authentically Berlin, **Prenzlauerberg** is the place to go. From U-Bahn Rosenthaler Platz, head up Weinbergsweg into Kastanienallee where you'll find many hip bars and restaurants. Bars usually open at 2200 and then close when the last guest leaves.

The club scene attracts top performers, be it a plethora of international DJs at the incredibly hip **Weekend Club**, or Kings of Leon at **O2 World**. Berlin also plays host to secret Geheimtip parties: part of the eastside nightlife. If you are lucky you might discover the location for favourites, such as the **Mittwochclub**, every Wed.

Classical music and opera
Berlin's classical music scene is world renowned. The **Berlin Philharmonic Orchestra** is based at the Berliner Philharmonie, *Herbert-von-Karajan-Str 1, T030 2548 8132, www.berliner-philharmoniker.de, daily 0900-1800.* Equally prestigious is the exquisitely restored **Staatsoper**, *Unter den Linden 7, T030 2035 4555, www.staatsoper-berlin.org*, where opera and ballet are performed. Unsold tickets are available for €13 before a performance.

Travel essentials

Getting there
Due to finally open after lengthy delays in spring 2014, **Berlin-Brandenburg International Airport** (T030 6091 1150, www.berlin-airport.de) will be the area's new international gateway, with state-of-the-art facilities and improved transport links. Located 20 km from the centre on a site adjacent to the existing **Schönefeld (Berlin-Brandenburg)** airport, the new airport will replace both Schönefeld and **Tegel (Berlin International)** airports, which are due to close. The Airport Express (RE7, RB14, RE9) will run every 15 mins between the airport and the central station (Berlin Hauptbahnhof), taking 30 mins. Alternatively there are excellent S-Bahn services (S9 and S45) to and from the city centre every 20 mins, also taking 30 mins. Tegel, 8 km northwest of the centre, is connected to the centre (Zoo station) by buses X9 (20 mins) and 109 (30 mins), via most of the hotels. Bus 128 is better for destinations to the north or east, while the JetExpressBus TXL goes to Alexanderplatz, Mitte (single €2.10). Taxis are plentiful and cost about €25 to Zoo Station or €35 to Mitte. A tip of 5-10% is normal. Opened for the 2006 World Cup, **Berlin Hauptbahnhof**, Europaplatz 1, www.hbf-berlin.de, is the state-of-the-art hub of Berlin's upgraded rail network, linking national and international services (including sleeper trains from Brussels) with the city's urban transport system. Almost all long-distance trains also stop at **Ostbahnhof**, Straße der Pariser Kommune 5 in Friedrichshain. There are 3 other long-distance stations (Gesundbrunnen, Südkreuz and Spandau), as well as regional stations. For details, see www.bahn.de.

Getting around
The extensive and speedy urban rail system consists of U-Bahn (underground) and S-Bahn (overground) trains. Both operate at night. Rail services are supplemented by the 'MetroNetz' of tram and bus routes. The city is divided into 3 travel zones: A, B and C. You are only likely to venture out to zone C if you're going to Potsdam. A ticket for any number of journeys in a 2-hr period costs €2.60. Day passes for zones A and B cost €6.70. Tickets and passes are available at the Tegel Airport office, at the BVG centre at Zoo Station (T030 19449, www.bvg.de) and from machines on all platforms. The **Berlin WelcomeCard** (starting at €18.50), available from Berlin Infostores, offers free transport in all zones and a 25% reduction on many sights. Taxis are plentiful, with ranks at most U-Bahn and S-Bahn stations in the suburbs; they can be hailed in the city centre. Fares start at around €2, then cost €1 per km.

Tourist information
Visit Berlin tourist offices, T030 250 025, www.visit berlin.de, are located at the Hauptbahnhof, daily 0800-2200; at Kurfürstendamm 22, Mon-Sat 1000-2000, Sun 1000-1800; at the Brandenburg Gate, Apr-Oct daily 0930-1800, Nov-Mar 09.30-1800; and in the Berlin Pavilion at the Reichstag, Apr-Oct daily 0830-2000, Nov-Mar daily 1000-1800. **New Berlin Tours**, www.newberlintours.com, offer excellent free tours of the city.

Ratings

Art and culture ☆☆☆
Eating ☆☆☆☆
Nightlife ☆☆☆
Shopping ☆
Sightseeing ☆☆
Value for money ☆☆☆
Overall city rating ☆☆☆

Bilbao

In an amazingly short time, and without losing sight of its roots, the dirty industrial city of Bilbao – a name that once conjured images of rusted pig-iron – has transformed itself with huge success into an exciting, buzzy, cultural hub. The Guggenheim Museum is the undoubted flagship of this triumphant progress. A sinuous fantasy of a building, it inspires not only because of what it is, but also because the city had the vision to put it there. While the museum has led the turnaround, much of what is enjoyable about Bilbao already existed. Bustling bar life, harmonious architecture, a superb eating culture and a sense of pride in being a working city. The exciting new developments, which improve and beautify the city, have only added to those qualities.

Reflections in the Palacio Euskalduna, Deusto.

Around the city

Casco Viejo (Old Town)

Tram Ribera/Arriaga. Metro Casco Viejo. Map F/G2.

Tucked into a bend in the river, Bilbao's Casco Viejo (Old Town) has something of the medina about it and evokes a cramped medieval past. Designer clothes shops occupy the ground floors where families once huddled behind the city walls, and an array of memorable bars serve up fine wine and elaborate bartop snacks, from delicious tortilla from a generations-old family recipe, to gourmet postmodern creations that wouldn't look out of place in the Guggenheim. Most Bilbaínos live and work elsewhere in the city and the true soul of the Casco emerges from early evening, when people descend on it like bees returning to the hive, strolling the streets, listening to buskers, debating the quality of the *pintxos* (snacks) in the bars, and sipping drinks in the setting sun.

The parallel **Siete Calles** (Seven Streets) form the oldest part of town (**Somera** is particularly interesting), with the slender spire of the graceful Gothic **Catedral de Santiago** rising from the

tightly packed maze. On the waterfront here is the **Mercado de la Ribera**, a lovely art deco market building with over 400 stalls of fruit, vegetables, meat and fish on three floors. **Plaza Nueva** will appeal to lovers of symmetry: its courtly, neoclassical arches conceal an excellent selection of restaurants and bars, serving some of the best *pintxos* in town. On Plaza Miguel de Unamuno is **Museo Vasco**, *T944 155423, 3, Tue-Sat 1100-1700, Sun 1100-1400, €3 (free on Thu)*, housing an interesting, if higgledy-piggledy, series of Basque artefacts. Across the square, the **Museo Arqueológico**, *Calzadas de Mallona 2, T944 040 990, Tue-Sat 1000-1400, 1600-1930, Sun 1030-1400, €3*, has a well-presented overview of Vizcaya's prehistory and history through material finds, including prehistoric artefacts found in caves around the province.

Atop a steep hill above the Casco Viejo is Bilbao's most important church, the **Basílica de Begoña**, *lift from C Esperanza; bear right, then turn right up C Virgen de Begoña*, home of Vizcaya's patron, the Virgin of Begoña. Take the steps back down to the old town; a charming descent.

La Ribera market.

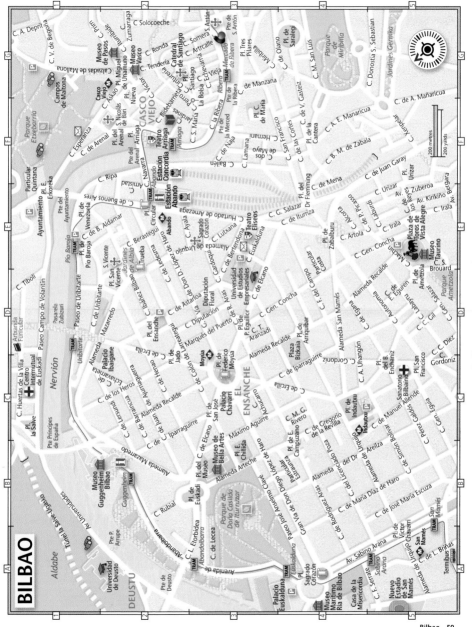

BILBAO

Around the city

Riverbank

The once-grim riverbank was completely redesigned as the focus of Bilbao's regenerative leap into the 21st century. If you only take one stroll in Bilbao, make it an evening *paseo* along the Nervión from the Casco Viejo west to the Guggenheim Museum (see below). Highlights on the way include the fin de siècle **Teatro Arriaga**, *Tram Arriaga*, and Calatrava's eerily skeletal **Zubizuri** **footbridge**, *Tram Uribitarte*.

Beyond the Guggenheim the bizarre **Palacio Euskalduna** opened in 1998 on the site of the last Bilbao shipyard and is now a major venue for concerts, particularly classical. Nearby is the **Museo Marítimo**, *Muelle Ramón de la Sota, T902 131000, www.museomaritimobilbao.org. Tue-Fri 1000-1800 (2000 summer), Sat and Sun 1000-2000,*

Out of town

At the mouth of the Nervión, 20 km from the centre, **Getxo** has a pretty old harbour and good beaches. The impressive **Puente Bizkaia**, a UNESCO World Heritage Site, zips cars and passengers across the estuary via a hanging 'gondola'. The rugged coast to the east is lined with great surf beaches and appealing fishing towns, such as **Mundaka**, a laid-back little surf village with one of Europe's most famous waves, and **Lekeitio**, a Basque fishing port with a picturesque harbour and good eating. Inland is the unmissable and thriving town of **Gernika**, the symbolic home of Basque nationalism. Its **Museo de la Paz**, *Pl Foru 1, T946 270 213, www.museodelapaz.org, Tue-Sat 1000-1400, 1600-1900 (1000-2000 in summer), Sun 1000-1400, €5*, is a moving but optimistic museum detailing the brutal aerial bombardment endured by the town on 26 April 1937.

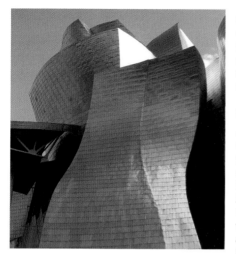

€6, Tram Euskalduna, a salty treat that includes a number of different boats as part of its exterior exhibition. Across the river from here is the university barrio of **Deusto**, while, just south, is the new **San Mamés stadium**, Pl Pedro Basterretxea, T944 411 445, www.athletic-club.net, Metro/tram San Mames, home of the fervently supported Athletico Bilbao.

Guggenheim Museum

Abandoibarra Etorbidea 2, T944 359 000,
www.guggenheim-bilbao.es.
Tue-Sun 1000-2000, Jul-Aug also Mon. Around €11, combined ticket, €13.50 including Museo de Bellas Artes. Tram Guggenheim. Map B2.

More than anything else, it is this building that has thrust Bilbao firmly on to the world stage. Frank Gehry's exuberant Guggenheim brings art and architecture together. It sits among the older riverfront buildings like some unearthly vehicle that's just landed. The titanium panels are paper thin and malleable, making the whole structure shimmer like a writhing school of fish.

Outside, a pool and fog and fire sculptures interact fluidly with the river. Jeff Koons' giant floral sculpture, Puppy, sits eagerly greeting visitors at the entrance. Inside, while most exhibits are temporary, enormous Gallery 104 holds Richard Serra's magnificent and interactive The Matter of Time, eight monumental structures of curved oxidised-steel, centred around *Snake*, whose curved sheets will carry whispers from one end to another.

El Ensanche

Across the river from the Casco Viejo, the new town was laid out in 1876 and has an elegant European feel to it. The wealth of the city is evident here, with stately banks and classy shops lining its avenues. Here you'll find the **Museo de Bellas Artes**, *Pl del Museo 2, T944 396 060, www.museobilbao.com, Tue-Sun 1000-2000, €6, Wed free, Metro Moyua,* which houses modern Basque art, older pieces and temporary exhibits. On the edge of El Ensanche is the bullring (*www.plazatorosbilbao.com*) and museum of **Vista Alegre**, *C Martin Agüero, T944 448 698, Metro Indautxu.*

Below: 'Puppy' by Jeff Koons.
Left: Guggenheim Museum.
Opposite page: Zubizuri footbridge.

Where to stay

Restaurants

Melià Bilbao €€€
Lehendakari Leizaola Kalea 29,
T944 280 000, www.melia.com.
Tram Abandoibarra.
This striking reddish giant
has excellent modern rooms
featuring really stylish bathrooms.
Chock-full of facilities.

Gran Domine €€
Alameda Mazarredo 61,
T944 253 300, www.gran
hoteldominebilbao.com.
Tram Guggenheim.
Inspiring modern hotel opposite
the Guggenheim with a façade
of tilted glass panels and a
delightful interior.

Indautxu €€
Pl Bombero Etxariz,
El Ensanche, T944 211 198,
www.hotelindautxu.com.
Metro Indautxu.
Comfortable Ensanche 4-star with
bags more character than most
business-level establishments.

Miróhotel Bilbao €€
Alameda Mazarredo 77, T946 611
880, www.mirohotelbilbao.com.
Tram Guggenhelm.
Close to the Guggenheim, with
some great views, this is a sleek
hotel with a pared-back feel not
without touches of whimsy.

Apartamentos Atxuri €
Av Miraflores 17, T944 667 832,
www.apartamentosatxuri.com.
Tram Atxuri.
These beautifully sleek
apartments occupy a modern
building just east of the
Casco Viejo.

Hotel Sirimiri €
Pl de la Encarnación 3, T944 330
759, www.hotelsirimiri.com.
Tram Atxuri.
Great hotel with a genial owner,
gym, sauna and free parking.

Iturrienea Ostatua €
C Santa María, T944 161 500,
www.iturrieneaostatua.com.
Tram Arriaga.
Beautiful pensión fitted out in
stone, wood and idiosyncratic
objects. Tasty breakfasts.

Casco Viejo is the best place to
head for *pintxos* (bar snacks) and
evening drinks, especially the
Plaza Nueva and around the
Siete Calles. In El Ensanche,
there's concentrations of bars
on Av Licenciado Poza, C García
Rivero and C Ledesma.
Restaurants are scattered
throughout the Casco Viejo,
Ensanche and Deusto.

Mina €€€
Muelle Manzana s/n, T944 795
938, www.restaurantemina.es.
Tram Ribera.
Perhaps the most enjoyable place
to eat in town, this restaurant faces
the Casco Viejo on the riverbank.
Expect creative combinations that
you haven't seen before and are
unlikely to again.

Porrue €€€
Alameda Rekalde 4, T944
231 313, www.porrue.com.
Tram Guggenheim.
Perfectly placed for a post-
Guggenheim special meal,
this intimate, romantic space is
decorated with contemporary
flair. The cuisine focuses on
seasonal ingredients. One of
the city's best.

Zortziko €€€
Alameda Mazarredo 17,
T944 239 743, www.zortziko.es.
This upmarket choice in the
business district focuses
on fairly traditional Basque
ingredients cooked to perfection
with modern techniques.

Kasko €€
C Santa María, Casco Viejo,
T944 160 311, www.restaurante
kasko.com
Tram Arriaga.

High-class but low-priced new
Basque food in this spacious
bohemian bar-restaurant in
the heart of the action.

Café-Bar Bilbao €
Pl Nueva 6, Casco Viejo,
T944 151 671.
Metro Casco Viejo.

Don't miss this sparky place
with top service and a selection
of some of the best *pintxos*
to be had in the old town, all
carefully labelled and irresistible.
Try them with a *txakolí* (a slightly
fizzy local wine).

El Globo €
C Diputación 8, T944 154 221,
Metro Moyúa.

There's an extraordinary variety
of cold and cooked-to-order hot
pintxos here; traditional bites
take their place alongside wildly
imaginative modern creations.

El Puertito €
García Rivero y Licenciado Poza,
T944 026 254, www.elpuertito.es.
Metro Indautxu.

On this fertile pintxo street in the
Ensanche, this is a top little place
to perk up your palate with
toothsome fresh-shucked oysters.

Right: Tram in Bilbao.
Opposite page: Modern Bilbao.

Travel essentials

Getting there
Bilbao International Airport, *T905 505505*, designed by Santiago
Calatrava, is 10 km northeast of the city. Buses run to the centre every
30 mins or so, taking 20-30 mins (€1.40). A taxi will cost about €25.
Brittany Ferries, *T0871 244 0744, www.brittany-ferries.co.uk*, run overnight
ferries between Bilbao and Portsmouth once or twice weekly. The ferries
arrive at Zierbena, 21 km from the centre of Bilbao. You can get a cab
either into town (€30) or to the closest metro stop, Santurzi, 3 km from the
port. The main Abando train station is centrally located across the river
from the Casco Viejo and is well connected by both metro and tram lines.

Getting around
Bilbao is reasonably walkable – the Guggenheim is an easy 20-min stroll
along the river from the old town – but the re-established **tram** line is
a handy alternative. It runs every 10-15 mins from Atxuri station along
the river, skirting the Casco Viejo and El Ensanche, with stops at the
Guggenheim and the bus station (Termibus) among other places.
A single costs €1.45. To reach destinations further afield, including Deusto,
Getxo and the beaches, use the fast, efficient **metro**. A single fare costs
from €1.50; a day pass is €4.60. **Euskotren** (T902-543210) services from
Abando and Atxuri stations link Bilbao with coastal towns and Gernika.
There are also buses from C Hurtado Amezaga, next to Abando station.

Tourist information
Bilbao Turismo, www.bilbao.net, is at Pl Circular 1, T944 795 760, daily
0900-2100. There are information centres near the **Guggenheim** at
Abandoibarra Etorbidea 2, Tue-Fri 1100-1800, Sat 1100-1900, Sun 1100-
1500, and at the **airport**, T914 710 301.

Ratings

Art and culture ☆☆☆☆☆
Eating ☆☆☆☆☆
Nightlife ☆☆
Shopping ☆☆☆
Sightseeing ☆☆☆☆☆
Value for money ☆☆
Overall city rating ☆☆☆

Bruges

Bruges is a miniature marvel, a perfectly preserved medieval city set upon a network of canals. Sometimes called the 'Venice of the North', it was, like its southern sister, at the centre of a huge trading empire during the middle ages. When the canals silted up, so did the trade, and Bruges was forced onto the sidelines of European history. Paradoxically, it was the centuries of neglect that preserved the old city intact and made it the magical time capsule so beloved by travellers. From the top of the medieval belfry, you can still gaze down over a picture-postcard huddle of red-roofed, gabled mansions and bridge-studded canals. Contemporary Bruges is now firmly on the tourist track, but there are numerous secret corners and quiet gardens to escape the hordes. After wandering the cobbled streets, taking a boat trip along the canals, or admiring the city's spectacular artworks (highlights include the Flemish Primitives at the Groeningemuseum, Memling at the Hospital Museum, or Michelangelo's *Madonna* in the Church of Our Lady), head to the city's cosy pubs to sample some famous Belgian beers. Gourmets are in for a treat, as Belgian cuisine is world-renowned. Bruges offers something for all budgets, from the punnets of golden *friet* (fries) dispensed from *frietkoten* on the street, to a dozen or so Michelin-starred restaurants.

Canalside houses.

At a glance

The historic centre of Bruges is small and compact, an egg-shaped warren of medieval streets neatly contained within a ring of canals. The bus and train stations are found next to each other on the southeastern edge of the old city, close to the modern **Concertgebouw** (concert hall) which also contains the main tourist information office. Shop-lined **Zuidzandstrasse** and **Steenstrasse** will bring you to the **Markt**, the heart of the city, a grand ensemble of gabled townhouses set around a huge cobbled square. It's dominated by the **Belfry**, the city's most famous landmark. A two-minute stroll east will bring you to the **Burg**, the political and administrative centre of Bruges for more than a thousand years, and the location of the gilded **Stadhuis** (city hall) and the magnificent **Heilig Bloedbasiliek** (Basilica of the Holy Blood). Behind the Burg is the **Vismarkt**, the wonderful 18th-century fish market, and the pretty little café-lined square of the **Huidevettersplein**. The main museums, including the **Groeningemuseum** and the **Memlingmuseum**, in the **Sint-Jan Hospital**, are found just to the south, close to a picturesque canal where you can pick up boat tours. Also here is the **Onze-Lieve Vrouwerk** (Church of Our Lady), with Michelangelo's sublime *Madonna and Child*. Follow the canal further south to the charming **Begijnhof**, a religious complex composed of whitewashed houses and a simple church, which provides a quiet retreat from the city bustle. On the opposite bank of the canal is the lush, watery expanse of the **Minnewater**, a dreamy park overlooking a lake. Another clutch of smaller sights and museums can be found northeast of the Markt: these include the **Kantcentrum**, where lace is still made according to ancient traditions, the **Volkskundemuseum** (Folklore Museum), and, near the old city gate of **Kruispoort**, a pair of traditional windmills, now a museum.

Markt

Map D4.

The bustling, commercial heart of Bruges is the Markt, an enormous cobbled square enclosed by gabled former guildhalls and dominated by the celebrated **Belfry** (see below). The old guildhalls are now cafés and restaurants, most with large terraces that are perfect for a spot of people-watching. One of the nicest cafés is the **Craenenburg** at Markt 16, which occupies the oldest original building to survive on the square. At the centre of the square is a 19th-century statue depicting the heroic guild-masters Jan Breydel and Pieter de Coninck, who led a famous rebellion against the French in 1302.

Belfort (Belfry)

Markt 7, T050 448 711.
Daily 0930-1700. €8, €6 concessions. Map D4.

The city's best-loved symbol is the medieval Belfry, which, at 83 m, is visible from almost everywhere. Built between the 13th and 15th centuries, the Belfry once doubled as a watchtower and treasury: money and charters were stored in medieval 'safes' still visible behind 13th-century wrought-iron gates, and guards kept a careful eye on fires and trouble-makers from their lofty vantage point. Nowadays, visitors climb the 366 steps to the top for panoramic views over the red-tiled rooftops and canals. The tower also contains the famous 47-bell Dumery carillon, which dates back to the mid-18th century, as well as the huge Triumphal Bell, which is only rung on special occasions.

Burg

Map D4.

Bruges began in the Burg, an elegant square named for the fortified castle ('burg') built by Baldwin Iron Arm, first Count of Flanders, in the ninth century. The castle has long gone, but the Burg is still the administrative and political heart of Bruges, and its

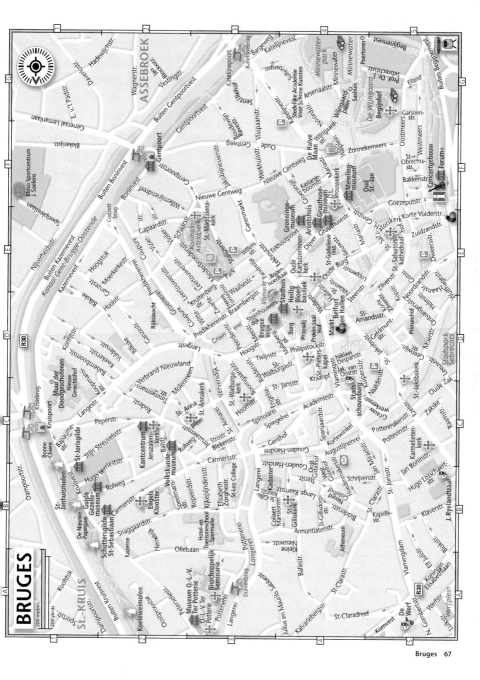

BRUGES

Around the city

southern end is dominated by some of the city's most spectacular historic buildings. These include the Gothic **Stadhuis**, which is Belgium's oldest city hall, and the 12th-century **Heilig Bloedbasiliek** (Basilica of the Holy Blood, see below). Facing the basilica is the gorgeously gilded 16th-century Civil Registry, which incorporates the Renaissance hall of the **Brugse Vrije** (Liberty of Bruges), *Burg 11a, T050 448 711, www.museabrugge.be, Tue-Sun 0930-1230 and 1330-1700, €4.* Here you can admire a lavish mantelpiece carved in honour of the Emperor Charles V, who visited Bruges in 1515.

Heilig Bloedbasiliek (Basilica of the Holy Blood)

Burg 10, T050 448 711, www.holyblood.com. Apr-Sep daily 0930-1200 and 1400-1700; Oct-Mar Thu-Tue 1000-1200 and 1400-1700, Wed 1000-1200. Museum €2. Map D4.

The 12th-century Basilica of the Holy Blood contains a crystal vial containing blood supposedly wiped from the body of Christ. Credited with miraculous powers, it is said to have been brought back to Bruges after the Second Crusade by the Count of Flanders in the mid-12th century. Every year on Ascension Day it is paraded through the streets of the city in a tradition that was first chronicled in 1291. More than 1600 locals dressed in historic costumes take part in the procession, which attracts enormous crowds of visitors and pilgrims. The vial is displayed on Fridays in the basilica's upper chapel, built in flamboyant late-Gothic style in the early 16th century and thickly covered with statues by Flemish artist Lancelot Blondel. In contrast, the lower chapel preserves one of the finest Romanesque interiors in Belgium, with rounded arches and plain stone walls. A pocket-sized museum next door displays the jewel-encrusted reliquary used to transport the vial during the Procession of the Holy Blood.

Above: Detail from façade of Heilig Bloedbasiliek.

Vismarkt (Fish Market)

Market Tue-Sat 0800-1300. Map D3.

Historically, the fishmongers of Bruges occupied a corner of the Markt square, but locals complained so bitterly about the stench that they were moved to splendid, purpose-built quarters in 1821. The elegant stalls, with their balustrades and broad counters, remain virtually unchanged, and stretch all the way around the square. Come in the mornings (except Sun and Mon) to catch the market in full swing, with stall-holders bellowing out their wares in time-honoured tradition. The arcades around the square are filled with terrace cafés, where you can watch the action in comfort.

Groeningemuseum

Dijver 12, T050 448 711, www.museabrugge.be.
Tue-Sun 0930-1700. €8, €6 concessions. Map E4.

One of the finest museums in Europe, this contains a spectacular collection of Flemish and Belgian art spanning six centuries. The highlight is the collection of Flemish Primitives, particularly the outstanding works by Jan van Eyck (1395-1441), Rogier van der Weyden (1399-1464), and Dirk Bouts (1410-1475). Among them, look out for Jan van Eyck's *Madonna with Canon van der Paele* (1436), considered the jewel of the collection. Not merely a religious painting, the extraordinary level of detail in the rich robes and decorations offers a fascinating glimpse into the prosperous world of Bruges under the Dukes of Burgundy. Other celebrated pieces include a gory *Last Judgment* by Hieronymus Bosch, and a few Surrealist works by René Magritte and Paul Delvaux.

Memling In Sint Jan Hospitaalmuseum (Memlingmuseum, St John's Hospital)

Mariastraat 38, T050 448 711, www.museabrugge.be.
Tue-Sun 0930-1700; pharmacy 1145-1400.
€8, €6 concessions. Map F4.

St John's, established in the late 12th century, is one of the oldest and best preserved hospitals in Europe. The cavernous old wards, where monks and nuns once tended to sick travellers, now display furniture, paintings, gruesomely rudimentary medical instruments and even a medieval ambulance. The chapel contains six outstanding works by 15th-century artist Hans Memling, including the masterful *St Ursula Shrine*, a large reliquary illustrating the martyr's life and unpleasant death.

Onze Lieve Vrouwekerk (Church of Our Lady)

Mariastraat, T050 448 743, www.museabrugge.be.
Church Mon-Sat 0930-1230 and 1330-1700,
Sun 1330-1700. Museum Tue-Fri 0930-1700,
Sun 1330-1700. €8, €6 concessions. Map A3.

This beautiful church of golden stone is adorned with a slender spire, which, at 122 m, is one of the tallest in Belgium. It contains the city's most celebrated treasure: a tender depiction of the *Madonna and Child* sculpted by Michelangelo in 1504. The white marble statue has been stolen twice – first by the French during the Napoleonic Wars and then by the Nazis – but was recovered each time. The church is also remarkable for the handsome Renaissance tombs of Charles the Bold (1433-1477) and his daughter, Mary of Burgundy (1457-1482).

Sint-Salvator-kathedraal

Steenstraat, T050 336 841, www.sintsalvator.be.
Cathedral Mon-Fri 1000-1300 and 1400-1730,
Sat 1000-1300 and 1400-1530, Sun 1130-1200
and 1400-1700; Treasury Sun-Fri 1400-1700.
Cathedral free; Treasury €2. Map E5.

The oldest church in Bruges, Saint Salvator's was begun in the 12th century and completed three hundred years later. It remained a simple parish church until the early 19th century, when it was raised to the status of cathedral and given a lavish neo-Gothic facelift. The city's first cathedral was demolished by French armies at the end of the 18th century. Its surviving treasures, including paintings, sculptures and tapestries, were transferred to St Salvator's and are displayed in the cathedral treasury.

Begijnhof

Begijnhof 24-30, www.monasteria.org.
Grounds daily 0630-1830. Museum Mon-Sat
1000-1700, Sun 1430-1700. Museum €2, €1.50
concessions. Complex or church free. Map G5.

The most serene and tranquil corner of old Bruges, the Begijnhof is a hushed, whitewashed monastic enclosure set around a tree-filled courtyard. The convent complex was established in 1245 for the Begijnen (Beguines in French), a lay order founded by the Countess of Flanders in the 12th century for the widows of crusaders, although most of the surviving buildings date from between the 16th and 18th centuries. It is now inhabited by a community of Benedictine nuns, but visitors are welcome to admire the gabled houses, the simple church, and to visit the museum which occupies one of the historic dwellings.

Minnewater

Map G4.

This canalized lake, overhung by willow trees, is the focus of an idyllic park, perfect for a quiet stroll. The grassy banks are filled with ducks and swans and trees form a gauzy canopy. It's hard to imagine that once this was a busy dock, where ships from across Europe would unload their exotic cargoes of silks and spices, and exchange them for prized Flemish cloth.

Below top: Begijnhof.
Bottom: Minnewater.

Best of the rest

Arentshuis (Brangwyn Museum)
Dijver 16, T050 448 763. Tue-Sun 0930-1700.
€4, €3 concessions.
An appealing museum set in an elegant 18th-century mansion, featuring the eclectic works of British artist Frank Brangwyn (1867–1956).

Astridpark (Queen Astrid Park)
Entrances on Gevangenisstraat and Minderbroedersstraat.
Map E3.
A small green lung in the heart of the city with meandering paths, a serene pond and verdant lawns.

Choco-Story
Sint-Jansstraat 7b, T050 612 237, www.choco-story.be.
Daily 1000-1700. €7, €6/4 concessions.
Learn about the history of chocolate and enjoy a special tasting.

De Halve Maan
Walplein 26, T050 332 697, www.halvemaan.be.
Apr-Oct Mon-Fri 1000-1600, Sat-Sun 1000-1700;
Oct-Mar Mon-Fri 1100-1500, Sat-Sun 1100-1600.
€5.50 including tasting. Map F4.
De Halve Maan (The Half Moon) is the only traditional brewery still operating in central Bruges and is famous for its 'Brugse Zot' (which means 'Bruges Fool') and 'Straffe Hendrik' beers, which are produced on the premises.

Gruuthusemuseum (Gruuthuse Museum)
Dijver 17, T050 448 711, www.museabrugge.be.
Tue-Sun 0930-1700. €8, €6 concessions.
A magnificent 15th-century mansion, built for the Lords of Gruut, with rooms decorated in period styles, and a magpie collection of artworks, tapestries and historic tools.

Jeruzalem Kirk (Jerusalem Church) and Lace Centre
Peperstraat 3a, T050 330 072, www.kantcentrum.eu.
Mon-Sat 1000-1700.
Watch lace being made the old-fashioned way, then head next door to the macabre Gothic church.

Volkskundemuseum (Folklore Museum)
Balstraat 43, T050 448 711, www.museabrugge.be.
Tue-Sun 0930-1700. €2.
A cluster of 17th-century almhouses converted into a charming folklore museum.

Where to stay

Central Bruges is so compact that most hotels and guesthouses are located within a 15-min walk of the Markt. Accommodation is generally pricy; if you're on a budget, consider one of the scores of delightful B&Bs. The tourist office has a comprehensive accommodation brochure, available in print, or online at www.brugge.be.

Pand Hotel €€€
Pandreitje 16, T050 340 666, www.pandhotel.com.
This bijou boutique hotel is the chicest address in town and perfect for a romantic break. The 18th-century mansion contains 26 supremely elegant, antique-filled rooms and suites, yet the atmosphere remains one of a gracious private home rather than a hotel. Sip a cocktail by the fire in winter, or relax in the plant-filled patio in summer.

Prinsenhof €€€
Ontvangerstraat 9, T050 342 690, www.prinsenhof.com.
An enchanting luxury hotel in the city centre, the Prinsenhof is located in a mansion built for 13th-century merchants. Traditional furnishings are complemented by contemporary amenities such as plasma TVs and spacious bathrooms, but the hotel's greatest strength is its thoughtful and attentive staff. Good, varied breakfasts are served, and there are several

excellent restaurants within a short stroll of the hotel.

Adornes €€
Sint-Annarei 26, T050 341 336, www.adornes.be.
If you're looking for tranquility, consider the appealing Hotel Adornes. It is tucked away on the banks of a canal in a quiet neighbourhood about a 10-minute walk to the Markt, and offers free parking and free use of bicycles to its guests. Friendly service, spotless rooms, and a copious buffet breakfast (included in the price) make this an excellent mid-priced option. Doubles €120–150.

Nuit Blanche Guesthouse €€
Groeninge 2, T0494 400 447, www.bruges-bb.com.
An artistically decorated guesthouse run by a painter in the historic heart of Bruges, this has antique-furnished rooms, canal views and an enchanting medieval garden.

Ter Duinen €€
Langeria 52, T050 330 437, www.hotelterduinen.eu.
Book early for a room at this captivating little hotel, set in a typical gabled mansion overlooking the canal. The hotel has an airy conservatory overlooking the garden, and tasteful guestrooms. It's located in a quiet neighbourhood about a 10-min stroll from the main sights. An excellent buffet

breakfast is served and the service is exceptional.

B&B Le Coquin €€-€
Noorweegse Kaai 43, T050 612 018, www.lecoquin.be.
A quiet, family-friendly B&B set 1.5 km from the centre of Bruges, this tranquil spot has canal views and is located near a bike path (bike rental can be organized). Prices (doubles are €95-105) include a generous breakfast, and there's a pretty terrace where you can relax on fine days.

Hotel Fevery €
Collaert Mansionstraat 3, T050 331 269, www.hotelfevery.be.
Comfortable, friendly and modestly priced, this family-run, eco-friendly hotel is about a 10-min walk from the Markt. There are just 10 simple guestrooms, and a decent breakfast is included in the price. The welcoming owners can arrange day trips or guided tours and are happy to make recommendations. Private parking is available for around €9 per day. Doubles €40-90.

Restaurants

Flemish and French cuisines dominate the local culinary scene, but there is a handful of international restaurants. Lunch is usually served between 1200 and 1400 and dinner from 1900 to 2100. Always reserve in advance: the most popular places fill up early.

De Karmeliet €€€
Langestraat 19, T050 338 259, www.dekarmeliet.be.
One of the finest restaurants in Belgium, with 3 Michelin stars and a host of other accolades, De Karmeliet excels on every front. The spectacular cuisine is complemented by the elegant, high-ceilinged dining room, superlative service, and magnificent wine list. Book early for a table on the romantic, ivy-covered terrace. If the prices are too daunting, consider chef Geert van Hecke's charming bistro, **Der Refter**, *Molenmeers 2, T050 444 900, www.bistrorefter.com.*

Bocarme €€
Cordoeaniersstraat 1A, T050 343 445, www.debocarme.be.
This elegant cellar restaurant is a romantic choice for dinner. The menu includes dishes such as scallops with lobster and lamb with a Bordelaise sauce, as well as a classic tarte tatin. The weekday set lunch is one of the best bargains in town at around €16. Closed Thu and Sun.

Kardinaalshof €€
St Salvatorskerkhof 14, T050 341 691, www.kardinaalshof.be.
The award-winning cuisine at this luxurious restaurant, which sits in the shadow of St Salvator's Cathedral, is complemented by elegant decor and charming service. Choose from a selection of set menus (from €52 for 4 courses to €88 for the 8-course option), and savour traditional local recipes like wild duck with chicory, pears and nuts, or lamb with olives.

Les Malesherbes €€
Stoofstraat 3-5, T050 336 924.
Tucked down an impossibly narrow side street, this cosy and romantic spot is a great address for tasty French favourites like cassoulet and *magret du canard*, or a selection of fresh fish. Tiny and family-run, it feels rather like being invited to someone's house for dinner. Charming service.

De Bron €
Katelijnstraat 82, T050 333 4536.
A relaxed and child-friendly vegetarian restaurant, this serves a good choice of daily specials, such as vegetable lasagne, made with organic produce where possible. They also do wonderful home-made cakes and a range of fresh juices.

Salade Folle €
Walplein 13, T050 349 443, www.saladefolle.com.
This restaurant isn't strictly vegetarian, but veggies will find plenty to choose from among the long list of soups, salads, quiches and pasta dishes. Some are made with organic produce. There are well priced set menus available at lunchtimes (€13) and weekend evenings (€24-28), and it's also a lovely spot for afternoon coffee and cakes.

Cafés and tea rooms
De Medici Sorbetiere €
Geldmunstraat 9, T050 339 341, www.demedici.com.
One of the most famous cafés in town, justly lauded for its thick hot chocolate (which comes as a DIY package – frothy, hot milk with chunks of chocolate to stir in). Their home-made ice creams and sorbets are a treat in summer, while the cakes are delicious at any time. They also serve light lunches – salads, toasted sandwiches and a couple of pasta dishes.

De Proeverie Tea Room €
Katelijnstraat 5-6, T050 330 837, www.deproeverie.be.
Scrumptious cakes and hot chocolate are the fare of choice in this wonderful tea room with an open fire, owned by the famous Sukerbuyc chocolate shop just across the street. The range of hot chocolates is enormous, with all kinds of unusual flavours – try the dark chocolate and orange. They are beautifully presented with a swirl of fresh cream and a little dish of chocolate treats.

Nightlife

If you're looking for nightclubs, best head to Ghent or Antwerp: the nightlife in Bruges is decidedly low-key, and focused largely on the city's traditional taverns. Try one of the hundreds of speciality beers, perhaps take in a little live music, and soak up the city's relaxing vibe. For a relatively small city, it packs a big cultural punch, with plenty of concerts, theatre and dance performances throughout the year. Most are held at the Concertgebouw (www.concertgebouw.be). To find out what's on, pick up a copy of the Agenda Brugge pamphlet from the tourist office or check out http://events.brugge.be.

Cactus Club
Sint-Sebastiaan 4, T050 332 014, www.cactusmusic.be.
From the people behind the city's excellent contemporary music festivals (Cactus, Klinkers, More Music!), the Cactus Club enjoys a well deserved reputation for its eclectic live music programme. Anything goes, from jazz and blues to reggae and R&B, and it also hosts regular club nights. The promoters also organize events at the Concertgebouw.

De Republiek
St-Jakobsstraat 36, T050 3402 29, www.derepubliek.be.
Downstairs from the Cinéma Lumière, this big, buzzy café-bar is a favourite with young locals, particularly on summer weekends when everyone piles out into the huge courtyard. It often has DJs at weekends, and it also serves food.

Staminee de Garre
De Garre 1, T050 341 029.
This old-fashioned bar, with exposed brick walls, beams and wooden furnishings is a mecca for beer aficionados, thanks to its carefully chosen list of exceptional Belgian beers, each served in its own special glass. The house speciality is Tripel de Garre, a fabulous – if incredibly strong – local brew. Order a platter of Flemish cheese as an accompaniment.

Travel essentials

Getting there
The nearest **international airports** to Bruges are in Brussels (www.brusselsairport.be, 110 km northeast of Bruges see page 83) and Charleroi (www.charleroi-airport.com, 150 km southeast of Bruges). Charleroi is smaller and is mainly used by low-cost airlines. From Brussels airport, there are regular train and bus links to the centre of Brussels, where you can change for trains to Bruges (total journey time 90 mins). From Charleroi airport, take the bus to Brussels or to Charleroi train station for onward connections (total journey time 2 hrs). Train timetables are available at www.b-rail.be.

For details of international **Eurostar** (www.eurostar.com, T08432 186 186) services between London and Brussels, see page 83.

Getting around
Bruges is compact, so few visitors will need to make use of the **bus** network, except for the shuttle bus between the train station and the centre. The main bus station is next to the train station, about a 10-min walk from the city centre. Bus tickets cost €1.30 in advance (from tobacconists and newsstands), or €2 on the bus. A one-day bus pass costs €5 in advance, or €7 on the bus.

Bruges is a bike-friendly city. Ask your hotel for bike rental or contact the following: **Bruges Bike Rental**, Niklaas Desparsstraat 17, T050 616 108, www.brugesbikerental.be, or **Bicycles Popelier**, Mariastraat 26, T050 343 2362, www.fietsenpopelier.be. Average costs are around €4 per hr, or €10-15 per day.

Driving is not recommended in Bruges. Leave your car at the multi-storey car park next to the train station (€3.50 for 24 hrs) and forget about it during your visit. Show your car park ticket at the bus ticket window to get a pass for the shuttle bus. Taxis cannot be hailed in the street, but there are convenient taxi stands at the train station and the Markt.

Tourist information
Concertgebouw, 't Zand, T050 444 646, visitbruges.be, daily 1000-1800.
Railway Station, Stationsplain, Mon-Fri 1000-1700, Sat and Sun 1000-1400.

Ratings

Art and culture ☆☆☆☆
Eating ☆☆☆☆☆
Nightlife ☆☆☆
Shopping ☆☆
Sightseeing ☆☆☆
Value for money ☆☆☆
Overall city rating ☆☆☆

Brussels

When visitors come to Brussels, it's rarely a case of love at first sight, but this is a city that soon gets under your skin. Despite its grey image, the 'capital' of Europe is not short of showpiece buildings or stunning works of art, and its shabby, slightly frayed feel could be regarded as part of its charm. The EU presence lends the city an upbeat, cosmopolitan atmosphere, while the Dutch-speaking minority adds a cultural cutting edge – and all the city's communities unite in their appreciation of the finer things in life. The cooking really is superlative, even in the humblest corner café; the beer is out of this world, and the local penchant for self-deprecating humour gives the nightlife an earthy, unpretentious vibe.

Maison du Cornet, Grand'Place.

At a glance

The core of Brussels is the plectrum-shaped **Pentagone**, home to the Upper and Lower Towns. At the Lower Town's heart is the Grand'Place, an awe-inspiringly opulent square graced with gilt-strewn guildhouses and a Gothic town hall. Around it bustle bars and restaurants in a warren of medieval streets known as the **Ilôt Sacré** ('Sacred Isle'). The **Upper Town**, otherwise known as the Royal Quarter, is almost oppressively monumental, its wide boulevards, mansions and palaces still lofty and inaccessible. The view back across town makes the uphill trudge worthwhile, however, and the Fine and Modern Arts Museums are essential viewing. Down rue de la Régence, under the shadow of the preposterously grandiose Palais de Justice, is the chic **Sablon** district, its main square lined with elegant houses, smart cafés and swish antiques shops. For something a little earthier, head into the **Marolles**, a traditional working-class area with a fabulous flea market. East of the Pentagone is the **European Quarter**, where quiet squares of stunning art nouveau architecture nestle amid the concrete colossi that house the EU institutions. To the south lie **St Gilles** and **Ixelles**, two characterful communes, laced with leafy squares, belle époque buildings, ethnic eateries and cosy cafés.

24 hours in the city

The die-hard Bruxellois breakfasts on beer, but a coffee on a **Grand'Place** terrace may have more appeal. Once you've drunk it all in, amble through the Ilôt Sacré, visiting the **Galeries St Hubert**, one of the world's first covered shopping arcades, and, if you can't wait the urge, paying homage to the **Manneken Pis**. Head up the Mont des Arts to the Upper Town, stopping at the art nouveau Old England building to visit the marvellous **Musical Instruments Museum**: the top-floor café is a good spot for lunch with a view. See the Bruegels and Magrittes at the **Fine and Modern Arts Museums**, then stroll down to the Sablon for a spot of window shopping; or, if you're an architecture buff, take a tram to **St Gilles** and visit the house of Victor Horta, the master architect of art nouveau. In the evening, head to the streets around tranquil **Place Ste Catherine** for fine fish and moules-frites in any of a dozen wonderful places before hunkering down for some serious beer appreciation in the bountiful bars of the Old Town.

Grand'Place

Map D2.

On this jaw-droppingly gorgeous square, it's hard to know where to stare first – at the exquisite Gothic **Town Hall**, with its curlicued masonry and soaring spire, or the glorious baroque **guildhouses**, honey-coloured and dripping with gilt and leaded glass.

Jean Cocteau called the square "the greatest theatre in the world", and its story is nothing if not dramatic: Louis XIV's artillery razed the square in 1695, but the doughty burghers rebuilt it in just four years. Each house belonged to a guild, and identifying the trade from the golden statues atop each building is all part of the fun. Victor Hugo lived at Nos 26-27 (known as '**The Pigeon**') during his exile from France; Marx brooded over the *Communist Manifesto* in the workers' café at No 9, ('**The Swan**'), now a swanky restaurant. The best terrace is at Nos 1-2, '**Le Roy d'Espagne**', formerly the bakers' guild. Drinks are not cheap, but the views are priceless.

Ilôt Sacré

The jumble of medieval streets around the Grand'Place has long been anything but sacred. Their names attest to intense mercantile activity – Butchers' Street, Herring Street, Spur-Makers' Street – and they remain a blur of shops, restaurants, bars and clubs. The eateries around rue des

Grand'Place.

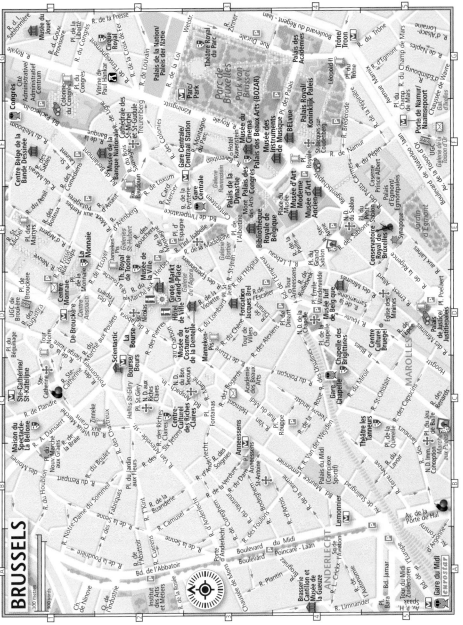

All hail the ale

Brewing is one of Belgium's grandest traditions, and the appreciation of a really good beer, poured reverently into its special glass, is one of the high points of any visit to Brussels. Even if you don't consider yourself an ale aficionado, you'll savour a trip to the **Brussels Gueuze Museum**, Q Cantillon brewery, rue Gheude 56, T02 521 4928, www.cantillon.be, Mon-Fri 0900-1700, Sat 1000-1700, €6, the capital's last bastion of traditional lambic production. The basis for Belgium's fabled fruit beers, lambic is the only brew to ferment spontaneously without yeast: the roof is left open to allow spores from the local atmosphere to infuse the liquid. Learn more on the brewery tour, marvelling at the musty ambience, the huge copper vats and the unbridled enthusiasm of the owner. Then it's tasting time: the *kriek* (cherry) and *framboise* (raspberry) beers are sharper, fruitier and more refreshing than the sweetened stuff on sale in most cafés. But the real deal is the *gueuze*, a complex blend of lambics that has a sharp, sour, almost vinegary taste. If you don't like it on the first try, buy 75cl bottles to take home and/or inflict on your nearest and dearest.

Bouchers, with vast seafood displays outside, are expert at relieving unwary tourists of their cash and are best avoided. (If that sounds bad, night-time visitors in the 19th century were considered lucky to leave with their lives!) That said, there are other great places to eat and drink, and the atmosphere can be positively Bruegelian. The **Galeries St Hubert**, one of the world's first covered shopping arcades, is an oasis of calm amid the surrounding hubbub; a cool, airy glass structure erected in 1847, it houses a theatre, a cinema, cafés and restaurants.

Belgian Comic Strip Center (Centre Belge de la Bande Desinée)

Rue des Sables 20, T02 219 1980, www.comicscenter.net.
Tue-Sun 1000-1800. €8. Map F1.

Tintin fans are in for a treat here; but there's more to *bande dessinée* than the intrepid boy reporter. While this marvellous museum, converted from a Horta-designed art nouveau department store, gives Hergé ample coverage, it's a great place to catch up on Belgium's other memorable comic-book creations. And, more ignominiously, the origins of the Smurfs. Parents be warned: they take the 'ninth art' seriously in Belgium, and the top-floor displays show just how grown-up the genre can be.

Manneken Pis

Rue de l'Etuve.
Map D3.

Symbol of Bruxellois irreverence, anti-war icon or shamelessly tacky photo opportunity? Here's your chance to decide, if you can force your way through the camcorder-wielding crowds that surround Brussels's smallest tourist attraction. Mystery surrounds his origins, but the pint-size piddler's current incarnation is a copy of a statue fashioned by Jérôme Duquesnoy in 1619 and smashed into smithereens two centuries later. He's often decked out in costumes donated by visiting dignitaries, from the Elector of Bavaria, in 1698, to Elvis.

Fine and Modern Arts Museums

Place Royale 1-2, T02 508 3211,
www.fine-arts-museum.be.
Tue-Sun 1000-1700. €8. Map E4.

These twin museums comprise the country's finest collection. The Fine is a conventional 19th-century gallery with a superb survey of works by the artists once grouped together as the 'Flemish Primitives': Van der Weyden, Memling, Bouts and, most important, Pieter Bruegel the Elder. It also boasts vast Rubens canvases and superbly observed smaller works. The Modern is an unusual subterranean spiral with the world's largest collection of works by the star Surrealist René Magritte; there's also a good sample of 20th-century greats – Picasso, Matisse, Bacon, Dalí – and Belgian masters: Paul Delvaux, Leon Spilliaert and Constant Permeke.

Above left: Manneken Pis.
Above right: Old England building.
Opposite page: Galeries St Hubert.

Musical Instruments Museum

Rue Montagne de la Cour 2, T02 545 0130,
www.mim.fgov.be.
Tue-Fri 0930-1700, Sat-Sun 1000-1700. €8. Map E5.

No prizes for guessing what's on show here – but the setting is a real surprise. The frills and flourishes of the ornate Old England building, a delightful art nouveau department store in glass and black iron, are an apt counterpoint to the exquisite craftsmanship of the exhibits. The painted pianos from pre-revolutionary France are a highlight, as are the weird and wonderful folk instruments. The top-floor restaurant has some of the best views in town.

Place du Grand Sablon

Map E4.

The Grand'Place may be the city's grandest square, but the Sablon has a little more class. Although the baroque houses lack their counterparts'

Stained-glass window in Notre Dame du Sablon.

flamboyance, they're still drop-dead gorgeous. The antiques shops at street level are reassuringly expensive, and the smart cafés and restaurants are perfect for observing how Brussels' other half lives. There's a wonderful Gothic church, **Notre Dame du Sablon**, at the square's southeastern side.

Place du Jeu de Balle

If you find the Sablon too stuffy, head downhill to the grittier, more ramshackle Marolles, a traditionally working-class district in the shadow of the preposterously overblown Palais de Justice. It sprawls around rues Blaes and Haute (on which Bruegel lived, at No 132), but its heart is the **flea market** on place du Jeu de Balle (Mon-Fri 0600-1400, Sat-Sun 0600-1500). Amid the mountains of tat, there are some serious bargains, especially for early birds.

Horta Museum

Rue Américaine 25, T02 543 0490, www.hortamuseum.be.
Tue-Sun 1400-1730. €8. Tram 81 or 92. Off map.

Victor Horta was perhaps the greatest exponent of art nouveau, and the house he built in St Gilles is an eloquent reminder of his philosophy and craftsmanship. Horta believed in total design, right down to the door knobs, but he never let the swirls and curls get out of control. Inside, the house is a symphony of burnished wood, stained glass, delicate wrought iron and covetable antiques.

European Quarter

Home to the Commission, the Council of Europe and the European Parliament, as well as countless NGOs, lobby groups, media organizations and multinationals, this district east of the Old Town is like an entirely separate city, one where English is the lingua franca, but where you'll hear dozens of languages on every street. If possible, time your visit for a weekday; the area's deserted at weekends and the relentlessly functional post-war office blocks can deaden the soul. Amid the glass, steel and concrete boxes, however, are two lovely squares, **place Ambiorix** and **place Marie-Louise**. The Hôtel St-Cyr, at 11 place Ambiorix, is so ridiculously ornate, it's beyond parody.

Where to stay

Although there are plenty of characterful establishments, Brussels depends primarily on business. That's great news for short-breakers, as rates plummet at the weekend. Expect reductions of at least 30% and often much more. Summer prices are also extremely keen. The Old Town has a good concentration of hotels; there are also good options in the European Quarter and Ixelles. Try www.bookings.be for late deals; for B&Bs, visit www.bnb-brussels.be or www.bedandbreakfastbelgium.com.

Amigo €€€
rue de l'Amigo 1-3, T02 547 4747, www.hotelamigo.com.
Part of Rocco Forte's exclusive portfolio, this is an immensely stylish establishment near the Grand'Place. Once a prison (the poet Paul Verlaine was incarcerated here after shooting his lover, Rimbaud), it's now a liberating mix of ancient and modern, with lush tapestries and Flemish masters complemented by top-quality contemporary fabrics and fittings.

Le Dixseptième €€€
rue de la Madeleine 25, T02 517 1717, www.ledixseptieme.be.
Don't be fooled by the discreet façade – this was once the Spanish ambassador's residence. Now it's really spoiling us with a superbly restored 17th-century interior, relaxed service and 24 dreamily luxurious, classically kitted-out rooms.

Theater Hotel Brussels €€
Rue Van Gaver 23, T02 350 9000, www.theaterhotelbrussels.com.
One of the city's boutique hotels, located, as the name suggests, in the theatre district. The building has been completely renovated, resulting in stylish but simple interiors with smooth lines and no frills. It's also handy for rue Nueve, the city's main shopping area, so not too far to carry the bags!

Villa Leopoldine €€
Renbaanlaan 52, T02 498 6706 30, www.villaleopoldine.be.
A charming guesthouse set in an idyllic location overlooking the Ixelles lakes in the heart of Brussels. There are only 5 rooms and suites, so guests benefit from their affable hosts' undivided attention and local knowledge. The locally sourced gourmet breakfasts are a sheer delight each morning, setting guests up for a day of sightseeing.

Welcome €€
rue du Peuplier 5, T02 219 9546, www.hotelwelcome.com.
Amid the fish restaurants of Place Ste Catherine is this wonderful little hotel with 17 recently re-furbished world-themed rooms. The Congo is all leopard-print fabrics; the Japan, sleek, stark and serene. It's too well done to be kitsch, and the owners have charm to spare.

2Go4 Hostel €
blvd Emile Jacqmain-laan 99, T02 219 3019, www.2go4.be.
A bright and cheerful 19th-century building, whose situation in the heart of the city make it a very popular choice for budget-conscious travellers who like to be in the thick of things. Private rooms and shared dorms available. The sister hostel, Grand Place, opened in 2013 only 20 m from its namesake market square.

Restaurants

Even the self-deprecating Bruxellois can't help being proud of their city's culinary prowess, and with good reason: it's almost impossible to have a bad meal here, unless you're foolish enough to succumb to the wiles of the waiters on rue des Bouchers. Brasseries, and cafés usually have an all-day menu, with staples such as omelettes and a range of *croques*. Portions are enormous, so go easy on the starters. Oh, and the *frites* are mighty fine, too.

Breakfast

Britxos €€
*rue de Savoie 13, T02 613 4890,
www.britxos.com. Sat 1100-1600,
Sun 1100-1900, closed Mon-Fri.*
Worth seeking out for a leisurely
weekend brunch experience. The
café's name is a fusion of 'British'
and 'pintxos' (the Basque term for
tapas). The atmosphere is relaxed,
with patrons encouraged to pull
up a seat and take their time,
sampling a selection of tasty
brunch options (brunch €25).

Het Warm Water €
*rue des Renards 25, T02 513 9159,
www.hetwarmwater.be. Sun-Tue
0800-1900, Thu-Sat 0800-2200.*
For brekkie, brunch and Belgian
specialities, with a side order of
authentic Marollien atmosphere,
you can't beat this place off place
du Jeu de Balle. It serves earthy,
homely cuisine – Brussels soup,
pottekees, cheese and endive
omelette – as well as croissants
and muesli. Brunch on Sun
(1100-1500) is a riotous affair.

Lunch

Le Paon Royal €€-€
*rue du Vieux Marche aux Grains 6,
T02 513 0868, www.paonroyal.
com. Tue-Sat 0800-2200.*
The Royal Peacock is the
quintessence of Brussels
bonhomie. Off Place Ste
Catherine, it's homely with a
country-pub feel, serving shrimp

croquettes, veal cooked in cherry
beer and eels in a pungent green
sauce. Lunchtime special €8.50.
Excellent beer too.

Dinner

Maison du Cygne €€€
*Grand'Place 9, T02 511 8244,
www.lamaisonducygne.be.*
One of Brussels finest
restaurants, serving traditional
French and Belgian cuisine. Step
back in time and experience an
elegant bygone era in stunning
surroundings. The quality of the
food matches the decor, so be
prepared to settle down for the
evening and enjoy. There are
over 10,000 wines to choose
from in the restaurant's cellar.
Reservations essential.

Bij Den Boer €€
*quai aux Briques 60, T02 512
6122, www.bijdenboer.com.
Mon-Sat 1200-1430
and 1800-2230.*
There are posher and trendier
places to eat fish in the Ste
Catherine area but this
resolutely old-fashioned
restaurant has rugged charm
aplenty. It's a sea of burnished
wood and check tablecloths,
with specials chalked up on
mirrors. House specialities
include mussels 5 ways, North
Sea bouillabaisse and poached
skate wing.

La Roue d'Or €€
*rue des Chapeliers 26,
T02 514 2554, www.resto.be.
Daily 1200-2400.*
Although its striking decor tips
a (bowler) hat to Magritte and
the Surrealists, the polished
wood and mirrors give the game
away: the Golden Wheel is
basically a brasserie, and a jolly
good one at that. Just off the
Grand'Place, it offers a mix of
French (cassoulet, *andouillette*)
and Belgian dishes (sausage and
stoemp, creamy fish or chicken
waterzooi), handling both
cuisines with aplomb. The
double-fried chips are to die for.

Travel essentials

Getting there
Brussels is well served by international trains: **Eurostar** (www.eurostar.com) runs from London to Brussels **Gare du Midi** (2 hrs 20 mins, returns from £69), while the high-speed Thalys service (www.thalys.com) links the city with Paris, Amsterdam and Cologne. The city has 2 airports. **Brussels International** (www.brusselsairport.be) is served by airlines from destinations throughout Europe. From the airport, there are 4 trains an hour to the city's 3 stations; the 20-min ride costs €7.60. A **taxi** costs €45 each way. **Brussels South (Charleroi;** www.charleroi-airport.com) is used by some budget airlines and is a 1-hr bus ride from the capital. Alternative routes from the UK include ferry services to Zeebrugge, Ostend (both an hour's drive from Brussels) and Calais (1½-2 hrs), or the EuroTunnel.

Getting around
The Pentagone is easily negotiable on foot; for journeys further afield, there's an excellent tram, bus and metro network, run by **Societé des Transports Intercommunaux Bruxellois (STIB/MIVB)**, online at www.stib.irisnet.be. A day pass (called 'Jump') for all forms of transport costs €6.50. You get free public transport with the **Brussels Card** (www.brusselscard.be), available at the Gare du Midi, the main tourist office and from hotels and museums. It offers free access to 32 museums in the city, a city map and guide and 25% discounts in shops, restaurants and bars across the city. A card costs €24 for 1 day, €34 for 2 days or €40 for 3 days. Cycling in the city centre is not recommended (given the tramlines, cobbles and traffic-clogged boulevards).

Tourist information
The **Visit Brussels** tourist office, rue Royale 2, T02 513 8940, www.visitbrussels.be, Mon-Fri 0900-1800, Sat-Sun 1000-1800, sells the **Brussels Card** (see above), maps and guides. There's also a room-finding service for visitors who arrive in the city without a hotel reservation. Note that most museums are closed Mon; some are also closed at lunchtime on other days.

Nightlife

With so many great beers to try, it's a good job Brussels is rammed with bars. The expat crowd stick to the European Quarter's Irish joints; leave them to it and focus on the Old Town. Place St Géry's terraces are a magnet for the beautiful people, but rue du Marché au Charbon has more edge; try samba and salsa at **Canoa Quebrada** (No 53), the boho **Au Soleil** (No 86) and the LHB haven **Belgica** (No 32).

The intersection of rue Dansaert and rue des Chartreux is another good crawling point: on the former, **L'Archiduc** (No 6) is a seriously cool art deco jazz bar; on the latter, **Le Greenwich** (No 7) is a classic old café where chess players congregate; and on nearby rue Orts, the **Beurs Café**, is a super-cool post-industrial space.

Beyond the Old Town, chaussée de Charleroi (tram 91 or 92) is lounge central. Try **Chelsea** (No 85) and **Kolya** (No 102). Off the main drag are 2 great conversions: **Khnopff**, *rue St Bernard 1*, a cooler-than-thou bar-restaurant; and the hugely romantic wine bar **Amadeus**, *13 rue Veydt*, in Rodin's studio. Beer buffs should head straight for **Chez Moeder Lambic**, *68 rue de Savoie* (pré-Métro Horta), a loveably scruffy St Gilles institution that stocks every Belgian brew you can think of. It's open till (at least) 0300 most nights. Those in search of the 'in-crowd' will find them at **The Flat**, *rue de la Reinette 12*, a bar and club with chic lounging rooms and resident DJs (Tue-Sat 1800-0300).

Ratings

Art and culture ☆☆☆☆
Eating ☆☆☆
Nightlife ☆☆☆☆
Shopping ☆☆☆
Sightseeing ☆☆☆☆☆
Value for money ☆☆☆
Overall city rating ☆☆☆☆

Budapest

Budapest bears the imprint of its communist past relatively lightly and shares much of the imposing grandeur of its Hapsburg neighbour, Vienna, although it is more derelict and more charming for it. The two cities Buda and Pest, joined administratively in the 19th century, are still kept apart by the grey sweep of the Danube. Above its waters lie belle époque buildings and the weathered stone of neoclassical and baroque mansions. The home of Liszt and Bartók has a rich musical heritage, as well as an underground arts and bar scene, not to mention beautiful mosaic Turkish baths where you can steam yourself back to life after a night on the town.

Stained-glass window, Mátyás Templon.

At a glance

Buda's Castle Hill rises just over 180 m oh the west side of the Danube to offer brilliant views of both the neighbouring hilltop, **Gellért**, to the south, and the low-level sprawl of **Pest** across the river to the east. Pest incorporates two-thirds of the city and is more dynamic and grimy than its west bank rival. The **Chain Bridge** links Castle Hill with **Belváros** on the east bank. This is where the medieval city grew up. It is bordered by a semi-circular series of roads (József Attila ut, Károly körút, Múzeum körút and Vámház körút), which together are dubbed the 'Little Boulevard'. Cutting straight through the inner city, parallel to the Danube, is the shopping street-cum-tourist zone, **Váci út**. To its northeast is **Deák Ferenc tér**, the starting point for the city's most important and grandiose thoroughfare, **Andrássy út**, which runs northeast for over 2 km to the city park, **Városliget**, and **Heroes Square** (Hösök Tere), focal point of the 1956 anti-Soviet uprising.

The **Great Boulevard** is a broader arc that apes the semi-circle of the Little Boulevard, running from Margit Hid (Margaret Bridge) at the toe-tip of **Margit Island** in the north, crossing Andrássy út at Oktogon, then looping back to the river at Petőfi Híd to the south of the city.

24 hours in the city

For an early morning view of Budapest's World Heritage status head for Buda's Castle District. Enter through the northern **Vienna Gate** (Bécsi kapu tér) and stroll past the ceramic roof of the **National Archives**, before exploring the cobblestone side streets and ducking west for a leafy walk along the ramparts. Have a late breakfast at **Ruszwurm**, then head on towards Holy Trinity Square to see the **Mátyás Church** and the **Fishermen's Bastion**. Take the funicular down the hill to the river and then take a tram south to the **Gellért** thermal spa for a swim and a pummel. After a snack lunch at the **Central Market** in Pest, head up Váci út, to reach **Szent István Bazilika**, then stroll along Andrássy út to the **House of Terror**. Recover from the horrors of the 20th century by contemplating the achievements of the Spanish masters at the **Museum of Fine Arts** on Heroes Square. Head back to the river for an early evening **cruise** before enjoying a recital at the **Opera House** or Liszt Academy. Supper could be something modishly Hungarian at **Menza**, followed by table football and a nightcap at one of the trendy **kerts**. Too down-at-heel? Try a bar on **Liszt Ferenc Square**, or the **A38 boat** on the river between Petőfi and Lágymányosi bridges, Buda.

Várhegy and Király Palota (Castle Hill and Royal Palace)

Map A3/B4.

A fortress was first built on Buda's unmistakable World Heritage hilltop following the Mongol invasion of 1241, which almost razed the settlements of low-lying Obuda and Pest. The Royal Palace occupies the southern slopes of the hill and commands regal views over the quays and boats of Pest, but, although the site was successfully defended over the centuries, its buildings proved to be less resilient. The palace was destroyed first in battle with the Turks in the 17th century and, again, during the German retreat at the end of the Second World War, and each time it was rebuilt in the architectural vernacular of the day. Today, its stately neoclassical buildings and stone parapets house a rash of cultural institutes: the **Hungarian National Gallery**, *T020 439 7331, www.mng.hu, Tue-Sun 1000-1800, HUF1400 (temporary exhibitions HUF3200)*; the **Budapest History Museum**, *T01 487 8800, www.btm.hu, Tue-Sun 1000-1800, HUF1800*; the **National Széchényi Library**, *T01 224 3700, www.oszk. hu, Tue-Sat 0900-2000*; and the **Ludwig Museum**, *T01 555 3444, www.ludwigmuseum.hu, Tue-Sun 1000-1800, from HUF600 (prices vary with exhibitions)*. Look out for the bronze sculpture of King Mátyás at the hunt, looking every inch like Errol Flynn. A funicular, the **Budavári Sikló** (HUF800) is a good way to climb to the top of the hill.

Castle Hill.

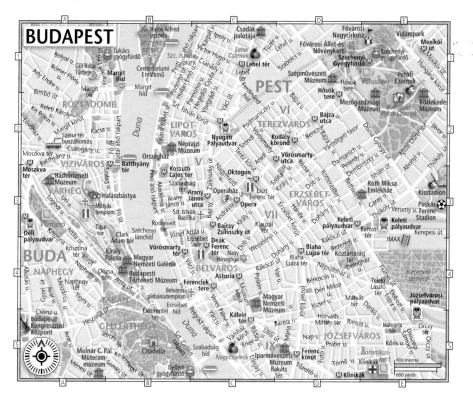

Mátyás Templom, Fishermen's Bastion and Várnegyed

Szentháromság tér, District 1, T01 355 3657.
Daily 0600-2000. HUF270-550 in summer. Map A3.

The two-thirds of Buda that wasn't taken up with palace buildings was left to the civilians. At the centre of this area is Holy Trinity Square (Szentháromság tér) and the lovely Mátyás Church, *www.matyas-templom.hu, Mon-Fri 0900-1700, Sat 0900-1300, Sun 1300-1700, HUF1000.* Painted with Asian and Turkish-influenced geometric heraldic motifs, the church has had to wear a number of religious hats down the ages. It was shared between Catholics and Protestants and became a Mosque during the Turkish occupation of 1541. The Gothic body of the church was built in the 13th century, the tower in the 15th. A facelift, timed to coincide with the 1896 millennium celebration, gave it back its eye-popping frescoes, medieval-style tiles and stained glass. The whole project was overseen by Frigyes Schulek, who also designed the neo-Romanesque trim to the church, the Halászbástya, known as the Fishermen's Bastion.

North of the square, in Várnegyed, are the squat merchants', noblemen's and courtiers' residences, painted umber, olive, yellow, ochre and cream. Heavy doors open on to courtyards, with wells and plane trees, and shallow stone reliefs decorate the façades. Parts of the area are medieval but much was rebuilt in the baroque and Louis XVI styles when the Turks left after the 1686 siege.

Above: Fishermen's Bastion.
Opposite page: House of Terror.

Orszaghaz (Parliament)

Kossuth Lajos tér, District 5, T01 317 9800.
Visits by guided tour only (tickets from gate 10),
English tours daily 1000, 1200, 1400 HUF2520.
Map C3.

The puffed-up Parliament building on the Pest
embankment is a splendid piece of pomp, modelled
on the Palace of Westminster, and it's as impressive
inside as out: full of frescoes and sculptures, deep
red carpets, stained-glass windows, hundred-
bulb chandeliers, four-tonne monolithic granite
colonnades and the crown, sceptre, orb and
sword of the Hungarian coronation.

Szent István Bazilika (St Stephen's Basilica)

Szent István tér, District 5, T01 311 0839.
Mon-Fri 0900-1700, Sat 0900-1300, Sun
1300-1700. Map C3.

Budapest's largest church, completed in 1905, is a
fat neoclassical building perfumed with the myrrh
of its votive candles and dominated by marble
(15 different types), mosaics and paintings. If Matyas
Church is Budapest's fussy Westminster Abbey, then
St Stephen's is the city's St Paul's. It is named after
the founder of the Hungarian state, Catholic King
Szent István, whose mummified arm is kept on the
left side of the chapel, and who sits carved from
Italian marble on the high altar. Go up to the dome
for amazing rooftop views of the **Postal Savings
Bank**, designed by Ödön Lechner. What appears at
street level to be an unremarkable white building,
reveals itself from above to be a perfect aesthetic
expression of the building's function: the bank's roof
is embroidered with bees, the symbol of saving.

Magyar Állami Operaház (State Opera House)

Andrássy út 22, District 6, T01 814 7100, www.opera.hu.
Map C3.

Hungary punches well above its weight in
terms of musical virtuosity, and the Hungarian
State Opera House is an appropriate physical
representation of the country's acoustic
refinement. The sphinx-flanked entrance
gives onto a Fabergé-egg of an interior. Built
in 1884 in neo-Renaissance style to Miklós Ybl's
design, the architecture is best enjoyed during
a ballet or opera performance. Tickets are
decidedly affordable by London standards.

Andrássy út

This UNESCO-protected boulevard runs for
2.5 km from inner-city Pest at Szent István's to the
Hösök Tere and **City Park** in the northeast. It was
built in the late 19th century at the time of the
administrative union of Buda, Óbuda and Pest, after
the Austro-Hungarian Compromise. Its buildings are

almost absurdly beautiful and can be divided loosely into three sections: closest to the Danube are four-storey residential blocks, then two-storey mansions give way to palaces and gardens the further out you get. Modelled on the Champs-Elysées and designed by Ybl, it is one of the world's finest urban landscapes. Look out particularly for the old **Postamúzeum** (Postal Museum) building at Andrássy út 3, which is notable for its wonderful architecture. The postal exhibits themselves were fairly uninspiring and have recently been re-located from this magnificent building to Benczur House.

Hósök Tere (House of Terror)

Andrássy út 60, District 6, T01 374 2600, www.terrorhaza.hu.
Tue-Sun 1000-1800, closed Mon. HUF2000. Map D1.

Brace yourself: this is sightseeing as harrowing 20th-century history lesson. Number 60 Andrássy

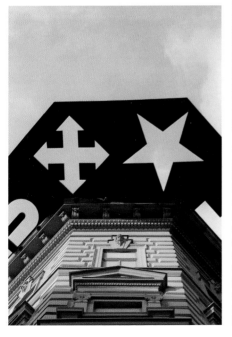

Buda bath time

Residents on the Buda side of the city have water pressure sloshing from their taps with the force of a hardly-harnessed Niagara: Budapest lies on top of somewhere between 80 and 120 active springs and wells from which 70 million litres of water burst forth daily. The medicinal properties of the city's naturally hot springs were recognized during the Turkish occupation and, by 1500, the Turks had bequeathed their Hungarian subjects some beautiful Ottoman baths, featuring high domes with shafts of light searing through the steam, and tile mosaics lining the 18°C plunge pools. Today, the baths remain a brilliant way to atone for a night on the Buda or Pest tiles, despite the off-putting appearance of most bathhouse staff. Baths tend to be single sex, although swimming pools are usually mixed. Specific treatments for rheumatism, physiotherapy and inhalation are available, but on weekends from April to September, most people head outside to lounge around and sunbathe with the papers, stirring only to complete extremely lackadaisical laps of the swimming pool. The best baths in town are: **Gellért**, *Kelenhegyi út 4-6, T01 466 6166, www.gellertbath.com, daily 0600-2000, from HUF4900,* which is full of art nouveau furnishings, mosaics and stained-glass windows; the neo-baroque **Széchenyi Spa**, *Állatkerti út 11, District 14, T01 363 3210, www.szechenyifurdo. hu, daily 0600-2200, HUF3800-4800,* which has chess boards in its pool, and the gay favourite, **Király Medicinal**, *Föutca 82-84, T01 202 3688, Mon, Wed, Fri 0700-1800 for women, Tue, Thu, Sat 0900-2000 for men, all day HUF4800 (includes massage), morning HUF2400.*

út was, from 1939 to 1944, the House of Loyalty, party HQ of the Hungarian Nazi Arrow Cross Party. Between 1945 and '56 it went on to become the head of the Soviet terror organizations ÁVO and ÁVH. Both were remarkable for their institutionalized brutality and the torture of subjects. The emphasis is on experience over mere exhibition. Nagging music and newsreel footage make this document of the crimes of the successive terror regimes so vivid as to turn your stomach. Documentary footage contrasts the order and iconography of the Nazi regime with the relative scrappiness of Soviet rule, but the museum has also been criticized for describing the atrocities

Best of the rest

Chain Bridge
The oldest bridge to span the Danube (1849) was designed by the engineer of Hammersmith Bridge, William Tierney Clark, and built by Scotsman, Adam Clark.

Dohány Street Synagogue
Dohány utca 2. Mar-Oct Sun-Thu 1000-1800, Fri 1000-1530, Nov-Feb Sun-Thu 1000-1600, HUF400-1000.
Central Europe's largest Jewish community gave rise to its largest synagogue. The Holocaust tree in the garden has metal branches and dog-collar leaves, bearing the names of Jewish lives lost.

Gellérthegy (Gellért Hill)
District 6.
A symbol of Austrian supremacy, this citadel was built after the 1848 revolution.

Liszt Ferenc Zeneakadémia
(Franz Liszt Academy of Music)
Liszt Ferenc tér 8, District 6, T01 462 4600, www.lisztacademy.hu.
Amazing art nouveau building and one of the city's main concert halls.

Margitsziget (Margaret Island)
The lungs of the city, a favourite destination for romantics and joggers.

Memento Park
Balatoni út/ Szabadkai utca, District 22, T 01 424 7500, www.mementopark.hu. 1000-sunset. HUF1500. From Ferenciek tér bus No 7 or No 173 to Etele tér, then Volan Bus (yellow to Diosd-Erd).
'The Disneyland of Communism' displays the vast statues that once lined the city's streets: Marx, Engels, Lenin, Hungarian labour movement heroes, plus the hammer and sickle.

of the latter in detail, while providing only relatively cursory treatment of the Nazi genocide.

Museum of Fine Arts.

Szépm vészeti Múzeum (Museum of Fine Arts) and around

Dózsa György út 41, Heroes Sq, District 4, T01 469 7100, www.szepmuveszeti.hu.
Tue-Sun 1000-1800. Map D1.

This imitation Greek temple at the City Park end of Andrássy út houses a collection of Spanish masters including seven El Grecos and five Goyas. Its walls also carry bleary oil paintings of saints, acts of martyrdom, beheadings and sermons. Outside, the **Millennium Monument** marks the 1000th anniversary of the Magyar Conquest, with Archangel Gabriel on top of a column and the seven tribal chieftains below. Across Heroes Square, the showcase for political gatherings and displays of Communist and Soviet might, sits the **Palace of Arts**. Behind is **City Park**, home to Széchenyi spa and the winter ice-skating rink.

Where to stay

Budapest has its share of charmless Soviet-style business hotels but there are some treats too. The city also has a strong homestay tradition, as well as serviced apartments, which are available for both long-term rental and short lets.

Corinthia Hotel €€€
Erzsebet korut 43, T01479 4000, www.corinthia.com.
A magnificent 5-star hotel in a central location right in the heart of the city. It effortlessly blends grandeur with modern and luxurious facilities, and the hotel spa is one of the finest in Budapest.

Four Seasons Hotel Gresham Palace €€€
Chain Bridge, Roosevelt tér 5-6, T01 268 6000, www.fourseasons.com/budapest.
The art nouveau/secessionist Gresham Palace was built to accommodate wealthy British aristocrats. Today, this landmark building is home to Budapest's most luxurious hotel. Rooms have huge fluffy pillows, giant bathrooms and the best views in Pest. There's also an infinity pool, gym, spa and flawlessly polished service.

Danubius Hotel Gellért €€
Szent Gellért tér 1, T01 889 5500, www.danubiushotels.com/hu.
The grand dame among Budapest's hotels. Its carpets can be dank, and it reeks of the Soviet era, but the views across

the Liberty Bridge are splendid, and it has character in spades. Rates include admission to the excellent on-site Gellért Thermal Baths (see page 89).

Casati Budapest Hotel €€
Paulay Ede u. 31, District 6, T01 343 1198, www.casati budapesthotel.com.
Formerly named 'Hotel Pest', the Casati opened its doors in Jun 2012 after a complete refurbishment. This 18th-century building now houses a 25-room contemporary boutique hotel with sleek and modern rooms. For adults only.

Mamaison Residence Izabella €€
Izabella út/ Andrássy út, T01 475 5900, www.mamaison.com.
This residential apartment in a 19th-century building has been exactingly refurbished. There are 38 suites with 1-3 bedrooms, plus kitchen, lounge and dining room. Room service, breakfast, laundry, concierge, AV system, sauna, pool room and home theatre are all available.

Trendy B&B Hostel €
Oktober 6 útca 19, T01 650 5992, www.trendybudapesthostel.com.
With most of the city's main sights and attractions on its doorstep, this designer hostel is the ideal base. The inexpensive rooms are themed and quirky yet large and spacious, with options for private bathrooms and a

family flat available. The owner brothers are affable hosts and a fountain of knowledge when it comes to places to go and things to do during your stay.

Restaurants

Hungarians know their way round a knuckle of ham, but the country that gave us goulash hasn't earned a place at the top table of global cuisine. Stout, artery-thickening dishes are the norm; most come soused in thick creamy sauces. That said, there is a lively metropolitan restaurant scene at the top end, serving fish fresh from Lake Balaton, and the countryside seems to produce so much fruit that the Hungarians have no option but to use it in spiced soups – a cool cinnamon-spiked peach broth is not uncommon in late summer. Cakes are a strong suit, as is *lángos*, a pizza-like dough that's fried, then smeared with sour cream and garlic.

Menza €€€
Liszt Ferenc ter 2, T01 413 1482, www.menzaetterem.hu.
Retro floral wallpaper sets the tone for this funky recreation of a Soviet-era canteen. Modern international touches influence the Hungarian dishes on the menu and there's a good wine list. An oh-so-cool compilation album is also available.

Nightlife

Café Kör €€
Sas utca 17, Szent István Bazilika,
T01 311 0053, www.cafekor.com.
Mon-Sat 1000-2200, closed Sun.
A cosy, ochre-walled bistro on
the heels of the Basilika that,
among a glut of high-price
showy restaurants, still attracts
locals as much as passing
sightseers. Flavours are
Hungarian (goulash and goose
liver, aubergine cream, cottage
cheese dumplings with hot
forest fruit sauce) with some
lighter European notes. Booking
is strongly recommended.
Also serves breakfast.

Gerbeaud €€
Vörösmarty tér 7, Deák Ferenc tér,
District 5, T01 429 9000,
www.gerbeaud.hu.
Daily 0900-2100.
A 150-year-old institution
dripping with chandeliers. The
café's signature dessert is a cake
with nuts, jam and apricot,
covered in chocolate. Once part
of the weekend ritual of the
middle classes, it is now firmly
etched on the tourist's itinerary.

Central Market Hall €
Fövám Krt 1-3, District 4.
Pile 'em high is the philosophy at
the cheap food counters ranged
around the top of the grand
Market Hall built in 1890. Mounds
of cabbage, stews of butter
beans, stringy pickles and plenty
of sordid-looking sausages.
Sophisticated it ain't.

Ruszwurm Cukrászda €
Szentháromság utca 7, Várhegy,
District 1, T01 375 5284,
www.ruszwurm.hu.
Daily 1000-1930.
A glory clock hangs behind the
old-world cherrywood counter
at this perfect Biedermeier relic.
Gilt chandeliers, velvet
banquettes, 19th-century
ornaments and chinaware –
this is the place for strudels,
gingerbread and salt cakes.

Tamp & Pull €
Czuczor Utca 3, T01 398 2472,
www.tamppull.hu.
Mon-Fri 0700-2000,
Sat 0900-1800.
A coffee-lover's idea of heaven.
The café takes its name from the
final 2 stages in the coffee-
roasting process and was
specially chosen by the owner,
four times Hungarian Barista
Champion Attila Molnar. The
man knows his coffee... try the
Tasting Menu to sample some
of the café's finest blends and
coffee types.

Bars and clubs
There are chi-chi metropolitan
sit-outs at **Liszt Ferenc Square**,
slightly seedier coffeeshops
along **Raday utca** and, in
summer, chic and dressy clubs
on **Margit Island**. The cool **A38
boat**, moored on the Buda side
between Lágymányosi and
Petöfi bridges, *T01 464 3940,*
www.a38.hu, is a Ukrainian stone
carrier ship that stages
cutting-edge concerts.
Ten out of ten for hipness,
though, goes to the *kerts*,
Budapest-style late-night
speakeasies that are set up in the
disused courtyards of the city's
derelict housing squares.
Unpopular with sleep-deprived
neighbours, they squat in
uninhabitable dwellings until
local opposition forces the
fridge, chairs, tables and,
invariably, *fussball* tables, to
move a few doors down to the
next condemned and neglected
ghost house. Understandably
shy of publicity, they seldom
have street signs or set
addresses, so ask a local to direct
you through the medieval
district or look out for a doorman
propped on a bar stool outside
an otherwise unassuming
doorway. The 2 longest-running
venues are **Szoda** in District 5,
and **Szimpla** in the Jewish
district, *Kazinczy utca 14, T01 261
8669, www.szimpla.hu*.
  **Tüzraktér Independent
Cultural Centre**, *Tüzoltó u 54-56,*

District 9, www.tuzrakter.hu, is the place for VJ festivals, avant-garde art, jazz and performance, while **AlterEgo**, Dessewffy utca 33, T01 345 4302, www.alteregoclub.com, is the hippest gay club in town with live shows and funky DJ sets.

Classical music and opera
The city has fistfuls of concert venues, from the **National State Opera** house and the art nouveau **Liszt Ferenc Academy** to the state-of-the-art Russell Johnson-designed

National Concert Hall at the Palace of Arts, Komor Marcell u 1, T01 455 9000, www.mupa.hu, home of the National Philharmonic Orchestra. Tickets are available at the box office and via the website.

Travel essentials

Getting there
Ferihegy International Airport (www.bud.hu) is 16 km southeast of the city, T01 296 9696. Terminal 1 serves low-cost airlines, while Terminal 2 serves most other airlines, including Hungary's **Malev**. A handy **airport minibus**, T01 296 8555, runs to any address in the city 0600-2200 (HUF3200 one way, HUF5500 return); it's cheaper than a taxi but you must book your return journey 24 hrs in advance. You can also travel by bus 200E to Kőbánya-Kispest metro station (HUF350 from machine, HUF450 on board).

Most international express trains plus domestic trains to and from the north use **Keleti pályaudur**, VIII Kerepesi út 2-6 (M3 metro); other main stations are **Deli pályaudur**, I Krisztina körút 37 (M2 metro), and **Nyugati pályaudur**, VI Teréz körút (M3 metro). Call T01 461 5400, www.mav.hu, for domestic services and T01 461 5500, www.elvira.hu, for international links, including Vienna, every 3 hrs (2½ hrs), Berlin (12 hrs) and Paris (16 hrs).

Getting around
Walking around Budapest is a pleasure, but the **public transport** network of buses, trams and trolleybuses, plus 3 metro lines, is excellent, cheap and runs 0430-2310. You can buy single journey tickets valid for 60 mins (HUF290) or booklets at newsagents, stations and stops. A 24-hr pass costs HUF1500 and 72-hr pass HUF3700. Tickets must be validated once on board; you face a HUF6000 on-the-spot fine if you travel without a ticket. The tourist office's **Budapest Card** gives you access to unlimited public transport in the city for 24 hrs (HUF4500), 48 hrs (HUF7500) or 72 hrs (HUF8900), as well as discounts on sights, activities and thermal baths.

Bikes can be rented from many of the city's hotels and from

Velo-Touring, T01 319 0571, www.velo-touring.hu. **Taxis** have yellow number plates and run on a meter; drivers will expect a 10% tip on top of the fare. Booking by phone is cheaper than hailing a cab on the street: try **Buda Taxi**, T01 233 3333; **Rádió Taxi**, T01 777 7777; **Fõtaxi**, T01 222 2222, or City Taxi T01 211 1111.

Tourist information
Budapest's **Tourinform** office is at Deák tér/Sütõ utca 2, T01 438 8080, www.budapest info.hu, daily 0800-2000. **Citytours**, T01 374 7050, www.citytour.hu, run a hop-on hop-off city tour, HUF5000, from 28 different bus and boat stops.

Exchange rate
Hungarian Forint (HUF): £1 = HUF358. €1 = HUF299 (Nov 2013).

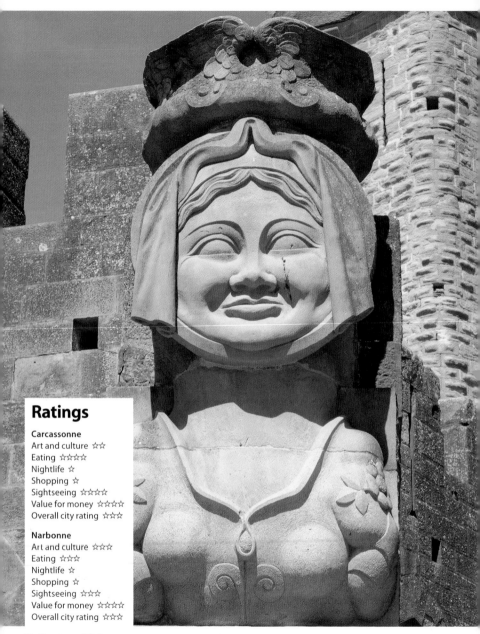

Ratings

Carcassonne
Art and culture ☆☆
Eating ☆☆☆☆
Nightlife ☆
Shopping ☆
Sightseeing ☆☆☆☆
Value for money ☆☆☆☆
Overall city rating ☆☆☆

Narbonne
Art and culture ☆☆☆
Eating ☆☆☆
Nightlife ☆
Shopping ☆
Sightseeing ☆☆☆
Value for money ☆☆☆☆
Overall city rating ☆☆☆

Carcassonne and Narbonne

This is a tale of two cities in France's sunny Languedoc region, two cities that had their golden age in the time of the medieval troubadours. First is Carcassonne, a spectacular city of arms with it storybook citadel perched high over the main invasion route between France and the Pyrenees. Captured (infamously by trickery) in 1209 by the dastardly Simon de Montfort and the Albigensian Crusaders, it would go on to become the seat of French royal power in Languedoc as well as the greatest and most impregnable citadel in Europe. A World Heritage Site since 1997 and the subject of both popular novels (notably Kate Moss's *Labyrinth*) and a board game, Carcassonne is currently enjoying a reputation as a top city break destination. It receives some four million visits a year and is buzzing with new boutique hotels, B&Bs and Michelin-starred restaurants.

Less than an hour away by train, yet far more peaceful and less-visited is Narbonne. This city of faith is one seat of Languedoc's powerful medieval archbishop. His former fortress-like palace towers over the city centre, the big chief of a handsome tribe of churches and museums that make Narbonne one of France's secret art cities. Other reasons to visit? An exceptional market, leafy promenades and sandy beaches a bus hop away.

Statue of Carcas, Cité de Carcassonne.

Carcassonne

Carcassonne's tower-girdled **Cité** is the famous bit. Underneath lies the tight-knit grid of the **Bastide St-Louis**, the 13th-century new town built for the locals after the French captured the Cité. Here you'll find the market, stylish B&Bs and restaurants, and the Canal du Midi.

Cité de Carcassonne

It's only by chance that the Cité is still there. Once it became obsolete as a fortress, the once-impregnable walls slowly crumbled and were on the verge of being cannibalized, when master restorer Eugène Viollet-le-Duc came to the rescue in 1853. The Cité has four gates, but only the elaborate **Porte Narbonnaise** is accessible by road. Start your exploration with **Basilique St-Nazaire** in place de l'Eglise, *Mon-Sat 0800-1145 and 1345-1800, Sun 0800-1045 and 1400-1700, free, map E6.* A Romanesque church begun on the order of Pope Urban V in 1096, it became a tall Gothic hybrid in the hands of the northern conquerors. Admire its enormous rose windows and the organ, which is the biggest in the south of France. A plaque marks the tomb of the hated Simon de Montfort, although his heirs transferred his body in 1224.

Cité de Carcassonne.

Château Comtal and the ramparts

1 rue Viollet-le-Duc, T04 6811 7070, www.carcassonne.monuments-nationaux.fr. Apr-Sep daily 0930-1830, Oct-Mar daily 0930-1700. €8.50. Guided tours €8.50-13. Map E5-6.

Built on Roman foundations, this castle became residence of the French *sénéchal* (the king's representative) and had to be fortified to protect him from the angry populace. Today, it houses sculptures and an exhibition on Viollet-le-Duc's restoration of the Cité. From Château Comtal, you can walk around most of the 3 km of walls with their 52 towers; the Pyrenees hover in the distance. The outer walls were built by Louis IX; the inner are Gallo Roman. Between them, **Les Lices** are where the knights would train and hold their jousts, today dramatically re-enacted in the **Grand Tournois de Chevalerie**, *T04 6810 2430, Jul and Aug daily1500 and 1645, €12.*

Bastide St-Louis

The working end of Carcassonne has at its core the Bastide St-Louis, a medieval 'new town' founded on the left bank of the Aude by Louis IX in 1247 to house the locals, who were bitter about the French occupation. Stand on the city's oldest bridge, the **Pont Vieux** (1320), for one of the most enchanting views of the Cité, above. Like all *bastides*, St-Louis is made up of a tight grid of streets around a central square, in this case, **Place Carnot**, where a lively market takes place on Tuesday, Thursday and Saturday mornings. Nearby on 1 rue de Verdun is the **Musée des Beaux-Arts**, *T04 6877 7370, mid-Sep to mid-Jun Tue-Sat 1000-1200 and 1400-1800, mid-Jun to mid-Sep daily 1000-1800, free, map C4.* It houses mostly French works, with canvases by Corot, Chardin and Courbet.

The evocative **Canal du Midi** flows past the north end of the bastide; take a scenic 90-minute cruise with **Hélios et Lou Gabaret**, *T04 6871 6126, www.carcassonne-croisiere.com, €8.50.*

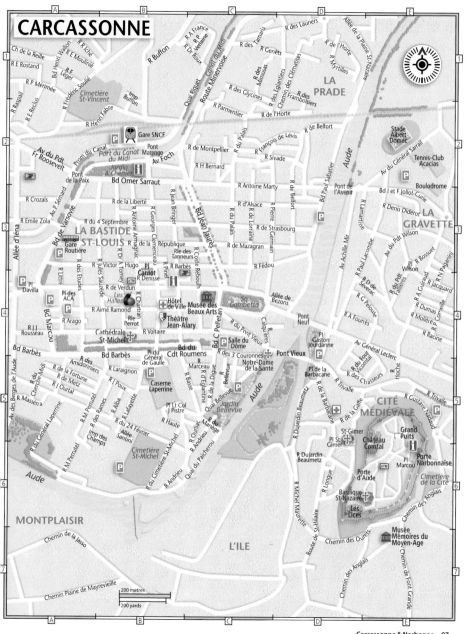

CARCASSONNE

Ch de la Reille
R E Rostand
Bd Henri Wallon   R R Iché
Bd Henri Wallon   R E Moulinié
R P Mérimée
Av du Pdt   R F Léger
Fr Roosevelt   R Frédéric Soulié
R Raspail   Cimetière St-Vincent
R E Reclus
R P Sémard
R Henri Fabre
R Buffon
R A France   R P
R Dr Roux   R Dr Verlaine
R des Lauriers
R des Tamaris   R des Genêts
R de l'Horte
R des Myrtilles
Allée de la Plaine St-Nazaire
LA PRADE

Quai Riquet   Route Minervoise   Canal du Midi
R des Glycines   R des Mimosas   R des Eglantiers
Chemin des Clématites   R des Framboisiers
R Parmentier   R de l'Horte

Gare SNCF
Prom du Canal   Port du Canal du Midi   Pont Marengo   Av Foch
Jardin A Chénier
Bd Omer Sarraut
R de Montpellier   R du Palais
R H Bernard   R François de Lévis   R Sivade
R Antoine Marty   R de Belfort
Pont de Belfort
R de l'Avenir
Bd Paul Sabatier
Aude
R Denis Diderot
Stade Albert Domec
Av du Général Sarrail
Tennis-Club Acacias
Bd J et F Joliot-Curie
Boulodrome
LA GRAVETTE

R Crozals
R Emile Zola
Bd de Varsovie
R de la Liberté
R du 4 Septembre
LA BASTIDE ST-LOUIS
Gare Routière
R des Etudes
R J J Rousseau
Bd Marcou
Pl Davilla
Pl des ACA
R Arago
Bd Barbès
R Littré
R Jules Sauzède
R V Victor Hugo
R A Tomey
R de Verdun
Pl Carnot
R Denisse
Les Halles
R Aimé Ramond
R Chartrand
Rue Perrot
Cathédrale St-Michel
R Voltaire
Georges Clemenceau
R de la Liberté
R Antoine Armagnac
R République
Rue des Tanneurs
R Barbès
R Coste Reboulh
Bd Jean Jaurès
R Jean Bringer
R du Palais
R de Lorraine
R d'Alsace
R Pierre Germain
R de Strasbourg
R de Mazagran
R Fédou
Sq Gambetta
Musée des Beaux Arts
Hôtel de Ville
Théâtre Jean-Alary
Bd du Cdt Roumens
Pl du Général de Gaulle
Allée de Bezons
Pont Neuf
R A Fournès
R du Pont Vieux
Salle du Dôme
R des 3 Couronnes
Notre-Dame de la Santé
Pont Vieux
Calquières
Pl Gaston Jourdanne
Pl de la Barbacane
Av Général Leclerc
R du Four Vicomtal
R des Chasseurs
R Trivalle
R Trivalle
R Gustave Nadaud
CITÉ MÉDIÉVALE
Av Achille Mir
R Paul Lacombe
R D de Séverac
R C Pelloux
R Dumas
R Mollère
R Racine
P R Bossuet
Wilson
Av du Pdt Wilson
R A Cuilrauд
R A Paganini
R du Pdt Faillières
R P Corneille
R Jacquard

R des Amidonniers
R de la Fortune
R de Metz
R J Ourtal
R J Poux
Bd Barbès
R Laraignon
R Marceau
Caserne Laperrine
R Basse
Av des Berges de l'Aude
R du Cherche-Midi
R Masséna
R du Général Laperrine
R M Pertuisé
R des Rames
Imp des Champs
R Alba
R Lafayette
R du 24 Février
Allée Santini
R Haute
Pl Lt Col J Pistre
Cimetière St-Michel
Quai du Paicherou
R d'Eglantine
R Andrieu
R Ourliac
Quai Bellevue
Jardin Bellevue
R du Manège
R Outfiac
R du Cimetière St-Michel
R Andrieu
Aude
R de la Barbacane
St-Gimer
Pl St Gimer
Château Comtal
Porte d'Aude
Basilique St-Nazaire
Les Lices
Grand Puits
Porte Narbonnaise
Pl Marcou
Cimetière de la Cité
Chemin des Anglais
Musée Mémoires du Moyen-Age
R Michel Maurette
Route de St-Hilaire
Chemin des Ouerts
R Dujardin Beaumetz
R Longue
R de la Gaffe

MONTPLAISIR
Aude
Chemin de la Jasso
L'ILE
Chemin des Anglais
Chemin de Font Grande
Chemin Plaine de Mayrevieille

200 metres
200 yards

Narbonne

Narbonne started out as the Roman capital of Languedoc and was a major port until the Aude silted up and changed direction. In 1686, the ancient riverbed was transformed into the **Canal de la Robine**. In the centre of town, the canal is spanned by the **Pont des Marchands**, the only bridge in France that is still lined with buildings. Underneath are the foundations of the Roman bridge that once carried the **Via Domitia** road from Rome to Spain; part of this ancient roadway has been uncovered in nearby Place de l'Hôtel-de-Ville (see below).

Palais des Archevêques

pl de l'Hôtel-de-Ville, T04 6890 3054.
Oct-May Wed-Mon 1000-1200 and 1400-1700; Jun-Sep daily 1000-1800. €4. Map C3.

The majestic 12th- to 14th-century Palais des Archevêques is an ecclesiastical fortress-palace surpassed only by the Papal Palace in Avignon. Its 41-m watchtower, **Donjon Gilles Aycelin**, has grand views over Narbonne. The palace also houses two museums. The **Musée Archéologique** features Bronze Age swords, Greek ceramics, and extremely rare Gallo-Roman frescoes. The **Musée d'Art et d'Histoire** occupies the 17th- and 18th-century apartments of the archbishops. On the walls are works by Salvator Rosa, Canaletto, Breughel and Veronese. A special Orientalist Gallery displays fascinating 19th-century paintings on North African and Middle Eastern themes.

Cathédrale St-Just-et-St Pasteur

rue Armand Gautier, T04 6832 0952.
Daily 0900-1200 and 1400-1800. Free. Map C3.

Begun in 1272 by Pope Clement IV, this Cathedral was designed to rival the Gothic masterpieces of the Ile de France, but construction came to an abrupt end in 1340, leaving a splendid 130-ft choir and transept, and a blank wall instead of a nave. Inside, there's an enormous organ in a madly ornate case, 13th- and 14th-century stained glass

Above: Pont des Marchands, Narbonne.

and a Gothic retable. The **treasury**, *Nov to mid-Jul Wed-Sat 1400-1745, mid-Jul to Oct Mon-Sat 1000-1200, 1400-1745, €2.20*, has remarkable 16th-century Flemish tapestries and illuminated manuscripts.

Horreum Romain

7 rue Rouget de Lisle.
Oct-May Wed-Mon 1000-1200 and 1400-1700; Jun-Sep daily 1000-1800. €4. Map D2.

The ancient geographer Strabo called Roman Narbonne the 'greatest emporium' in the south of France. These subterranean granaries from the first century BC were hollowed out in the form of a giant 'U' and were used to store arms, grain, oil and wine at a constant 12-14°C.

Left bank

On the left bank of the Canal de la Robine is the splendid **Halles** (covered market), dating from 1905, and the 13th-century church of Notre Dame-de-Lamourguier. The latter houses the **Musée Lapidaire**, *Pl Emile Digeon, Oct-May Wed-Mon 1000-1200 and 1400-1700, Jun-Sep daily 1000-1800, €4, map C5*, the second-largest museum of stone inscriptions outside Rome. A short walk west leads to the handsome Renaissance townhouse, the **Maison des Trois-Nourrices** (1558), and to one of the oldest Gothic churches in the south, the **Basilique St Paul-Serge**, *T04 6890 3065, Mon-Sat 0900-1200 and 1400-1800, free, map A3*, built in 1180. The interior is wonderfully atmospheric; ask to visit the crypt (AD 250), containing the oldest Christian sarcophagi in Gaul.

Maison Natale de Charles Trénet

13 av Charles-Trénet, T04 6890 3066.
Oct-May Wed-Mon 1000-1200 and 1400-1700; Jun-Sep daily 1000-1800. €6. Map A2.

Singer/songwriter Charles Trénet (1913-2001) donated his birthplace to the city on the condition that it didn't become a museum. Instead the house has remained as it was, with its piano, old photos and furnishings, accompanied by Trénet's greatest hits.

Beaches

It's a 30-minute journey by city bus from Narbonne to the long sandy beaches of **Narbonne Plage** and **Gruissan Plage**. Gruissan is famous for its **Plage des Pilotis**, lined with beach huts on stilts, used in the sultry French cult film *Betty Blue* (1986).

Listings
Where to stay

Restaurants

Carcassonne
Hôtel 111 €€€
290 av Général Leclerc, T04 6811 1111, www.hotel111.com.
In the modern town, a new avant-garde hotel with a striking 10-m 'human aquarium' pool, spa and sauna, and a contemporary Michelin-starred restaurant, Michel del Burgo.

Hôtel de la Cité €€€
pl Auguste-Pierre Pont, T04 6811 9871, www.hoteldelacite.com.
Sumptuous rooms, pool, gardens and restaurant in the former bishop's palace, with bags of medieval atmosphere.

Hôtel du Château €€€
2 rue Camille St-Saens, T04 6811 3838, www.hotelduchateau-carcassonne.com.
Small and well equipped, with attractive grounds just under the medieval walls, plus a heated pool (Easter-Nov) and year-round jacuzzi. At the lower end of this price bracket.

Hôtel Montmorency €€
9 rue Camille St-Saens, T04 6811 9670, www.lemontmorency.com.
Just a few mins from the Cité, 20 quiet if rather small rooms and use of the pool and jacuzzi at the nearby Hôtel du Château.

Le Grand Puits €
8 pl du Grand Puits, T04 6825 1667, http://legrandpuits.free.fr.
These simple rooms in the Cité

sleep up to 5 and some have kitchenettes.

Narbonne
Hôtel La Résidence €€
6 rue 1er Mai, T04 6832 1941, www.hotel-laresidence-narbonne.fr.
A reworking of a 19th-century hotel in the heart of Narbonne, offering classic rooms in soft pastels and wine tastings in the bar.

Hôtel de France €
6 rue Rossini, T04 6832 0975, www.hotelnarbonne.com.
Charming, well-equipped 15-room hotel on a quiet street in the centre.

Hôtel du Midi €
4 av de Toulouse, T04 6841 0462, www.hoteldumidi.net.
Recently refurbished bright rooms (including family rooms) in the historic centre, a short walk from the train station.

Carcassonne
La Barbacane €€€
Hotel de la Cité, Pl Auguste-Pierre Pont, T04 6871 9871, www.hoteldelacite.com.
Closed Tue, Wed.
The hotel restaurant offers fabulous dining in a splendid medieval hall. The exquisite classics include Charolais beef with foie gras and sole glazed in Champagne.

Le Parc Franck Putelat €€€
Chemin des Anglais, T04 6871 8080, www.franck-putelat.com.
Closed Sun, Mon.
One of France's rising culinary stars, chef Franck Putelat runs this laid-back, stylish restaurant in a garden at the foot of the Cité. Menus feature classics (truffled Bresse chicken) and exceptional wines.

Comte Roger €€

14 rue Saint-Louis, T04 6811 9340,
www.comteroger.com.
Closed Sun, Mon.

Amid the tourist throngs in the Cité, this place offers classy cuisine in a contemporary setting with tables out in a pretty garden. Excellent fixed-price lunches, but be sure to book in summer.

L'Atelier de Robert Rodriguez €€

39 rue Coste-Reboulh, T04 6847 3780, www.restaurantrobert rodriguez.com.
Closed Sun, Wed.

Intimate bistrot in the Bastide St-Louis, focusing on well-prepared French classics (foie gras, cassoulet, wild sea bass) and a superb choice of wines. Splurge on an all-truffle menu from Dec to Feb.

Le Saint Jean €

1 pl St Jean, T04 6847 4243,
www.le-saint-jean.eu.
The terrace of this bar-restaurant overlooking Viollet-le-Duc's witch-hatted towers is an oasis of calm in the Cité, for a simple lunch, snack or *salade composée.*

Narbonne

La Table de Saint-Crescent €€€

68 av du Général Leclerc, T04 6841 3737, www.la-table-saint-crescent.com.
Closed Sat lunch, Sun eve and Mon.

One of Languedoc's top gourmet restaurants is hidden away in

Travel essentials

Getting there

Carcassonne Airport, T04 6871 9646, www.aeroport-carcassonne.com, is linked to the city by the Navette Aeroport shuttle service, T04 68 47 82 22, €5. Alternatively, **Toulouse-Blagnac Airport**, T08 2538 0000, toulouse.aeroport.fr, has shuttles (www.tisseo.fr) every 20-40 mins to Toulouse train station, €5, with frequent rail links to Carcassonne (40 mins, €15.60) and Narbonne (1 hr 20 mins, €24), www.voyages-sncf.com.

Getting around

Both cities can easily be explored on foot, although in Carcassonne you may want to take a bus (single €1) from the Ville Basse to the Cité, T04 6847 8222, www.carcassonne-agglo.fr. From Narbonne train station, frequent buses (single €1) go to the beaches in summer: P1 to Gruissan Plage or P2 to Narbonne Plage, T04 68 90 18 18, www.citibus.fr.

Tourist information

Carcassonne: 28 rue de Verdun, T04 6810 2430, www.tourisme-carcassonne.fr. **Narbonne**: 31 rue Jean Jaurès, T04 6865 1560, www.narbonne-tourisme.com. Save money with a day pass to the museums.

a former oratory with a terrace and garden. Lionel Giraud's extraordinarily inventive cuisine makes great use of the prime local ingredients. There are good-value weekday lunches, too.

Brasserie Co €€

1 bd du Docteur Ferroul, T04 6832 5525, www.brasserie-co.com.
Chic art-deco bar and brasserie near the Halles, where locals meet for a meal or a coffee on

the terrace. The dishes are a cut above typical brasserie fare, featuring the likes of *foie gras en millefeuille au caramel de figues.*

Chez Bébelle €

Les Halles, 1 bd du Docteur Ferroul, T06 8540 0901.
Daily 0600-1400.

Located in Narbonne's beautiful market, this is a fun place for lunch. Owner Gilles Belzon was a rugby player and makes great steaks.

Ratings

Art and culture ☆☆☆
Eating ☆☆☆☆
Nightlife ☆☆☆☆
Shopping ☆☆☆☆
Sightseeing ☆☆☆
Value for money ☆☆
Overall city rating ☆☆☆

Copenhagen

For years Copenhagen was known as the capital of the land that gave us Lego, Lurpak and the egg chair. There were hints of Scandinavian sensuality and liberation but to say it had 'understated chic' hardly raised the blood pressure. The most famous people to hail from the city were an existentialist philosopher and a writer of maudlin fairy tales. But in the last decade, Copenhagen has found itself well and truly in the spotlight. Scandinavian cuisine has never been more fashionable or more celebrated thanks to the ground-breaking culinary genius of Noma, frequently rated as the best restaurant in the world. What's more, the Danes have discovered a previously untapped talent for gritty TV crime dramas, notably *Forbrydelsen* (*The Killing*). As well as unleashing a trend for patterned knitwear, the series revealed a compelling dark side to Copenhagen that adds unexpected shade and substance to the city. Copenhagen's appeal still lies in its manageable scale, laid-back vibe and ever-so-literate awareness of design, but these qualities are now layered with a modish undertone that makes the city more than a little sexy.

Nyhavn.

Around the city

Tivoli Gardens

Vesterbrogade 3, T3315 1001, www.tivoli.dk.
Mid Apr-late Sep daily 1100-2300. Hallowe'en
and Christmas holidays daily 1100-2300. Kr75.
S-tog København H. Map A7.

First opened in 1843, Tivoli pleasure gardens remain
Denmark's most visited attraction and a national
institution (most visitors are Danes). The tweeness
has encouraged Disneyfication, but a glimmer of
the original Orient-inspired magic still pervades.
There is an ancient rollercoaster amongst the
modern fairground rides, as well as fainter echoes
of times past, such as the 1949 spiral lamp by Poul
Henningsen near Tivoli Lake. Henningsen also
designed the stunning Glassalen, with its hint of
camp. When twilight descends, the Turkish façade
of Restaurant Nimb is subtly illuminated, while
outside is the silent fountain inspired by Niels Bohr,
Danish winner of the Nobel Prize for physics. The
Chinese-style Pantomime Theatre plays host to a
genuine ghost of *commedia dell'arte*.

NyCarlsberg Glyptotek

Dantes Plads 7, T3341 8141,
www.glyptoteket.dk.
Tue-Sun 1100-1700. Kr 60, Sun free.
S-tog København H. Map B7.

This is one of Copenhagen's must-see galleries,
founded by the Carlsberg brewing magnet Carl
Jacobsen at the end of the 19th century. Like other
world-class museums, it contains too much to take
in on a single visit, including extensive ancient near

East and Mediterranean collections. At its heart is
the magnificent glass-domed Winter Garden, where
Roman sarcophagi and contemporary Danish
sculptures share the space with giant tropical palm
trees. The 19th-century French Impressionists are
housed in a purpose-built wing, added in 1996.

Nationalmuseet

Ny Vestergade 10, T3313 4411,
www.natmus.dk.
Tue-Sun 1000-1700. Free. S-tog København H.
Map B7.

Denmark's National Museum showcases four
floors of world cultural history and, although the
emphasis is on Denmark, it also has an expansive
ethnographical collection and a floor devoted to
near Eastern and Classical antiquities. Highlights
include some astounding 3000-year-old artefacts,
Viking silver ornaments, jewellery, coins and skin
cloaks, an Eskimo hunter's anorak made of sealskin
and a metope from the outer frieze of the
Parthenon, purchased by a Danish naval officer
in the 17th century.

Tivoli Gardens.

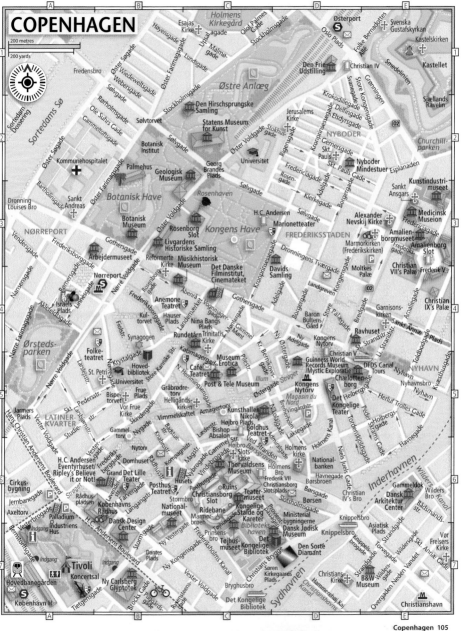

COPENHAGEN

200 metres
200 yards

Around the city

Slotsholmen

The island of Slotsholmen (www.ses.dk) is where
Bishop Absalon first built a stone castle in 1167.
Today it is crowded with buildings that chart the
evolution of the city from the 12th century to the
present. At its heart is **Christiansborg Slot**,
*Christiansborg Slotsplads, T3392 6492, www.christians
borg.dk, map C6, May-Sep daily 1000-1700, Oct-Apr
Tue-Sun 1000-1700 ruins Kr40, reception rooms Kr80,*
the 20th-century incarnation of a palace first built
by Christan VI in the 1730s. It now houses the
Danish parliament, Royal Reception Rooms and an
absorbing exhibition on the excavation of
Absalon's original fort. There are tours of the Royal
Reception Rooms in English daily at 1500.

Among the many other museums and
interesting buildings here, seek out the 17th-
century **Børsen** (stock exchange), with its whimsical
decorations; **Den Sorte Diamant** (Black Diamond),
*Søren Kierkegaards Plads 1, T3347 4747, www.kb.dk,
map D7, Mon-Sat 0800-2100 (tours available),* a
stunning black-granite and smoked-glass extension
to the Royal Library, and the peaceful enclave of
the **Bibliotekshaven** (Royal Library Garden).

Strøget and the Latin Quarter (Latiner Kvarter)

The wide open space of **Rådhuspladsen** is best
explored before mid morning, when there's only
a gentle buzz of commuters. Dominating the
late 19th- and early 20th-century square is the
brown-brick **Rådhuset** (City Hall), *T3366 2582,
access to tower late-Aug to Dec Mon-Fri 1100 and 1400,
Sat 1200, Kr20, S-tog Vesterport, map D4.* Check out the
fine views from the tower and the intricate cogs and
wheels of Jen Olsen's World Clock near the entrance.

Copenhagen's most hyped street,
pedestrianized **Strøget**, runs northeast from here.
By lunchtime, its cafés, restaurants and cobbled
squares heave with people and street performers.
To get away from the crowds, explore the narrow
side streets where medieval Copenhagen
developed. For a more tangible feel of the past,
move on a few centuries and explore the Latin
Quarter around the university with some grand

19th-century churches and a studious atmosphere.
Strøget continues its long, shop-laden route along
Østergade to Kongens Nytorv; the small streets to
the north are filled with speciality stores and
restaurants. Købmagergade caters to hedonists and
consumers, with more prestigious shops and the
now closed Museum Erotica. Also here is the
Rundetårn, *Købmagergade 52a, T3373 0373,
www.rundetaarn.dk, May-Sep daily 1000-2000,
Oct-Apr Thu-Mon 1000-1800, Tue and Wed 1000-2100, ,
Kr25, Metro/S-tog Nørreport, map C4,* built as an
observatory by Christian IV. Ascend the spiral
walkway for good views of the city centre.

Frederiksstaden

A populist atmosphere characterizes the north side
of the **Nyhavn canal**, where colourful Dutch-style
houses and a cluster of eateries encourage visitors

to sit on the quayside and soak up the sun. Around the corner, on stately Bredgade, the mood changes abruptly amidst the many reminders of inherited influence. Frederiksstaden, laid out by Frederik V in the mid-18th century, has many palaces and churches, including the Danish royal residence at **Amalienborg Slot** and the remains of an old fortress, **Kastellet**. The **Frihedsmuseet**, chronicling Danish resistance to Nazi occupation, is currently closed after a fire in April 2013. Fortunately none of the archives were damaged and the building is to be rebuilt over the next few years. It is worth visiting the **Kunstindustrimuseet**, *Bredgade 68, T3318 5656, www.designmuseum.dk, Tue, Thu-Sun 1100-1700, Wed 1100-2100, Kr60, map E3*, with its exquisite collections of decorative art.

Rosenborg

West of Frederiksstaden lies the much-visited **Rosenborg Slot**, *Øster Voldgade, T3315 3286, www.dkks.dk, Nov-Apr Tue-Sun 1100-1600, May daily 1100-1600, Jun-Aug daily 1000-1700, Sep-Oct daily 1000-1600, Kr80, Metro/S-tog Nørreport, map C3*, built by Christian IV in the 17th century. The castle is stuffed full of overblown furniture, tapestries and trinkets and is surrounded by the manicured greenery of the Kongens Have (Royal Gardens).

To the northwest are two top-notch art galleries: the esteemed **Statens Museum for Kunst**, *Sølvgade 48, T3374 8494, www.smk.dk, Tue-Sun 1000-1700, Wed 1000-2000, closed public holidays, free, S-tog Østerport, map C2*, which houses the national collection of major works of European art; and the lesser-known but highly rewarding **Den Hirschsprungske Samling**, *Stockholmsgade 20, T3542 0336, www.hirschsprung.dk, Tue-Sun 1100-1600, Kr 95, S-tog Østerport, map C2*, a veritable treasure trove of Danish art from the last two centuries.

The polis and the politics

Across the water from Slotsholmen is the island of Christianshavn and the multi-faceted community of Christiania. Much more than a bohemian social experiment, Christiania is a buzzing area that mixes anarchists with hard-nosed dealers, and canny careerists with 21st-century hippies. It came into existence over 40 years ago, when hippies and activists moved into abandoned military buildings. Over the years, it has experienced numerous clashes with the authorities but now up to 1000 people work or live here tax-free, many in homes they have designed and built themselves. Christiania attracts visitors intrigued by the possibility of an alternative community flourishing in the heart of a modern bourgeois state. The makeshift entrance and a few down-and-outs can be off-putting but, around Pusher Street, you'll find cafés and stalls selling jewellery and T-shirts. A few years ago numerous types of cannabis were on sale here but a major clean-up campaign has stopped the open selling of drugs on the streets. While you're here, don't miss the baroque splendour of **Vor Frelsers Kirke**, with its wacky external staircase that twists around a spiral tower.

Opposite page: Gold statue on City Hall.
Below left: Nyhavn's colourful houses.
Below right: Rosenborg.

Where to stay

The main hotel areas are Vesterbro and Frederiksberg, where smart and comfortable double rooms can be found for below Kr1000. Classier hotels tend to be around Nyhavn and Kongens Nytorv.

Hotel D'Angleterre €€€
Kongens Nytorv 34, T3312 0095, www.dangleterre.com.
Over 250 years old, this luxurious 5-star hotel is definitely the city's finest. Steeped in tradition and oozing elegance, it occupies a prime spot on King's Square and offers guests a fabulous spa experience and top-notch dining options.

Nimb €€€
Bernstorffsgade 5, T8870 0000, www.nimb.dk.
Originally built in 1909 as an Arab fantasy castle, this 5-star boutique hotel was completely refurbished, inside and out, in 2007. The result is a seriously stylish hotel with just 14 rooms and a Michelin-starred restaurant.

Andersen Hotel €€
Helgolandsgade 12, T3331 4344, www.andersen-hotel.dk.
The city's latest design hotel is hip and chic, but the price won't break the bank. Ask for 'CONCEPT24' when booking if you would like to have your room for 24 hrs from whatever time you check in.

Hotel CPH Living €€
1C Langebrogade, T6160 8546, www.cphliving.com.
A unique and stylish floating boutique hotel, located in the city's harbour area. The maritime theme is continued throughout the interior and up top is a private sun deck for taking in the harbour views on a sunny day.

CABINN City €
Mitchellsgade 14, T3346 1616, www.cabinn.com.
Pristine, budget rooms: tiny but perfectly formed, with all you need contained in an amazingly small space. Very central, with a good coffee bar and 24-hr reception. Possibly the best value in town.

Restaurants

Gammel Strand has some upmarket fish restaurants and cafés. Nyhavn offers a more democratic mood for wining and dining, while in Vesterbro you'll find everything from Danish bakeries to kebab shops. Værnedamsvej, off Vesterbrogade, has several non-touristy places.

Amass Restaurant €€€
Refshalevej 153, T4358 4330, www.amassrestaurant.com.
Tue-Thu 1800-0000, Fri-Sat 1200-1600 and 1800-2400.
This is the newest addition to the city's already exciting restaurant scene. Chef and owner, Matt Orlando, has worked at some of the world's finest restaurants, including Noma. Table 153 is a communal experience.

Noma €€€
Strandgade 93, Christianshavn, T3296 3297, www.noma.dk.
Tue-Sat 1200-1600 and 1900-0030.
Set in a converted 18th-century warehouse overlooking the harbour, this ultra-minimalist room lets the excellent and twice Michelin-starred Scandinavian cuisine do all the talking. Often rated as the best restaurant in the world.

Restaurant Godt €€€
Gothersgade 38, T3315 2122, www.restaurant-godt.dk.
Tue-Sat 1800-2400.
A small and intimate venue, so booking is essential. The husband and wife team serve up some of the city's finest Scandinavian cuisine to rave reviews. The menu changes on a daily basis using the best locally sourced ingredients.

Nytorv Restaurant and Café €€-€
Nytorv 15, T3311 7706, www.nytorv.dk.
Daily 1100-2200.
One of the city's oldest restaurants, this is one of the few places left specializing in the much-heralded *smørrebrød* (open sandwich). At lunch, it's full of Danes tucking in.

Rizraz €
Kompagnistræde 20,
T3315 0575, www.rizraz.dk.
Daily 1130-2400.
A vast warren of a place with a huge all-you-can-eat vegetarian buffet as well as meat dishes. Possibly the best value in town.

Nightlife

Copenhagen boasts a lively, ever-changing bar and club scene, based around Vesterbro, Nørrebro, Østerbro and the centre. The great thing is that the city is small enough to allow you to sample a selection of several venues in any one night. The most popular club in town is **Vega**, *Enghavevej 40, T3325 7011, www.vega.dk,* in Vesterbro, which incorporates a nightclub at weekends, plus a lounge bar, concert venue and cocktail bar. In Nørrebro head to **Rust**, *Guldbergs gade 8, T3524 5200, www.rust.dk,* another multi-venue place where good music takes precedence over the weekly cattle market. In the city centre, **Hive**, *Skindergarde 45-47, T2845 7476, wwwø.hivecph.dk,* is one of the city's most exclusive clubs, attracting the 'beautiful people'. Kødbyen (aka the Meatpacking District), near the main station, is home to some of the city's hottest clubs, including **Bakken Kbh**, *Flaesketorvet 19-21, www. bakkenkbh.dk,* with its weekend party atmosphere and live music.

Travel essentials

Getting there
Copenhagen International Airport, T3231 3231, flight information T3247 4747, www.cph.dk, is 9 km from the city and 12 mins from Central Station by high-speed train, departing every 10 mins (Kr36). The metro runs between Terminal 3 and Central Station with a journey time of 14 mins (Kr36). City bus services 5A, 35 and 36 cost about the same as the train but take 55 mins. At night bus 96N runs every 30 mins to 1 hr from Terminal 3 to the city centre (Kr45). A taxi from outside the arrivals hall will cost about Kr180-200. International trains arrive at **København H central station**, T7013 1415, www.dsb.dk; long-distance coaches also arrive here.

Getting around
Public transport tickets cover buses, S-Tog trains and the metro, within designated zones. The basic ticket costs Kr24 and is valid for up to 1 hr within any 2 zones (which covers most of the sights and places of interest). Tickets and maps showing the zones are available from machines or ticket offices in train stations and from bus drivers. A new electronic Travel Card system that does away with the current zones is due to be introduced in the near future. If you intend to do a lot of travelling about the city you can buy a *klippekort*, valid for 10 rides or a 24-hr unlimited travel card (Kr130). Another alternative is to buy a **Copenhagen Card**, which offers unlimited travel in greater Copenhagen and free admission to some museums and sights (www. copenhagencard.com). It's valid for 24-120 hrs and costs Kr299-749. It is also easy to get around the various sights on foot. From Central Station it takes about 30 mins to walk the length of Strøget and reach Nyhavn. From around Istedgade or Vesterbrogade it takes 20 mins to reach Slotsholmen.

Tourist information
Wonderful Copenhagen tourist office, T7022 2442, www.visitcopenhagen. com, is on the corner of Vesterbrogade and Bernstorffsgade, close to Central Station. May-Jun and Sep Mon-Sat 0900-1800; Jul-Aug Mon-Sat 0900-2000, Sun 1000-1800; Oct-Apr Mon-Sat 0900-1600, Sat 0900-1400. There is a smaller tourist office at the airport.

Exchange rate
Danish Kroner (Kr). £1 = Kr8.94. €1 = Kr7.46 (Nov 2013).

Copenhageners don't start to kick up their heels until at least 2400-0100, particularly at weekends, but lounge bars such as glam cocktail joint **Ruby**, *Nybrogade 10, T3393 1203,* and **The Jane**, *Grabrodretorv 8, T6969 6000,* will keep you in an intimate and inviting atmosphere until then. Special one-off and try-out club and bar nights are plentiful. The weekly *Copenhagen Post*'s 'In & Out' guide, *www.cphpost.dk,* contains a good day-by-day rundown in English.

Ratings

Art and culture ✩✩✩
Eating ✩✩✩
Nightlife ✩✩✩✩
Shopping ✩✩
Sightseeing ✩✩✩
Value for money ✩✩
Overall city rating ✩✩✩

Dublin

Dublin has been riding one hell of a rollercoaster in recent decades. In the 1990s, Ireland's capital regained a European presence that it had last experienced in the 18th century, metamorphosing, with the help of Euro money, from struggling provincial backwater to the city that never slept. But when the money dried up, the Celtic Tiger lost its roar and looked as though it was going to limp away with its tail between its legs. And yet, a few years on from the financial crash, Dublin's appeal for visitors remains undimmed. Plane-loads still arrive in the city looking for hedonism, history and the perfect pint. They come for the city's rich literary heritage and its earthy good humour, for its Georgian architecture and high-tech arts centres, its wood-panelled Edwardian pubs and designer bars. Underneath the sophisticated gloss, the fiddly-diddly music and the political wheeler-dealing, they find a city whose secrets are still waiting to be explored. And through the heart of it all snakes the Liffey: dark, unfathomable and just a little bit muddier than we'd like to admit.

Stone carving on Dublin Castle.

Around the city

Trinity College

College Green, www.tcd.ie.
Campus tours summer daily 1015-1540; winter Fri, Sat and Mon 1015-1540, Tue-Thu on demand, Sun 1135-1515. €10 with Book of Kells. Map D4.

Trinity College is a time capsule of smooth lawns, cobblestones, statuary and formal buildings, reminiscent of Oxford's dreaming spires. It was founded in 1592 by Elizabeth I in an attempt to prevent young Protestant intellectuals of the Pale going to Europe and discovering Catholicism. In Library Square is the **Campanile**, beside which is a Henry Moore statue, *Reclining Connected Form*. To the right is the highlight of the campus, the 18th-century **Old Library**, home to the **Book of Kells Exhibition**, *T01 896 2320, Mon-Sat 0930-1700, May-Sep Sun 0930-1630, Oct-Apr Sun 1200-1630, closed for Christmas and New Year, €9*. Two pages of the ninth-century illuminated manuscript are on show each day, accompanied by displays explaining its religious symbolism and manufacture. Upstairs is the magnificent 65-m Long Room, where 200,000 of the library's oldest books are held.

Across Fellowes Square is the Arts Block, built in 1980 and showing collections of conceptual and avant-garde art in its **Douglas Hyde Gallery**, *T01 896 1116, www.douglashydegallery.com, Mon-Fri 1100-1800, Thu 1100-1900, Sat 1100-1645, free, map D4.*

Trinity College Campus.

At a glance

Georgian **Grafton Street** runs from Trinity College south to St Stephen's Green. This area and the streets to the east are the centre of tourist Dublin, where you'll find most of the most significant sights and the city's best restaurants and hotels. **Temple Bar**, with its ancient, redeveloped streets, Dublin Castle and Christchurch Cathedral lie to the west, while to the southwest is an odd mishmash of areas, loosely defined as the **Liberties** and barely touched by the Celtic Tiger phenomenon of the 1990s.

North of the Liffey, **O'Connell Street**, one of the city's oldest and grandest boulevards, is now cluttered with shop signs and statuary. It's less tourist-focused than areas south of the river but has a great deal to offer thanks to its powerful historical associations and impressive literary connections. You'll also find much of the city's cheapest accommodation here. Northwest of the Liffey is a relatively unvisited area with a long history, an ancient church, the city's Four Courts and **Smithfield market**. Further west still are the old **Collins Barracks**, which house a branch of the National Museum, and, beyond that again, is **Phoenix Park**, the largest enclosed public space in Europe. Victorian and Edwardian **Ballsbridge**, southeast of the centre, is the poshest part of Dublin with some good restaurants and lively bars.

24 hours in the city

Start your day with a full Irish breakfast at the **Kingfisher** on Parnell Street. Here you'll find a mix of locals and tourists all tucking in to a hearty spread. Spend the morning marvelling at the collection of gold in the **National Museum**, followed by a quick peek at the Picasso in the **National Gallery** and a really classy lunch at The Commons. In the afternoon stroll around the shops and alleys of Temple Bar before hopping on a bus to the **Guinness Storehouse** to enjoy a bird's eye view of the city – and a pint of Guinness to boot. In the evening head back to Temple Bar to sample some traditional Irish fare at Gallagher's Boxty House. After dinner enjoy a drink at Oliver St John Gogarty's, where you've a good chance of catching some traditional Irish music, or grab a cab over to the Brazen Head, Dublin's oldest bar. The next port of call for nightowls should be **Old Harcourt Street**, where the clubs get going around 2300. POD, Crawdaddy and Tripod are some of the hippest joints in town.

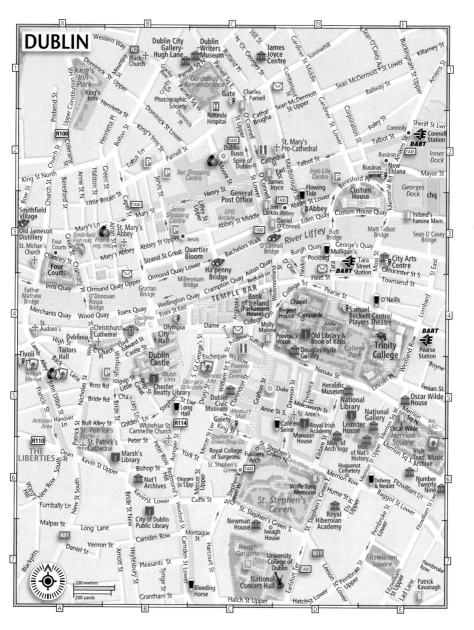

DUBLIN

Around the city

Leinster House and the museums

Map D5.

The area south of Trinity College and east of Kildare Street is tightly packed with museums and other places to visit. At its heart is **Leinster House**, which is home to the Republic's two Houses of Parliament: the Dáil and the Seanad. The house was built around 1745 by James Fitzgerald, Earl of Kildare (later Duke of Leinster), as an escape from Parnell Square in north Dublin, which had become a little too nouveau riche for his liking. In the 19th century, Leinster House was sold to the Royal Dublin Society, which added two new wings on either side, designed in 1884-1890 by Deane and Son, to house the **National Library**, *Kildare St, T01 603 0200, www.nli.ie, Mon-Wed 0930-1945, Thu and Fri 0930-1645, Sat 0930-1245, free*, and the archaeology collections of the **National Museum of Ireland**, *T01 677 7444, www.museum.ie, Tue-Sat 1000-1700, Sun 1400-1700, free*. The museum is full of wonderful things, including a stunning hoard of Bronze Age gold, guarded by two stone *sheela-na-gigs*. Upstairs, you'll find Viking and medieval artefacts, a display of ancient Egyptian embalming techniques and 'The Road to Independence' exhibition.

National Gallery

Merrion Sq (entrance via Clare St), T01 661 5133, www.nationalgallery.ie.
Mon-Wed, Fri and Sat 0930-1730, Thu 0930-2030, Sun 1200-1730. Free. Map E5.

Merrion Square, the Georgian heartland of Dublin, was once home to Daniel O'Connell at No 58, W B Yeats at 82 and Oscar Wilde at No 1. (Look out for his flamboyant statue sprawling nearby.) On its western side is the country house façade of Leinster House and the entrance to the National Gallery, where the big names of European art are well represented. There are works by Caravaggio, Degas, El Greco, Fra Angelico, Goya, Mantegna, Monet, Picasso, Rembrandt, Tintoretto, Titian, Velasquez and Vermeer for starters. Then there is also a decent display of English art and a marvellous collection by Irish artists. Although the gallery always functioned on a hand-to-mouth basis, more prosperous times saw the opening of a Millennium Wing in 2002.

St Stephen's Green

Map C/D6.

Nowadays the city's playground, St Stephen's Green, south of Trinity College, has had many incarnations over the centuries. Until the 1660s it was an expanse of open ground where people grazed their cattle and public executions took place. As the surrounding area began to be developed, the green was partly fenced in and became a park. In 1814 the public were excluded and only residents of the grand houses overlooking the park could use it. In 1877 Lord Ardilaun, one of the Guinness family, introduced a bill to Parliament making it a public park again and put up the cash to make it happen. Now it's great for a picnic on a sunny day, with occasional music from the bandstand.

Dublin Castle

Dame St, T01 645 8813, www.dublincastle.ie.
Guided tours of the State Apartments and Medieval Undercroft Mon-Sat 1000-1645, Sun 1200-1645; €4.50; the castle may be closed at short notice for Government business. Map B5.

It is difficult to surmise from the hand-tufted carpets and 18th-century plasterwork that this

Above: Kilmainham Gaol.
Opposite page: Oscar Wilde statue in Merrion Square.

Republican city

Built in 1792 and opened just in time to incarcerate any surviving rebels of the 1798 uprising, **Kilmainham Gaol**, *Inchicore Rd, T01 453 5984, www.heritageireland.ie. Apr-Sep daily 0930-1800, Oct-Mar Mon-Sat 0930-1730, Sun 1000-1800. €6*, saw hundreds of men suffer and die for their belief in independence in the uprisings of 1798, 1803, 1848, 1867, 1916 and 1922. Most of the big names in Republican history spent time in here and some of them died here. The last man to walk out was Eamon de Valera at the end of the Civil War in 1923, whereupon the gaol was closed. Forty years later a group of history buffs decided to restore it and Kilmainham was opened to the public. A museum covers the early 20th-century political history of Ireland, prison memorabilia and a guided tour. It takes you around the dungeons, tiny cells, the chapel where Joseph Plunkett was married three hours before his execution and the grim yard where Connolly, Plunkett and 15 other leaders of the 1916 uprising were executed.

was once Dublin's biggest stronghold, built in 1204 to defend the city against the native Irish. It must have looked the part, too, because, apart from a Fitzgerald attack in 1534 and an aborted attempt at seizing it in 1641, the castle has seen very little action. The most exciting thing to take place here must have been the night during the Black and Tan War, when Michael Collins infiltrated the records office. In 1922 the castle was officially handed over to him as commander in chief of the Irish army. The guided tour explores the State Apartments then passes into the Upper Yard, where you can see the Statue of Justice over the gateway, unblindfolded and with her back to the city she should have been defending. Until she was mended in the 1980s, her scales of justice regularly tipped when they filled with rainwater. From here you visit the Undercroft, where you can see the remains of Viking fortifications, part of the old medieval city wall, the moat, postern steps for deliveries and a dribble of the River Poddle itself.

Housed in a beautifully converted clocktower within the castle walls is the stunning **Chester Beatty Library**, *T01 407 0750, www.cbl.ie, map B5,*

Oct-Apr Tue-Fri 1000-1730, Sat 1100-1730, Sun 1300-1700, May-Sep also Mon 1000-1730, closed public hols, free, a priceless collection of cultural and religious treasures – icons, papyrus texts, Buddhas and ancient copies of the Bible and the Koran – bequeathed to the state by the Irish-American mining magnate, Chester Beatty.

Christchurch Cathedral

*Christchurch Pl, T01 677 8099,
www.christchurchdublin.ie.*
Jun-Sep Mon-Sat 0900-1900, Sun 1230-1430, 1630-1900, Oct-Feb Mon-Sat 0900-1700, Sun 1230-1430, Mar-May Mon-Sat 0900-1800, Sun 1230-1430, 1630-1800. €6. Map A4.

This is Dublin's oldest building, pre-dating the castle by a century or so. However, the original wooden construction is long gone and, although the crypt, north wall and south transept date from the 12th century, most of what you see is 19th-century stone cladding. Inside there are lovely faux ancient floor tiles, a 16th-century replica of the tomb of Strongbow (Richard de Clare, the Norman conqueror of Ireland) and lots of stuff to admire in the 'Treasures of Christchurch' exhibition in the crypt. If you stand in the choir by the bishop's throne and look back towards the entrance, you'll notice that the north wall (to your right) is seriously out of kilter.

Temple Bar
Map C4.

The landmark **Ha'penny Bridge** over the River Liffey is a cast-iron footbridge built in 1816 and named after the toll levied on it until 1919. On the south side of the bridge, **Merchant's Arch** leads into the hub of streets and alleys that define Temple Bar. Nowadays a vibrant tourist ghetto, this network of narrow lanes, named after its 17th-century developer, Sir William Temple, criss-crosses between the river and Dame Street and from Fishamble Street to Fleet Street. Despite all the redevelopment, a few remnants of the old city are still intact. Look out for Sunlight Chambers, on the corner of Parliament Street and Essex Quay, with multi-coloured terracotta reliefs displaying the benefits of soap.

The **Gallery of Photography**, *Meeting House Sq, T01 671 4654, www.galleryofphotography.ie, Tue-Sat 1100-1800, Sun 1300-1800, free*, is a carefully lit, purpose-built venue with a permanent collection of 20th-century Irish photographs, plus changing monthly exhibitions by Irish and international artists. The **Irish Film Centre** on Eustace Street shows art house films in a post-modern conversion of a Quaker Meeting House.

O'Connell Street and around

Most of the hyped tourist spots are in the southern half of the city but the north has lots to offer and fewer crowds; there is also a more genuine, earthy feel to it because it is less geared up to the tourist market. The area has strong historical and literary associations and boasts some of the city's earliest Georgian buildings.

The **General Post Office**, O'Connell Street's most famous building, was gutted by fire and shelling in 1916 and suffered further damage in 1922 during the Civil War before being rebuilt in 1929. Inside the functioning post office is a series of paintings depicting scenes from the 1916 Easter Rising.

At the north end of O'Connell Street are the excellent **Hugh Lane Gallery**, *Charlemont House, Parnell Sq North, T01 222 5550, www.hughlane.ie, Tue-Thu 1000-1800, Fri and Sat 1000-1700, Sun 1100-1700, free, map B1*, with its fine collection of modern art, and the attractive **Dublin Writers' Museum**, *18-19 Parnell Sq, T01 872 2077, www.writersmuseum.com, Mon-Sat 1000-1700, Sun and public holidays 1100-1700, later opening Jun-Aug, €7.50, map C1*.

Nearby, homage can be paid to Dublin's most famous writer at the **James Joyce Centre**, *35 North Great George St, T01 878 8547, www.jamesjoyce.ie, Mon-Sat 1000-1700, Sun 1200-1700, closed Christmas and New Year, €5, map C1*.

Best of the rest

Guinness Storehouse
St James' Gate, T01 408 4800, www.guinness-storehouse.com. Sep-Jun daily 0930-1700; Jul-Aug daily 0930-1900. €14.85.
A temple to the famous Irish drink and brand.

James Joyce Museum
Sandycove, 13 km south of the centre, T01 280 9265, www.jamesjoycetower.com. Apr-Aug Tue-Sat 1000-1700 (closed 1300-1400), Sun 1400-1800. Closed on Mon. Free; donations welcome.
A Martello tower houses literary memorabilia associated with Joyce and *Ulysses*.

National Museum of Decorative Arts and History
Collins Barracks, Benburb St, T01 677 7444, www.museum.ie. Tue-Sat 1000-1700, Sun 1400-1700. Free.
A former military barracks houses exquisite pieces from the Museum of Ireland's decorative arts collection.

St Patrick's Cathedral
Patrick's Cl, T01 453 9472, www.stpatrickscathedral.ie.
Despite its ugly exterior, the national cathedral of the Church of Ireland is worth a look due to its interesting history and its links with Jonathan Swift, who was dean here in the 18th century.

Where to stay

Hotel rooms in Dublin don't come cheap. Grafton St and Temple Bar form Dublin's chief accommodation area and prices here are pretty high, with no B&Bs. North of the river is a concentration of more affordable guesthouses – the top end of O'Connell St, around Parnell Sq, has some interesting options – but the central location and proximity of the bus and railway station mean they tend to fill up most quickly. Ballsbridge, southeast of the city centre, has a great range of top-notch hotels, quality guesthouses and a cluster of good restaurants.

The Clarence €€€
6-8 Wellington Quay, T01 407 0800, www.theclarence.ie.
Owned by U2's Bono and the Edge, the Clarence has preserved its original wood panelling amidst modish embellishments like leather-clad lifts and Egyptian cotton on the king-size beds in the individually designed bedrooms. Friendly staff, a bookless lounge called the Study and original artwork contribute to the strange mix of the spartan and the sybaritic.

Morrison €€€
15 Ormond Quay, T01 887 2400, www.morrisonhotel.ie.
This classy building sits unobtrusively on the banks of the river and vies with the Clarence for Dublin's hippest hotel award. It has recently undergone a complete refurbishment at the hands of Irish architect, Nikki O'Donnell. It is chic and modern, with more than a nod to Ireland's illustrious roll call of musical legends. On Sat evenings the hotel plays host to new talent and live acts in its bar, Quay 14.

Dylan €€€-€€
Eastmoreland Pl, T01 660 3000, www.dylan.ie.
A chic boutique hotel whose 44 bespoke bedrooms manage to retain an intimacy sometimes lost in larger hotels. The decor is funky yet elegant, and the Dylan restaurant offers a menu of sumptuous contemporary Irish cuisine. Its location, a short stroll from the RDS and the Aviva Stadium, makes it an upmarket choice for sports enthusiasts.

Merrion Hall €€
56 Merrion Rd, T01 668 1426, www.merrionhall.net.
A quiet, welcoming place with 4-poster beds, an ample lounge area, private gardens and a library of tourist literature. Award-winning breakfasts are served in the serene, sunny breakfast room.

O'Callaghan Stephen's Green Hotel €€
1-5 Harcourt St, T01 607 3600, www.stephensgreenhotel.ie.
A new arrival on the Dublin hotel scene, offering 4-star comforts at affordable prices. The building blends Georgian splendour with a modern glass atrium, and the location is superb for exploring the city. Some rooms overlook the 9 acres of parkland that make up St Stephen's Green, yet it's only a short stroll from the thick of things in Grafton St.

Castle Hotel €
2-4 Gardiner Row, T01 874 6949, www.castle-hotel.ie.
A real find, this is a lovingly restored Georgian building that offers so much more and, at better value, than some of the faceless hotels in town, including an elegant lounge and comfortable rooms. Michael Collins is said to have used room 201, originally No 23, as one of his safe houses during the War of Independence. Parking available.

The Times Hostel €
8 College St, T01 675 3652, www.timeshostels.com.
Stay in the heart of the city at budget prices but don't expect to get much sleep. A great choice for those wanting somewhere to lay their head for a few hours after a night sampling Dublin's club and music scene until the wee small hours. Temple Bar, O'Connell Street and Grafton Street are all on its doorstep. Lively and bustling with free dinner offer on Wed.

Restaurants

While many of Temple Bar's restaurants are fun, fashionable and relatively inexpensive places to enjoy a meal, the area from St Stephen's Green to Merrion Square is where the real money tends to dine. Don't even look at the menus if you're on a tight budget but for seriously fine dining and splashing out, this is the place to eat.

Chapter One €€€

19 Parnell Sq, T01 873 2266,
www.chapteronerestaurant.com.
A foodie's delight located in the basement of the Dublin Writers Museum. For a truly unique dining experience, guests can book the Chef's Table and watch this Michelin-starred team create their culinary magic at close hand. The 6-course tasting menu (€85) with accompanying champagne will allow you to experience a wide range of glorious Irish dishes, all served with flare and panache.

Thorntons €€€

Fitzwilliam Hotel, St Stephen's Green, T01 478 7000,
www.fitzwilliamhoteldublin.com.
Acclaimed chef Kevin Thornton serves up his innovative signature dishes in a contemporary setting overlooking the Green. Considered by many of Ireland's foodies to be one of the city's finest restaurants, Thorntons is Michelin starred and has an extensive wine list with dozens of fine wines available by the glass.

Cleaver East €€

6-8 East Essex St, T01 531 3500,
www.cleavereast.ie.
Having established himself as the chef with the Midas touch, Oliver Dunne opened his 3rd restaurant in summer 2013. So far so good. A contemporary menu of tasting plates, ranging from barbecued pork belly to lobster dumplings, are attracting the punters in their droves.

Gallagher's Boxty House €€

20-21 Temple Bar, T01 677 2762,
www.boxtyhouse.ie.
Sells the eponymous filled potato pancakes, plus lots more Irish-sourced edibles. Vegetarians will do well here. It has an old-fashioned country-kitchen feel to it, with newspapers and books to read.

Nico's €€

53 Dame St, T01 677 3062.
Ask anyone involved in the food business in Dublin where they like to eat, and they'll mention here. Good traditional Italian food, white cloths, Chianti bottles and bustling waiters.

Tante Zoe's €€

1 Crow St, T01 679 4407,
www.tante-zoes.com.
Established over 20 years ago in Temple Bar and still going strong, this is a lively Cajun/Creole restaurant with a legion of fans. The best gumbo and jambalaya this side of the Atlantic!

Gruel €

68a Dame St, T01 670 7119,
www.gruel.ie.
Very popular inexpensive restaurant that serves hearty hot meals, such as beef hotpot and pan-fried sea trout, as well as simpler filled rolls and soups. Bare boards and plain tables inside.

Nightlife

Pubs, bars and clubs are what Dublin does best. Tourists flock to Temple Bar to party well into the early hours every night of the week. Elsewhere, the liveliest streets are South Great George's and Camden, which, from Thu evening, turn into a huge street party. Old Harcourt St is the centre of clubland. Most clubs serve drinks until 0200 and close around 0300. For up-to-date entertainment listings, check on noticeboards or consult the excellent *Event Guide*.

Live music pours out of many pubs and bars in Dublin: try **Bruxelles**, *7/8 Harry St*; **The Porterhouse**, *16-18 Parliament St*; **Whelan's**, *25 Wexford St*; or the **Cobblestone**, *North King St*. The cool kids head to the **Button Factory**, *Curved St, Temple Bar*, the city's hippest music venue. There are also great venues for comedy and drama, including iconic names such as the **Abbey Theatre**, *26 Lwr Abbey St, T01 878 7222*, and the **Gate Theatre**, *1 Cavendish Row, T01 874 4045*. Cultural festivals include the **Jameson Dublin Film Festival** (www.jdiff.com) in spring and the **Dublin Theatre Festival** (www.dublintheatrefestival.com) in autumn.

Travel essentials

Getting there
Dublin International Airport, T01 814 1111, www.dublinairport.com, is 12 km north of the city centre. **Aircoach**, www.aircoach.ie, runs to and from city centre hotels 24 hrs daily. Tickets can be bought on board and cost €7 single or €12 return, journey time 35 mins. A taxi costs about €25. At the mouth of the Liffey, **Dublin Port** is used by ferries to and from Holyhead (Terminal 1) and Liverpool (Terminal 3); bus 53/53A runs into the centre. Other ferry services use **Dun Laoghaire** harbour, 30 mins south of the city and accessible on the DART.

Getting around
The centre of Dublin is easy enough to negotiate on foot but if you get tired, local buses run by **Dublin Bus**, T01 873 4222, www.dublinbus.ie, are frequent and cheap; fares (exact change only to the driver) start at 95c for a short hop within the city. Dublin now has a bus corridor with a city centre zone for public transport only that operates during rush hours. Fares within the zone at these times of day are only 65c. A 1-day Rambler pass costs €6.90 (3- and 5-day passes €15 and €25.00 respectively). An excellent bus map of the city is available free from Dublin Bus or the tourist office. **Dublin Bus Tours**, www.dublinsightseeing.ie, operate the hop-on, hop-off Dublin City Tour, which starts on O'Connell Bridge. The complete tour takes over an hour and visits 16 sights around the city. A ticket (€18) includes discounts at each of the sights and is valid for a day. The electric tram system, the **Luas**, www.luas.ie, is designed for commuters, but the red line, from Connolly Street through the shopping streets north of the river and then along the quays to Phoenix Park and Heuston station, can be useful. Tickets are available at each stop; a single ticket is valid for only 90 mins, a return for the whole day. The all-zone combi ticket for bus and Luas costs €8.30 for 1 day. The **DART** (Dublin Area Rapid Transit), T01 850 366222, www.irishrail.ie, is a suburban rail service that links the coastal suburbs with the city centre. It is useful for travel between the south and north of the city and for transport to some suburban areas. There are taxi ranks on O'Connell Street, Dame Street and St Stephen's Green.

Tourist information
Dublin Tourism Centre, St Andrew's Church, Suffolk St, www.visitdublin. com, Mon-Sat 0900-1730, Sun 1030-1500, offers accommodation advice and bookings, ferry and concert tickets, car hire, bureau de change, free leaflets and guidebooks for sale. There's also a **Temple Bar information centre** at 12 East Essex St, www.dublinstemplebar.com.

Ha'Penny Bridge at night.

Ratings

Art and culture ☆☆☆☆
Eating ☆☆☆☆
Nightlife ☆☆☆
Shopping ☆☆☆
Sightseeing ☆☆☆☆
Value for money ☆☆
Overall city rating ☆☆☆☆

Dubrovnik

Backed by rugged limestone mountains and jutting out into the Adriatic Sea, Dubrovnik is one of the world's finest and best-preserved fortified cities. For centuries it was the centre of the maritime Republic of Ragusa. Its gargantuan walls and medieval fortresses enclose a historic centre characterized by town houses with terracotta roofs, monasteries with cloistered gardens, and baroque churches with copper domes. The old town is traversed by the main pedestrian promenade, Stradun (Placa), which is paved with glistening white limestone and lined with open-air cafés. In 1979, the city became a UNESCO World Heritage Site.

Tourism has a long history here, and the sights, hotels and restaurants are all geared to foreign visitors. Dubrovnik is now considered one of Europe's most exclusive destinations – be aware that prices are almost double what they would be anywhere else in Croatia. Throughout the high season the city heaves with visitors, attracting more than its share of international celebrities. The good news is that it is now also a winter destination, with year-round flights from London. Come in the low season to enjoy the city's attractions without the crowds.

View through gate of city wall.

Around the city

Gradske Zidine (City walls)

T020 638800, www.citywallsdubrovnik.hr.
May-Sep daily 0800-1900; Oct-Apr daily
1000-1500. kn90.

The highlight of any visit to Dubrovnik has to be
a walk around the city walls. To reach them, climb
the steps immediately to your left after entering
the old city through the 16th-century **Vrata od
Pila** (Pile Gate). To walk the full circuit, 2 km, you
should allow at least an hour. The walls, as they
stand today, follow a ground plan laid down in the
13th century. However, they were reinforced with
towers and bastions by Italian architect Michelozzo
di Bartolomeo, following the fall of Constantinople
to the Turks in 1453. On average, the walls are 24 m
high and up to 3 m thick on the seaward side, 6 m
on the inland side.

City of Dubrovnik.

At a glance

All Dubrovnik's major attractions are in the car-free
old town, which is encircled by medieval walls.
There are two main entrances into the old town:
Pile Gate in the west and Ploče Gate in the east;
these are connected by Stradun (Placa), the main
pedestrian thoroughfare. To the east of the old town
rises **Mount Srdj**, the peak of which can be reached
by cable car. Some 3 km west of the old town lies
Gruž port, with daily ferries to the nearby Elafiti
islands. Opposite Gruž is **Lapad Peninsula**, where
you'll find several beaches and a concentration of
big, modern, mid-range hotels.

Stradun

Until the 12th century, Stradun (also known as
Placa) was a shallow sea channel, separating the
island of Laus from the mainland. After it was filled
in, it continued to divide the city socially for
several centuries, with the nobility living in the
area south of Stradun, while the commoners lived
on the hillside to the north. It forms the main
thoroughfare through the old town, running
300 m from **Pile Gate** (map A2) at the western end
to the old port. The white limestone paving stones
date from 1468, though the buildings on either
side were constructed after the earthquake of
1667; the ground floors were used as shops with
residential accommodation above. Stradun still
serves as the city's main social hub, where locals
conduct their morning and evening promenades
and meet at rather pricey open-air cafés. On
Poljana Paska Miličevića, just inside Pile Gate, is
Velika Onofrio Fontana (map B2), a polygonal
cistern designed by the Neapolitan builder
Onofrio de la Cava to bring water into town from
the River Dubrovačka, 20 km away. Completed
in 1444, it is rimmed with 16 spouting masks and
topped with a dome.

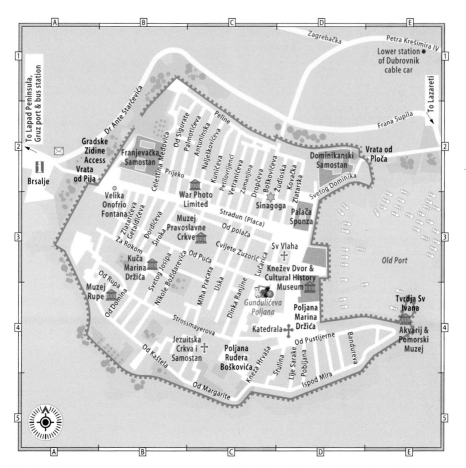

Franjevačka Samostan

Placa 2, T020 321410.
Apr-Oct daily 0900-1800; Nov-Mar daily
0900-1700. kn30. Map B2.

At the western end of Stradun, this Franciscan
monastery is centred on a delightful cloister from
1360; its late Romanesque arcades are supported
by double columns, each crowned with a set of
grotesque figures. There's also an internal garden
filled with palms and Mediterranean shrubs.

There's a small museum displaying early laboratory
equipment, ceramic bowls and medical books
used in the monastery's pharmacy; it was founded
in 1318 and is said to be the oldest institution of its
kind in Europe.

Knežev Dvor (Rector's Palace)

Pred Dvorom 3, T020 321422, www.dumus.hr.
May-Sep daily 0900-1800; Oct-Apr Mon-Sat
0900-1600. kn70 (ticket valid for entry to
4 museums). Map D4.

Left: Aerial view of the old town.
Right: Beach near Dubrovnik.

Behind the **Church of St Blaise** (Sv Vlaha), the Rector's Palace was home to the rector (or governor) of the Republic. The rector was obliged to reside in the palace throughout his one-month term in office; he could only leave for official business, and his family remained in their own home. The building dates from the 15th century, though the arcaded loggia and internal courtyard, combining late-Gothic and early-Renaissance styles, were largely built after the 1667 earthquake.

In the courtyard (where classical music concerts are held during the Summer Festival) stands a bust of Miho Pracat (1528-1607), a powerful merchant and ship owner from the nearby island of Lopud, who left his wealth to the Republic for charitable purposes when he died. Next to the courtyard is a series of large rooms where the Great Council and Senate held their meetings; a plaque over the entrance reads *'Obliti privatorum publica curate'* (Forget private affairs, and get on with public matters).

Upstairs, the rector's living quarters now accommodate the **Cultural History Museum**, offering an idea of how people once lived in the Republic of Ragusa. Exhibits include a curious collection of clocks, each one stopped at quarter to six, the time at which Napoleon's men took the city on 31 January 1806, marking the fall of the Republic.

Katedrala (Cathedral)

Poljana Marina Držića, T020 323459 (Treasury).
May-Oct Mon-Sat 0900-1700, Sun 100-1700;
Nov-Apr Mon-Sat 1000-1200 and 1500-1700, Sun 1100-1200 and 1500-1700. Treasury kn15. Map D4.

The original 12th-century cathedral on this site is said to have been sponsored in part by Richard the Lionheart of England out of gratitude for having been saved from a shipwreck on the nearby island of Lokrum on his return from the Crusades in 1192. That building was destroyed in the 1667 earthquake, so what you see today is a splendid baroque structure with three aisles and a cupola, designed by Andrea Buffalini of Rome in 1671. The light but rather bare interior contains a number of paintings, notably a large polyptych above the main alter depicting *The Assumption of Our Lady*, attributed to the Venetian master, Titian (1485-1576). Adjoining the cathedral, the **Treasury** displays 138 gold and silver reliquaries. Pride of place is given to the skull of St Blaise in the form of a bejewelled Byzantine crown; an arm and a leg of the saint are also on show.

Tvrdja Sv Ivana (St John's Fortress)

Map E4.

St John's Fortress guards the entrance to the old city port. In previous centuries, the port was closed at night by stretching a chain from the fortress across to Kaše, a breakwater built in the 15th century. The ground floor of the fortress now houses the **Aquarium**, *T020-323978, May-Oct daily 0900-2000, Nov-Apr Tue-Sun 0900-1600, kn40*, where several saltwater pools and well-lit tanks display a variety of Adriatic fish and other underwater life.

Above the Aquarium, on the first floor the **Maritime Museum** (**Pomorski Muzej**), *Damjana Jude 2, T020 323904, www.dumus.hr, May-Sep Tue-Sun 0900-1800, Oct-Apr Tue-Sun 0900-1600, kn70 (ticket valid for entry to 4 museums)*, traces Dubrovnik's seafaring past.

Lokrum

www.lokrum.hr.
15 mins by boat from the old port. kn60.

A short boat ride east of the old port, you'll find the lush island of Lokrum, site of a Benedictine Monastery, founded in 1023. Legend has it that when French authorities began closing down religious institutions in the early 19th century, local Benedictines placed a curse upon anyone who should try to possess Lokrum. A succession of subsequent owners died mysterious and horrific deaths, one being the unfortunate Archduke Maximilian von Hapsburg, who bought the island in 1859, only to be taken prisoner and shot in Mexico in 1867. Maximilian built a summer house here, surrounded by a botanical garden filled with exotic plants and peacocks. Even now, locals remain superstitious about Lokrum, and while it is a popular bathing area during daylight hours, no one stays on the island after sunset. There are some decent beaches on the southwest side of the island, plus a small saltwater lake. You'll find a restaurant within the former monastery, and there's also a seasonal café.

Beaches

The nearest bathing area to the old town is **Banje Beach**, between the city walls and Lazareti, where the fancy Eastwest Beach Club offers sun-beds and umbrellas on a stretch of golden (imported) sand, plus DJ-music, masseurs and a rather expensive bar-restaurant. A 20-minute walk further down the

Best of the rest

Dubrovnik Cable Car
Frana Supila 35a, T020 325393, www.dubrovnikcable car.com. Jun-Aug daily 0900-2400, Sep 0900-2200, Oct and Apr-May 0900-2000, Nov and Feb-Mar 0900-1700, Dec-Jan 0900-1600. kn50 (single). Map E1.
The cable car whizzes visitors to the peak of **Mount Srdj** (405 m) in just three minutes. From the top, you have an amazing bird's-eye view of the old town and out to sea.

Palača Sponza
Luža, T020 321032.May-Oct daily 0900-2100; Nov-Apr daily 0900-1500. Free (ground floor only). Map D3.
Sponza Palace was designed by Paskoje Miličević in 1522 and displays a blend of Renaissance and Venetian-Gothic architecture. It was one of the few buildings to survive the 1667 earthquake and now houses the state archives and temporary exhibitions.

War Photo Limited
Antuninska 6, between Placa and Prijeko, T020 322166, www.warphotoltd.com. Jun-Sep daily 1000-2200; May and Oct Tue-Sun 1000-1600; closed Nov-Apr. kn30. Map C3.
This is a beautifully designed two-floor gallery dedicated to photo-journalism from war zones around the world. Emotionally gruelling but well worth a visit.

coast, you'll find the more peaceful **Sveti Jakov Beach** in a bay backed by cliffs; the pebble beach is approached down a long flight of steps. West of the old town, on Lapad Peninsula, **Lapad Cove** is popular with guests staying in the big modern hotels nearby.

Where to stay

There are only 2 (very expensive) hotels within the old town walls, but you also have a decent choice of rooms and small self-catering apartments to rent. Most of the luxury hotels lie along the coast, southeast of the old town. The majority of mid-range hotels are to be found on Lapad Peninsula, close to Gruž port.

Hotel Bellevue €€€
Pera Cingrije 7, T020 330100, www.adriaticluxuryhotels.com.
Built into a cliff face overlooking the sea, halfway between the old town and Lapad Peninsula, this chic hotel has 81 rooms plus 12 spacious suites with jacuzzis. Facilities include a pebble beach in the bay below, and a luxurious spa and wellness centre with a sea-view indoor pool.

Villa Dubrovnik €€€
Vlaha Bukovca 6, T020 500300, www.villa-dubrovnik.hr.
A 15-min walk from the old town, on the coast, this modern minimalist hotel is sophisticated and luxurious. There are 50 rooms and 6 suites, all with wooden floors and sliding windows opening onto private sea-view terraces. Service is discreet and personalized, and there's a spa and a private bathing area.

Amoret Apartments €€
Dinka Ranjine ulica, T020 324005, www.dubrovnik-amoret.com.
Occupying three 17th-century stone buildings in the old town,

Amoret has 15 double rooms, each with wooden parquet flooring and antique furniture, free Wi-Fi, and a kitchenette so you can cook. The owner, Branka Dabrović, is full of local advice.

Berkeley Hotel €€
Andrije Hebranga 116A, T020 494160, www.berkeleyhotel.hr.
The Berkeley has 16 spacious suites and studios (with kitchenettes), plus 8 double rooms, all with wooden floors, slick furnishing, flatscreen TV and internet. There's also a new outdoor pool. 'Stay and Cruise' combines several nights at the hotel with a few days exploring the Elafiti islands by motorboat.

Karmen Apartments €€
Bandureva 1, T020 323433, www.karmendu.com.
For a quaint hideaway in the old town, try this delightful little guesthouse run by the Van Bloemen family, who also own the **Hard Jazz Café Trubador**. The 4 light and airy apartments offer views onto the old harbour. The entrance is down a narrow side street between the Rector's Palace and the Aquarium.

Fresh Sheets Hostel €
Sv Simuna 15, T091 799 2086, www.freshsheetshostel.com.
This friendly hostel is run by a Canadian-Croatian couple and offers 4-bed and 8-bed dorms, plus a private double room with

sea views. There's a kitchen area in reception, where guests can make a do-it-yourself breakfast.

Restaurants

Breakfast

Pučić Palace €€
Ulica od Puca 1, T020 326000, www.thepucicpalace.com.
Non-residents are welcome to eat at this luxurious boutique hotel in the old town. Breakfast includes freshly squeezed juice, oven-warm pastries and eggs Florentine served on the lovely Defne upper-level terrace; in winter it moves down to the ground floor **Café Royal**.

Buffet Škola €
Antuninska ulica bb, T020 321096.
Ideal for brunch, this tiny family-run eatery does scrumptious sandwiches made from delicious freshly baked bread, locally produced *sir iz ulja* (cheese in oil) and *pršut* (dried ham), plus home-made apple strudel.

Lunch

Bota Oyster & Sushi Bar €€€
Od Pustijerne bb, T020 324034, www.bota-sare.hr.
Unusual for Dalmatia, this chic but unpretentious eatery offers beautifully presented sushi made from fresh, locally caught Adriatic seafood, including fresh oysters cultivated by the owners themselves in nearby Ston.

Lokanda Peškarija €€
Na Ponti bb, T020 324750, www.mea-culpa.hr.
This informal Dalmatian seafood eatery is next to the covered fish market. Inside there's a candlelit dining space with exposed stonework and wooden beams, but the best tables are outside with sea views.

Dinner
Kopun €€€
Poljana Rudera Boskovića 7, T099 212 1751, www.restaurantkopun.com.
On a tranquil square in front of the Jesuit church, Kopun serves traditional Croatian dishes with a contemporary twist. The house speciality is capon cooked with honey and wild orange.

Nishta €€
Prijeko bb, T020 322088, www.nishtarestaurant.com.
While most restaurants in this pretty stone alley are tourist traps, this welcoming vegetarian eatery is a real find. It borrows influences from afar to conjure up an eclectic menu, including tasty gazpacho, falafels and burritos.

Taj Mahal €€
Gučetića 2, T020 323221.
Despite its name, this eatery specializes in Bosnian dishes. Come here for *čevapi* (minced beef rissoles) and pork skewers, plus *krompiruša* and *zeljanica* (filo-pastries filled with either potato or spinach and cheese).

Travel essentials

Getting there
Dubrovnik Airport, T020 773100, www.airport-dubrovnik.hr, lies 21 km southeast of the city centre at Čilipi. It is served by a regular shuttle bus (kn35), which drops passengers at Pile Gate and at the main bus station next to Gruž port (see below), from where there are ferries to the Elafiti islands. Alternatively, a taxi to town will cost you around kn300.

Getting around
The old town is pedestrian-only. It is a joy to explore on foot, though you should wear comfortable walking shoes, as most streets are cobbled and there are steep steps in places. Many mid-range hotels are located on the Lapad Peninsula, approximately 3 km west of the old town opposite Gruž port. Buses 1A and 1B run from Pile Gate to the main **bus station** at Gruž port, Obala pape Ivana Pavla II 44, T060 305070, www.libertasdubrovnik. com, while buses 4 and 6 run from Pile Gate to Lapad. Dubrovnik's buses are cheap and frequent but often crowded (single fares are kn12 when bought from a kiosk; kn15 bought from the driver; one-day pass kn30).

Tourist information
The main tourist information centre is at Brsalje 5, T020 312011, www.tzdubrovnik.hr, daily 0800-2100, close to Pile Gate, just outside the city walls. In addition, there is a tourist information centre close to the bus station, overlooking Gruž port, Obala Ivana Pavla II 1, T020 417983, www.visitdubrovnik.hr, daily 0800-2100.

Nightlife

Generally considered a couples' destination, Dubrovnik offers a nightlife that is low-key and romantic; think candlelit bars with outdoor tables set against medieval stone buildings. Many people's favourite Dubrovnik bar is Buža, *Od Margarite, www.cafe buza.com*, accessed through a small doorway in the city walls. Tables are arranged on terraces set into the rocks looking out to sea. Wine lovers should also look in at D'Vino, *Palmotićeva 4a, www.dvino.net, daily till 0200.* This friendly little wine bar has a fine selection of over 60 local and imported wines. They also do platters of cheese and/or cured meats. For an after-dinner nightcap, try **Hard Jazz Café Trubadour**, *Bunićeva Poljana 2, T020 323476.* Inside, it's crammed with old furniture, candles, jazz memorabilia and signed photos; in summer it stages occasional live jazz concerts on a small stage out front. For glamorous late-night clubbing, try **Eastwest**, *Frana Supila bb, www.ew-dubrovnik.com*, in a 1970s modernist building, overlooking the old harbor.

Ratings

Art and culture ☆☆☆☆☆
Eating ☆☆☆☆☆
Nightlife ☆☆☆
Shopping ☆☆☆
Sightseeing ☆☆☆☆☆
Value for money ☆☆☆
Overall city rating ☆☆☆☆☆

Edinburgh

Few cities make such a strong impression as Edinburgh. Scotland's ancient capital is undeniably one of the most beautiful cities in Europe, with a grandeur to match Paris or Prague, Rome or Vienna. Fittingly, such a setting provides the stage for the Edinburgh Festival, the biggest arts event on the planet. But Edinburgh is more than just the sum of its arts. Its Hogmanay party is the largest celebration in the northern hemisphere, and the arrival of the new Scottish Parliament has brought confidence and vitality to a city that was always thought of as being rather straight-laced. Edinburgh's famous pursed lip has gone, replaced by a broad smile. The city is learning how to have fun, how to be stylish and, heaven forfend, how to be just a wee bit ostentatious.

Edinburgh houses.

Edinburgh Castle

T0131 225 9846, www.edinburghcastle.gov.uk.
Apr-Sep daily 0930-1800; Oct-Mar daily 0930-1700. £16, £9.60-£12.80 concessions. Map C3.

The city skyline is dominated by the castle, sitting atop an extinct volcano and protected on three sides by steep cliffs. Until the 11th century the castle was Edinburgh, but with the development of the royal palace from the early 16th century, it slipped into relative obscurity. Though mobbed for much of the year, and expensive, the castle is worth a visit. It encapsulates the history of a nation, and the views from the battlements are spectacular. The highlight is the Crown Room, where the 'Honours of Scotland' are displayed, along with the Stone of Destiny, the seat on which the ancient kings of Scotland were crowned.

The Royal Mile

Map C/D3.

Running down the spine of the Old Town, from the castle to the Palace of Holyroodhouse, is the Royal Mile. The 1984 regal yards comprise four separate streets: Castlehill, Lawnmarket, the High Street and the Canongate. Along its route is a succession of tourist attractions – some more worthy of the description than others – as well as many bars, restaurants, cafés and shops selling everything

Edinburgh Castle.

At a glance

South of Princes Street is the **Old Town**, a medieval Manhattan of high-rise tenements running from the castle to the Palace of Holyroodhouse. This dark and sinister rabbit warren of narrow alleys and wynds is still inhabited by the ghosts of the city's past. North of Princes Street is the elegant, neoclassical **New Town**, built in the late 18th and early 19th centuries to improve conditions in the city. The eastern New Town is bordered by Broughton Street, which forms one side of the so-called '**Pink Triangle**', the pumping heart of the city's gay scene. Here you'll find hip bars and clubs as well as a neighbourly, laid-back atmosphere. Looming over the Pink Triangle is **Calton Hill**, whose summit and sides are studded with sublime Regency terraces and bizarre monuments. The **West End** is a seamless extension of the New Town, with perfect neoclassical symmetry and discreet old money.

Northeast of the city centre is **Leith**, Scotland's major port until the shipbuilding and fishing industries decanted south. Neglected and ignored for years, Leith has undergone a dramatic transformation and now warehouse conversions, gourmet restaurants, bars and bistros jostle for position along its waterside.

24 hours in the city

Plan your day over breakfast at **Café Hub** on Castlehill, then take a leisurely stroll down the length of the historic **Royal Mile** before landing back in the present with a bump at the award-winning **Scottish Parliament** building. Head back up the Royal Mile for lunch at **Off The Wall**, then stretch your legs with a walk up **Calton Hill** for the stupendous views of Arthur's Seat, the Castle and across the Firth of Forth to the hills of Fife. Afterwards, indulge in some indoor aesthetic appreciation at the **National Gallery of Scotland**, then hop on a bus down to Ocean Terminal for a fascinating tour of the **Royal Yacht Britannia**. From here it's a short stroll to **Leith** for an alfresco aperitif on the quayside, followed by a superb dinner at **The Kitchin**. Then take a cab back to the centre for a nightcap in your hotel or some late-night action in one of the many bars on or around George Street in the New Town.

from kilts to Havana cigars. This is the focus of the city's tourist activity, especially during the festival when it becomes a mêlée of street performers, enthralled onlookers and alfresco diners and drinkers. One of the main points of interest is the medieval High Kirk of St Giles, conspicuously placed on the High Street.

Palace of Holyroodhouse

T0131-556-5100, www.royalcollection.org.uk. Apr-Oct daily 0930-1800; Nov-Mar daily 0930-1630. £11, £6.65-10 concessions. Map D3.

At the foot of the Royal Mile lies Edinburgh's royal palace. The present structure largely dates from the late 17th century when the original was replaced by a larger building for the Restoration of Charles II, although the newly crowned monarch never set foot in the place. Opposite the Palace of Holyroodhouse is the **Scottish Parliament** building, *www.scottish.parliament.uk*, which opened in October 2004 after years of delay and spiralling costs.

Holyrood Park

Map D/E3.

Edinburgh is blessed with many magnificent open spaces but Holyrood Park tops them all. The main feature is the 237-m-high Arthur's Seat, the igneous core of an extinct volcano. It is a genuine bit of wilderness right in the centre of Scotland's capital and well worth the climb for the stupendous views. Another dominant feature on the skyline is the precipitous Salisbury Crags, directly opposite the south gates of Holyrood Palace.

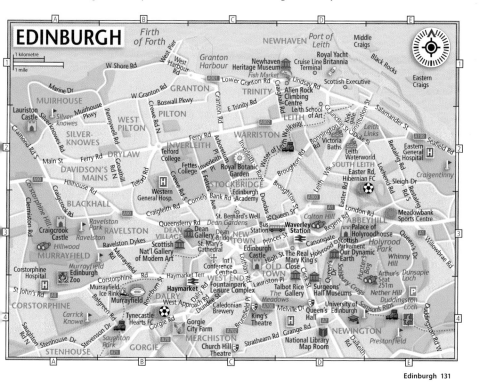

Secret city

The spirits who haunt the vaults and tunnels of old Edinburgh have long drawn tourists to the capital. Recent research has revealed that there may be something really going on beneath the city's streets. A detailed study into paranormal activity was carried out as part of the Edinburgh International Science Festival. Volunteers entered the network of ancient tunnels and reported paranormal activity, such as hearing loud breathing, seeing figures and being touched or grabbed. **Mercat Tours** (www.mercattours.com) runs tours of the 200-year-old haunted vaults. If that isn't enough to frighten the living daylights out of you, check out the **City of the Dead Haunted Graveyard Tour** (www.blackhart.uk.com), which involves being locked in a haunted graveyard at night with a bloodthirsty poltergeist. Tours start from the Mercat Cross, next to St Giles Cathedral on the High Street.

Museum of Scotland and Royal Museum of Scotland

Chambers St, T0300 123 6789, www.nms.ac.uk.
Daily 1000-1700. Free. Map D3.

The Museum of Scotland is a treasure trove of intriguing and important artefacts, displayed chronologically from the basement up to the sixth floor. Though coverage is at times patchy and incomplete, the museum does help to take the mystery out of Scottish history and makes for a pleasurable few hours.

Its elderly neighbour, the Royal Museum, holds an extensive and eclectic range of artefacts, from Classical Greek sculptures to stuffed elephants and Native North American totem poles, all housed in a wonderful Victorian building.

National Gallery

The Mound, T0131 624 6200,
www.nationalgalleries.org.
Fri-Wed 1000-1700 (1000-1800 in Aug),
Thu 1000-1900. Free. Map C3.

At the junction of The Mound and Princes Street
are two impressive neoclassical buildings, the
National Gallery and the Royal Academy, connected
by the WestonLink, which provides more exhibition
space and a striking café that overlooks Princes
Street Gardens. The former houses the most
important collection of Old Masters in the UK
outside London and boasts many masterpieces
from almost every period in Western art.

National Portrait Gallery

1 Queen St, phone, website and opening times as
for National Gallery.
Free. Map D3.

The first of its kind in the world, this gallery houses
a collection of the great and the good of Scottish
history in a fantastical French Gothic medieval
palace, modelled on the Doge's Palace in Venice.

Calton Hill

Map D3.

Calton Hill, at the east end of Princes Street, is
another of Edinburgh's extinct volcanoes and well
worth climbing for some of the best views in the
city as well as for the monuments at the top. These
form the four corners of a precinct and make for a
strange collection. The most famous is the National
Monument, built to commemorate the Scots who
died in the Napoleonic Wars.

Scottish National Gallery of Modern Art

775 Belford Rd, phone, website and
opening times as for National Gallery.
Free. Map B3.

About 20 minutes' walk from the West End is the
Scottish National Gallery of Modern Art, featuring

The world's greatest arts festival

Every year Edinburgh plays host to the world's
biggest arts festival, when the capital bursts into
life in a riot of entertainment unmatched anywhere
else. Over a million tourists descend on the city to
experience a brain-sapping variety of acts performed
in a frightening variety of venues. The Edinburgh
Festival is actually a collection of different festivals
running alongside each other, from the end of
July through to the beginning of September. The
International Festival (T0131 473 2000) tends to
be a fairly highbrow affair and features large-scale
productions of opera, ballet, classical music, dance
and theatre performed in the larger venues. **The
Fringe** (T0131 226 0000) features everything from
top-class comedy to Albanian existentialist theatre
performed in a lift. Also coming under the festival
heading are the **International Jazz and Blues
Festival**, **International Book Festival**, **International
Film Festival** and **Military Tattoo**. For details of
all the events and links to other websites, see
www.edinburghfestivals.co.uk.

Opposite page: Edinburgh from Calton Hill.
Below: Museum of Scotland.

everything from the Impressionists to Hockney. It's particularly strong on Expressionism, with works by Picasso, Cézanne, Matisse, Magritte, Mondrian, Kandinsky, Klee, Giacometti and Sickert all displayed, as well as the big names from Fauvism, Surrealism, Abstract Expressionism and Cubism. Alongside these are British greats like Francis Bacon, Helen Chadwick and Damien Hirst. Opposite, the Dean Gallery houses one of the most complete collections of Dada and Surrealist art in Britain.

Best of the rest

Our Dynamic Earth
Holyrood Rd, www.dynamicearth.co.uk. Mar-Nov daily 1000-1730; Jul-Aug 1000-1800; Nov-Mar Wed-Sun 1000-1730. £11.50, £7.50-9.75 concessions. Map D3.
Hi-tech virtual journey through time with strong environmental message.

The Real Mary King's Close
Warrinston's Close, High St, T0845 070 6244, www.real marykingsclose.com. Apr-Oct daily 1000-2100; Aug daily 0900-2300; Nov-Mar Sun-Thu 1000-1700, Fri-Sat 1000-2100. £12.95, £7.45-11.45 concessions. Map D3.
Authentic and spooky insight into 17th-century town life.

Rosslyn Chapel
7 miles south of the city, www.rosslynchapel.org.uk. Mon-Sat 0930-1700, Sun 1200-1645. £9, £7 concessions, children free.
This 15th-century chapel is featured in the *Da Vinci Code* and is said to be the last resting place of the Holy Grail.

Surgeon's Hall Museums
9 Hill Sq, T0131 527 1649, www.rcsed.ac.uk. Mon-Fri 1200-1600. £5. Map D4.
Fairly grotesque but fun look through the keyhole of surgical history.

Talbot Rice Gallery
Old College, www.trg.ed.ac.uk. Tue-Sat 1000-1700 (daily during the festival). Free. Map D3.
The University's collection of Renaissance paintings, housed in a wonderful neoclassical building.

Water of Leith and the Botanic Gardens

Botanic Gardens: East gate, Inverleith Row, www.rgbe.org.uk.
Daily till dusk. Gardens free, glasshouse £4.50, £1-3.50 concessions. Map C2.

If the weather's fair, one of the finest pleasures this city has to offer is the walk along the bucolic Water of Leith. The Water of Leith Walkway runs from the western outskirts of the city, all the way to the docks at Leith, but the most beautiful section starts from below Belford Bridge and takes you to the gorgeous Royal Botanic Gardens. South of the gardens is **Stockbridge**, one of the city's most beguiling corners, with a jumble of antique shops and second-hand bookstores.

Royal Yacht Britannia

Ocean Terminal, Leith, T0131 555 5566, www.royalyachtbritannia.co.uk.
Apr-Jun and Oct daily 0930-1600; Jul-Sep daily 0930-1630; Nov-Mar daily 1000-1530. £11, £7.50-10.50 concessions. Britannia Tour bus from Waverley Bridge or buses 11, 22, 34, 35 and 36 from Princes St. Map D1.

The *Britannia* is a fascinating attraction and shows the Windsors in a strangely downbeat manner. The relatively steep entrance fee is well worth the outlay. The tour offers a genuine insight into the lives of Britain's best-known family and the sight of Her Majesty's bedroom, more in keeping with a Berkshire guesthouse than a Head of State's private quarters, comes as a real shock.

Leith waterfront.

Where to stay

Edinburgh has a huge selection of places to stay. Most of the upscale accommodation is in the New Town, West End and around Calton Hill. Many city centre hotels offer good low-season deals, especially at weekends, and also offer a standby room rate throughout the year. You'll need to book well in advance during the festival or at Hogmanay. Check out the Visit Scotland website, *www.visitscotland.com*, for full accommodation options and booking. For a cheaper city centre option, try Premier Inn, *www.premierinn.com*.

21212 €€€
3 Royal Terr, T0845 22 21212, www.21212restaurant.co.uk.
Edinburgh's only Michelin-starred restaurant with rooms has certainly made its mark. The chef, Paul Kitching, brings passion and inventiveness in abundance to the dining room, and the 4 guest rooms in this classic townhouse below Calton Hill are the last word in indulgence, from the effortlessly tasteful decor to the impeccable service. Expensive but worth every penny for a truly unique experience.

Hotel Missoni €€€
1 George IV Bridge, T0131 220 6666, www.hotelmissoni.com.
Those who find bright colours and angles interrupt their sleep might want to give it a miss. But for those who love modernity and clever design, the Missoni is the ultimate Edinburgh hotel. The bar and restaurant, *Cucina*, are so good you won't want to leave but, most charmingly, the thoughtful extras make you feel genuinely pampered.

Scotsman Hotel €€€
North Bridge, T0131 556 5565, www.thescotsmanhotel.co.uk.
The former offices of *The Scotsman* newspaper have been transformed into this state-of-the-art boutique hotel. Each room is distinctive and has been furnished with great attention to detail, with original art, DVD and internet. Services and facilities include valet parking, screening room, bar, brasserie and restaurant, breakfast room, private dining rooms and health club and spa.

Apex Waterloo Place €€€-€€
27 Waterloo Pl, T0131 523 1819, www.apexhotels.co.uk.
Just up the stairs and round the corner from Waverly train station, it offers superb value for money without skimping on quality or style. A king-sized bed, fluffed-up bedding, flat-screen TV, free Wi-Fi, a breakfast fit for a king and a little rubber duck to take home all come as standard. Check for deals.

Ten Hill Place €€€-€€
10 Hill Pl, T0131 662 2080, www.tenhillplace.com.
Close to the Festival Theatre, this hotel is technically a 3-star but you'd never know it. Large, bright rooms with big beds and spotless bathrooms (although the glass doors on these may panic some). Breakfasts are bountiful and the staff eager to keep everyone happy.

Restaurants

Nightlife

Edinburgh has a wide range of culinary options. Most of the upmarket restaurants are in the New Town, though there are also some excellent places to be found around the Royal Mile and in Leith, which has fish restaurants and dockside bistros. During busy periods, such as the festival, it's best to book ahead.

Breakfast

Heller's Kitchen €€
15 Salisbury Pl, T0131 667 4654, www.hellerskitchen.co.uk.
Try this modern and spacious place for something a wee bit different and imaginative. Their sumptuous American-style pancakes, for instance, which come with smoked bacon or fresh fruit.

Valvona & Crolla €€
19 Elm Row, T0131 556 6066, www.valvonaandcrolla.com.
Great home cooking and the best cappuccino in town. The perfect place for a big Sat brunch and very popular. Authentic Italian deli.

Lunch

La Favorita €€
325-331 Leith Walk, T0131 554 2430.
Bit of a walk from the centre but worth it for Edinburgh's finest pizza. Buzzy atmosphere and excellent service. Best to book a table, especially during the festival, though they also deliver.

Petit Paris €€
38-40 Grassmarket, T0131 226 2424.
The checked tablecloths, French staff and accordion music will kid you into believing you are in Paris rather than the Grassmarket. The menu includes authenticities such as *cocotte* (stew) and *saucissces de Toulouse*. They even hold fondue and *moules* parties!

Dinner

Dubh Prais €€€
123b High St, T0131 557 5732.
The understated grandeur at Dubh Prais (pronounced doo prash) makes for a fine but not overly pricey dinner, with wood panelling, starchy white tablecloths and staff that appear and disappear just when you want them to. Serving all manner of beasts that have fed on Scottish grass or swam in its seas, there really is no better place to sample the finest game, salmon, beef and lamb.

The Kitchin €€€
78 Commercial Quay, T0131 555 1755.
Tom Kitchin, one of the UK's most celebrated chefs, slept on Paris floors to learn his trade. Edinburgh's all the better for his return with this chic but cheerful restaurant that serves sumptuous, inventive dishes. Bookings essential.

Edinburgh has more pubs and bars per square mile than any other European city. The prime drinking venue is George St and the streets running north and south of it. Another good destination is the area at the top of Leith Walk known as the 'Pink Triangle'. For more raucous boozers, head to Lothian Rd and the Grassmarket. The club scene has improved dramatically, and any self-respecting raver will be supplied with the latest dance floor tunes spun by some of the UK's top DJs.

For movie fans, the legendary **Filmhouse**, *88 Lothian Rd, T0131 228 2688, www.filmhousecinema. com*, is the UK's most famous regional cinema and the hub of Edinburgh's International Film Festival. The café-bar is a good place to hang out. **The Jazz Bar**, *1A Chambers St, T0131-220 4298, www.thejazzbar. co.uk*, hosts gigs and jam sessions 7 days a week. Expect a varied programme – including blues, soul, funk and acoustic – alongside some emerging and established jazz artists.

The **Traverse Theatre**, *Cambridge St, T0131 228 3223, www.traverse.co.uk*, is the city's most exciting theatre venue and commissions works from contemporary playwrights from Scotland and all over the world.

Travel essentials

Getting there
Edinburgh International Airport, T0844 481 8989, is 8 miles west of the city centre. An Airlink bus (www.lothian buses.com) to and from Waverley Bridge leaves every 10 mins, takes 30 mins and costs £3.50 one way, £6 return. A taxi to Princes St costs around £25.

There are direct trains to **Edinburgh Waverley** from London King's Cross (4½ hrs), Birmingham (5 hrs) and Manchester (3½ hrs). Fares vary widely depending on the time of travel; for times, fares and bookings, contact National Rail Enquiries, T0845 748 4950, or www.thetrainline.co.uk. Scotrail, T0845 601 5929, www.scotrail.co.uk, runs the overnight Caledonian Sleeper service from London Euston (7 hrs).

Getting around
Most of what you'll want to see lies within the compact city centre, which is easily explored on foot. Public buses are generally good and efficient. Princes Street is the main transport hub and you can get a bus to any part of the city from here. An excellent way to see the sights is to take one of the tours on board an open-top double-decker bus with a multilingual guide. These depart every 20 mins from Waverley Bridge, the first one leaving around 0930 and the last one between 1600 and 1730, depending on the time of year. Tickets are valid for the full day and you can hop on and off any of the company's buses at any of the stops. Tickets cost from £10 from Guide Friday Tours, www.stuckonscotland.co.uk, or £13 from Edinburgh Bus Tours, T0131 220 0770, www.edinburgh tour.com.

Taxis are not cheap, costing from around £5 for the very shortest of trips up to around £12 from the centre to the outskirts. They also tend to be scarce at weekends so book ahead if you need one.

Tourist information
The main tourist office is at 3 Princes St, on top of Waverley Market, T0845 225 5121, www.edinburgh.org, Mon-Sat 0900-1700, Sun 1000-1700 (Jul-Aug till 1900). It has a full range of services, including currency exchange, and will book hotel rooms, provide travel information and book tickets for various events and excursions. There's also a tourist information desk at the airport, T0845 225 5121, in the international arrivals area. For details of entertainment listings in the city, pick up a copy of *The List* from any newsagent.

Ratings

Art and culture ☆☆☆☆☆
Eating ☆☆☆
Nightlife ☆
Shopping ☆☆☆
Sightseeing ☆☆☆☆☆
Value for money ☆☆☆
Overall city rating ☆☆☆

Florence

For all its reputation as one of the world's most beautiful cities, Florence can seem impenetrable to the first-time visitor: a city of cramped traffic, swarms of tourists, street-hawkers and markets selling enormous quantities of leather belts and aprons decorated with the anatomy of Michelangelo's *David*. But it's a city that people come back to. There's good Tuscan food and wine (if you know where to look), beautiful countryside all around and a history that includes the birth of the Renaissance. But it's the art and architecture that, rightly, are most celebrated. From super-star exhibits such as Botticelli's *Birth of Venus* to the marginally less well known but no less impressive cloisters in Santa Croce and frescoes in Santa Maria Novella, Florence has it all. And, if you need a new belt, there are few better places to buy one.

The hand of Michelangelo's *David*.

At a glance

Many visitors arrive in the city at Santa Maria Novella, the city's train station and main transport hub. The city centre spreads out southeast beyond it along the northern bank of the river Arno. To the immediate east, the area of San Lorenzo has streets crowded with market stalls. Just northeast of here is the Galleria dell'Accademia, home to many of Florence's statues. The Duomo, Florence's biggest landmark, lies a little further south, below which a regular grid of streets stretch towards the river and make up the heart of the antique district. At the western edge of this grid, Palazzo Strozzi is a hulking Renaissance building, while to the south Piazza della Signoria competes with the Duomo to be the city's centre point; it's surrounded by grand buildings including the Palazzo Vecchio and the Uffizi, Florence's great art gallery. Nearby, the Ponte Vecchio, Florence's oldest bridge, leads across the river to the **Oltrarno**. This is one of the most satisfying areas of the city to wander around and has a more laid-back feel than the rest of Florence. There's a market next to the church of **Santo Spirito** on some days of the week. The main attraction, though, is the enormous **Palazzo Pitti** and elegant **Giardino di Boboli**. Up a steep hill from here is **San Miniato al Monte**. Back on the northern bank of the Arno, to the east of Piazza della Signoria, is the spectacular Gothic basilica of Santa Croce and an area of interesting narrow streets and considerably fewer visitors.

24 hours in the city

Start with a coffee and a pastry from a café. Stand at the bar to drink it, since many of Florence's cafés will charge you a small fortune to sit down. Then take some time to wander across the **Ponte Vecchio** before the crowds descend. You can also stop off in **piazza della Signoria** for the obligatory photo of the copy of Michelangelo's *David*. If you plan to visit the **Uffizi**, start early to get a good place in the queue and allow the whole morning. Alternatively, the **Galleria dell'Accademia, Bargello** or the museums and galleries of the **Pitti Palace** will give a taste of Renaissance art with less queuing. Find a restaurant in the **Oltrarno**, on the other side of the river, for lunch and follow it up with a stroll in the **Giardino di Boboli**, or a climb up the hill to **San Miniato al Monte**. In the late afternoon, visit the spectacular **Duomo** and the **Battistero** and climb to the top of either the Campanile or the Cupola and survey the city from above, ideally with the sunshine glowing off the rooftops. Head to **Santa Croce** in the evening – if you can get there before it closes at 1730, have a look around the interior and the cloisters. Otherwise sit for a while on the steps while people gather for *aperitivi* before drinking one or two of your own. There are some good eating options around here, too, and you shouldn't miss an ice cream from **Vivoli**. If you want to keep going into the night, bars around Piazza Santa Croce are a good place to start.

Duomo and Battistero

piazza del Duomo, T055 230 2885, www.operaduomo.firenze.it.
Duomo Mon-Wed and Fri 1000-1700, Thu 1000-1530, Sat 1000-1645 (1st Sat of month 1000-1530), Sun 1330-1645; free. Campanile daily 0830-1930; €6. Cupola Mon-Fri 0830-1900, Sat 0830-1740; €8. Combined ticket for all of the Duomo's attractions €23, valid for 4 days. Map C2.

Florence's tallest building is still its pink-and-white, marble-clad cathedral. Filippo Brunelleschi's dome was completed in 1463 and, at the time, was the biggest in the world with a span of 42 m. Brunelleschi constructed the octagonal ribbed dome without scaffolding, using bricks inside a marble skeleton. Both the cupola and the separate campanile can be climbed; there are 414 steps up

Duomo.

the bell tower and 463 steps to the top of the dome. The campanile was designed by Giotto in 1334 but not completed until after his death.

The interior of the Duomo doesn't quite match the extraordinarily beautiful exterior, although Vasari's 16th-century frescoes of the Last Judgement on the inside of the dome are spectacular.

Just to the west of the Duomo, the **Battistero** (baptistry), *Mon-Sat 1215-1900, Sun 0830-1400, €4, map B2*, may date from as early as the fourth century, making it the city's oldest building. The interior has 13th-century mosaics and a font where Dante was baptized. The highlights, however, are the famous 14th- and 15th-century brass doors, by Pisano and Ghiberti. Those in situ are now copies; the originals are in the **Museo dell'Opera del Duomo**, *piazza del Duomo 9, T055 230 2885, Mon-Sat 0900-1930, Sun 0900-1345, €6.*

Piazza della Signoria

Map B3.

At the heart of the city, piazza della Signoria is a busy square that buzzes with tourists milling

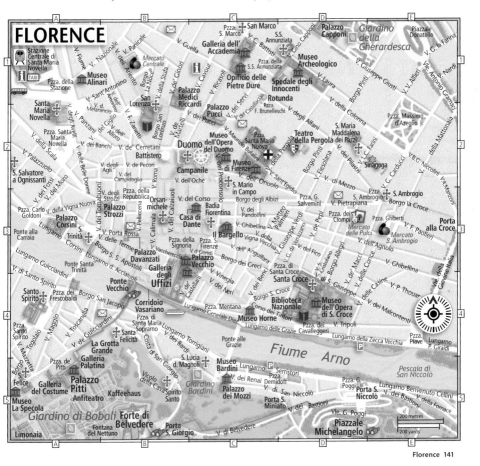

Around the city

Ponte Vecchio.

The Fountain of Neptune.

around the Renaissance and Roman statues and fountains. A replica of Michelangelo's *David* gets the most camera clicks, but there is also the *Fontana di Nettuno* (Neptune Fountain) by Ammannati (1575) and the *Rape of the Sabine Women* by Giambologna (1583), carved, remarkably, from a single block of marble.

On the southern edge of the piazza, opposite the 14th-century, statue-filled **Loggia dei Lanzi**, is the **Palazzo Vecchio**, *T055 276 8224, Oct-Mar Fri-Wed 0900-1900, Thu 0900-1400, Apr-Sep Fri-Wed 0900-2400, Thu 0900-1400, €10*. Originally the town hall, it also served as the residence of Duke Cosimo de Medici. Nowadays visitors can wander through some of its grand rooms.

Galleria degli Uffizi

piazzale degli Uffizi, T055 294 883 (bookings), www.polomuseale.firenze.it. Tue-Sun 0815-1850. €6.50, €11 during exhibitions. Map B3/4.

Some of the longest queues in the art world are to be found outside the Uffizi gallery, so allow several hours to get in. Booking ahead is highly recommended but even this is unlikely to mean you will be able to swan straight in.

Once inside the hallowed halls of Renaissance art, highlights include: Sandro Botticelli's *Birth of Venus*, Titian's *Venus of Urbino*, Artemisia Gentileschi's *Judith Beheading Holofernes*, Michelangelo's *Holy Family*, three Caravaggios, three Leonardos and two Giottos.

The Giorgio Vasari-designed building was finished in 1581 and was originally intended to house the offices (hence the name) of Florentine magistrates. It suffered significant damage as a result of a car bomb in 1993.

Ponte Vecchio

Map B4.

Best known for the jewellers' shops which line its sides, the Ponte Vecchio is the only Florentine bridge to have survived the Second World War. There have been shops on the bridge since it was built in 1345 – it was possibly constructed in this way in order to avoid taxes. These days the shops are expensive tourist traps, but the bridge itself remains one of the city's iconic symbols.

Palazzo Pitti and Giardino di Boboli

piazza Pitti.
Palazzo Tue-Sun 0815-1850. *Garden* closing time varies with dusk. Combined ticket to museums and garden €11.50. Map A5.

Started in 1457, the Palazzo Pitti was built by a banker, Luca Pitti as a conscious effort to outdo the Medicis, the most powerful family in Renaissance Florence. However, the enormity of the project practically bankrupted the Pitti family, and the Medicis themselves moved into the palace in 1550. Already grandiose, the palace was further extended over the years, the most recent additions being the wings added in the 18th century. During Florence's brief position as capital of Italy in the 19th century, the Palazzo Pitti served as the main royal residence.

The contemporary palace houses several museums. The **Galeria Palatina**, *T055 238 8614*, contains many great works of Renaissance art, including paintings by Titian, Botticelli and Veronese. The **Appartamenti Monumentali** are examples of overblown opulence, and there are also museums dedicated to costume, porcelain and gold and silver.

Behind the Palazzo Pitti, **Giardino Boboli** is a large formal garden offering a peaceful, relaxed and often pleasantly cooler counterpoint to the stresses of the city centre. The gardens are the setting for musical and theatrical events in summer.

San Miniato al Monte

via Monte alle Croci.
Summer daily 0800-1930. Winter daily 0800-1230 and 1500-1730. Free.

High on a hill to the southeast of the city centre, the church of San Miniato is one of Italy's most beautiful Romanesque buildings. Construction began in 1013, and the church has changed little in the last 1000 years. The striking exterior is decorated with green and white marble. Inside, the choir is raised above

Excursions: Fiesole

In the hills to the northeast of Florence, Fiesole was once a more important power base than Florence itself and still likes to think of itself as a little bit superior. Certainly cooler, Fiesole is also more laid-back and has great views over Florence in the valley below as well as some sights of its own. The town has a **Duomo**, which dates back to the 11th century, as well as the archeological remains of a Roman theatre. The **Museo Archeologico**, *via Portigiani 1, T055 5961293, summer Wed-Mon 1000-1900, winter Thu-Mon 1000-1600, €12*, contains pieces that were uncovered at this site. The winding walk along via Vecchia Fiesolana to **San Domenico** is a scenic one, but many visitors choose not to move far from the central **piazza Mino**, which has plenty of good bars and restaurants. Bus No 7 goes between Santa Maria Novella train station in Florence and Fiesole every 15 minutes.

the crypt, creating a two-tier design, all of which is bathed in light. The nave is inlaid with mosaics and the walls have faded frescoes.

Just down the hill, **piazzale Michelangelo**, *map D5*, an otherwise unremarkable car park, affords great views over the Arno and across the city. The place fills with tourists and local couples around sunset.

San Miniato al Monte.

Boboli Gardens.

Best of the rest

Bargello
via del Proconsolo 4, T055 238 8606.
Daily 0815-1400, closed 2nd and 4th Mon in
month. €4, €6 during exhibitions. Map C3.
Built in 1255, the Bargello was used as a prison but
now holds Renaissance sculpture by Michelangelo,
Donatello, Sansovino and others.

Capella Brancacci
piazza del Carmine, Oltrarno, T055 276 8558.
Wed-Mon 1000-1700, reservation required. €6.
This small chapel within the church of Santa Maria
del Carmine contains some of Masaccio's 15th-
century frescoes. Visits are limited to 15 minutes.

Museo di San Marco
piazza San Marco 3, T055 238 8608.
Mon-Fri 0815-1350, Sat and Sun 0815-1650. €4.
This 15th-century Dominican monastery contains
superb works by Fra Angelico.

San Lorenzo
piazza San Lorenzo, T055 216634.
Mon-Sat 1000-1730, Sun 1330-1730. €4.50. Map B2.
In the middle of Florence's market district,
surrounded by Leonardo aprons and fake designer
belts, San Lorenzo was the Medici's church in
the 15th century. Brunelleschi, Donatello and
Michelangelo all worked on it.

Santa Croce
piazza Santa Croce, T055 246 6105.
Mon-Sat 0930-1730, Sun 1430-1730. €6. Map D4.

Containing the tombs of several famous
Florentines, including Michelangelo, Galileo and
Machiavelli, the Gothic basilica of Santa Croce
is one of Florence's most important churches.

To the right of the altar, Giotto's frescoes in the
Bardi and Peruzzi chapels are the highlights of
the interior. Brunelleschi's 15th-century Secondo
Chiostro (second cloister) is serenely beautiful and
the Capella dei Pazzi (also by Brunelleschi) is
another fine example of Renaissance architecture.
There is a statue of Dante outside the basilica and
a funerary monument to him inside, although he
was actually buried in Ravenna.

Santa Maria Novella
piazza Santa Maria Novella, T055 219 257.
Mon-Thu 0900-1730, Fri 1100-1730,
Sat 0900-1700. €5. Map A2.

Built by the Dominicans in the 13th and 14th centuries,
the church of Santa Maria Novella holds a startlingly
colourful fresco cycle by Ghirlandaio, illustrating
the life of John the Baptist. Other highlights include
Masaccio's *Trinità*, famous for its pioneering use of
perspective, and the *Chiostro Verde*, so-called because
of the green pigment used for the frescoes by the
artist, Paolo Uccello. The Romanesque-Gothic
façade (by Leon Battista Alberti) was added in 1470.

Galleria dell'Accademia
via Ricasoli 60, T055 294 883 (bookings).
Tue-Sun 0815-1850. €6.50 (€11 during
exhibitions). Map C1.

Famously containing Michelangelo's masterful
statue of David, sculpted in 1504 (when the artist
was 29 years old), the Accademia also holds
unfinished Michelangelo sculptures intended
for the tomb of Pope Julius II.

Giotto's frescoes in Santa Croce.

Where to stay

Hotels in Florence tend to be expensive and, with notable exceptions, service can be below par; the city's popularity means that it is a seller's market and standards tend to suffer.

Gallery Hotel Art €€€
vicolo dell' Oro 5, T055 27263, www.lungarnocollection.com.
A contemporary luxury hotel near the Ponte Vecchio, Gallery Hotel Art has over 70 elegant rooms and suites, plus a well-stocked library and a trendy international bar serving fusion food. The place is decorated in muted tones and holds photography and art exhibitions.

JK Place €€€
piazza Santa Maria Novella 7, T055 264 5181, www.jkplace.com.
A real fire and antique furniture meet hip design in coffee and caramel tones in this 20-room hotel on piazza Santa Maria Novella. There's an immaculate roof terrace, cakes are served in the courtyard and you'd be hard-pushed not to feel eminently fashionable, in a refined Florentine kind of way.

Residenza d'Epoca in piazza della Signoria €€€
via dei Magazzini 2, T055 239 9546, www.inpiazzadellasignoria.com.
A stylish residence with 10 rooms and 3 self-catering apartments. The decor is uncluttered and the rooms,

some with views of the piazza della Signoria, have free Wi-Fi.

Casa Howard €€
via della Scala 18, T06 6992 4555, www.casahoward.com.
The elegant recipe of the well-known Rome hotel has been repeated in Florence – a handful of individually designed (and loosely themed) rooms, creating an intimate and homely feel. The owners have a personal and idiosyncratic style, with plenty of quality fabrics and artefacts from around the world.

Torre Guelfa €€
borgo Santi Apostoli 8, T055 239 6338, www.hoteltorreguelfa.com.
Draped 4-poster beds, wooden floors, a roof terrace (at the top of the eponymous 13th-century tower) with views over the Florentine rooftops make Torre Guelfa good value. Its location near the Ponte Vecchio makes it an even better choice.

Pensione Scoti €
via De' Tornabuoni 7, T055 292 128, www.hotelscoti.com.
Almost opposite Palazzo Strozzi, Pensione Scoti is a smart, friendly, antique place with frescoes and large, simple, old-fashioned rooms.

Residenza Johanna 1 €
via Bonifacio Lupi 14, T055 481896, www.johanna.it.
The cheapest of a group of 5 residenze in Florence (the

others are Johanna II, Johlea I and II and Antica Dimora Firenze). Johanna is especially good value, with antiques and parquet floors. Service is friendly, though staff all go home at 1900.

Restaurants

An abundance of good-quality fresh produce lies at the heart of Tuscan cuisine, and Florence's restaurants do well from it. Eating out is not especially cheap, although there are still some traditional trattorias to be found, which cater to a local market rather than the tourists.

Alla Vecchia Bettola €€
Via Luigi Ariosto 34r, T055 224 158. Closed Sun and Mon.
Communal eating on benches at marble-topped tables is the style at this excellent traditional trattoria just off piazza Tasso near Santo Maria del Carmine. A daily changing menu offers top Tuscan food.

Fuori Porta €€
via del Monte alle Croci 10/r, T055 234 2483, www.fuoriporta.it.
Perfectly placed for those who plan to visit San Miniato al Monte but never make it up the hill, Fuori Porta is a wine bar that serves excellent light meals too. The outside tables are popular and, inside, you can gaze on (and of course consume) some

of the enormous selection of wine on offer.

La Canova de Gustavino €€
via della Condotta 29, T055 239 9806, www.gustavino.it.
Next door to sophisticated Gustavino, this is its more traditional sister offering classic Tuscan dishes such as *ribollita* and *pappa al pomodoro*.

Da Benvenuto €
via della Mosca 16/r, T055 214833, www.trattoriabenvenuto.it.
Closed Sun.
Simple but reliably good (and reliably good-value) Tuscan food in the centre of Florence.

Da Vinattieri €
via Santa Margherita 6r.
Daily from 1000.
Traditional hole in the wall serving panini with tripe, the local speciality, as well as *lampredotto* (cow's stomach), which is generally accompanied by a glass of red wine. Plenty of

locals come here, and it's a real slice of old Florence.

Il Pizzaiuolo €
via dei Macci 113, T055 241171.
Closed Sun.
An authentic Neapolitan pizza place in Santa Croce, Il Pizzaiuolo fills up quickly in the evenings with those eager for their mouthwatering discs of tomato and mozzarella. In a city not renowned for its pizzas, this is a beacon of excellence.

'Ino €
via dei Georgofili 3r/7r, T055 219208, www.ino-firenze.com.
Close to the Uffizi, this is a great little wine and sandwich bar. Come for fresh cheeses, meats and panini.

Osteria Santo Spirito €
piazza Santo Spirito 16/r, T055-238 2383.
A friendly and colourful place in the corner of the attractive piazza, which has attempted to reinvent the traditional osteria in a contemporary style. Popular with travellers.

Vivoli
Via Isole delle Stinche 7, T055 292334.
Closed Mon.
Quite rightly one of Italy's most celebrated gelaterias, serving ice cream of the highest quality in generally old-fashioned flavours.

Fra Angelico

Fra Angelico, known in Italy as Beato Angelico (the 'blessed' Angelico), is one of the most celebrated of the early Renaissance artists. Born Guido di Pietro c1387, he became a Dominican friar in 1407, together with his brother. He spent time in Cortona and in the Dominican community at Fiesole, working all over Tuscany as well as in Rome. Fra Angelico was a talented artist, influenced by Giotto, and his paintings are notable for their tenderness and glorious colours. The artist prayed before starting work and his art was meant to stimulate prayer and meditation. John Ruskin once said that Fra Angelico was ' not an artist…[but] an inspired saint'. He died in 1455 and is buried in Rome.

Nightlife

Bars and clubs

Much of Florence's nightlife takes place around piazza Santa Croce, with other lively pockets in the Oltrarno. Clubs loosen up a little and move outside in the heat of summer, but for the rest of the year, well-dressed chic predominates.

Aperitivi, usually drunk between 1900 and 2100, are often accompanied by generous buffets of complimentary snacks. Drinks are correspondingly more expensive, but at places like **Negroni**, *via dei Renai 17,* you can just about nibble your way to an evening's sustenance. After *aperitivi*, cocktails (or, increasingly, wine bars) take over, followed by dancing the night away at locations such as **Tenax**, *via Pratese 46 79/r,* which is out by Peretola airport.

Live music

The pop, rock and jazz scenes have become livelier in recent years, belying Florence's conservative reputation. Record shops are the best places to find out what's going on. Tourist offices have details of classical concerts at the **Accademia Bartolomeo Cristofori**, *via di Camaldoli 7/r, T055 221 646, www.accademiacristofori.it,* and other venues. For opera and ballet head to the **Teatro del Maggio Musicale Fiorentino**, *via Solferino 15, T055 2779350, www.maggiofiorentino.com.*

Travel essentials

Getting there

Florence's **Amerigo Vespucci Airport**, T055 306 1300, www.aeroporto.firenze.it, is 4 km from the centre of Florence. A taxi to the centre will cost you €25; alternatively the Volainbus (every 30 mins, €5) connects with Santa Maria Novella railway station. Vespucci is a small airport, so flying to Pisa's **Galileo Galilei Airport**, T050 849 111, www.pisa-airport.com, may be cheaper. Trains run regularly from the airport to Pisa Centrale, where you change for a train to Florence. The main station is **Santa Maria Novella**, Piazza Stazione, www.trenitalia.it, which also serves as the hub for the city's buses. A new high-speed train station is being built on the site of the city's ex-slaughterhouse at Belfiore at a cost of hundreds of millions of euros.

Getting around

The city centre is small and walking it is the only sensible way to get around. Taxis can be found at ranks, but they are notoriously few and far between; buses work reasonably well, but often get snarled up in traffic jams; cars are not allowed in some parts of the centre and trying to park is next to impossible.

Tourist information

Azienda Promozionale Turistica, via Cavour 1, T055 290 832, www.firenzeturismo.it, Mon-Sat 0830-1830, is helpful and has free maps as well as information on opening hours, prices and tours. There are also offices at Santa Maria Novella station, T055 212 245, Mon-Sat 0900-1900, Sun and public holidays 0900-1400, and at the airport, T055 315 874, Mon-Sat 0900-1900, Sun 0900-1400.

Ratings

Art and culture ☆☆☆☆
Eating ☆☆☆☆☆
Nightlife ☆☆☆
Shopping ☆☆☆☆☆
Sightseeing ☆☆☆☆
Value for money ☆☆☆
Overall city rating ☆☆☆☆

Istanbul

With over 25 centuries of uninterrupted history, including periods as the capital of three world empires – Roman, Byzantine and Ottoman – Istanbul is an undisputed cultural heavyweight. Castles, mosques, churches, seminaries, bazaars and palaces, plus some world-class museums: it has them all. Add to that a superb backdrop, cleaved by the waters of the continent-dividing Bosphorus and the Golden Horn, with minarets and domes punctuating the skyline and the taste of salt in the air. Modernity and tradition rub shoulders at this ancient meeting place of east and west, ensuring that the cosmopolitan human landscape, with its vibrant café culture, is no less beguiling. Istanbul has taken on the mantle of one of Europe's coolest cities with confident aplomb . Be prepared – Istanbul will surprise, amaze, entertain and confound you, all in the space of an afternoon.

Interior of the Blue Mosque.

At a glance

Home to the Byzantine Emperors and Ottoman Sultans, **Sultanahmet** is Istanbul's historic heart. If you are only visiting for a few days, much of your time will be spent here. The area has a concentration of the city's main sights within a short stroll of its most atmospheric accommodation – think boutique Ottoman. Within walking distance are the **Grand Bazaar** and the teeming streets of **Eminönü** (where the Bosphorus ferries dock) and the **Spice Bazaar**. It's easy to spend several days exploring this part of the city, although a lot more awaits north of the Golden Horn. Across the Galata Bridge, in what was the European quarter in Ottoman times, **Galata** and **Beyoğlu** have many of the city's best bars and restaurants. Formerly seedy and run-down, the narrow backstreets off pedestrianized **Istiklal Caddesi**, Istanbul's main shopping street, are dotted with atmospheric eateries, galleries and bars. At the north end of Istiklal Caddesi is **Taksim Square**. A nexus for public transport, this wide expanse is undergoing extensive redevelopment. In 2013 it served as the centre for political protests, sparked by a local campaign to save adjacent Gezi Park. A short cab ride north is **Nişantaşı**, an upmarket shopping district ideal for a spot of retail therapy. Down beside the Bosphorus, a string of suburbs are great to explore. The cobbled streets of **Ortaköy** lead to a waterside square overlooked by lively cafés and bars. Beyond the continent-spanning Bosphorus Bridge, things get progressively more exclusive, as you head towards the upmarket Bosphorus 'village' of **Bebek**, with its diminutive mosque, cafés and restaurants overlooking the expensive yachts moored offshore. Nearby is the Ottoman castle of Rumeli Hisarı, built in preparation for the conquest of Constantinople during the mid 15th century. A string of equally bucolic villages lining the Asian shore can be reached either by ferry, or via the brand-new Marmaray railway, inaugurated in late 2013, which zips under the Bosphorus, connecting the strait's western and eastern shores.

24 hours in the city

Have a lazy breakfast on your hotel roof terrace while drinking in the fantastic view. If your lodgings are one of the few in the Old City that don't have one, then try the **Hotel Uyan**. Be enthralled by the soaring symmetry of the **Sultanahmet (Blue) Mosque**, before jumping on a tram to shopaholic heaven – the **Grand Bazaar**. With lightened wallet and bag of souvenirs in hand, weave your way down through the backstreets to **Eminönü** and the **Spice Market**. Take refuge from the hustle and relax over a late lunch at **Pandeli Restaurant**. Afterwards, wander past the fishermen on the **Galata bridge** before catching the Tünel funicular up to Galata and the other main shopping hub of Istanbul, **Istiklal Caddesi**. The Genoese watchtower in Galata is a great place to enjoy the sunset and a well-earned beer. After dark, jump in a taxi to **Ortaköy**, where in summer you can dine alfresco on the main square. Alternatively, the bars and clubs of Beyoğlu await those wanting to imbibe or boogie until the wee hours.

Topkapı Palace (Topkapı Sarayı)

Sultanahmet Meydanı, Sultanahmet, T0212 512 0480, www.topkapisarayi.gov.tr. Mid-Apr to Sep Wed-Mon 0900-1900; Oct to mid-Apr Wed-Mon 0900-1700. TL25. Harem Tour TL15. Map C5.

Home of the Ottoman sultans and centre of their empire, the Topkapı Palace is one of the world's most important historical collections, as well as being one of the most popular sights in the whole country. Each year tens of thousands wander through its many halls, apartments and pavilions. Entered through the imposing Imperial Gate (Bab-i Humayun), the palace sprawls over a series of large courtyards, with the Harem, inviolate residence of the Sultans, their wives and concubines, at its core. Things can get very crowded so it is wise to visit early in the day and buy your ticket for the Harem tours, which depart every 30 minutes, as soon as you arrive. With so many other things to see, you should allow at least half a day for your wanderings. Highlights include the newly renovated palace kitchens and the dazzling artefacts in the Imperial Treasury.

Haghia Sophia (Aya Sofya)

Ayasofya Meydanı, T0212 522 1750, www.ayasofyamuzesi.gov.tr.

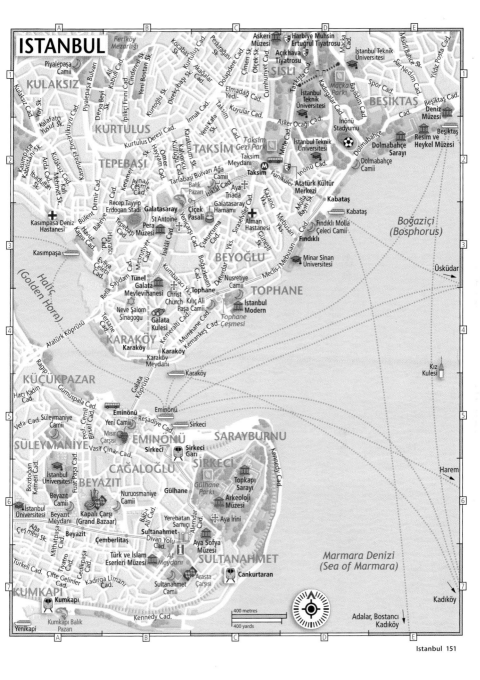

Around the city

Mid-Apr to Sep Tue-Sun 0900-1900; Oct to mid-Apr Tue-Sun 0900-1700. TL25. Map C6.

The pinnacle of Byzantine architectural achievement was built in AD 537 at the behest of Emperor Justinian, eager to prove the pre-eminence of his 'New Rome'. Towering over the city's rooftops and topped by a whopping 30 m-wide dome, the cathedral enthralled Byzantine visitors then and continues to do so today. Despite a sacking by the Crusaders in 1204, its conversion into a mosque in 1453, then a museum in 1935, the building has a great collection of precious and ancient mosaics, some only recently rediscovered beneath Ottoman plaster. But it is the venerable atmosphere that can't help but impress.

Sultanahmet Mosque (Sultanahmet Camii)

At Meydanı Caddesi, Sultanahmet.
Daily 0900-1900. TL5-10 donation suggested. Map B7.

The gracefully cascading domes and sharp, soaring minarets of the Sultanahmet Mosque, better known as the **Blue Mosque**, rise evocatively above the well-kept gardens of Sultanahmet Square. Built by Sultan Ahmet in 1616, it was the last of the great imperial mosques, an architectural milestone marking the beginning of the Ottoman Empire's long, inexorable decline. Controversially, the Sultan had six minarets built, instead of the usual four, an act that many saw as a mark of disrespect to the Mosques of the Prophets in Mecca, which were also graced with a half-dozen towers. As a functioning mosque you enter through a special entrance and must be dressed appropriately – shawls can be borrowed to cover exposed arms and female heads at the door. Inside, the walls are gaudily decorated with 20,000 patterned Iznik tiles, hence the building's western name.

Museum of Turkish and Islamic Art (Turk ve Islam Eserleri Muzesi)

At Meydani 46, Sultanahmet, T0212 518 1805.
Mid-Apr to Sep 0900-1900; Oct to mid-Apr 0900-1700. TL10. Map B7.

The museum boasts a fascinating collection covering the Middle East and Central Asia, from earliest Islamic times through to the present day. The exhibits range from ivory to calligraphy to mosaics and ceramics, and are well labelled and organized. All are housed in a 16th-century palace constructed by Ibrahim Paşa, the Grand Vizier to Suleyman the Magnificent, before he was strangled at his master's behest. Undergoing thorough renovations at the time of writing, the museum is due to reopen to the public in early 2014. Outside the museum, **At Meydani** was once the Byzantine Hippodrome, an arena where ceremonies, parades and races were held.

Top: Harem, Topkapı Palace.
Bottom: Imperial Gate of palace.

Grand Bazaar (Kapalı Çarşı)

Beyazıt Meydanı, www.grandbazaaristanbul.org.
Mon-Sat 0830-1930. Map B6.

With over 4000 shops connected by a maze of covered streets and passageways, the Grand Bazaar is the largest retail area of its kind in the world. Surrender yourself to the inevitability of getting lost and just wander, browsing shops selling clothes, carpets, gold and silver, household goods and souvenirs, stopping to practise your haggling skills. Each type of shop is concentrated in a particular area, with silver and antique merchants occupying the İç Bedestan, the historic heart of the bazaar. If you need a break, there are several cafés within the bazaar.

Çemberlitaş Hamamı

Vezirhan Caddesi 8, T0212 522 7974,
www.cemberlitashamami.com.tr.
0600-2400. TL54-137, plus 10% tip. Map B6.

The perfect antidote to a day's sightseeing is a steam clean, followed by a massage in one of the city's many Turkish baths. Built in 1584 by master architect Mimar Sinan, and with separate sections for men and women, the Çemberlitaş Hamamı is one of the most atmospheric, as well as being close to the Grand Bazaar and Sultanahmet. Towels and cloths to wrap around you while bathing are provided, and refreshments are also available. Pricey, but a real experience.

Egyptian Bazaar and Eminönü

Mon-Sat 0800-1900. Map B5.

Also known as the **Spice Market**, this busy arcade lined with shops selling spices, imported foods, souvenirs and herbal remedies, such as the somewhat dubious 'Turkish Viagra', gets its name because it was built with money raised through custom duties from Cairo. The market is part of the **Yeni Camii** (New Mosque) complex, which is surrounded by the bustling district of Eminönü. Bosphorus ferries dock at the quayside and the air

Best of the rest

City Walls
You can walk much of the 6.5 km length of the restored city walls, although it's best not to do it alone.

Dolmabahçe Palace
Dolmabahçe Caddesi, Beşiktaş, T0212 236 9000, www. dolmabahce.gov.tr. Tue-Sun 0900-1600. TL40; TL20 harem only. Ostentatious home of the last Ottoman sultans.

Galata Tower
Galata Sq. Daily 0900-1900, T212 293 8180. TL13.
A medieval Genoese watchtower with a great view.

Istanbul Modern
Meclis-i Mebusan Caddesi, Liman İşletmeleri, Sahası Antrepo 4, Karaköy, www.istanbulmodern.org. Tue-Wed and Fri-Sun 1000-1800, Thu 1000-2000. TL15.
Istanbul's first modern exhibition space is set on the Bosphorus waterfront in a converted warehouse.

Leander Tower (aka the Maiden's Tower)
www.kizkulesi.com.tr. Daily 1000-1900.
Catch the ferry from Kabataş to this tiny tower bobbing in the Bosphorus. Photo opportunities aplenty and Bond fans may recognize it from *The World Is Not Enough*.

Museum of Innocence
Çukurcuma Caddesi, Dalgıç Çıkmazı 2, Beyoğlu, www.masumiyetmuzesi.com. Tue-Thu and Sat-Sun 1000-1800, Fri 1000-2100. TL25.
One of the most enchanting museums in the city has three floors of vintage Turkish knick-knacks, collected by Nobel prize-winning author of *The Museum of Innocence*, Orhan Pamuk.

Süleymaniye Mosque
Prof Dr Sıddık Sami Onar Caddesi, Tahtakale, Fatih. Sat-Thu 0900-1900.
The city's grandest mosque – fully refurbished in 2010 – was designed by Ottoman architect Mimar Sinan.

Yerebatan Sarnıcı
Yerebatan Caddesi 13, Sultanahmet, www.yerebatan.com. Daily 0900-1830. TL10.
Underground cistern featured in the Bond film *From Russia With Love*.

Above left: Bosphorus Bridge.
Above right: Rumeli Hisarı fortress.

is filled with the smell of juicy kebabs and the sound of itinerant traders hawking their wares from the pavements.

Istiklal Caddesi and Beyoğlu

In Ottoman times Beyoğlu was home to the city's Greek, Armenian and European communities, and many of their churches and consulates remain. With the departure of these communities after the establishment of the Turkish Republic, the area fell on hard times, though it has enjoyed a Bohemian renaissance in recent years. Beyoğlu's narrow streets, running off the main shopping thoroughfare of Istiklal Caddesi, are studded with cutting-edge restaurants, cafés and bars.

Ortaköy

Ortaköy is the first of the Bosphorus 'villages' on the European shore. Cobbled streets lined with cafés, shops and market stalls lead down to a small square overlooked by the baroque **Büyük Mecidiye Mosque**, which looks like a wedding cake when lit up at night. On sunny days, the cafés are crowded, as are the bars at night. Further north, some of the city's most upmarket nightspots overlook the straits.

Rumeli Hisarı and Bebek

Yahya Kemal Caddesi 42, Rumelihisarı.
Thu-Tue 0900-1630. TL5. Bus 25E from Kabataş or bus 40 from Taksim.

In preparation for his attack on Constantinople in 1453, Sultan Mehmet had castles built on either side of the Bosphorus to prevent supply ships reaching the city. The larger of these was Rumeli Hisarı, on the European shore north of Bebek, overlooking a bend in the Bosphorus. Today you can walk the restored 15-m-thick battlements and take imaginary pot-shots at passing ships. There are several excellent little cafés nearby or stroll along the coastal path to the genteel Bosphorus 'village' of Bebek, which attracts a well-heeled crowd.

Excursion: Princes' Islands

Off Istanbul's Asian shore are a collection of nine islands, which were a place of exile in Byzantine and Ottoman times, later becoming home to wealthy families from the city's Greek and Armenian minorities. The islands are graced with many beautiful wooden houses, churches and a Greek Orthodox monastery. They also remain blissfully car-free, with horse carts the only means of transport. The largest, **Büyükada**, is the most interesting and you can explore it by rented bicycle or hire a horse-drawn phaeton. A tour of the island takes a couple of hours on foot, passing by Leon Trotsky's home – he wrote *The History of The Russian Revolution* while living here – and the hilltop St George's Monastery.

There is a beach club on the far side of the island with a small beach for cooling off. Ferries depart from Kabataş's Adalar pier regularly for the 90-minute crossing. Tickets cost TL4.5.

Where to stay

Istanbul has an excellent choice of accommodation from budget hotels to atmospheric Ottoman boutique places and luxury international chains. Prices are now on a par with other major European cities and. Booking in advance is advisable at any time of year. Many top-notch beds are found along the Bosphorus. The city's most famous hotel is the **Pera Palace**, www.jumeirah.com, built in 1882 for visitors arriving on the Orient Express

Çiragan Palace €€€
Çiragan Caddesi 32, Beşiktaş, T0212 326 4646, www.kempinski.com.
This five-star on the edge of the Bosphorus is truly glorious and is housed inside the former Turkish parliament building. It has the city's finest swimming pool, as well as a spa and several excellent restaurants including Tuğra, widely considered Istanbul's best.

Adahan €€
General Yazgan Sokak 14, T0212 243 8581, www.adahanistanbul.com.
Housed in a beautifully restored late 19th-century apartment building, Adahan is the epitome of eco-chic. Guestrooms boast custom wooden furnishings, undyed linens and olive oil bath products. Buffet breakfast is served in the panoramic rooftop dining room and on the terrace.

Empress Zoe €€
Akbiyik Caddesi 10, Sultanahmet, T0212 518 2504, www.emzoe.com.
Incorporating the ruins of 15th-century Turkish baths, the Zoe is exquisitely decorated, with modern frescoes and wall hangings and small but comfy and well-furnished rooms. There is a scenic roof terrace bar and a lovely garden.

The House Hotel €€
Bostanbaşı Caddesi 19, Beyoglu, T0212 252 0422, www.thehousehotel.com.
Perfectly located inside a century-old 4-storey mansion in Istanbul's coolest quarter. Composed of 20 ultra-hip suites, rooftop bar and art deco interiors, and complemented by top-notch service. There are now 2 additional House Hotels, located in Ortaköy and Nişantaşı.

Istanbul Sweet Home €€
Various locations in Beyoglu, www.istanbulsweethome.com.
This neat concept involves a dozen designer apartments, most with awesome views over Istanbul, rented out by the week in hip Beyoğlu locations. Flats range from the sophisticated to the sumptuously traditional. All have great kitchens, while some have Turkish baths and vast outdoor terraces.

Hotel Uyan €€-€
Utangaç Sokak 25, Sultanahmet, T0212 516 4892, www.uyanhotel.com.
A good choice for budget travellers. It's set in a converted corner house with clean en suite rooms. The scenic roof terrace has stunning views.

Side Hotel €
Utangaç Sokak 20, Sultanahmet, T0212 517 2282, www.sidehotel.com.
A well-managed place with a selection of simple pension rooms, or more expensive hotel suites, most with their own bathrooms.

Restaurants

Istanbul's restaurant scene has come on in leaps and bounds in recent years, with a crop of talented new Turkish chefs adding to the existing mix of superb traditional *meyhane* (the city's equivalent of a taverna), kebab houses and fish restaurants. Dining out is generally great value for money, though prices in some of the top-notch establishments are on a par with – or may exceed – prices in other European cities. Alcohol is available in the vast majority of the city's restaurants.

For a great evening out visit the raucous area of Kumkapı, on the coast south of Beyazit and the Grand Bazaar, which is crowded with meze and fish restaurants, where diners are entertained by gypsy street musicians. The *meyhane* of Nevizade Sokak, reached down the Balık Pazarı from Istiklal Caddesi, are very popular with local diners.

Breakfast

Fes Café €
Halıcılar Caddesi 62, Grand Bazaar, T0212 528 613, www.fescafe.com.
At the heart of the bazaar, this trendy café is a good spot for a cappuccino and a snack.

Dârüzziyafe €€
Şifahane Sokak 6, Fatih, T0212 511 8414, www.daruzziyafe.com.tr.
Set in the grand old gardens and kitchens of the Süleymaniye Mosque, this is classic Ottoman dining at its most atmospheric. Choose from around 60 classics, from chicken and walnut stew to lamb shish. Sherbets and juice only, no hard stuff.

Lunch

Haci Abdullah €€
Atıf Yılmaz Caddesi 9/A, T0212 293 8561, www.haciabdullah.com.tr.
In a sidestreet off Istiklal Caddesi, this is a grandfather of the Istanbul restaurant scene, having served Ottoman-Turkish cuisine for over 110 years. It's also known for its pickles and preserves which are displayed in colourful jars along the walls. No alcohol served.

Pandeli €€
Misir Çarşısı (Egyptian Bazaar), Eminönü, T0212 527 3909, www.pandeli.com.tr.
This atmospheric restaurant, housed in century-old dining room above the entrance to the Spice Market, serves traditional Turkish dishes at lunchtime only.

Dinner

Mama Shelter €€
Istiklal Caddesi 50, T0212 252 0200, www.mamashelter.com
A brand-new addition to the city's uber-hip rooftop dining scene. The menu is pan-Mediterranean, ranging from stuffed vine leaves to Turkish coffee crème brûlée.

Imroz €€
Nevizade Sokak 24, T0212 249 9073, www.krependekiimroz.com.
A local favourite since it opened in 1941, Imroz is one of the best fish and meze restaurants on a street crowded with excellent *meyhane*. Expect live music and pleasantly raucous patrons.

Nightlife

You certainly won't be bored after dark in Istanbul. Beyoğlu has a diverse collection of bars and clubs, catering for tastes from jazz to Turkish folk and techno. Pick up a copy of local magazine *Time Out Istanbul* (www.timeoutistanbul.com/en) for details of the best nightspots.

If you want to see where Istanbul's rich and famous strut, visit one of the super-clubs overlooking the Bosphorus in Kuruçeşme. Try **Reina**, *Muallim Naci Caddesi 44, Kuruçeşme, www.reina.com.tr*, but dress up and be prepared for a vertiginous bar bill. Call ahead to get on the guest list.

Babylon
Şehbender Sokak 3, Asmalımescit, Beyoğlu, www.babylon.com.tr.
A live venue which hosts top international and Turkish acts, as well as club nights.

Hocapaşa Culture Center
Hocapaşa Culture Center Ankara Caddesi, Hocapaşa Hamam Sokak 3.B, Sirkeci, T0212 511 4626, www.hodjapasha.com.
Authentic whirling dervish performances, as well as a regular schedule of traditional Turkish folk dance.

Shopping

Istanbul has to be one of the great shopping cities of the world, up there, in its own unique way, with New York and Milan. The **Grand Bazaar** is of course a good place to start, but there are other areas to check out including **Arasta Bazaar** (www.arastabazaar.com), beside Sultanahmet Mosque, for carpets, handicrafts and Iznik tiles. The **Istanbul Handicraft Centre**, *Nuruosmaniye Caddesi 32,*

T0212 520 9192, *www.istanbul handicraftcenter.com*, has artisans onsite producing various traditional Ottoman crafts.

Istaklal Caddesi, the city's main drag, has a mix of department stores, clothing shops (like Mavi Jeans) and some good bookshops. For antiques, the Beyoğlu district of Çukurcuma, east of Istiklal Caddesi, is dotted with little treasure troves, though remember there are restrictions on exporting real antiquities. **Nişantaşi** has international and home-grown fashion labels along Abdi Ipekci Caddesi and Tesvikiye Caddesi.

Across the Bosphorus Kadiköy's streets are dotted with some of the city's most authentic shops, stocking everything from seasonal produce, dried spices and trays of sweet baklava to cosmetics and clothing outlets.

Travel essentials

Getting there
Ataturk Airport, www.ataturk airport.com, is 25 km west of the city centre. The journey by taxi into Sultanahmet or Taksim takes 30-60 mins depending on the traffic, and costs TL40-55 (taxis are metered). Havaş (www.havas. net) operates an airport bus into Taksim (every 30 mins, TL10). The cheapest way to Sultanahmet is by tram (TL6, every 5 mins), change at Zeytinburnu. The **Sabiha Gökçen Airport**, www.sgairport.com, is located on the Asian side of the city. Many low-cost carriers, such as easyJet and Pegasus, fly here. Havaş buses (allow an hour's journey time, TL10) connect the airport with Istanbul's city centre.

Getting around
To get around the Old City all you need is your feet and an occasional ride on the modern **tram**, which passes Aksaray, Beyazit and the Covered Bazaar, Sultanahmet Square and Topkapı Palace (Gülhane) before terminating in Eminönü. Tokens can be bought at each station and cost TL3.

The 19th-century **funicular railway**, known as the Tünel, climbs steeply up to Istiklal Caddesi from the north side of the Galata bridge (straight on at the end of the bridge and then bear left at the first main junction). Tokens can be bought from the ticket booths in either station, TL3. There's also a picturesque little tram that will take you the length of Istiklal Caddesi, from Tünel to Taksim Square, without stopping. For longer journeys, taxis are fast and cheap, but avoid road travel during rush hour, and don't fall for the old taxi driver ruse where your TL50 note is swapped for a TL5 note!

Ferries regularly cross the Bosphorus from Eminönü and Karaköy to the suburbs of Uskudar and Kadiköy on the Asian shore. Tickets cost TL3 and the crossing takes about 15 mins. There are also 3 daily cruises up and down the Bosphorus to the Black Sea. These depart at 1030 and 1330 from Eminönü's Bogaz Hatti pier,with an extra sailing at 1200 during the summer. Tickets cost TL25 and the trip takes over 6 hrs, including a stop for lunch.

Tourist information
The most convenient offices are in the arrivals hall at Ataturk Airport, T0212 663 0793; Sultanahmet Sq, at Divan Yolu 3, T0212 518 1802; and in Sirkeci Station, Eminönü, T0212 511 5888. They can provide basic maps, brochures and information on current events, although not much else. For listings and city information buy a copy of *Istanbul: The Guide* (*www.theguideistanbul.com*).

Exchange rate Turkish Lira (TL). £1 = TL3.29. €1 = TL2.74 (Nov 2013).

Visas These can be bought at the airport before customs. It's £10 for Brits, or €15 for most other nationalities. Remember to have cash ready to pay for it.

Ratings

Art and culture ☆☆☆
Eating ☆☆☆
Nightlife ☆☆☆☆☆
Shopping ☆☆☆
Sightseeing ☆☆
Value for money ☆☆☆☆☆
Overall city rating ☆☆☆☆

Lisbon

With its back to Europe and its soul in the 15th century, scrupulously self-effacing Lisbon has long kept a low profile while its neighbours strutted their stuff. During nearly 50 years of solitude, Salazar smothered the city in a conservative mantle, but it emerged from its cocoon in the 1990s, thanks to European funding, a stint as City of Culture in 1994 and Expo '98, which saw the arrival of the futurist Parque das Nações. Appropriately, given Portugal's sea-faring, imperialist history, old and new worlds now sit comfortably side by side in the capital. Lisboetas emerge from riverside warehouse conversions and fashion boutiques to board arthritic trams that still chug up ludicrous gradients, zigzagging past squat dwellings, hole-in-the-wall grocers and ancient Roman walls.

Padrão dos Descobrimentos.

At a glance

Square and spare, Lisbon's downtown, **Baixa**, is the city's commercial nexus, a grid of thrusting thoroughfares that stretch from **Rossio**, the city's central reference point, south to handsome **Praça do Comércio**, Lisbon's medieval city gateway. To the west is gentrified **Chiado**. North of Rossio **Avenida da Liberdade** leads to **Praça Marques de Pombal**. **Parque Eduardo VII**, and, further north, the unassailable **Museu Calouste Gulbenkian**. West of Chiado, the **Bairro Alto** has always been Lisbon's Latin quarter, where sleek bars and *fado* houses line labyrinthine alleyways. Chiado's backyard to the west is the earthy neighbourhood of **São Bento**, which gives way to smarter **Estrela** and haughty, diplomatic **Lapa**. East of Baixa is **Alfama**, a maze of medieval Moorish streets where it all began. **Mouraria** to the north is the cradle of *fado*. A few kilometres west of the centre, stretching along the Tagus, **Belém** sees Portugal's imperial triumphs made stone. To the northeast, meanwhile, suburban sprawl gives way to sleek modernism at **Parque das Nações**, site of Expo '98.

Rossio

Map C1/2.

All roads seem to lead to Rossio, Baixa's central square, formally known as Praça Dom Pedro IV. The neoclassical **Teatro Nacional de Dona Maria II**, built in 1846 by Fortunato Lodi, occupies the north side of the square. During the 18th century this was the site of the Palace of the Inquisition. To the northwest are the interlocking horseshoe arches of **Rossio station**, designed in 1887 and betraying a late 19th-century nostalgia for the period of the Discoveries. Adjacent to Rossio, **Praça da Figueira** retains more endearing old-world charm.

Baixa Pombaline

South of Rossio is the grid of streets that form the Baixa Pombaline (Lower Town), constructed following the devastation of the 1755 earthquake. One of Baixa's main thoroughfares, **Rua Augusta** is lined with touristy pavement cafés, international chain stores and leather emporiums, culminating in the overarching splendour of the **Arco de**

Vitória, gateway to **Praça do Comércio**. This square was the crowning glory of the enlightened despot Marques de Pombal's vision for a model city and was designed to out-pomp the most regal of Europe's squares. The showpiece is a bronze equestrian statue of King Dom José I. On the north side of the square, nestling beneath the arcaded colonnades, is one of Lisbon's most famous literary landmarks, **Café Martinho do Arcado**.

On Rua Santa Justa, just south of Rossio, **Elevador de Santa Justa**, *daily 0700-2145, map C2, €5*, is one of Lisbon's most iconic and memorable images. Designed by an apostle of Eiffel, Raoul Mesnier du Ponsard, the 45-m vertical wrought-iron lift was built to link the Baixa with Largo do Carmo.

Alfama

Alfama is Lisbon's spiritual heart. It's the old Moorish quarter where ribbons of alleyways coil into blind alleys and crooked alcoves. Ancient trams take you to the **Miradouro de Santa Luzia** and **Largo Portas do Sol** from where the views of the city below are breathtaking; look out for the pristine baroque **Panteão Nacional de Santa Engrácia** and the twin bell towers of the **Igreja de São Vicente da Fora** rising amidst clusters of squat houses to the east. Encircling the church on Saturday or Tuesday is the 'thieves' flea market, **Feira da Ladra**, where you can buy your own piece of crumbling Lisbon, a fireman's T-shirt, or a traditional basket. Surrounded by seafood restaurants, tour group-orientated *fado* houses and neighbourhood grocers, the **Casa do Fado e da Guitarra Portuguesa**, *Largo do Chafariz*

Praça do Comércio.

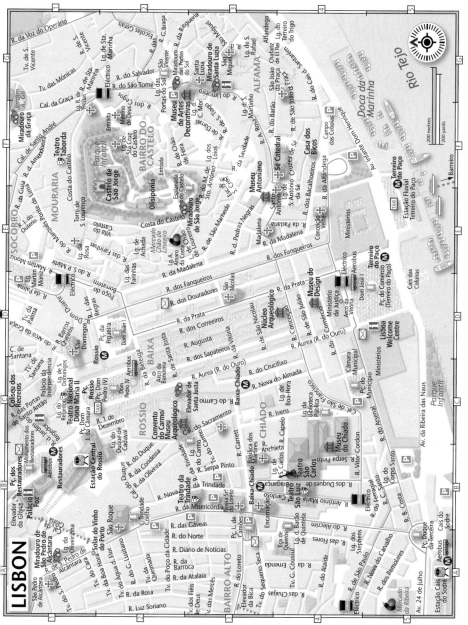

LISBON

Around the city

de Dentro 1, T21 823 470, www.museudofado.pt,
Tue-Sun 1000-1800, €5, tells the history of the
national song. A short bus ride away, set in the
tranquil Madre de Deus Convent, the **Museu
Nacional do Azulejo,** *Rua de Madre de Deus 4,
T21 810 0340, www.museudoazulejo.pt, Tue-Sun
1000-1800, €5, free on Sun 1000-1400,* houses the
finest collection of *azulejo* tiles in the country.

Castelo de São Jorge

T218 800 620, www.castelodesaojorge.pt.
Nov-Feb daily 0900-1800; Mar-Oct daily
0900-2100. €7.50. Bus 37. Map E2.

Dominating the skyline above the Alfama is the
iconic, if a little Disneyfied, Castelo de São Jorge.
First fortified by the Romans, it served as the
Moorish royal residence until it was captured by
Portugal's first king, Afonso Henriques, during the
Reconquest in the 12th century. The Moorish
fortified palace remains, as do extensive walls and
ramparts affording stunning views over the city.
Living history exhibitions are supplemented by
guided tours and family-friendly events.

Chiado

In Chiado, 19th-century old-world elegance
prevails. Devastated by fire in 1988, Chiado has
been born again and now SoHo-style wrought-
iron architecture is juxtaposed with the rococo
elegance of the **Teatro Nacional de Sao Carlos,**
Rua Serpa Pinto, T21 325 3000, www.tnsc.pt, map B4.
Rua Garrett is studded with high-fashion
boutiques and art nouveau jewellery stores.
The literary legacy of Fernando Pessoa still
hangs in the air, his spirit immortalized in stone
at **Café A Brasileira** (see page 164).
   From Rua Garrett, Calçado do Sacramento leads
to one of the most atmospheric buildings in the
city, the vast, ruined **Convento do Carmo,** *T21 347
8629, Oct-Apr Mon-Sat 1000- 1700, May-Sep Mon-Sat
1000-1800, €3, map C3.* The 15th-century Gothic
church was all-but destroyed by the 1755
earthquake, leaving the flying buttresses of the vast

Cannon at Castelo de São Jorge.

nave reaching up to the open sky. Heading south
along Rua Serpa Pinto towards the river, the **Museu
do Chiado,** *T21 343 2148, www.museudochiado-
ipmuseus.pt, Tue-Sun 1000-1800, €4, free on Sun
1000-1400, map B/C4,* is one of the finest exhibition
spaces for Portugal's 19th- and 20th-century artists.

Bairro Alto

In Lisbon's 'High Town', peeling doorways reveal
sleek bars, gritty *tascas* and *fado* houses. Here you'll
also find baroque magnificence in the Jesuit **Igreja
de São Roque,** *Largo Trindade Coelho, www.
museu-saoroque.com, T21 323 5381, Tue-Sun
0930-1700, museum €2.50, free Sun until 1400, map A/
B2,* and exotic gardens at the **Jardim Botânico,** *Rua
da Escola Politécnica, www.mnhc.ul.pt, May-Oct
daily 0900-2000, Nov-Apr daily 0900-1800, €1.50.*
Connecting the Baixa with Bairro Alto, the
Elevador da Glória wheezes up to the stunning
Miradouro de São Pedro de Alcântara, *map A1.*
   On the southern edge of the Bairro Alto, **Santa
Catarina** has some of the most endearing streets
in the city. The Miradouro de Santa Catarina offers
views across the Tagus and is the site of the acclaimed
Design and Fashion Museum (MuDe), *Rua Augusta
24, T21 888 6117, www.mude.pt, Tue-Sun 1000-1800.*

Belém

Belém, spreading west along the banks of the Tagus,
is a tremendous heap of 15th- and 16th-century
marvels, built to celebrate Vasco da Gama's
discovery of the sea route to India. It is also one

of the loveliest places in the city, with riverside walkways, expansive parks and views upriver to the **Ponte 25 de Abril** suspension bridge. The **Mosteiro dos Jerónimos**, *Praça do Império, T21 362 0034, www.mosteirojeronimos.pt, Oct-May Tue-Sun 1000-1730, May-Sep Tue-Sun 1000-1830, church free, cloisters €7, free Sun 1000-1400*, astounds with its sublime cloister where fantastical sea creatures and maritime emblems writhe in milky stone. By the river, the monumental **Padrão dos Descobrimentos** celebrates the thrust and ambition of Portugal's Age of Discovery, while, to the west, the **Torre de Belém**, *Av de Brasília, T21 362 0034, www.torrebelem.pt, Oct-Apr Tue-Sun 1000-1730, May-Sep Tue-Sun 1000-1830, €5, free Sun 1000-1400*, looks more like a chess piece washed ashore than a defensive fort.

Museu Calouste Gulbenkian

Av da Berna, 45a, T21 782 3000, www.gulbenkian.pt. Tue-Sun 1000-1745. €4, free Sun. Metro São Sebastião.

As monumental in its scope as in its quality, the Museu Calouste Gulbenkian, lies in its own serene, 7 ha garden and houses an outstanding collection of Western and Eastern art of the major periods from 2800 BC onwards.

Also north of the city centre is the decorative art museum, **Casa-Museu Dr Anastácio Gonçalves**, *Av 5 de Outubro, T21 354 0823, www.cmag.imc-ip.pt, Tue 1400-1800, Wed-Sun 1000-1800, €3, Metro Saldanha/Picoas*. It's worth visiting for its swirling art nouveau façade alone.

Torre de Belém.

Excursion: Sintra

About 30 km from Lisbon is the UNESCO World Heritage site of Sintra. Poets have raved and pagans have revelled in its Elysian Fields, recaptured from the Moors in 1147. It's an ethereal landscape where castles rise from emerald mountain ranges. On sloping terraces, carpeted with lush pine forests, erupts a rhapsody of Bavarian kitsch in the form of the slapstick **Palácio da Pena**, *T21 910 5340, Jul to mid-Sep Tue-Sun 1000-1900; mid-Sep to Jun Tue-Sun 1000-1700, last entry 30 mins before closing, €13.50*, the epitome of 19th-century decadence. In the valley are the cobble-stone streets and Moorish courtyards of **Sintra Vila**, the old quarter – all very chocolate box, but nonetheless alluring. The tourist magnet, however, is the sublime **Palácio Nacional**, *Largo Rainha Dona Amelia, T21 910 6840, www.pnsintra.imc-ip.pt, daily 0930-1900, last admission 30 mins before closing, €10*, a 14th-century royal palace steeped in Arabian myths and the imprint of cavorting kings. Trains run from Sete Rios to Sintra every 15 mins (journey time 45 mins; €3.90 return). The Scotturb bus No 434 runs every 20 mins from Sintra train station through Sintra Vila to the Palácio da Pena (€5). A combined 1-day train and bus ticket costs €12. It takes a good hour to walk up to the palace. For further information visit the tourist office at **Sintra station**, *www.cm-sintra.pt, daily 0900-1900*.

Parque das Nações

For Expo '98, this industrial wasteland was transformed into a modernist playground, united by the theme 'The Oceans, a Heritage for the Future'. Catch one of the cable cars that glide up to the city's highest viewpoint, the **Torre de Vasco da Gama**, currently being converted into a luxury hotel. From the park, the 17-km **Ponte Vasco Da Gama** spans the River Tagus; it's the longest bridge in Europe.

Attractions include the **Oceanarium**, *T21 891 7002, www.oceanario.pt, Mar-Oct 1000-2000, Nov-Mar 1000-1900, last entry 1 hr before closing, €13*, the largest in Europe, and **Pavilhão do Conhecimento Ciência Viva**, *Alameda dos Oceanos, T21 891 7100, www.pavconhecimento.pt, Tue-Fri 1000-1800, Sat-Sun and hols 1100-1900, €8*, an interactive science museum.

Where to stay

The most idiosyncratic places to stay are in Alfama, with its charming guesthouses, arty *pensões* and a few sleeker 4-star options. Bairro Alto is in the heart of the night-time action. Many rooms overlook Rossio and Praça da Figueira, but this area is noisy. Av da Liberdade has most of the really swanky choices.

Hotel Avenida Palace €€€
Rua 1 de Dezembro 123, T21 321 8100, www.hotelavenidapalace.pt.
Decadence and luxury combine to create one of the city's finest 5-star experiences. Superb central location.

Tiara Park Atlantic €€€
Rua Castilho, off Parque Eduardo VII 149, T21 381 8700, www.tiara-hotels.com.
Contemporary rooms and the highest standards. Sweeping views out over the Tagus.

Hotel Metrópole €€
Praça do Rossio, 30, T21 321 9030, www.hotelmetropolerossio.com.
Unrivalled views over Rossio, a stately 1920s classic with characterful rooms. Great value.

Chill Out Hostel €
Rua Nogueira e Sousa 8, T21 246 8450, www.lisbon chillouthostel.com.
This place is a short stroll from the main attractions making it an ideal base. Breakfast is included and there's free Wi-Fi. Dorms and private rooms available.

Pensão Ninho das Águias €
Costa do Castelo, 74, Alfama, T21 885 4070.
Just below the walls of Castelo de São Jorge is one of the best *pensãos* in the city, offering comfortable rooms, some en suite. Proud owner Luís is utterly charming and devoted to the history of the place and the city in general.

Restaurants

Chiado offers traditional cuisine; Alfama is *fado* tour-group territory, and Bairro Alto has soul food, Portuguese staples and poly-cultural delicacies. Dinner is eaten late; in Bairro Alto restaurants stay open until around 0200.

Eleven €€€
Rua Marques Fronteira, T21 386 2211, www.restauranteleven.com.
Mon-Sat 1230-1500, 1930-2300.
A location overlooking the port and an impressive collection of Portuguese contemporary art inside help to make this the ideal choice for special occasions. The tasting menu makes the most of the region's local produce, changing with the seasons.

Gambrinus €€€
Rua Portas de Santo Antão 23e 25, Baixa, T21 342 1466, www.gambrinuslisboa.com.
Daily 1200-0130.

One of Portugal's best seafood restaurants and a local institution. Tantalizing flavours, served by knowledgeable and friendly staff.

100 Maneiras €€
Rua do Texeira 35, T21 099 14 75, www.restaurante 100maneiras.com.
The 10-course, prix-fixe menu features inventive international cuisine using local ingredients in a low-key setting.

Antiga Pastelaria de Belém €
Rua de Belém 90, www.pasteisdebelem.pt.
Daily 0800-2300.
Around 10,000 salivating locals come to worship each day at the shrine of the most famous bakery in Portugal. The best way to spend 75c in Lisbon.

Café A Brasileira €
Rua Garrett, Chiado, T21 346 9541.
Daily 0800-0200.
The best place for a coffee and a pastry. The former stomping ground of Lisbon's literati is now a popular gay meeting point.

Café Martinho da Arcada €
Praça do Comércio, 3, T21 887 9259, www.martinhodaarcada.pt.
Mon-Sat 0700-2300.
The oldest café in Lisbon, dating from 1782, is an essential stop on the trail of Fernando Pessoa. There's an expensive restaurant or you can simply order a *bica* and a *pastel de nata*.

Nightlife

The Bairro Alto is the best place to kick-start an evening. Its cobbled streets hold hundreds of bars, eateries, clubs and shops. Start along the main Rua da Atalaia and explore the down-to-earth *tascas*, sleek gay joints (**Sétimo Céu**), jazz bars (**Catacombas**), lounge clubs (**Caffe Suave**, **Clube da Esquina**) and funky discos (**Bicaense**) that come to life after 2200. Check out the views from the terrace at **Miradouro de Santa Catarina** or at the **Noo Bai** rooftop bar. **B.leza** has the best African rhythms, with live music every night in Largo Conde Barão. Av 24 de Julho has the larger, more commercial venues, like **Kremlin** or **Main**. East of the 25 de Abril bridge, the Docas district of renovated warehouses has bars and clubs serving up latino sounds and tall drinks. Finally, **Lux Frágil** (www.luxfragil.com), in the docks, is high-tech and offers the best DJs and performances.

Finding authentic *fado* is tricky. Still, you may stumble across raucous amateur *fado vadio*, with no formal programme, but an orgy of catharsis.

Travel essentials

Getting there
Lisbon's **Portela Airport**, *T800 201 201, www.lisbon-airport.com*, is 6.5 km from the city centre. The **AeroBus**, *www.yellowbustours.com*, is the cheapest way to reach the city centre, departing every 20 mins (0700-2300) making stops en route, including Saldanha, Marquês de Pombal, Praça dos Restauradores, and arriving in Rossio in around 20-25 mins, before terminating at Cais do Sodré railway terminal. A ticket costs €3.50 and is valid on the transport network for 1 day. Buses 22, 44, 45 and 83 also operate 0600-2130 to the centre (€1.35), and bus 45 runs until 0010 from outside the Cais de Sodré terminal. Bus 5 links the airport to Oriente Station. A taxi to the city centre costs approximately €10 (ensure metre is on). There is a minimum charge of €2.35 for daytime bookings and €2.50 for nightime.

Getting around
Most of the main sights of the Baixa, Bairro Alto, Chiado and Alfama can be reached on foot, but there's also an efficient network of orange **buses** run by Carris, T21 361 3000, www.carris. pt. A simple (1-way) ticket bought on board costs €1.75. A ride on one of Lisbon's ancient emblematic **trams** is the most enjoyable way to get around. Tram 28 is an unofficial tourist tram that runs from Praça Martim Moniz downtown (map D1) to Campo de Ourique, uptown, with 30 hop-on, hop-off stops at key sights en route. The super tram No 15, runs from Praça da Figueira (map D2) to Belém and then on to Ajuda Palace. Bright yellow Carris

booths provide maps of bus and tram routes. Lisbon's **metro**, with 4 lines, is fast and efficient. It's best used if you are going to the north and west of the old city. A rechargeable card, '7 Colinas' costs an initial 50c and can then be credited to cover Carris buses and trams (eg one zone for €1.25 or a day for €5) or the entire network including the metro. **Taxis** are cheap; a trip from Rossio to the northern suburbs should be no more than €5. Fares are higher after 2200. There are ranks near Baixa-Chiado Metro station and Largo de Camões, or call Radio Taxis, T21 793 2756.

Tourist information
The main office is the **Lisboa Welcome Centre**, *Praça do Comércio, T21 031 2810, www.visitlisboa.com, daily 0900-2000*, with other information points around the city. **Ask Me Lisboa**, *www.askmelisboa. com*, has information on sports, the arts, palaces and museums.

Ratings

Art and culture ☆☆☆☆☆
Eating ☆☆☆☆☆
Nightlife ☆☆☆☆☆
Shopping ☆☆☆☆☆
Sightseeing ☆☆☆☆
Value for money ☆☆
Overall city rating ☆☆☆☆☆

London

Somewhat to its own surprise, London is still one of the world's great cities. It's not the loveliest in the world, nor the most antique, romantic, or mysterious. Far from exotic, it's not the richest, largest, or even the most happening place on the planet either. Notwithstanding all of this, it's impossible to resist. Civilized, improvised, sophisticated and alive, London wins everyone over in the end. Most definitely the capital of the UK, and very British, it's also a global city that has grown up thanks to other nations. Perhaps the world's best advert for multiculturalism, London's fusion of flavours is an invigorating one, with little discord and enormous cultural energy, showcased most recently at the 2012 Olympics.

The Romans, who founded Londinium in the first century AD, failed to pass any of their order on to their successors, who have developed various centres of power, commerce and entertainment over the centuries. London's streets, despite their enormous extent, are small, haphazard and human in scale. But they hold a world of artistic wonder within their mixed-up planning. The city still does tradition, with its Tower, Buckingham Palace and Trooping the Colour, but there's a new London, whose self-confidence is exemplified in the Shard, St Pancras International station and the re-developed Olympic Park. With its expansive green spaces, river views and murky weather, with its thriving culture and driven soul, this teeming muddle works its way into your heart.

St Paul's Cathedral from One New Change.

At a glance

Trafalgar Square is usually considered to be the centre of the city, with **Whitehall** and **Westminster**, the seat of government, immediately to the south. From the square, **The Strand** runs east to **St Paul's Cathedral** and the **City**. Just north of the Strand is **Covent Garden** and, to the northwest of Trafalgar Square, **Leicester Square** and **Shaftesbury Avenue** are the showbiz centre of the West End with **Chinatown** next door. Beyond, **Soho** is the West End's late-night party zone, with **Oxford Street** forming its northern boundary. **Regent Street** separates **Soho** from **Mayfair** to the west, the swankiest end of town with the gentleman's clubland and royal stamping ground of **St James's** next door. Between these two areas, **Piccadilly** heads west to Hyde Park Corner with panache. West of here, **Knightsbridge** and **South Kensington** boast luxury shopping and a trio of great museums. **Regent's Park** and **London Zoo** are northeast of Hyde Park, above **Marylebone** with its low-brow tourist attractions around **Baker Street**. **Bloomsbury**, to the east, is the academic heart of London, home to the British Museum. Further east are **Holborn**, with its Law Courts, and buzzing **Clerkenwell**. South of the river, **Southwark**, **Bankside** and **Borough** are laden with attractions and reached either from St Paul's across the Millennium Bridge, or along the river from the **South Bank** and the London Eye. Out in the East End, some of London's most happening nightlife is in **Shoreditch**, **Hoxton**, **Brick Lane** and **Spitalfields**, while further east still is the Queen Elizabeth Olympic Park. **Greenwich**, across the river from **Docklands**, has the National Maritime Museum and Royal Observatory.

24 hours in the city

An easy three-mile stroll takes in many of London's major sights. From **Trafalgar Square**, walk down Northumberland Avenue to the Embankment and cross over the Golden Jubilee footbridge to the **South Bank**. Take a ride on the **London Eye**, then walk along the river, past the **Royal Festival Hall** and **Waterloo Bridge**, to **Tate Modern** and Shakespeare's **Globe Theatre** before heading over the Millennium Footbridge to **St Paul's Cathedral**. After a look around St Paul's, the restaurants and clubs of **Clerkenwell** and **Smithfield** or **Shoreditch** are close at hand for an evening's entertainment.

Trafalgar Square

WC2.
Tube Charing Cross, Leicester Sq. Map D4.

Trafalgar Square is considered the centre of London. Linked to Westminster and Parliament by the breadth of Whitehall, this is where the administrative offices of government meet the people. **Nelson's Column**, **Landseer's Lions** and the two large fountains give the square some dignity, inspiring a sense of occasion. The pedestrianized north side of the square provides access to the **National Gallery**, *T020 7747 2885, www.nationalgallery.org.uk, Sat-Thu 1000-1800, Fri 1000-2100, free*, one of the world's most comprehensive fine art collections, with more than 2000 Western European paintings dating from the 13th century to 1900. Behind it is the **National Portrait Gallery**, *St Martin's Pl, T020-7306 0055, ext 216, www.npg.org.uk, Sat-Wed 1000-1800, Thu-Fri 1000-2100, free*.

Parliament Square

SW1.
Tube Westminster. Map D5.

At the heart of the City of Westminster, Parliament Square is bordered by two iconic buildings of the British state. The **Palace of Westminster**, *T0844 847 1672, www.parliament.uk/visiting/, guided tours Sat 0915-1630, also mid-Sep to early Oct Tue-Fri 0915-1630, £16.50*, incorporates the Houses of Parliament and

Trafalgar Square.

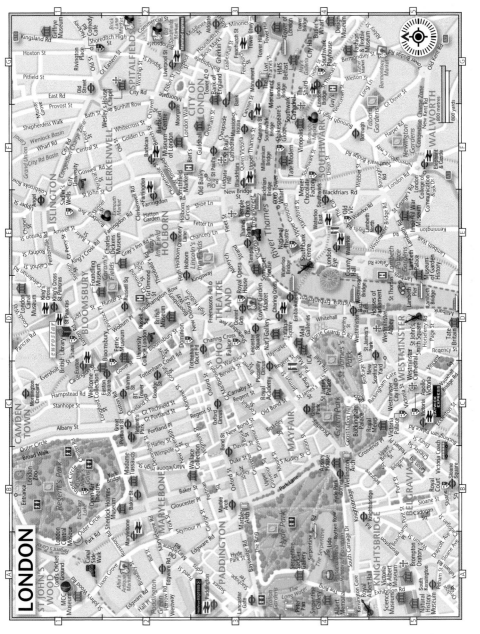

LONDON

Around the city

the Elizabeth Tower (Big Ben). Most of the neo-Gothic parliament buildings were constructed in 1860, following a devastating fire, but medieval Westminster Hall, dating from 1097 is still intact. South of the square is **Westminster Abbey**, *T020 7654 4834, www.westminster-abbey.org, Mon, Tue, Thu, Fri 0930-1630, Wed 0930-1900, Sat 0930-1430, Sun for services only, £18*, which dates in part from the 13th century. Highlights include: the vast central nave (over 30 m high); the Coronation Chair, used to crown nearly every English monarch since 1308; Henry VII's Chapel (or Lady Chapel); and Poet's Corner, with its monuments to Shakespeare, Chaucer and other cultural luminaries.

Buckingham Palace and St James's Park

T020 7766 7334, www.royalcollection.org.uk. Late Jul-Sep daily 0945-1830. £19. Tube Green Park, St James's Park, Hyde Park Corner. Map C4.

The Queen's official London residence is open to the paying public for two months of the year and, despite the high admission prices and long queues, it attracts thousands of people from all over the world. Next door to the palace visitors' entrance and open year round, the **Queen's Gallery**, *T020 7766 7334, daily 1000-1730 (last admission 1630), closed Oct, £9.50*, displays changing selections from the Queen's collection of Old Masters and portraiture, an extraordinary array founded by Charles II. The **Changing of the Guard** takes place daily on the Palace forecourt at 1130 from 1 April to the end of July and on alternate days for the rest of the year.

St James's Park, stretching out east from the palace, is the finest and most carefully laid out of the Royal parks (others include Hyde Park, Green Park, Regent's Park and Kensington Gardens). A wander around reveals surprising but carefully orchestrated vistas at every turn. Guided tours are given by its warden from April to September.

South Kensington Museums

SW7.
Tube South Kensington. Map A5.

Although they are located tantalisingly close together, the temptation to 'do' all three of these great museums in a day should definitely be resisted. Even two could prove too rich a treat.

The **Science Museum**, *Exhibition Rd, T0870 870 4868, www.sciencemuseum.org.uk, daily 1000-1800,*

Top right: Houses of Parliament and Westminster Abbey.
Bottom right: Buckingham Palace from St James's Park.

free, prides itself on being one of the most forward-thinking, interactive and accessible museums in the country. The Wellcome Wing is particularly worth visiting, with four floors dedicated to cutting-edge science. A new Media Space gallery opened in 2013 to explore the relationships between photography, art, science and technology.

The **Natural History Museum**, *Cromwell Rd, T020 7942 5000, www.nhm.ac.uk, daily 1000-1750, until 2230 on last Fri of month, free*, housed in an extraordinary orange and blue terracotta building, is an academic research institution that is now seriously fun packed. Divided into Life Galleries and Earth Galleries, it tells the history of our planet through a successful combination of venerable artefacts and child-friendly attractions, including stuffed mammals and an animated, life-sized tyrannosaurus rex.

The **Victoria and Albert Museum**, *Cromwell Rd, T0870 906 3883, www.vam.ac.uk, Sat-Thu 10-1745, Fri 1000-2200, free*, was founded in 1857 with the aim of educating the populace in the appreciation of decorative art and design by exhibiting superb examples of these. Not a narrow nationalistic enterprise, its remarkable collection was gathered, like the British Museum's, from all corners of the globe. In recent years the V&A has shrugged off a slightly fusty reputation with some cutting edge modern exhibits.

British Museum

Great Russell St, WC1, T020 7323 8000, www.britishmuseum.org.
Sat-Thu 1000-1730, Fri 1000-2030; Great Court Sat-Thu 0900-1800, Fri 0900-2030. Free (donations appreciated), prices of temporary exhibitions vary. Tube Tottenham Court Rd. Map D2.

Open to the public for free since 1753, the British Museum is one of the world's greatest cultural institutions. Norman Foster's redevelopment of the **Great Court** in 2000 turned the museum's long-hidden central quadrangle into the largest covered square in Europe. A beautiful lattice-work canopy of 3312 unique panes of glass wraps itself around the dome of the famous **Reading Room**, free-standing once again at the heart of the museum.

On entering the Great Court from the south, pick up a floorplan and get your bearings. Head to the **west wing** for Ancient Egypt, the Ancient Near East and Ancient Greece; the **east wing** for the Enlightenment and the King's Library; and the **north wing** for ethnography, Asia and the Americas. The upper floors are devoted to Ancient Rome, Europe, prehistory, Ancient Egypt, the Ancient Near East and the Japanese and Korean collections. It would be quite impossible to see everything in one day, so, apart from the guided and audio tours, it's worth joining one of the free daily 30- to 40-minute eyeOpener gallery tours.

St Paul's Cathedral

T020 7236 4128, www.stpauls.co.uk.
Mon-Sat 0830-1630, Sun worship only. £16 including cathedral crypt and galleries. Organ recitals Sun 1700, free. Tube St Paul's. Map F3.

Standing proud at the top of Ludgate Hill is St Paul's Cathedral. At least the fifth church on the site, construction started in 1675 and took about 35 years to complete. Hemmed in by other buildings, Sir Christopher Wren's colossal church still impresses. The redevelopment of Paternoster Square has opened up new views of St Paul's, reflecting its cleaned Portland stone in plate-glass office blocks, while the **Millennium Bridge** provides a neat approach from Tate Modern. It's definitely worth climbing up to the **Whispering Gallery**, around the base of the inner dome, and then continuing up the dizzying cast-iron stairway to the open-air **Golden Gallery** to soak up the tremendous wraparound views.

South Bank

SE1.
Tube Westminster, Waterloo. Map E4.

The **London Eye**, *T0870 500 0600, www.londoneye.com, Sep-Mar 1000-2030, Easter and Jun-Aug 1000-2130, Apr and May 1000-2100, £19.20, private capsule £440*

Best of the rest

Imperial War Museum
Lambeth Rd, T020-7416 5320, www.iwm.org.uk, map E5.
Daily 1000-1800. Free.
Dedicated to the history of 20th-century warfare and refurbished to mark the centenary of the First World War.

London Zoo
Regent's Park, T020 7722 3333, www.zsl.org, map B1.
Summer daily 1000-1730, winter daily 1000-1630 (last admission 1 hr before closing). £21-25, cheaper online.

Museum of London
150 London Wall, T0870 444 3852, events T020 7814 5777, www.museumoflondon.org.uk, map F2.
Daily 1000-1800. Free.
A refreshing visual approach to the social history of the city. There's another site in London Docklands.

Queen Elizabeth Olympic Park
E20, T0800 0722 110, queenelizabetholympicpark.co.uk.
Summer daily 0600-2200, winter daily 0600-1900.
Tube Stratford, Stratford International.
The Olympic Park is re-opening as the centrepiece of a 560-acre redevelopment project. Lawns, gardens, play areas and waterways are set around eye-catching sport, entertainment, shopping and cultural venues.

Royal Academy of Arts
Piccadilly, T020-7300 8000, www.royalacademy.org.uk.
Sat-Thu 1000-1800, Fri 1000-2200, map C3.
Attention-grabbing exhibitions of contemporary art.

The Shard
Joiner St, SE1, T0844 499 7111, www.theviewfromtheshard.com. Summer daily 0900-2200, winter Sun-Wed 1000-1900, Thu-Sat 1000-2200. £24.95. Tube London Bridge. Map G4.

At 306 m high, Renzo Piano's shimmering glass pinnacle is the tallest building in the European Union. Views from the observation deck on the 72nd floor are outstanding.

Somerset House
Strand, T020 7845 4600, www.somersethouse.org.uk, map E3. Daily 1000-1800 (last admission 1715). Courtauld Gallery £6, other exhibitions vary.
An ice rink in winter and fine art and antiques all year in the Courtauld and Gilbert Collections or Hermitage Rooms.

Tate Britain
T020 7887 8888, www.tate.org.uk/britain, map F4.
Daily 1000-1800, free, prices for exhibitions vary.
Ancient and contemporary British art.

(advance booking available online), is a vast spoked white observation wheel beside Westminster Bridge that dominates the London skyline. Over 100 m in diameter, it's visible from unexpected places all around the city. There's no denying its novelty value or even, perhaps, its beauty. The half-hour 'flight' in one of its surprisingly roomy capsules, moving at 25 cm per second, provides superb 25-mile views over the city.

Next door to the Eye, the magisterial **County Hall** now houses the highly acclaimed **London Aquarium**, *T0871 663 1679, www.visitsealife.com, daily 1000-1900, £23.70*, and the relocated **London Dungeon**, *www.thedungeons.com, Mon-Wed, Fri 1000-1700, Thu 1100-1700 (extended hours Sat, Sun and hols), £24.60*. Downstream is the **South Bank Centre**, the largest arts complex of its kind in Europe. Apart from the main Royal Festival Hall (page 176), it also houses other concert venues, an exhibition space, the Poetry Library, the National Theatre (page 177), the National Film Theatre (page 176) and the cutting-edge **Hayward Gallery**, *T020 7960 4200, www.southbankcentre.co.uk, Mon 1200-1800, Tue, Wed, Sat, Sun 1000-1800, Thu, Fri 1000-2000, price varies.*

Tate Modern

Bankside, SE1.
Ticket bookings T020 7887 8888; information
T020 7887 8008, www.tate.org.uk.
Sun-Thu 1000-1800, Fri and Sat 1000-2200
(last admission 45 mins before closing). Free
(charges for special exhibitions around £15).
Tube Southwark or Blackfriars. Map F4.

Tate Modern is one of the most spectacular and
popular of London's attractions. The converted
Bankside Power Station houses the Tate's collection
of international modern art from 1900 to the present.
A great solid box of brick with a single free-standing
square chimney front centre, the power station was
decommissioned in 1986 and left desolate until Swiss
architects Herzog and de Meuron were appointed to
adapt the building to its current role. The immense
Turbine Hall is an astonishing space for specifically
commissioned artworks on a grand scale, with the
rest of the main collection permanently arranged in
galleries along one side. Free guided tours leave from
Level 3 at 1100 (Poetry and Dream) and 1200 (Material
Gestures), and from Level 5 at 1400 (States of
Flux) and 1500 (Energy and Process).

Tower of London

EC3, T0844 482 7777, www.hrp.org.uk.
Tue-Sat 0900-1730, Sun and Mon 1000-1730.
£21.45. Tube Tower Hill. Map G3.

The Tower was built 900 years ago not to protect
Londoners but to subdue them, a role it played
until the mid-19th century. Nowadays, some
dismiss it as a tourist trap, but it makes an
enormous effort to elucidate its wealth of historical
associations and bring the old buildings to life with
a mix of bare Norman stonework and 21st-century
three-dimensional virtual tours. Highlights include
the Norman **White Tower**, the **Royal Armouries**
and the **Crown Jewels**. Nearby is the neo-Gothic
extravagance of **Tower Bridge**.

Greenwich

SE10.
Cutty Sark DLR or overland train from Charing
Cross or London Bridge to Greenwich train station.

With its 18th-century architecture, expansive views
and royal associations, Greenwich has attracted
visitors for centuries. Flanking the Renaissance
Queen's House, the **National Maritime Museum**, *Park
Row, T020 8858 4422, www.nmm.ac.uk, daily 1000-1700
(extended hours in summer), free*, is dedicated to
Britain's sea-faring history. Uphill from here, in
Greenwich Park, is the **Royal Observatory**, *T020 8858
4422, www.nmm.ac.uk, daily 1000-1700 (extended hours
in summer), free*, home of Greenwich Mean Time.

Explore antique shops and market stalls in the
village, and, on the waterfront, the 19th-century
tea clipper **Cutty Sark**, *T020 8312 6608, www.rmg.
co.uk/cuttysark, daily 1000-1700 (extended hours in
summer)*, fully restored after fire damage and set
in a striking glass gallery.

It is now possible to travel by cable car
across the Thames on the **Emirates Air Line**,
*www.emiratesairline.co.uk, Mon-Fri 0700-2100,
Sat 0800-2100, Sun 0900-2100, from £3.20 one way.*
The 'Air Line' runs between Greenwich (Tube
North Greenwich) and the Royal Docks (Tube
Royal Victoria), affording wonderful views of
the O2 arena, Greenwich Park and Canary Wharf.

Right: Cutty Sark.
Opposite page: The Shard.

Where to stay

Accommodation doesn't come cheap in London – even at the budget end – but, if it's luxury, pampering and romance you're after, you'll be spoilt for choice. We've left out the really obvious big-hitters, like Claridge's, The Dorchester and The Savoy, in favour of more intimate, cosy or romantic options. All are centrally located.

Dukes €€€
St James's Pl, SW1, T020 7491 4840, www.dukeshotel.com.
With 90 comfortable, old-fashioned rooms and a health club, this is a very discreet luxury hotel with a cosy bar that mixes devastating Martinis.

Hazlitt's €€€
6 Frith St, W1, T020 7434 1771, www.hazlittshotel.com.
Many people's London favourite with 23 individual period rooms of great character, in memory of the London essayist. No restaurant or bar but plenty nearby in the liveliest streets of Soho.

Malmaison €€€
18-21 Charterhouse Sq, EC1, T0844 693 0656, www.malmaison.com.
With 97 differently shaped rooms, this hotel is comfortable, easygoing but quite flash.

The Rookery €€€
Peter's Lane, Cowcross St, EC1, T020 7336 0931, www.rookeryhotel.com.
A renovated old-fashioned townhouse hotel with 33 rooms in an antique building and a crow's nest of a penthouse.

St Martin's Lane €€€
45 St Martin's Lane, WC2, T020 7300 5500, www.morganshotelgroup.com.
Formerly Ian Schrager's media favourite, designed by minimalist Philippe Starck. The restaurant does classic French and modern European on the side and, for drinking, there's the awesome Light Bar and the Seabar.

B&B Belgravia €€
64-66 Ebury St, SW1, T020 7259 8570, www.bb-belgravia.com.
Slick and minimalistic in a way that you wouldn't usually associate with a B&B; cut-price contemporary chic.

Number Sixteen €€
16 Sumner Pl, SW7, T020 7589 5232, www.numbersixteenhotel.co.uk.
42 rooms in 4 small townhouses. Elegant privacy and the most salubrious (and expensive) of the set in this dainty little stucco street. Part of the successful Firmdale group.

One Leicester Street €€
1 Leicester St, WC2, T020 3301 8020, oneleicesterstreet.com.
This 2013 re-brand of what was the St John Hotel offers subtle minimalism, a central situation and a superb restaurant run by Tom Harris, the Michelin-starred disciple of Fergus Henderson of St John restaurant.

Tophams Belgravia €€
28 Ebury St, SW1, T020 7730 3313, www.tophamshotel.com.
A charming, small country house-style hotel, family-run with very friendly service.

Restaurants

London's restaurant scene continues to mature at a heady rate. The range of excellent food on offer in almost every setting and price bracket can be baffling. A good meal has become an integral part of a top night out. But the city is a notoriously pricey place in which to eat compared to much of Europe. This is partly compensated by the sheer variety of cuisines available – from Argentina to Yemen via Poland and New Zealand.

Balthazar €€€
4-6 Russell St, WC2, T020 3302 1155, www.balthazarlondon.com.
The newly opened London branch of the über-fashionable Manhattan faux-French brasserie serves New York staples like steak frites in a sumptuously lit setting.

Gymkhana €€€
42 Albemarle St, W1, T020 3011 1021, gymkhanalondon.com.
Michelin-starred Karam Sethi's new venture (inspired by the colonial British gymkhana club house) serves modern Indian cooking prepared in a tandoor oven or over a sigri charcoal grill.

There is a lavish feast menu (including Goan suckling pig) available for groups.

Hutong €€€
Level 33, the Shard, 31 St Thomas St, SE1, T020 7478 0540, www.aquahutong.co.uk.
Situated high in the Shard, this is London's current best table with a view. The restaurant is the European branch of a much-vaunted Hong Kong eaterie, serving northern Chinese food. London twinkles at your feet.

Andrew Edmunds €€
46 Lexington St, W1, T020 7437 5708, www.andrewedmunds.com.
Excellent modern European cooking at reasonable prices is served up in a cosy, candlelit atmosphere. Booking ahead strongly recommended.

The Eagle €€
159 Farringdon Rd, EC1, T020 7837 1353.
One of the first pubs to go gastro, cooking up excellent modern European food.

St John €€
26 St John St, EC1, T020 7251 0848, www.stjohngroup.uk.com.
Especially good offal and freshly baked bread are served up in a stark former smokery celebrating 'nose to tail' eating. St John Bread and Wine, 94-96 Commercial St, T020 7251 0848, is the cheaper, no-frills version.

Union Street Café €€
47-51 Great Suffolk St, SE1, T020 7592 7977, gordonramsay.com.
Gordon Ramsay's 1st venture south of the river is an informal dining room set in a brightly lit converted warehouse. The Mediterranean dishes are made from ingredients sourced from artisan producers at nearby Borough market.

India Club €
143 Strand, WC2, T020 7836 0650. Closed Sun.
Pay up to £15 for old-style curries at formica tables on linoleum floors with yellow walls. A very Indian institution, since 1950. Bring your own booze.

Lahore Kebab House €
2 Umberston St, E1, T020 7488 2551, www.lahore-kebabhouse.com. Daily till 2330.
A 30-year-old family-owned informal restaurant set in the Pakistani and Bangladeshi quarters of East London. Delicious and authentic Pakistani dishes attract a multicultural crowd. Bring your own alcohol.

Time Out London (www.timeout.com), a weekly magazine, has the latest entertainment listings.

Bars and clubs
London has a busy bar, pub and club scene. Some traditional pubs still boast genuine Victorian interiors and a genuinely local crowd (**The Gunmakers**, *12 Eyre St, EC1*; the **Princess Louise**, *208 High Holborn, WC1*). Others have changed into smart gastro pubs (**Anchor and Hope**, *36 The Cut, SE1*; **Norfolk Arms**, *23 Leigh St, WC1*). Hot on their heels are a string of bars and speakeasies in the West End and Hoxton, including quirky **Mr Fogg's**, *15 Bruton Ln, W1, www.mr-foggs. com*, and the tiny **Cellar Door**, *Zero Aldwych, WC2*. In Soho, new bars and gay clubs rub shoulders with old-timers like the **French House**, *49 Dean St, W1*.

There are myriad nightclubs, too. These include vast mainstream venues like the well-established **Ministry of Sound**, *103 Gaunt St, SE1*, and glitzy, gaudy **Rise**, *1 Leicester Sq, WC2, www.risesuperclub.com*, as well as smaller venues in London's most fashionable nightlife quarters, currently around Mayfair and Hoxton. The former is largely conservative, exclusive, expensive and often for members only. Hoxton (EC2) is more democratic, cutting-edge and creative with an eclectic spread of bars and clubs, including the artsy **Book Club**,

Travel essentials

Getting there

London Heathrow Airport, T0844 335 1801, is 15 miles west of central London. Piccadilly Line tube trains run every 5-9 mins (roughly 0630-0100), journey time 50 mins. Heathrow Express, T0845 600 1515, www. heathrowexpress.co.uk, runs to Paddington Station, every 15 mins (0510-2340), journey time 15 mins, £20 single, £34 return. A black cab costs £45-75 (45 mins-1 hr).

    London Gatwick Airport, T0870 000 2468, 28 miles south of the capital. Gatwick Express, T0845 850 1530, www.gatwickexpress.com, to and from London Victoria every 15 mins (hourly at night), £19.90 single, 34.90 return. Taxi around £75-100, about 1 hr.

    London Luton Airport, T01582-405100, 30 miles north of central London. Regular trains to and from London Bridge, Blackfriars, Farringdon and King's Cross stations. A taxi takes 50 mins and costs around £75-100.

    Stansted Airport, T0870 000 0303, 35 miles northeast. Stansted Express, T0845 850 0150, every 15 mins to Liverpool Street, 45 mins, £23.40 single, £32.80 open return. A taxi takes 1-1½ hrs and costs about £75-100.

    There are 5 main national train stations: King's Cross serves Scotland and northeast England; Euston serves the northwest; Paddington serves Wales and the west; Waterloo serves the south of England; and Victoria serves the southeast. **Eurostar**, www.eurostar. com services to the continent operate from St Pancras International, adjacent to King's Cross. For train times and ticket prices call **National Rail Enquiries**, T08457-484950, or www.nationalrail.co.uk.

Getting around

London's public transport network consists of mainly buses and the underground (known as the Tube). It is fairly efficient, but expensive. Single Tube fares in Zone 1 (most of central London) cost £4.50 and single bus fares £2. Daily travelcards, for buses and the Tube, cost £7.30 off-peak, £8.80 peak. Or buy an Oyster card, for the cheaper single fares on public transport. For 24-hr information on public transport and tickets call T020-7222 1234, or visit www.tfl.gov.uk. The Tube is faster, but buses are good for sightseeing as you travel around town. Car drivers must pay a congestion charge (£10) in central London Mon-Fri 0700-1800; see the website above. Public bicycles can be hired from cycle stations throughout central London by using a credit card. The first 30 mins are free. Instructions and pricing details can be found on the Transport for London website (www.tfl.gov.uk).

Tourist information

Britain and London Visitor Centre (BLVC), 1 Lower Regent St, SW1 (Piccadilly Circus tube), Mon 0930-0630, Tue-Fri 0900-0630, Sat-Sun 1000-1600; Jun-Sep Sat 0900-1700, Sun 1000-1600. **London Information Centre**, in Leicester Sq, T020 7292 2333, www.london town.com, daily 0800-2300. **City Information Centre**, St Paul's Churchyard, south side of the cathedral, T020 7332 1456, Apr-Sep daily 1000-1800; Oct-Mar Mon-Fri 0930-1700, Sat 0930-1230.

100-106 Leonard St, and avant garde **Xoyo**, *32-37 Cowper St.*

Cinema

Sofas and wine-coolers make **Aubin Cinema**, *64-66 Redchurch St, E2, T0845 604 8486, www.aubin cinema.com*, London's classiest movie house. Also worth seeking out are the **Curzon Soho**, *99 Shaftesbury Av, W1, T020 7292 1686, www.curzoncinemas.com*; the **ICA Cinema**, *Nash House, The Mall, SW1,*

T020 7930 3647, www.ica.org.uk, for very rare or independent films, and the **National Film Theatre** (**NFT**), *South Bank, SE1, T020 7928 3535, www.bfi.org.uk*, home to the British Film Institute. Nearby is the **BFI London IMAX**, *Waterloo, SE1, T0870 787 2525, www.bfi.org.uk.*

Classical music and dance

The **South Bank Centre**, *SE1, T0870 380 4300, www.southbank centre.co.uk*, encompasses the

Royal Festival Hall, for large-scale orchestral and choral concerts, plus the Queen Elizabeth Hall and Purcell Room for chamber music groups. Classical music can also be heard at **Wigmore Hall**, *36 Wigmore St, W1U, T020 7935 2141, www.wigmore-hall. org.uk*, and at the **Barbican Centre**, *Silk St, EC2Y, T020 7638 8891, www.barbican.org.uk*, home of the London Symphony Orchestra. The **Royal Albert Hall**,

Kensington Gore, SW7, T020 7589 8212, www.royalalberthall.com, is a grand setting for the annual BBC Proms and other performances. Ballet and opera are performed at the bastion of high culture that is the **Royal Opera House**, *Bow St, WC2E, T020 7304 4000, www.royalopera house.org*, and also at the state-of-the-art **Sadler's Wells and Lilian Baylis Theatre**, *Rosebery Av, EC1R, T020 7863 8198, www.sadlerswells.com.*

Jazz, rock and pop

The biggest names in rock and pop perform at the **O2 Arena** on the Greenwich Peninsular (www. tho2.co.uk) or at **Wembley Arena** (www.wembleyarena.co.uk). Other pop and rock venues include **Koko**, *1a Camden Rd, NW1, T0870 432 5527, www.koko. co.uk*, and the **O2 Academy Brixton**, *211 Stockwell Rd, T020 7771 2000, www.o2academy brixton.co.uk*. For jazz, head to legendary **Ronnie Scott's**, *7 Frith St, W1, T020 7439 0747, www.ronniescotts.co.uk*, or the **Jazz Café**, *3 Parkway, NW1, T020 7916 6060, www.jazzcafe.co.uk.*

Theatre

The heart of theatreland is still the **West End**, with its diet of hit musicals and popular drama. Discount tickets are sold from a booth in Leicester Sq. **Off-West End** theatres are often a better bet for thought-provoking productions or new drama.

Those with a particular good reputation include the **National Theatre**, *South Bank, SE1, T020 7452 3000, www.nationaltheatre. org.uk*, which has three stages for all styles and sizes of production; the **Almeida**, *Almeida St, Islington, N1, T020 7359 4404, www.almeida. co.uk*; the **Donmar Warehouse**, *41 Earlham St, WC2, T020-7240 4882, www.donmar warehouse. com*; the **Royal Court Theatre**, *Sloane Sq, SW1, T020 7565 5000, www.royalcourttheatre.com*; the **Old Vic**, *The Cut, SE1, T0844 871 7628, www.oldvictheatre.com*; and the **Young Vic**, *The Cut, SE1, T020 7922 2922 , www.youngvic.org*. The **Globe Theatre**, *21 New Globe Walk, SE1, T020 7401 9919, www. shakespearesglobe.com*, is also worth visiting for its authentic Elizabethan architecture and innovative open-air productions.

Shopping

The difficulty is knowing where to begin. **Oxford St** and **Regent St** have **Selfridges, Hamleys, Liberty** and other large department stores and big brand shops. **Tottenham Court Rd** is good for computers and electronics. Head to **Charing Cross Rd** and **Bloomsbury** for new and second-hand books and **Soho** and **Carnaby St** for urban streetwear. **Covent Garden** is good for clothes, specialist foods, toys, toiletries and gifts. Visit **Bond St** and **Mayfair** for couture fashion and expensive jewellery. For bespoke boots, suits, smoking requisites, wine and other clubby male accessories, go to St James's and **Savile Row**. For crafts and independent designers, visit **Clerkenwell**. Knightsbridge has high street fashion and **Harrods**. **Chelsea** and **Notting Hill** are good for one-off, independent fashion labels, second-hand clothes, music, books and gifts. See also Markets, below.

Markets

London's markets often show the city at its best: lively enclaves of character and creativity. Here are the main ones: **Berwick Street**, W1, Mon-Sat 0900-1700), fabrics and food; **Borough**, SE1, Fri 1200-1800, Sat 0900-1600, organic food; **Brick Lane**, E1, Sun 0700-1400, just about everything; **Camden**, NW1, daily 0900-1800, furniture, gifts, clothes, accessories and general mayhem; **Columbia Road**, E1, Sun 0800-1400, flowers; **Leather Lane**, EC2, Mon-Fri 1030-1400, cheap clothes, accessories, fruit and veg; **Portobello Road**, W11, Sat 0800-1800, antiques, second-hand clothes and bric-a-brac; **Spitalfields**, E1, Mon-Fri 1000-1600, Sun 0900-1700, clothes, books, organic food, jewellery and bric-a-brac.

Ratings

Art and culture ☆☆☆☆☆☆
Eating ☆☆☆☆☆
Nightlife ☆☆☆☆☆☆
Shopping ☆☆☆
Sightseeing ☆☆☆☆☆
Value for money ☆☆☆
Overall city rating ☆☆☆☆

Madrid

Madrid is not a city of half-measures: Europe's highest, youngest, sunniest capital likes to boast Desde Madrid al Cielo ('from Madrid to Heaven'), with a matter-of-fact assumption that when you've seen Madrid, the only place left is Heaven. The city is as famous for what it lacks as for what it boasts – there's no great river, no architectural marvels, no immediate picture- postcard charm. But what it does have, it has in spades: a fabulous collection of western art held in the Prado, the Thyssen and the Reina Sofía; a crooked old centre where almost every alley is stuffed with excellent tapas bars and restaurants; a famously intense blue sky; and an even more intense nightlife that makes most other cities look positively staid.

Plaza Mayor de Madrid.

At a glance

The leafy, elegant **Paseo del Prado** sits on the eastern side of the city, where the three big museums – the Prado, the Centro de Arte de Reina Sofía and the Thyssen-Bornemisza – are conveniently clustered. West of here is **Puerta del Sol**, Madrid's crossroads, and the cheerful, bohemian barrio of **Santa Ana**, which slopes downhill back towards the Prado. **Plaza Mayor**, west down Calle Mayor, is the grand heart of old Madrid. The area around it, sprinkled with old palaces and monasteries, is known as **Madrid de los Austrias** (Hapsburg Madrid). To the west is the enormous Bourbon **Palacio Real** and the city's beautifully restored Opera House. South of Plaza Mayor are the multicultural, edgy, traditionally working class districts of **La Latina** and **Lavapiés**, with a great flea market on Saturdays. North of the **Gran Vía, Chueca** and **Malasaña** are sweetly old-fashioned by day and unstoppably wild by night. Swanky **Salamanca**, east of here, is an elegant 19th-century grid scattered with upmarket restaurants and designer boutiques.

24 hours in the city

Have breakfast on the **Plaza de Oriente**, with views of the Palacio Real. Spend a few hours seeing the highlights at one of the big three museums – the Goyas at the **Prado**, Picasso's *Guernica* at the **Reina Sofía** or the Italian Primitives at the **Thyssen**. Trawl around the old-fashioned tapas bars in the **Plaza Santa Ana** for lunch, followed by a siesta under the trees in the **Parque del Retiro**. Take a look at some of the new galleries springing up in trendy **Chueca** or go shopping at its quirky fashion boutiques. Soak up the atmosphere at a traditional restaurant, such as **Casa Paco**, followed by flamenco at **Casa Patas**. Alternatively, check out the Madrid club scene: celebrity spot at Vanila, or hop onto a podium at **Kapital**. Finish up with some traditional *churros con chocolate* at the **Chocolatería San Ginés**.

Museo del Prado.

Museo del Prado

Paseo del Prado, T91 330 2800, www.museoprado.mcu.es.
Mon-Sat 1000-2000, Sun 1000-1900.
€14, €7 concessions, free Mon-Sat 1800-2000, Sun 1700-1900, Abono Paseo del Arte €24.80.
Metro Banco de España. Map D3.

The Prado houses one of the world's greatest art collections, a dazzling display of European art spanning seven centuries. When it opened in 1819, it was one of the very first public art museums, infused with the spirit of the Enlightenment and shored up by royal whim (Queen Isabel of Braganza had been impressed with the Louvre and wanted one for Spain). The collection encompasses several thousand works of art, and the sheer scale can make it a daunting prospect. Pick out some highlights or favourite painters rather than trying to see it all in one go. The museum's strength is its magnificent collection of Spanish masterpieces dating from the 12th to the 19th centuries, including works by Zurbarán, Velázquez and Goya. A contemporary extension by Rafael Moneo has added more galleries, including a striking space which incorporates a 16th-century cloister.

Museo Thyssen-Bornemisza

Paseo del Prado 8, T91 420 3944, www.museothyssen.org.
Tue-Sun 1000-1900. €9, €6 concessions, temporary exhibitions extra, free Mon 1200-1600, Abono Paseo del Arte €24.80.
Metro Banco de España. Map C3.

Across Plaza de Cánovas del Castillo from the Prado is the **Thyssen-Bornemisza**, which perfectly complements its 'big brother'. It plugs the gaps left by the Prado, with a vast collection of western European art spanning eight centuries, as well as offering a dazzling selection of early 20th-century masters, from Braque to Kandinsky, to whet your appetite for the Reina Sofía. There's a charming garden café and a fabulous rooftop restaurant, El Mirador.

Museo Nacional Centro de Arte Reina Sofía

*C Santa Isabel 52, T91 467 5062,
www.museoreinasofia.es.*
Mon, Wed-Sat 1000-2100, Sun 1000-1430.
€6 for permanent collection and temporary
exhibitions, €3 for temporary exhibitions only,
free Sat 1430-2100 and Sun 1000-1430; Abono
Paseo del Arte €24.80. Metro Atocha. Map C/D4.

Housed in a former hospital close to Atocha
station, Reina Sofia has been beautifully
remodelled to hold the nation's collection of
20th-century art. A stunning extension with glossy
red curves by Jean Nouvel houses a library and a
superb café-restaurant. It's a graceful, light-filled
building set around a quiet interior courtyard, with
a pair of panoramic glass lifts which are almost an
attraction in themselves. The second and fourth

floors are devoted to the permanent exhibition
and the first and third floors are used for temporary
exhibitions which are usually excellent. The
undoubted highlight is Picasso's celebrated
Guernica (second floor), whose sheer scale and
emotional power cannot fail to impress.

Museo Nacional Centro de Arte Reina Sofía.

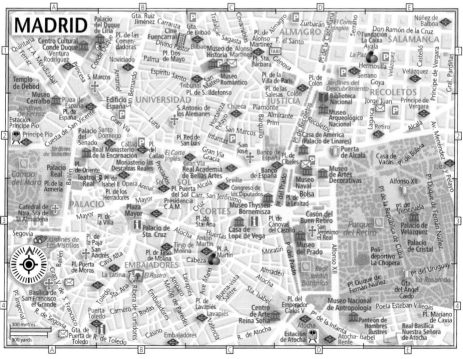

Around the city

Parque del Retiro

Metro Banco de España/Retiro.

This dreamy expanse of manicured gardens, lakes, shady woods and pavilions was once the garden of the Palacio Real del Buen Retiro and is the perfect escape from the city bustle. At the centre is a vast lake (*estanque*), with a sprinkling of kiosks and boats for hire. At the southern end of the park, take a peek at the bizarre *Ángel Caído* (Fallen Angel), one of only three monuments in the world to Satan, caught midway in his fall from Paradise. Ricardo Velázquez designed the elegant **Palacio de Velázquez** and **Palacio de Cristal** in 1882. The pavilions are now used for the Reina Sofía's temporary art exhibitions.

Plaza Santa Ana

Metro Antón Martín. Map C3.

This square, flanked by restaurants, bars, theatres and hotels, has been the heart of the Barrio de las Letras for centuries. It's been overhauled a dozen times and the latest restoration confirms Madrid's predilection for public squares.

Although not especially pretty, the square's charm lies in its vibrancy and constant animation; the pavements are lined with dozens of tapas bars complete with turn-of-the-20th-century fittings; it's one of the most popular places in Madrid for a tapas crawl (*tapeo*). On summer nights the pavements are dense with tourists, locals walking their dogs and elderly *Madrileños* sitting on benches. There are few reminders that this neighbourhood was once home to Cervantes, Lope de Vega, Quevedo and other great writers of the Golden Age, but you can visit Lope de Vega's delightful home, the **Casa-Museo Lope de Vega**, *C Cervantes 11, T91 429 9216, Tue-Sun 1000-1500 (last entry 1400; visits must be booked in advance), free, map C3.*

Below left: Ángel Caído.
Below right top: Palacio de Cristal.
Below right bottom: Parque del Retiro.

Plaza Mayor and around

Metro Sol. Map B3.

The Plaza Mayor is vast, a huge cobbled expanse surrounded by elegant arcades and tall mansions topped with steep slate roofs. When it's bright and sunny, it's packed with terrace cafés, souvenir shops and sun-worshipping tourists; the only time you might see a *Madrileño* in the Plaza Mayor is on a Sunday morning when a stamp and coin market is held here.

Building of the square started in 1617 to designs by Felipe II's favourite architect, Juan de Herrera. This was the ceremonial centre of Madrid, a magnificent backdrop for public spectacles, coronations, executions, markets, bullfights and fiestas. (It is riddled with the subterranean torture chambers of the Inquisition, which used the square for *autos-da-fé*, the trial of suspected heretics.) Before the square was built, a market was traditionally held in front of the **Casa de la Panadería**, the old bakery, which is now the most eye-catching building on the square. It was repainted in 1992 by Carlos Franco who covered it with a hippy-trippy fresco of floating nymphs. Arched passages lead off from here to some of 17th-century Madrid's most important thoroughfares – **Calle Toledo**, **Calle Mayor** and **Calle Segovia**. Other street names still echo the trades that were once carried out here, such as **Calle Cuchilleros** (Street of the Knife Sharpeners), which incorporates part of the old city walls. This is where you'll find the traditional *mesones* (inns), which grew up to cater for merchants and travellers arriving at the city gates. **Casa Botín**, at Cuchilleros 17, opened in the 16th century and claims to be the oldest restaurant in the world.

Palacio Real

C Bailén s/n, T91 454 8803,
www.patrimonionacional.es.
Oct-Mar daily 1000-1800; Apr-Sep daily 1000-2000. €11, €6 concessions, free to EU citizens Oct-Mar Mon-Thu 1600-1800 and Apr-Sep Mon-Thu 1800-2000; guided visits €7, audioguide €4. Free entry with Madrid Capital Bono 48h (see page 187). Metro Opera. Map A2.

Palacio Real Madrid.

All about Almodóvar

Pedro Almodóvar arrived in Madrid in the late 1960s; he was just 16 but he already knew that he wanted to be a film-maker. Franco had closed Spain's only film school, so Almodóvar started making shorts on super-8. In 1978, three years after Franco's death and the year Spain signed a new democratic constitution, he made his first full-length film and began work on *Pepi, Luci, Bom*, whose subsequent success allowed Almodóvar to found his own production company. The Movida Madrileña was just getting into its stride: the city's youth, making up for decades of repression, turned music, fashion, design and art upside down, and no one knew the city's anarchic subculture better than Almodóvar. Madrid has been a recurrent feature of his work ever since, appearing in his movies as regularly as the 'las chicas de Almodóvar', the select band of actresses he favours. In 2000, Almodóvar hit the big time, winning an Oscar for *Todo Sobre Mi Madre* (All About My Mother). The subversive director became the toast of the Hollywood establishment, cementing his success with a string of successful films including *Hable con ella* (Talk to her, 2002), *La Mala Educación* (Bad Education, 2004), *Volver* (2006), *Los Abrazos Rotos* (Broken Embraces, 2009), and *La Piel que Habito* (The Skin I Live In, 2011).

Around the city

In 1734, after a fire destroyed the original Moorish alcázar, Felipe V saw a chance to build something grander and commissioned the most prestigious architects of the day to create this monumental pile. Early plans for a palace four times the size of the current one were rejected but the finished structure is still built on a staggering scale; it's no surprise that Juan Carlos I and family have chosen to live in the more modest Palacio de Zarzuela on the city's outskirts. The visit includes the offical salons, the historic pharmacy, the Royal Armoury and the Picture Gallery. The Royal Palace is used for official functions and can be closed at short notice; if two flags are flying, the King is at home and you won't be allowed in.

El Rastro

C Ribera de Curtidores.
Metro Tirso de Molina or Puerta de Toledo. Map B4.

South of Plaza Mayor, the districts of La Latina and Lavapiés have traditionally been home to Madrid's poorest workers and immigrants. It's here that Madrid's famous flea market, El Rastro, takes place every Sunday morning. Stalls wind all the way up **Calle Ribera de Curtidores** and sell everything from tacky clothes and souvenirs to leather goods, underwear, arts and crafts and kites. The street name means Tanner's Alley and recalls the pungent

El Rastro.

Best of the rest

Monasterio de las Descalzas Reales
Reales 1 Pl de las Descalzas, T91 454 8800, www.patrimonionacional.es. Guided tour only Tue-Sat 1000-1400 and 1600-1830, Sun 1000-1500 (last entry 1hr before close). €7, €4 concessions, free with Madrid Capital Bono 48h (see page 187). Metro Sol.
A 16th-century convent for blue-blooded nuns, with a remarkable collection of tapestries and other artworks.

Museo Arqueológico Nacional
C Serrano 13, Salamanca, T91 577 7912, www.man.mcu.es, Tue-Sat 0930-2030, Sun 0930-1500, free. Metro Serrano.
Spain's most complete archaeological museum, with a collection spanning millennia.

Museo del Traje
Avda de Juan de Herrera 2, T91 550 4700, http://museo deltraje.mcu.es. Metro Moncloa or Ciudad Universitaria. Tue-Sat 0930-1900, Sun 1000-1500, until 2230 Thu in July and Aug. €3, €1.50 concessions, free Sat 1430-1900, Sun.
A slick modern museum dedicated to the history of fashion, set in beautiful gardens and with a stylish café-restaurant.

Parque del Oeste
C Ferraz s/n. Metro Ventura Rodríguez.
This cool, shady park spreads along the western flank of the city, north of the Plaza de España. It's most surprising sight is the Templo de Debod, a 2000-year-old gift from Egypt.

trades which took place down here, out of sight (and smell) of the smart neighbourhoods at the top of the hill. Rastro itself refers to the sticky trail of blood left when the meat carcasses were hauled through the streets. The surrounding shops are mainly devoted to antiques and bric-a-brac, although you'll still find plenty of leather goods, and, although the neighbourhood is still a little shabby, it's in the process of regeneration. The atmosphere on a Sunday is wonderful; after the stallholders have packed up, everyone heads to the surrounding bars for tapas and a well-earned cold beer. Watch out for your bags, though; El Rastro is notorious for pickpockets.

Where to stay

Madrid has an enormous range of accommodation, from swanky upmarket places to family-run *pensiones*. The grander options are mostly concentrated in Salamanca, while the Puerta del Sol area is where you'll find most budget options. If travelling in Jul and Aug, try to find somewhere with a/c. Book as far in advance as possible and bring industrial strength earplugs – Madrid is noisy.

Hotel Urban €€€
Cra de San Jerónimo 34, T91 787 7770, www.hotelurban.com. Metro Sevilla.
One of the city's hottest hotels is set in a striking glassy contemporary building, with ultra-luxurious rooms, a pool, gym, sauna and excellent restaurant.

Orfila €€€
C Orfila 6, Salamanca, T91 702 7770, www.hotelorfila.com. Metro Alonso Martínez.
A luxurious 19th-century mansion offering discreet 5-star luxury. It has a beautiful, flower-scented terrace, a charming salón de té, and a renowned restaurant.

Galiano €€
C Alcalá Galiano 6, Salamanca, T91 319 2000, www.hotelgaliano. com. Metro Colón.
Delightful, antique-filled hotel housed in a (much modernized) former palace, with spacious rooms and a leafy, central location.

Hostal Gala €€
Hostal Gala, Costanilla de los Ángeles, T91 541 9692, www.hostalgala.com.
A handsomely modernized *hostal*, with charming staff, and stylish rooms, some with their own sitting rooms. The amenities include a/c, free Wi-Fi, and use of a microwave and fridge.

Hotel Mario €€
C Campomanes 4, T91 548 8548, www.room-matehoteles.com. Metro Opera.
Part of a small chain of slickly designed hotels, all offering minimalist decor, friendly service, good central locations and excellent value. Recommended.

Abracadabra B&B €
C Bailen 39, T656 859 784, www.abracadabrabandb.com. Metro La Latina.
Handy for the Royal Palace, this friendly and inviting B&B is stuffed with artworks and bric-a-brac gathered from around the world by the globe-trotting owners. Nothing is too much trouble for the staff, and a delicious breakfast is included.

Hostal Cervantes €
C Cervantes 34, Santa Ana, T91 429 8365, www.hostal-cervantes.com. Metro Antón Martín.
A great favourite. Friendly owners have made it feel like a home from home. There's a cosy lounge, each room has been decorated with pretty blue prints and all have en suite bathrooms.

Restaurants

The streets around the Plaza Santa Ana – just 5 mins' walk from the Prado – are densely packed with all kinds of bars and restaurants. There are lots of traditional restaurants around the Plaza Mayor; head to the pretty 19th-century Mercado San Miguel just off the square to find plenty of gourmet tapas bars and produce stands. Some of the cheapest and best tapas bars are in La Latina and Lavapiés.

Cafés and tapas bars
La Perejila
C Cava Baja 25, T91 364 28 55. Metro La Latina.
The house speciality at this charming, convivial tapas bar is delicious *perejilas* (meatballs), but you'll find all the classic Spanish staples plus some more creative options. It's also a great spot for a pre-lunch *vermut* (vermouth).

Lolina Vintage Café
C Espíritu Santo 9, www.lolinacafe.com.
A bright, colourful café-bar in the Malasaña neighbourhood, with retro furnishings, including original handpainted wallpaper from the 1950s. On the menu are salads, quiches, tarts, soups and cakes.

Nightlife

Taberna de la Dolores
Pl de Jesús 4, T91 429 2243.
Daily 1100-0100, Fri and Sat
1100-0200. Metro Antón Martín.
Beautiful, century-old tiled tapas
bar – one of the most *típico* in
the city. The traditional tapas
include Galician-style octopus,
croquetas and *tostadas*.

Restaurants

La Terraza de Casino €€€
La Terraza de Casino,
C Alcalá 15, T91 521 8700,
www.casinodemadrid.es.
Mon-Fri 1330-1600 and
2100-2345, Sat 2100-2345.
Closed Aug and public hols.
This sumptuous 19th-century
building has a stunning
panoramic terrace and contains
one of Madrid's most spectacular
restaurants with Paco Roncero,
a disciple of super-chef Ferran
Adrià, at the helm. The cuisine is
as exciting and creative as you
would expect. Be prepared to pay
around €100 per head for an
unforgettable experience.

Zalacaín €€€
C Álvarez de Baena 4, T91 561 4840.
Mon-Fri 1300-1600, 2100-2400,
Sat 2100-2400.
Metro Gregorio Marañón.
This celebrated formal restaurant
has garnered all kinds of stars and
awards under the direction of chef
Benjamín Urdiáin. The Basque
cuisine is complemented by a
refined setting, perfect service
and a spectacular wine list. Jacket
and tie obligatory for men.

Casa Paco €€
Pl Puerta Cerrada 11, T91 366 3166.
Mon-Sat 1330-1600 and
2000-2400. Metro La Latina.
A resolutely old-fashioned bar
with a restaurant at the back.
Waiters in long aprons serve
hearty stews, Madrileña classics,
and good wines.

Casa Perico €€
C Ballesta 18, T91 532 81 76.
Metro Gran Vía.
Family-run and friendly, this
charmingly old-fashioned spot
serves classic favourites from
succulent grilled meats and
sturdy stews to home-made
rice pudding and *natillas*.

Delic €
Plaza de la Paja s/n, T91 364 54 50,
www.delic.es.
Metro La Latina.
A trendy spot on one of Madrid's
prettiest squares, this arty café
serves light meals and gorgeous
cakes. It morphs into a lively
cocktail bar in the evenings.

La Isla del Tesoro €
C Manuel Malasaña 3,
T91 593 1440.
Daily 1330-1600 and 2000-
2400. Metro Bilbao.
A cheerful spot for vegan,
macrobiotic and vegetarian
food. The *menú del día* (€11)
features the cuisine of a different
country each day.

In Madrid it's possible to start
dancing on Fri night and not
stop until Mon morning. Some
of the best clubs are **Nasti Club**,
C San Vicente Ferrer 33, a popular
underground address for indie
music on Fri and Sat nights; the
gay party Ohm on Fri night at
Bash, *Pl Callao 4*, and Mondo for
funk and electronica on Thu
nights at **Sala Stella**, *C Arlabán 7.*
Elsewhere, the Paseo de
Castellano is famous for its
summer *terrazas* where you can
drink and dance outside. Madrid
also has hundreds of *discobares*
spread all over the city. Santa
Ana and Huertas get packed,
especially in summer, and
though not especially
fashionable *barrios*, you are
guaranteed a good time. The
streets around Plaza de la Paja,
in the Plaza Mayor and Los
Austrias area, are packed with
fancy tapas joints but there's also
a healthy sprinkling of down-to-
earth bars. There are some very
funky bars tucked away in the
old working-class districts of La
Latina and Lavapiés, while to the
north of Gran Vía are 2 formerly
run-down neighbourhoods that
have become the focal point of
the city's heady nightlife: Chueca
is the heart of the gay district
and stuffed with some
ultra-stylish places – such as
Acuarela, *C Gravina 10* and
Liquid, *C Barquillo 8*, while
Malasaña is popular with
students and younger people
looking for a good time. For the

latest news, see www.clubbing spain.com. If you want to catch some flamenco, try the **Casa Patas**, *C Cañizares 10, T913 69 04 96, www.casapatas.com*, or **Cardamomo**, *C Echegaray, 15, T913 69 07 57, www.cardamomo.es*.

Shopping

As a general guide, you can find almost anything you want in the streets around C Preciados: department stores, chain stores and individual shops selling everything from hams to traditional Madrileño cloaks. The northwestern neighbourhoods of Argüelles and Moncloa, particularly around C Princesa, are also good for fashion chains. Smart Salamanca has plenty of designer boutiques and interior decoration shops, while Chueca is full of hip, unusual fashion and music shops.

Arrivals Hall at Barajas Airport.

Travel essentials

Getting there
Madrid's **Barajas Airport** is 12 km northeast of the city (airport information T902 404704, www.aena-aeropuertos.es). The most useful local bus lines into the city centre include No 101 for the Metro de Canillejas, and the No 200 (from all terminals) for Av de América; each costs €1.50. The yellow Exprés Aeropuerto (€5 single) runs 24 hrs a day from Plaza de Cibeles, Atocha station, and terminals T1, T2 and T4. Metro line 8 runs from Terminal 2 and Terminal 4 to Nuevos Ministerios in the city centre (€2). If you'll be using public transport during your stay it's best to get a **Metrobús ticket** (see below), but you'll have to pay a €3 supplement for journeys to and from the airport. Taxi ranks are outside all arrival halls. A taxi into the city costs around €25-30. Long-distance trains (including an overnight service from Paris d'Austerlitz) arrive at **Atocha station** (metro line 1), T902 320 320, www.renfe.com.

Getting around
Almost all Madrid's sights are clustered in the centre, an enjoyable stroll from each other. However, if you're in a hurry, the **buses** and **metro** are cheap, efficient and user-friendly. A few places – the museums dotted around the Salamanca district and the Ventas bullring, for example – are a bit further afield but are all accessible by public transport. A single trip by bus costs €1.30 or €1.50 by metro; the **Metrobús ticket** (which can be shared) costs €12 for 10 journeys. Tourist passes cost €8.40 to €35.40 for 1-7 days' unlimited use of the bus and metro in Zone 1 (the most useful for visitors). You can buy tickets at metro stations; the Metrobús ticket is also sold at tobacconists (estancos). Pick up free bus and metro maps from tourist offices, metro and bus stations. Information in English is available by calling T010 or online at **www.ctm-madrid.es**. Good bus routes for sightseeing include: No 2 from Plaza España, along the Gran Vía to the Retiro; No 3 for an overview of the centre, from Puerta de Toledo to Chueca; No 5 from Puerta del Sol up Paseo de la Castellana to Plaza de Castilla; No 21 down Pintor Rosales in the northeast, through Chueca and to the Ventas bullring.

Tourist information
The main office is in the Casa de la Panadería, Pl Mayor 27, T91 454 4410, daily 0930-2030. There are other branches (all open daily 0930-2030) at Plaza de Colón (underground); Plaza de Cibeles; Plaza de Callao; Paseo del Arte on the corner of C Santa Isabel, and at **Barajas Airport**, Terminals 2 and 4 (daily 0900-2000). Staff can provide a basic map of the city and a copy of *Es Madrid Magazine*, a pocket-sized magazine with helpful local information and listings. There's also a free English-language monthly newspaper *InMadrid* (www.inmadrid.com), with plenty of bar and club listings. Useful websites include: www.madrid.org, www.descubremadrid.com and www.esmadrid.com. The **Madrid Capital Bono 48h** ticket offers free entrance to the Palacio Real de Madrid, Descalzas Reales, Encarnación, Panteón de Hombres Ilustres and the Real Sitio de El Pardo and gardens for €25 (€11 concessions) and is valid for 48 hrs.

Ratings

Art and culture ☆☆☆☆
Eating ☆☆☆
Nightlife ☆☆☆
Shopping ☆☆☆
Sightseeing ☆☆☆
Value for money ☆☆☆
Overall city rating ☆☆☆

Marseille

With its international atmosphere, urban chaos and thriving counter-culture, much of Marseille is exactly what the rest of Western Provence is not: no snoozy afternoons, ambling retirees or seafront promenades here. But for many visitors, this contrast is exactly what makes the city so appealing.

Marseille was the first part of Provence to be colonized by Greek traders in around 600 BC. Over the following two and a half millennia, the city has welcomed wave upon wave of Romans, Jews, Spaniards, North Africans, South Americans and Vietnamese, creating a vibrant ethnic mix and contributing to a strongly innovative culinary tradition. Annual urban festivals crowd the city's calendar to complement its impressive music, theatre and 21st-century art scenes. A huge-scale, long-term urban regeneration project, Euroméditerranée, *www.euromediterranee.fr*, combined with a year as European Capital of Culture in 2013 has endowed Marseille with brand-new exhibition spaces, eateries and accommodation options by the dozen.

Ceiling of Basilique de Notre-Dame-de-la-Garde.

At a glance

Marseille is divided into 16 *arrondissements*, or neighbourhoods. Visitors will spend most of their stay in and around the **Vieux Port**, the city's natural harbour. East of here, Boulevard La Canebière rolls slowly uphill to Palais Longchamp, criss-crossed by popular shopping streets. Just beyond here lies the off-beat district surrounding **cours Julien**, a hub of restaurants, bars and organic produce markets. **Le Panier**, Marseille's pretty old town, is perched just north of the Vieux Port. It's primarily a pedestrian neighbourhood under slow and steady gentrification and is dotted with up-and-coming ateliers. To the west, Marseille's former **docklands** have been completed redeveloped over the past few years and now include a new 3-km seafront esplanade and the long-awaited **Musée des Civilisations de l'Europe et de la Méditerranée** (MuCEM, see page 193). During summer, the action moves southwards, as locals hit the city beach, **Plage des Catalans**, and the **Plages du Prado**, a strip of sand due south of the city centre.

Vieux Port.

Vieux Port

Metro Vieux Port.

It was here that the Greeks are said to have dropped anchor and founded the ancient metropolis of Massalia. Today, Marseille's old port remains the city's hub, and bars and restaurants crowd the pedestrian streets that wind their way through this lively quarter.

The harbour itself is packed with pleasure boats and is flanked by 17th-century **Fort St-Nicolas** and **Fort St-Jean**. Frequent ferries (see page 193) run to the Château d'If and the nearby Calanques. As day breaks, fishermen drag their catch on to the **quai des Belges**, setting up stalls for the daily fish market; chefs and locals soon arrive, shopping for local red mullet, rockfish and the makings of Marseille's classic fish soup, *bouillabaisse.*

Musée Cantini

19 rue Grignan, T04 9154 7775,
http://musee-cantini.marseille.fr.
Tue-Sun 1000-1800. €5.
Metro Estrangin-Préfecture. Map E5.

Located within a beautiful 17th-century former private home (fully renovated in 2013), the Cantini Museum's permanent collection covers the 20th-century masters comprehensively, including works by Paul Signac, Vassily Kandinsky, Picasso and Francis Bacon.

Palais Longchamp

bd Montricher/bd de Longchamp.
Metro Cinq-Avenues-Longchamp, bus 81, T2.
Map H1.

An imposing, colonnaded building, Palais Longchamp was completed in 1869 as a glorious celebration of the city's new aqueduct which brought torrents of drinking water from the Durance River, 80 km inland.

Within one wing of the building, the **Musée d'Histoire Naturelle**, *T04 9114 5950, www.museum-marseille.org, Tue-Sun 1000-1800, €6*, charts the area's indigenous flora, fauna and fossils. The other wing is home to the **Musée des Beaux-Arts**, *T04 9114 5930, http://musee-des-beaux-arts.marseille.fr, Fri-Wed 0900–1900, Thu 1200-2300, entrance fee*

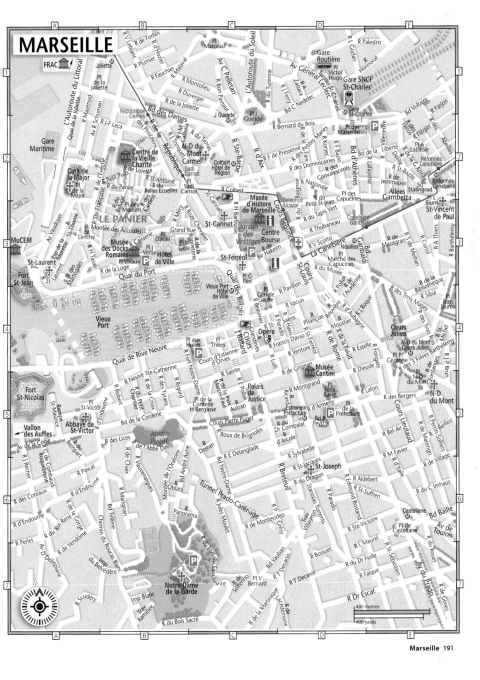

MARSEILLE

Best of the rest

Abbaye de St-Victor
3 rue de l'Abbaye, T04 9611 2260, www.saintvictor.net.
Daily 0900-1900. Basilica free, crypts €2.
Metro Vieux Port, bus 82, 83. Map B5.
On the southern side of the Vieux Port, this 13th-century abbey houses a creepy necropolis, as well as the famous 'Black Madonna' statue.

Fonds Régional d'Art Contemporain de Marseille (FRAC)
20 bvd de Dunkerque, T04 9191 2755, www.fracpaca.org.
Tue-Sat 1000-1800, Sun 1400-1800. €5.
Metro and tram Joliette, bus 35, 49, 82.
Designed by Japanese architect Kengo Kuma, the new FRAC shelters one of Marseille's finest contemporary art venues.

Musée Grobet-Labadié
Bvd Longchamp, T04 9162 2182, http://musee-grobet-labadie.marseille.fr. Tue-Sun 1000-1800. €5.
Metro Cinq-Avenues, tram Longchamp, bus 81. Map H1.
Just south of Palais Longchamp, this quirky former home shows how well-heeled locals of the previous century lived.

Vallon des Auffes
Bus 83.
Petite, pastel and a striking contrast to Marseille's often-gritty streets, this neighbourhood southwest of the old port has fishing boats, charming cottages and sublime restaurants.

varies, which reopened in 2013 after more than seven years of renovations. Blockbuster exhibitions, such as the recent 'Le Grand Atelier du Midi: Van Gogh a Bonnard', are now held here.

Le Panier

Metro Vieux Port.

A warren of steeply inclined alleys makes up Le Panier, Marseille's original old town, located on the north side of the Vieux Port. This was the area first settled by the Greeks. The name ('the breadbasket') may date back to a market.

An association with poverty plus waves of immigration gave Le Panier an edgy reputation.

In 1943, occupying Nazis believed the area to be a bastion of Resistance fighters and gave 24 hours' notice before bombing half the district to rubble: the legacy of this destruction can be seen in the 1950s architecture that swamps the neighbourhood's southern side.

Le Panier is still home to a sprinkling of historical sights, including tiny **Eglise St-Laurent** (map B3) and the 19th-century **Cathédrale de la Major** (map B2/3), said to have been inspired by Istanbul's Hagia Sophia. At Le Panier's highest point are three remaining stone bases from the 15 16th-century windmills that once crowned pretty **place des Moulins** (map C3).

Centre de la Vieille Charité

2 rue de la Charité.
Tram République Dames, bus 55, T2. Map C2.

Designed as a poor house during the 17th century, la Vieille Charité came close to condemnation during the mid-20th century. It was only through the ambitious efforts of architect Le Corbusier that the magnificent structure – four pale, arcaded wings around a freestanding chapel – still exists. Today, the centre houses the **Musée d'Archéologie Méditerranéenne**, *T04 9114 5859, www.marseille.fr, Tue-Sun 1000-1800, €5*, home to a large ancient Egyptian collection, and the **Musée d'Arts Africains, Océaniens et Amérindiens (MAAOA)**, *T04 9114 5838, www.marseille.fr, Tue-Sun 1000-1800, €5*, as well as the art house cinema, Le Miroir.

Le Panier.

Musée des Civilisations de l'Europe et de la Méditerranée (MuCEM)

1 esplanade du J4, T04 8435 1313, www.mucem.org.
Summer Wed-Thu and Sat-Mon 1100-1900, Fri 1100-2200; winter Wed-Thu and Sat-Mon 1100-1800, Fri 1100-2200. €5; additional fee for temporary exhibitions.
Metro Vieux Port, buses 49, 60 and 82. Map A3.

Sprawling over the refreshed 17th-century Fort St-Jean, its various gardens and a cubic, concrete, lace-effect edifice designed by architect Rudy Riciotti, MuCEM has taken Marseille by storm since it opened to the public during summer 2013. The museum showcases folk art, culture and traditions of the Mediterranean. After absorbing the wealth of culture, stop for a break at Michelin-starred chef Gérard Passédat's superb onsite restaurant, La Table du Môle (*www.passedat.fr*).

Basilique de Notre-Dame-de-la-Garde

Rue Fort du Sanctuaire, T04 9113 4080, www.notredamedelagarde.com.
Apr-Sep daily 0700-1915; Oct-Mar daily 0700-1815. Free. Bus 60. Map C7.

Also referred to as 'La Bonne Mère' ('the Good Mother'), the cathedral's 10-m gilded Madonna has been casting a protective eye over the city's fishermen since its consecration in 1864.

Château d'If

T06 0306 2526, www.if.monuments-nationaux.fr.
Daily mid-May to mid-Sep 0930-1810; mid-Sep to mid-Mar Tue-Sun 0930-1645; Apr-May daily 0930-1645. €5.50.

Built under François I in 1524, Château d'If served as both an island fortress and a prison, but it's perhaps best known as the fictional setting for Alexandre Dumas' *Le Comte de Monte-Cristo*. To visit the Château, hop aboard the **Frioul If Express**, *1 quai des Belges, T04 9611 0350, www.frioul-if-express. com, €10.10 return*, a frequent ferry service that runs from the Vieux Port.

Travel essentials

Getting there
Marseille Provence Airport, T04 4214 1414, www.marseille-airport.com, is 25 km west of the city centre. Its second hanger-type terminal, MP2, is used by budget airlines. Shuttle buses, www.navettemarseilleaeroport.com, run between the airport and Marseille's bus station (map E1) next to Gare St-Charles, every 15-20 mins (25 mins). High-speed trains from Paris and Lille (connections to Eurostar) arrive at **Gare St-Charles** (map E1/2).

Getting around
Marseille is a hilly town, although the energetic will have no problem navigating the downtown area on foot. There are two **metro lines**, www.rtm.fr, linking Gare St-Charles with the Vieux Port (M1) or the Stade Vélodrome and points south (M2). There are also two tram lines and an extensive network of buses. The same ticket is valid for travel on buses, trams or on the metro; a single ride on any of these costs €1.50. If you plan to make significant use of public transport, it's worth buying a carnet of tickets (10 rides €13). You can buy tickets in metro stations, on the bus or from automatic kiosks at each tram stop.

Tourist information
Marseille's tourist information office is located at 11 la Canebière, T0826 500 500, www.marseille-tourisme.com, daily 0900-1900. If you plan to buckle down for some heavy sightseeing, pick up a **City Pass**, which offers free entrance to more than a dozen sights, return boat trips to Château d'If and all public transport for one (€22) or two days (€29).

Where to stay

Hôtel-Dieu €€€
1 pl Daviel, T04 1342 4242,
www.ihg.com.
Metro Vieux-Port.
Opened in 2013, the 5-star Hotel
Dieu stretches over a former
18th-century hospital. Its sleek
guest rooms have superb views
over the Vieux Port.

Hôtel Le Corbusier €€
280 bd Michelet, T04 9116 7800,
www.hotellecorbusier.com.
Metro Rond-Point-du-Prado.
Designed by Swiss architect Le
Corbusier in the late 1940s. Cabin
rooms and studios are spread
over 2 floors, and there's a brand-
new contemporary art space,
MAMO (www.mamo.fr), on the
hotel's rooftop.

Hôtel Péron €€
119 corniche JF Kennedy, T04
9131 0141, www.hotelperon.com.
Bus 83.

Friendly, family-run spot
between downtown Marseille
and Vallon des Auffes. Funky
1960s decor throughout; best
are the corner rooms, which
look out over Château d'If.

Mama Shelter €€
64 rue de la Loubière, T04 8435
2000, www.mamashelter.com.
Metro Notre Dame du Mont.
Tucked into the offbeat cours
Julien quarter, this sunny
enclave – complete with
contemporary guestrooms
and an on-site pastis bar –
was created by innovative
designer Philippe Starck.

Aux Vieux Panier €€-€
13 rue du Panier, T04 9191 2372,
www.auvieuxpanier.com.
Metro Vieux Port, tram Sadi
Carnot.
This Le Panier bed and breakfast
boasts just 5 contemporary rooms,
each one designed by a different
international artist. Panoramic
rooftop terrace to boot.

Restaurants

Breakfast
Green Bear Coffee €
17 rue Glandevès, T04 9104 0691,
www.greenbearcoffee.com.
Mon-Sat 1100-1530.
Metro Vieux Port.
All-organic, tiny brunch bar
tucked behind the Vieux Port.
Daily offerings include a choice
of savoury tarts and a gluten-free
apple *tarte tatin.*

Oscar's €
8 quai Rive Neuve, T04 9133 2886.
Daily 1000-2130.
Metro Vieux Port.
The Vieux Port's favourite New
York-style locale, serving up
bagels, doughnuts and big cups
of coffee.

Lunch
Bar de la Marine €€
15 quai de Rive Neuve, T04 9154
9542. Daily 0700-0200.
Metro Vieux Port.
This portside bar featured in
Marcel Pagnol's novels, *Marius,*
Fanny, and *César.* Good salads
('La Marine' features red mullet,
sardines and salmon) and
steak haché.

Le Grain du Sel €€
39 rue de la Paix Marcel Paul,
T04 9154 4730.
Tue-Sat 1200-1400, Fri-Sat
2000-2200. Metro Vieux Port.
Produce at Chef Pierre Giannetti's
innovative eatery is farm-fresh, and
lunchtime menus (€15.50-18.50)
are a steal. Highly recommended.

Dinner
Restaurant Le Rhul €€€
269 corniche J F Kennedy,
T04 9152 5454, www.hotel-
restaurant-le-rhul.com.
Daily 1200-1400 and 1900-2200.
Bus 83.
One of the city's top spots to dine
on traditional fish stew, *bouillabaisse*.
As favoured by Jacques Chirac
and French celebrities.

Toinou €€
3 cours St-Louis, T08 1145 4545,
www.toinou.com.
Daily 1100-2300.
Metro Vieux Port.
Oysters, urchins, crab and plenty
more at this relaxed seafood
specialist, a Marseillaise favourite
for over 4 decades.

Chez Etienne €
43 rue de Lorette.
Mon-Sat 1230-1400 and
2000-2300. Metro Vieux Port,
tram Sadi Carnot.
Tucked away in Le Panier,
Etienne's brief yet delectable
menu includes anchovy and
cheese pizza, squid, *côte de bœuf*
and a smattering of starters.

Shopping

As the South of France's largest city, it's little surprise that
Marseille is packed with plenty of spots that will keep retail
junkies thoroughly thrilled.

Packed with one-off boutiques, galleries, bars and terraced
restaurants, the neighbourhood around pedestrianized **cours Julien**
is a great place to window shop, while **rue Paradis** and **rue St-Ferréol**
are lined with high-end boutiques. For lamps, furnishings and
kitchenware from the 1950s, try **d+ design**, *52 rue de Lorette*;
architecture fiends will adore the tomes on sale at **Librairie-Galerie
Imbernon**, *280 bd Michelet, Le Corbusier 357, www.editionsimbernon.
com.* For dashing, Asian-inspired threads, head to **Antoine & Lili**,
38 rue Montgrand, www.antoineetlili.com; while the brand-new **Les
Baigneuses**, *3 rue de l'Eveche, www.lesbaigneuses.com*, stocks their
own unique range of beautifully retro swimwear.

Top regional souvenirs range from locally produced soaps
at **La Compagnie de Provence Marseille**, *18 rue Francis Davso,
www.compagniedeprovence.com*, to navettes, the city's famous
orange-blossom biscuits at **Four des Navettes**, *136 rue Sainte,
www.fourdesnavettes.com*. Note that most shops are open Mon
or Tue to Sat from around 1000 until 1900.

Nightlife

Get the local late-night lowdown
with one of these free newspapers: *L'Hebdo* (French,
www.marseillehebdo.com),
COTE (French/English, www.
cotemagazine.com) or *Ventilo*
(French, www.journalventilo.fr).
La Caravelle, *34 quai du Port,
www.lacaravelle-marseille.com*,
shakes up aperitifs and amazing
tapas overlooking the Vieux Port,
while petite vodka bar **Le
Polikarpov**, *24 cours Honoré
d'Estienne d'Orves, www.
lepolikarpov.com*, boasts
temporary art installations and
live DJs most weekends. Jazz fans
should hit **Le Cri du Port**, *8 rue du
Pasteur Heuzé, www.criduport.fr*,

or **Le Pelle-Mêle**, *8 pl aux Huiles*,
for regular live concerts.
Late-night clubbing favourites
include the **New Cancan**, *3-7 rue
Sénac, www.newcancan.com*, the
city's best gay club, and port-side
Trolleybus, *24 quai Rive Neuve,
www.letrolley.com*.
The **Opéra Municipal de
Marseille**, *2 rue Molière, http://
opera.marseille.fr*, showcases
opera and ballet performances;
Théâtre National de la Criée,
*30 quai Rive Neuve, www.theatre-
lacriee.com*, stages premier
theatre within the city's former
fish market. For both club nights
and theatre performances, also
check out the alternative arts
centre **La Friche la Belle de Mai**,
41 rue Jobin, www.lafriche.org.

Ratings

Art and culture ☆☆☆
Eating ☆☆☆☆
Nightlife ☆☆☆☆☆
Shopping ☆☆☆☆☆☆
Sightseeing ☆☆
Value for money ☆
Overall city rating ☆☆☆

Milan

The epitome of style and sleek design, Milan's often grey, subdued city streets are an unlikely backdrop for its glitzy population of models, designers and chic businessmen. This northern Italian metropolis is a functional modern mix of football, fast cars, money and separatist politics, where industriousness is held in high esteem. Milan, however, is a city with hidden beauty. The city's courtyards, if you manage to catch a glimpse of them, are famously attractive. The city's most jaw-dropping vistas can be taken in from the roof of the Duomo. And there is a lively Milanese cultural life, too – from the grand opera of La Scala to hip modern music venues. As a city, Milan goes against what its fashion industry might suggest: in the end, it's what's under the surface that counts.

Galleria Vittorio Emanuele II.

Around the city

The **Duomo**, *piazza del Duomo, T02 7202 2656, www.duomomilano.it, daily 0700-1900, free; access to roof daily 0900-1900 (until 2200 in summer), €12 lift, €7 steps, Metro Duomo,* is the centrepoint of the city. Started in 1386, the mammoth cathedral was not completed until Napoleon ordered the addition of the façade in the 19th century. Intricately Gothic, the pale marble building has over 3000 statues, many on tall slender spires, best appreciated from the roof. Inside, a nail purportedly from Christ's cross hangs from the ceiling.

A cathedral to the gods of shopping sits right beside the Duomo. The grand **Galleria Vittorio Emanuele II** links the northern side of the piazza del Duomo with the piazza della Scala, location of the world-famous opera house. A vast, cross-shaped, vaulted arcade, it was opened by the eponymous first king of Italy in 1867. It is now filled with pricey cafés and equally expensive shops. Milanesi come to strut and stroll; tourists come to marvel at the enormity of the place and, near the centre, to spin on the balls of the mosaic bull (a symbol of nearby Turin) for good luck.

South of the cathedral sits the city's newest cultural addition, the **Museo del Novecento**, *Palazzo dell'Arengario, via Marconi 1, T02 4335 3522, www.museodelnovecento.org, Mon 1430-1930, Tue-Wed, Fri and Sun 0930-1930, Thu and Sat 0930-2230, €5,* which houses a superb collection of 20th-century Italian art, including works by Modigliani, Morandi and De Chirico.

Radiating out from the Duomo are several pedestrianized shopping streets, such as corso Vittorio Emanuele II, though the highest concentration of designer togs is to be found in the Quadrilatero della Moda, a neighbourhood just north of here that's encompassed by via Manzoni, via della Spiga, via Monte Napoleone and via Sant'Andrea. Both the **Giardini Pubblici**, a public park boasting a kids' playground and pony rides, and the **Galleria d'Arte Moderna**, *Villa Reale, via Palestro 16, T02 8844 5947, www.gam-milano.com, Tue-Sun 0900-1300 and 1400-1730, free, Metro Palestro,* sit to the northeast. The latter houses works by Renoir, Picasso and Matisse in Napoleon's one-time residence. Beyond the Giardini Pubblici is Stazione Centrale, the city's central train station.

To the northwest of the Duomo is the imposing façade of **Castello Sforzesco**, *piazza Castello 3, T02 8846 3700, www.milanocastello.it, various museums*

Roof of the Duomo.

Tue-Sun 0900-1730, €3, free Fri after 1400, Metro Cairoli, Cardorna Triennale or Lanza, which houses half a dozen smaller museums dedicated to ancient art, Egyptian artifacts, antique musical instruments and archaeology. The grounds surrounding the castle form the city's largest public park, Parco Sempione, with the outstanding **Triennale Design Museum**, viale Alemagna 6, T02 724 341, www.triennale.it, Tue-Wed and Fri-Sun 1030-2030, Thu 1030-2300, €8, sitting at its heart.

Between the castle and the Giardini Pubblici, the area of Brera has some of the city's oldest and most interesting streets and an excellent gallery in the **Pinacoteca di Brera**, Via Brera 28, T02 7226 3264, www.brera.beniculturali.it, Tue-Sun 0830-1915, €6, Metro Lanza. Highlights include paintings by Raphael, Caravaggio and Bellini.

Leonardo da Vinci's Last Supper, known as the **Il Cenacolo Vinciano**, T02 9280 0360, www.cenacolo vinciano.net, Tue-Sun 0815-1830, €8, book by telephone or online, Metro Conciliazone, Cadorna Triennale, is located in the refectory of the Convent of Santa Maria delle Grazie, to the west of the centre. The already enormous popularity of Leonardo's innovative and dramatic masterpiece has been enhanced by the success of The Da Vinci Code and visitors must book a week in advance for their chance to see it. Most hotels in Milan will be happy to make a booking by telephone on behalf of their guests.

To the south of the centre, the **Navigli** still has remnants of Milan's old canal system and has become one of the best areas of the city for eating, drinking and shopping.

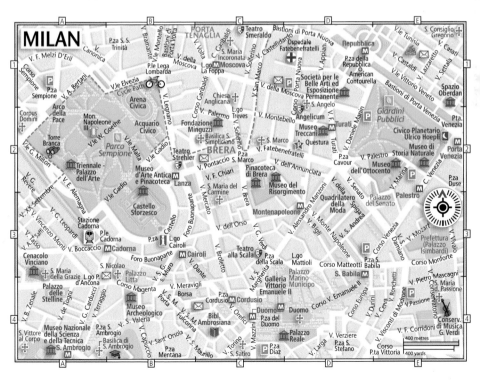

Where to stay

Many of the cheaper places to stay are in the area east of the station. Central hotels tend to be on the expensive side and often cater to a business clientele.

Château Monfort €€€
corso Concordia 1, T02 776761, www.hotelchateaumonfort.com.
Just east of the Quadrilatero della Moda, this sumptuous hotel combines sleek contemporary design with seriously romantic touches. There's a luxurious Pañpuri spa on site too.

The Yard €€€-€€
piazza XXIV Maggio 8, T02 8941 5901, www.theyardmilano.com.
Visitors with an eye for design should make a beeline for this guesthouse in the Navigli neighbourhood. There are 9 suites and 3 small apartments. Antique travel posters add to the funky ambience.

Antica Locanda Leonardo €€
corso Magenta 78, T02 4801 4197, www.anticalocandaleonardo.com.
A traditional, smart and friendly place west of the centre, with wooden floors, a garden and contemporary art.

Ariston €€
largo Carrobbio 2, T02 7200 0556, www.aristonhotel.com.
Bio-architecturally designed, though a little blandly, the Ariston purifies the Milanese air. Bicycles are available for guests to use and it's only 400 m from the Duomo.

Hotel Charly €€-€
via Settala 76, T02 204 7190, www.hotelcharly.com.
Located just a 5-min stroll from Stazione Centrale, it offers basic, relatively inexpensive rooms in 2 adjacent villas overlooking a leafy garden.

Restaurants

The Brera area is home to many of Milan's best restaurants. The Navigli, to the south, offers traditional, down-to-earth places.

10 Corso Como €€€
corso Como 10, T02 2901 3581, www.10corsocomo.com.
Closed Mon.
A complex incorporating a café, photography gallery, bookshop, and fashion and perfume boutiques, Corso Como 10 really comes into its own in the evenings, when the who's who of Italian fashion troop into its courtyard restaurant to consume trendy food. It's also a good – if pricey – spot for breakfast.

Al Pont de Ferr €€
ripa di Porta Ticinese 55, T02 8940 6277, www.pontdeferr.it.
Since being awarded a Michelin star in 2012, chef Matias Perdomo's country-style cooking is perhaps a little more gourmet. However patrons still relish his good-value, traditional dishes, such as steamed baccalà salt cod, or Sicilian scallops.

Joia €€
via Panfilo Castaldi 18, T02 2952 2124, www.joia.it.
Closed Sun.
A rarity in Italy: a hip, inventive, gastronomic vegetarian eatery.

Latteria San Marco €
via San Marco 24, T02 659 7653.
Closed Sat and Sun.
A small traditional eatery in an ex-dairy in Brera serving a changing menu of Milanese food. Popular with locals and good for lunch; be prepared to wait.

Spontini €
corso Buenos Aires 60, T02 204 7444, www.pizzeriaspontini.it.
The enormously thick and tasty pizza slices in this popular and noisy place only come in 2 versions – big and bigger. There's good beer on tap, and it's handy for hotels near the station.

Nightlife

The tourist office produces the bilingual monthly *Milanomese*, with details of events and concerts. You can download a copy from their website.

Bars and clubs
At *aperitivo* time, many bars offer free nibbles with your drink and these can sometimes constitute a meal in themselves. Later on, Milan has a wider selection of nightclubs than most Italian cities, as well as some hip bars.

Most clubs stay open until at least 0400. Bars tend to close between midnight and 0200. The best areas for bars are **Brera** (the most unconventional), the **Navigli** (good on summer evenings when the area is closed to traffic) and **corso Como** (the hippest). Notable nightspots include iconic **Plastic**, *via Gargano 15*, purportedly a favourite venue of Andy Warhol, Freddie Mercury and Prince; and fashion-tastic **Hollywood**, *corso Como 15, www.discoteca hollywood.com*, which pulls in footballers and models. In summer much of the nightlife decamps to **Idroscalo**, a lake near Linate airport.

Opera
Teatro alla Scala
Via Filodrammatici 2, T02 7200 3744, www.teatroallascala.org. Probably the world's most famous opera house. Tickets, costing €13-210, can be booked online.

Travel essentials

Getting there
Malpensa, T02 232 323, www.sea-aeroportimilano.it, Milan's main airport, is connected to the central station by bus every 20 mins (www.malpensa shuttle.it, journey time around 50 mins, €10 one-way, €16 return). A taxi costs a fixed rate of €90, or you can travel by train every 30 mins (www. malpensaexpress.it, 40 mins to Cadorna station, €11 single, €15 return). **Linate airport**, T02 232 323, www.sea-aeroportimilano.it, the most central, is connected to piazza San Babila by city bus 73 every 10 mins (www.atm-mi.it, about 30 mins, €1.50). Alternatively, Starfly buses run between Linate and the central station every 30 mins (€4). A taxi to the centre costs around €25. **Orio al Serio**, www.orioaeroporto.it, just outside Bergamo and used by Ryanair, has 3 bus connections to Milan central station, approximately every 30 mins, with Autostradale (www.airportbusexpress.it, €9, pay in advance or book online), Orio Shuttle (www.orioshuttle.com, from €3.50, book online) and Terravision (www.terravision.eu. International trains (including TGVs and sleeper services from Paris) arrive at **Milano Centrale**, piazza Duca d'Aosta, www.trenitalia.com.

Getting around
Much of the city centre's main sights are within easy walking distance of the Duomo. The **metro** (www.atm-mi.it) is an efficient way of getting to and from the station, or down to the Navigli. There are 4 colour-coded lines: red, lavender, green and yellow. Single tickets (€1.50) allow travel on buses and trams for 90 mins but only one metro journey. Day tickets (€4.50) give the freedom to use any mode of transport.

Tourist information
The main tourist office, T02 7740 4343, www.visitamilano.it, is at piazza Castello 1, just outside Castello Sforzesco.

Shopping

The line between Milanese street and catwalk is a fine one and it's not hard to spot the fashion set striding with hauteur around the city centre. The most famous area for Milan's designer clothing industry is the **Quadrilatero della Moda** or **Quadrilatero d'Oro** (Golden Square), an area just to the north of piazza della Scala. This neighbourhood has all the big names from Armani to Zenga and should be visited just for some window gazing Other parts of the city are also worth visiting: the more leftfield **Navigli** is excellent for bargains, as is **corso Buenos Aires**, east of the station. **Via Durini** has some pretty slick Italian designer kitchenware and furniture stores.

Ratings

Art and culture ☆☆☆☆☆
Eating ☆☆☆☆
Nightlife ☆☆
Shopping ☆☆
Sightseeing ☆☆☆☆☆
Value for money ☆☆☆☆
Overall city rating ☆☆☆

Naples

Naples, wedged between the world's most famous volcano and the deep blue sea, is beautiful and ugly in equal measure. A world away from the genteel islands of Ischia and Capri that grace its bay, the city can be intimidating: it's anarchic and only sporadically law-abiding; the traffic is terrible, and peace and quiet are hard to find. But it's an amazingly vivacious city; the pizzas are fantastic; music is ingrained in its culture; its natural setting is extraordinary, and the treasure trove of historical and artistic sights hidden away in its narrow streets is overwhelming. Ask an Italian from the north about Naples, and they will throw up their hands in despair. But probe these gentrified folk a little more, and they may start to reveal a fascination with the siren-like capital of the south.

Neapolitan graffiti.

Around the city

Santa Lucia

The grandest part of the city is around the giant
and slightly barren **piazza del Plebiscito**, with
its curved colonnade and vast, imposing space
dotted with kids playing football. Vesuvius can
be glimpsed between the grand 17th- and
18th-century buildings. The **Palazzo Reale**,
*T848 800 288, www.palazzorealenapoli.it, Thu-Tue
0900-1900, Royal Apartments €4, palace courtyard
and gardens free, map C5*, was built at the beginning
of the 17th century for Spanish viceroys and
extended by the Bourbons in the 18th century.
Behind the church of **San Francesco di Paolo**, the
hill of Monte di Dio is where the original settlement
of Parthenope was founded in around 680 BC by
Greeks from nearby Cuma; tightly packed housing
now characterizes the area. One of Naples'
smartest shopping areas, **Via Chiaia**, runs north of
the hill to piazza Trento e Trieste, the location of
Naples' great opera house, **Teatro di San Carlo**,
*T081 797 2468, www.teatrosancarlo.it, Mon-Sat
1030-1230, 1430-1630, Sun 1100-1230, €5*, tours
throughout the day except during performances.

South of Santa Lucia, **Castel dell Ovo**, *Mon-Sat
0830-1800, Sun 0830-1345, free*, juts out into the bay.
The island was first fortified by the Romans, but the
current structure dates from the 15th century. The
surrounding jetties, houses, restaurants and bars on
Borgo Marinari are heaving on summer evenings.

Centro Storico

This is the true heart of Naples; its dark, narrow
streets are greasy, irregularly paved and
overflowing with scooters, people and noise. Now
a UNESCO World Heritage Site, the area still follows
the ancient Greek and Roman layout of Neapolis,
with three main east–west streets, or *decumani*.
Long, straight **Spaccanapoli** ('split Naples') is made
up of vias Benedetto Croce, San Biagio dei Librai
and Vicaria Vecchia, and was once the *decumanus
inferior* of the Greek city, while **via dei Tribunali**
to the north was the *decumanus major*.

The most interesting part of Spaccanapoli begins
at piazza del Gesù, with the late 16th-century Jesuit

church of **Gesù Nuovo**, *T081 557 8111, daily 0630-1300, 1600-1900, map C3.* Its brutal armoured exterior gives little hint of its spectacular interior. Next up, away from the chaotic plethora of bars, restaurants and small shops, are the city's inconceivably peaceful and colourfully tiled 14th-century cloisters of **Santa Chiara**, *via Santa Chiara 49/c, T081 797 1231, www. monasterodisantachiara.com, Mon-Sat 0930-1730, Sun 1000-1430, €6, map C3.*

Other highlights of the Centro Storico include three 17th- and 18th-century spires or obelisks, which look like enormously elongated wedding cakes: **Guglia dell'Immacolata** in piazza del Gesù, **Guglia di San Domenico Maggiore**, in a piazza of the same name, and **Guglia di San Gennaro**, in piazza Riario Sforza, adjacent to the Duomo. The

13th-century **Duomo**, *via del Duomo 149, Mon-Fri 0800-1230, 1630-1900, Sun 0800-1330, 1700-1930, Scavi del Duomo €3, map D2,* is slightly less of a focus than cathedrals in other Italian cities but still a grand building. Its chapels are especially interesting, one holding the famous remains of San Gennaro, the city's patron saint. Another, the fourth-century Cappella di Santa Restituta, is one of the city's oldest buildings. Under the building, in the Scavi del Duomo, some fascinating ancient remains have been unearthed.

Cappella Sansevero, *via de Sanctis 19, T081 551 8470, www.museosansevero.it, Wed-Sat and Mon 1000-1740, Sun 1000-1310, €7, map C3,* originally built in 1590 but remodelled in the 18th century, is also worth a visit for some virtuoso allegorical marble

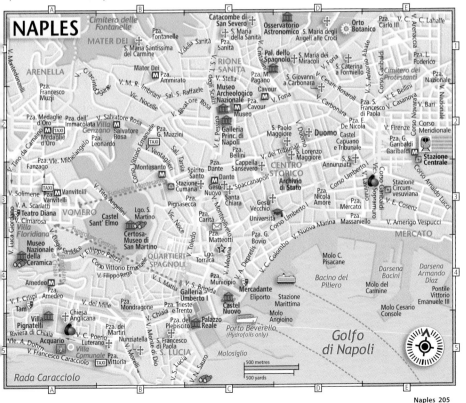

sculptures, notably *Disillusion* by Francisco Queirolo (1704-1762), and an amazingly life-like *Veiled Christ* (1753) by Giuseppe Sanmartino.

Amongst numerous places to wander, via **San Gregorio Armeno**, running north perpendicular to Spaccanapoli, is worth a visit. All year round, shops spill their wares out onto the pavements: thousands upon thousands of nativity scene figures vie for space with models of fruit baskets, mini electrically pumped water features and the occasional mechanized man drinking beer or chopping meat. Above you, angels suspended from ceilings and doorways stare down lovingly.

Quartieri Spagnoli and Via Toledo

Via Toledo, Naples' bustling high street, runs between piazza del Plebiscito and piazza Dante. To its west, the narrow streets of the Quartieri Spagnoli are among the city's poorest areas and form the Camorra heartland. There's a fascinating **market** every day on via Pignasecca towards piazza Montesanto. Via Toledo, meanwhile, heads north to the **Museo Archeologico Nazionale di Napoli**, *piazza Museo 19, T081 440 1466, www.cir.campania.beniculturali.it, Wed-Mon 0900-1930, €6.50, map C2*. From enormous grandiose marble statues to small homely paintings, and from erotic oil lamps to a mosaic made of a million pieces, this is a staggering collection and gives an insight into the look and feel of the ancient Roman world.

Mercato di Porta Nolana

Map E3.

Just to the west of the **Circumvesuviana Terminal**, this extraordinary piece of Neapolitan theatre spills out every morning onto via Cesare Carmignano and via Sopramuro. It's a heady mix of fish, fruit and veg, pirated DVDs, bread, olives, contraband cigarettes, cheap beer, toy helicopters and fishing rods.

La Sanità and Capodimonte

Beyond the Museo Archeologico the road continues to the fine, green Parco di Capodimonte, where the **Reggia di Capodimonte**, *via Capodimonte, T081 749*

Top: Palazzo Reale.
Bottom: Villa Comunale Park.

Pompeii and Herculaneum

There's a reason why Pompeii is the most famous of Vesuvius' victims. It may not be as well preserved as Herculaneum, but its sheer scale is staggering. Here is an entire Roman town, once home to as many as 20,000 people, ruined, yes, but in many ways extraordinarily intact; a city stopped dead in its tracks in AD 79. Much of the wonder of the place is to be had simply by strolling around, looking into ordinary houses. Some of the most prosaic aspects are also the most arresting: tracks on the roads where carts have worn down the stones, shop signs advertizing their wares, mosaics warning you to 'beware of the dog'. *T081 857 5347, www.pompeiisites.org. Apr-Oct 0830-1930, last entry 1800; Nov-Mar 0830-1700, last entry 1530. €11, 3-day ticket for Pompeii, Herculaneum, Oplontis and Stabia €20.*

Deep below the level of the surrounding contemporary city, Herculaneum (Ercolano) is extraordinarily unscathed. Much more than Pompeii's mixture of ash and pumice, Herculaneum's mud solidified and sealed the town below, preserving organic substance and the upper storeys of houses. *Corso Resina 6, Ercolano, T081 857 5347. Apr-Oct 0830-0730, last entry 1800; Nov-Mar 0830-1700, last entry 1530. €11.*

9111, www.museo-capodimonte.it, Thu-Tue 0830-1930, €7.50 (1400-1700, €6.50), houses the Bourbon and the Farnese art collections. On a bus there you might not even notice Dickensian **La Sanità**. Home to the city's ancient catacombs, it lies below and is bypassed by the bridge built by the French in 1808.

Chiaia, Mergellina and Posillipo

To the west of the centre the genteel Caracciolo seafront curves around to the yacht-filled marina of Mergellina, beyond which rises the exclusive residential area of Posillipo. Chiaia is a more laid-back area of bars, cafés and restaurants and some green spaces, notably the **Villa Comunale** park.

Certosa di San Martino

Largo San Martino 5, T081 229 4541, www.polomusealenapoli.beniculturali.it. Thu-Tue 0830-1930. €6.

Perched high above Naples, in Vomero, is this 14th-century Carthusian monastery with exceptional views. It now houses the excellent **Museo di San Martino** and is one of Naples' most satisfying sights, containing interesting paintings, an elegant cloister, an exhibition of *presepi* (nativity scenes), one of Naples' most spectacular churches and terraced gardens. The hulking **Castel Sant'Elmo** is next door.

Where to stay

Costantinopoli 104 €€€
*via S Maria di Costantinopoli
104, T081 557 1035,
www.costantinopoli104.com.*
Near piazza Bellini, this pristine
and stylish place has a tranquil
courtyard garden with a small
pool. Don't miss one of its
famously good breakfasts.

Caravaggio €€
*piazza Riario Sforza 157,
T081 211 0066,
www.caravaggio hotel.it.*
Modern rooms in a 17th-
century building. Cosy feel
and amiable staff.

Soggiorno Sansevero €€
*via Foria 42, T081 033 1012,
www.albergosansevero.it.*
In the heart of the Centro Storico,
large rooms in a handsome old
palazzo at a good price.

Hotel Piazza Bellini €€
*via Santa Maria di
Costantinopoli 101, T081 451732,
www.hotelpiazzabellini.com.*
Situated in an 18th-century palazzo,
this central hotel has contemporary
rooms, some with good views of
the city, and free Wi-Fi.

The Fresh Glamour €
*via Donnalbina 7, T081 020 2255,
www.thefresh.it.*
Unfussy modern rooms in the
heart of Naples, some suitable
for families.

Restaurants

Pizzeria Brandi €€
*salita Sant'Anna di Palazzo 1-2,
T081 416 928, www.brandi.it.*
Daily 1230-1500, 1930-0100.
Inventors of the ubiquitous pizza
Margherita. Also has a selection
of traditional Neapolitan fare.

Caffè Letterario Intra Moenia €
*piazza Bellini 70, T081 451 652,
www.intramoenia.it.*
Daily 1000-0200.
A literary café with a
decent menu and a cultured
atmosphere. Exhibitions, literary
meetings, concerts and poetry
evenings happen here and
there's also internet access.

Da Michele €
*via Sersale 1, T081 553 9204,
www.damichele.net.*
Mon-Sat 1000-2400.

The purists' pizzeria supreme.
There are 2 choices, Margherita
or Marinara, and service is
lightning quick with no frills.

La Cantina di Via Sapienza €
*via Sapienza 40/41, T081 459 078,
www.cantinadiviasapienza.it.*
Mon-Sat 1200-1530.
Great home cooking in a popular
lunch-only eatery. Try a delicious
and great-value bowl of *penne
aum aum*, with tomato,
aubergine and mozzarella.

La Vecchia Cantina €
*vico San Nicola alla Carità 14,
T081 552 0226.*
Mon and Wed-Sat 1200-1600,
1900-2200, Sun 1200-1600.
Busy, traditional family place
with lots of good fish dishes
and exquisite *torta caprese*.

Osteria della Mattonella €
via G Nicotera 13, T081 416541.
Mon-Sat 1300-1500, 1930-2330.
Tucked away up the hill from
the piazza del Plebiscito. You
may need to knock on the door
and wait to be let in. Fast, friendly
and informal service combined
with fairly simple but delicious
Neapolitan fare.

Nightlife

Areas which buzz until late are:
around **piazza Bellini** and via
Benedetto Croce in the Centro
Storico; **Borgo Marinari** (in
summer), by the Castel dell'Ovo;
Chiaia, mainly to the west of
piazza dei Martiri; and **Mergellina**.
   Bar Gambrinus, via Chiaia
1 (piazza Trento e Trieste), T081
417 582, 0800- 0130, is Naples'
most refined bar and worth
a visit for the luscious Liberty
interior and the exceedingly
good cakes.

Travel essentials

Getting there
Naples Airport, T081 751 5471, www.gesac.it, is 5 km from the centre.
Alibus runs every 20 mins to piazza Garibaldi (central train and bus station)
and piazza Municipio, by the port (€3). Taxis to Centro Storico costs around
€20. International trains, including sleeper services from Paris, arrive at
Napoli Centrale station on piazza Garibaldi, northeast of the centre.

Getting around
The city is a fairly manageable size and, despite the crazy traffic, walking
is the best way to get around the Centro Storico. There are also useful
bus routes: R2 goes from piazza Garibaldi along corso Umberto I to
piazza Trento e Trieste; R3 runs from piazza Carità to Mergellina past
piazza Trento e Trieste and the Chiaia seafront; R4 runs north from
the port to the Museo Archeologico. Linea 2 of the metro is useful for
connecting piazza Garibaldi to Montesanto, Chiaia (piazza Amadeo) and
Mergellina. For travel information on the city and local area, see www.
unicocampania.it. Tickets, valid for 60 mins, cost €1.30 each, but it's also
possible to buy a day ticket (Giornaliero) for €3.70 (€3.10 at weekends).
Four **funicular railways** go to Vomero, Centrale (via Toledo to piazza
Fuga), Chiaia (via del Parco Margherita to via Cimarosa), Montesanto
(piazza Montesanto to via Morghen) and Mergellina (via Mergellina to via
Manzoni). The **Circumvesuviana**, www.vesuviana.it, runs from Naples'
piazza Garibaldi around the bay to Sorrento every 30 mins, stopping at
Torre Annunziata (for Oplontis), Pompeii (Pompei Scavi)
and Herculaneum (Ercolano).

Tourist information
The main office is **Azienda autonoma di soggiorno**, cura e turismo,
piazza del Gesù, T081 551 2701, www.inaples.it, Mon-Sat 0900-2000,
Sun 0900-1500; there's also an office at via San Carlo 9, T081 402 394 The
useful bilingual monthly publication, *Qui Napoli*, is free and full of up-to-
date information. An ArteCard, www.campaniartecard.it, costs €21, lasts
3 days and provides reductions on public transport as well as free entry
to 3 museums or attractions, with 50% off remaining sites from a list of 40.

Ratings

Art and culture ☆☆☆☆☆
Eating ☆☆☆☆☆
Nightlife ☆☆
Shopping ☆☆☆
Sightseeing ☆☆☆☆☆
Value for money ☆☆☆
Overall city rating ☆☆☆☆☆

Nice

Nice is justly described as the Queen of the Riviera. The city is blessed with 300 days of sun per year and boasts all the trappings you would expect: rows of palm trees, pavement cafés on every corner and a medley of outdoor markets.

A clement climate has been the historical constant in this city of 350,000. In ancient times, Greeks and Romans came, saw and planted olives and vines. Medieval governorship under the Turin-based House of Savoy gifted the city its Italianate architecture, a ritzy cathedral, the Ligurian-style native cuisine and a hefty dose of *la dolce vita*. At the turn of the century Nice became the Côte d'Azur's tourism hub, as Europe's nobility followed Queen Victoria on her long winter vacations to the bourgeois suburb of Cimiez. Painters including Matisse and Chagall succeeded onto this exclusive stage, creating an art-filled legacy that runs at full force today.

The 5-km-long Promenade des Anglais wraps Nice's southern flank and epitomises the city's liberal ethic. This seaside walkway is a daily procession of strollers and sightseers, 'bladers and bikers, joggers and snoggers. By night it's similarly *en fête*. A postprandial pageant of buskers, beer hawkers and wide-eyes visitors wander along the prom'. Down below, drums, guitars and impromptu singsongs chorus from the seashore, while games of beach volley are played into the early hours. Nice is alfresco, decadent, and a touch showy, and doesn't worry about getting up in the morning.

Nice port.

At a glance

Bordered by the Mediterranean to the south, the **Promenade des Anglais** runs right along the shore . Planes and private jets glide almost overhead and land at the airport at its western end, while sailboats, yachts and ferries to Corsica putter out from **Nice Port** at its eastern extremity. But Nice's main action emanates out from the **Vielle Ville** (Old Town). A warren of pastel walls and lavender-blue shutters, it serves as a picturesque reminder of Nice's Italian connections.

The **Colline du Château** towers above the old town and the port. It's a vast public park with a children's playground, *boules* runs and astounding views. This panorama takes in the suburb of **Cimiez** in northern Nice, where the museums of Chagall and Matisse flank the Roman archaeological ruins of Nikaia, the original settlement from which Nice takes its name.

Place Massena, spliced by Nice's tramline, lies at the city's geographical heart. Several public parks – renovated completely in 2013 – radiate out from it, as does the wide shopping boulevard of **Avenue Jean Médécin**. At the end of the road lies the Gare SNCF, where trains for Antibes, Monaco and Cannes – and even Paris, Italy and Brussels – wind their way past every half-hour or so.

Top: Promenade des Anglais.
Above: Cours Saleya.

Vielle Ville

It's not just stores selling Niçois-style home-made pasta and *pistou* pesto sauce that remind visitors of life across the Italian border. Take an evening *passeggiata* along the narrow lanes of the Old Town and you may notice other influences including local dialect Nissart, a Ligurian tongue, shouted from window to window as you wander beneath. The Old Town's crowning glory, the Italian-styled **Cathédrale Sainte-Réparate** on place Rossetti, is a baroque gem adorned with towering frescoes.

Decades ago guidebooks warned against visiting this area after dark, it being generally perceived as a warren of prostitutes, drug dealers and vice. These seedy elements have slowly been replaced by one-off boutiques and scores of galleries. The best of these art studios line **rue Droite**, which bisects the old city from north to south. Also along this pretty street is the **Palais Lascaris**, *15 rue Droite, Wed-Mon 1000-1800, free,* one of a dozen palatial dwellings that once belonged to local nobles, and the only one open to the public. Inside the restored mansion are heavy frescoes, statuary and 17th-century objets d'art.

Bathed in the sunshine a block back from the beach is the **Cours Saleya**, the Old Town's most prestigious street. This avenue of much-coveted mansions starts with the golden façade of Matisse's former home on Place Charles Félix and passes westwards through lines of plane trees, cafés and market stalls as far as Nice's rococo opera house. In addition to organic fruit and vegetables (Tue-Sun 0700-1230), the avenue hosts a fragrant flower market (Tue-Sun 0800-1800) and a great antiques fair (Mon 0900-1800), at which linen, cutlery and ceramics filched from hotels and stately homes across Provence can be found. At lunchtime, the market pitches give way to the outdoor tables of the surrounding restaurants, which in turn become

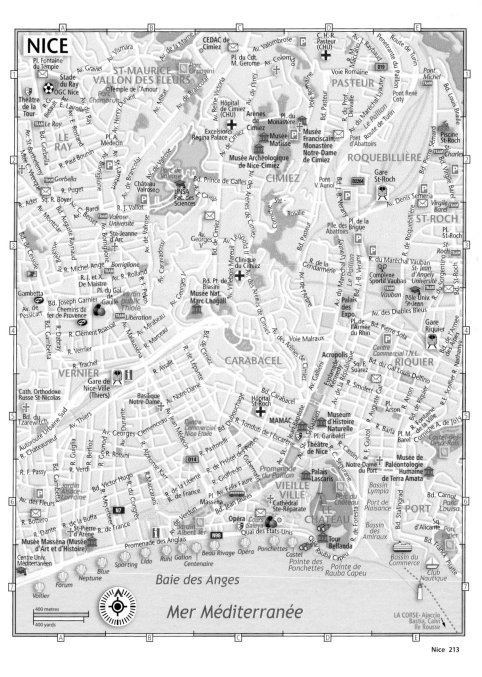

aperitif spots in the evening and dining terraces at night. On the Cours Saleya's seaward side are the **Galerie de la Marine** and the **Galerie des Ponchettes**, *59 & 77 quai des Etats Unis, Tue-Sun 1000-1800, free*, two fine-art galleries with cracking temporary exhibitions.

Musée Masséna

65 rue de France, T04 9391 1910.
Wed-Mon 1000-1800. Free. Map A6/7.

Formerly a neoclassical palace, then a local museum, the Musée Masséna reopened in 2008 as an asset-rich historical study of Nice. The mansion overlooks the sea and the Promenade and its fun and varied exhibits are bathed in glorious sunlight. The 1920s era is covered by newspaper accounts of parties at the time, menus from dinner dances, and street plans showing which buildings were owned by which particular Russian count or American millionaire. Paintings of Nice from a bygone age and artefacts from the city's famed Carnaval illuminate other periods.

Much is made on the ground floor of the Masséna family, regional aristocrats whose name still cuts ice in Nice (and secures dinner reservations in a jiffy). The empire-style villa was built in 1898 for Victor Masséna and was designed by Hans-Georg Tersling, who also had a hand designing – among other grand Riviera buildings – Monaco's Hotel Metropole and the Palais Carnoles in Menton.

Musée d'Art Moderne et d'Art Contemporain (MAMAC)

Place Yves Klein, T04 9713 4201,
www.mamac-nice.org.
Tue-Sun 1000-1800. Free. Map D5.

The MAMAC, as it's commony known, is a light-filled steel and glass edifice, surprisingly in harmony with the 300-year-old buildings of place Garibaldi and the Old Town immediately to the south. The permanent collection chronicles the history of Pop Art and French Modern Art. Andy Warhol is represented (not least in his amusing rejection letters from the

New York Museum of Modern Art), as is Robert Indiana (LOVE imagery) and Roy Lichtenstein.

The collections of the so-called Nice school of art include Yves Klein and Niki de Saint Phalle, each of whom have a dedicated room; the former includes a video installation of Klein shocking Paris society by daubing naked ladies with paint, while Saint Phalle's is filled with an army of mirror-covered humanoids. The museum is noted for its strong temporary exhibitions that take up the entire first floor: recent highlights have included Anish Kapoor and renowned local sculptor Louis Cane.

Catédrale St Nicolas

Av Nicolas II, T04 9396 8802,
www.cathedrale-russe-nice.fr.
Tue-Sun 0900-1200, 1400-1800. Free. Map A5.

During the late 19th and early 20th centuries, Russian visitors were as common on the Riviera as they are today. One of their legacies is this onion-topped cathedral, dazzlingly high from the outside, intoxicatingly beautiful – and hazy with incense – on the inside. No expense was spared in its construction during the last days of the tsars; the walls are covered with fine frescoes, tiles from Florence and icons from distant Moscow.

The leafy grounds hum with Russian voices, descendents of the White Russians who patronized the church after its construction in 1912. In mid-2013 the church was ruled to be the property of the Russian government, following a long-running dispute with Nice's century-old Russian community, who claimed it as their own. The Russian government softened the blow by pledging more than €15 million towards the church's upcoming restoration.

Musée Matisse

164 av des Arènes de Cimiez, T04 9381 0808,
www.musee-matisse-nice.org.
Wed-Mon 1000-1800. Free. Bus no 15. Map C2.

Originally from the Picardy region in northern France, Matisse had a long-term love affair with Nice. A quote on the wall of this Italianate villa, which serves as France's national Matisse museum, sums up his reason why: "When I opened my window and thought how I was going to have the light before my eyes every day, I couldn't believe my luck". The colourful displays cover his early Parisian period right up to his productive last years when he designed his masterpiece, the Chapelle du Rosaire in Vence, the workings of which form one of the key exhibits here.

In his later days Matisse lived in the fabulous **Palais Regina** building, a few minutes' walk west of the museum in the sumptuous *quartier* of **Cimiez**. The suburb's art deco mansions are juxtaposed with the remains of Nice's original Roman settlement Cemenelum, which can be found dotted around the **Musee Archeologique de Nice-Cimiez**, *160 av des Arènes, T04 9381 5957, Wed-Mon 1000-1800, free, map C2*. The ruins include paved streets and an amphitheatre.

Musée National Message Biblique Marc Chagall

Av du Docteur Ménard, T04 9353 8720, www.musee-chagall.fr.
Wed-Mon, May-Oct 1000-1800, Nov-Apr 1000-1700, bus No 15. €8. Map B4.

Russian-born Marc Chagall was a creative and playful artist. In the words of Picasso: "When Matisse dies Chagall will be the only painter left who understands what colour really is." The museum's permanent collection is devoted to biblical themes, a subject the artist returned to frequently throughout his life. The museum is particularly unique as it was the first in France to be designed by a living artist: an artistic vessel created to display a specific set of artworks. The powerful, vibrant paintings are exhibited exactly as Chagall planned to have visitors view them.

Colline du Château and the Port

Chateau Park: daily Jun-Aug 0800-2000, Apr-May and Sep 0800-1900, Oct-Mar 0800-1800. Free. Map E6.

The **Colline du Chateau**, *Jun-Aug daily 0800-2000, Apr, May, Sep 0800-1900, Oct-Mar 0800-1800, free, map D6*, separates the Port from the Old Town. It was formerly the defensive bastion of Nice; a cannon still fires off from the top at midday – be aware, it's deafening if you're nearby. Now the Colline is where locals come to read books, jam on guitars and let their children run free in the state-of-the-art playground. The clutch of cafés at the top have cracking views and are a just reward for the climb up from any of the three staircases dotted around the Old Town. Those with pushchairs might prefer to take the elevator next to the Hotel Suisse at the eastern end of the Promenade des Anglais. Of additional interest are the flamboyant graves in the **Christian and Jewish cemeteries**: only the rich and powerful made it up here. Note the preponderance of Italian names on the gravestones, a clue as to Nice's ethnological history.

Below the Colline du Chateau to the east is Nice's elegant Port, home to a historic fishing fleet and more than a few floating gin palaces. Ringed by great restaurants, it's a wonderful place to stroll and generally just hang about on a sunny day.

Catédrale St Nicolas.

Around the city

On the western edge of the Port is the **Quartier des Antiquaires** (most shops open Tue-Sat), hemmed in by rue de Foresta to the west and rue Cassini to the north. Over 100 antique shops trade 1950s Milanese furniture, medieval daggers, vintage musical instruments and contemporary art. The tiny **Marché aux Puces** flea market (Tue-Sun 1000-1800) on place Robilante is less pricey.

Further east, past the Corsica Ferries terminal, a path descends from the road, leading to a score of sandy coves and grottos on the **Cap de Nice**. This is a locals-only swimming area and makes a gorgeous snorkelling and picnicking spot. A coastal path now winds eastwards all the way to the seaside village of Villefranche, a blissful two-hour hike.

Musée International d'Art Naïf Anatole Jakovsky

Château Sainte-Hélène, Av de Fabron, T04 9371 7833.
Wed-Mon 1000-1800, bus No 9, 10, 23, 34. Free.

Anatole Jakovsky was an art critic who put his money where his mouth was. His love of *art naïf* – vivid, playful and often cartoony images set on canvas or sculpted – inspired his collection of around 600 pieces from the last few centuries. And, very kindly, he gifted it all to the city of Nice, where it now resides in a pink art deco palace, the Château Sainte-Hélène.

Kids will love the bright colours inside, the giant sculptures in the garden and, perhaps best of all, the excellent minigolf course just up the road (Parc Carol de Roumaine, 25 av de Fabron, T06 0766 4219).

Best of the rest

Libération market
Map A-B4.

Where the Niçois come to shop, Libération is Nice's most colourful fruit and vegetable market. Find organic bites, fresh fish and artisanal cheese to take home on the plane. Surrounding restaurants are superb.

Musée Beaux Arts
33 avenue des Baumettes, T04 9215 2828,
www.musee-beaux-arts-nice.org.
Tue-Sun 1000-1800, free. Map C6.

The city's fine arts museum is blessed with Rodin sculptures and Raoul Dufy paintings, all exhibited in a late 19th-century mansion formerly owned by Ukrainian princess Elisabeth Kotchoubey.

Parc Phoenix
405 Promenade des Anglais, T04 9229 7700,
www.parc-phoenix.org.
Apr-Oct 0930-1930, Oct-Mar 0930-1800, €2.

Tropical wildlife from parrots to butterflies and giant lizards. Find rainforest conditions under a huge glass hemisphere, plus outdoor gardens, streams and lakes. Kids adore it.

Théâtre de la Photographie
27 bl Dubouchage, T04 9713 4220,
www.tpi-nice.org.
Tue-Sun 1000-1800. Map B2.

An old movie theatre is the setting for a collection of black-and-white prints of Nice from yesteryear, plus challenging photography exhibitions from around the world.

Where to stay

Hotels fill up fast each summer, so an advance booking at one of these recommended places is essential. Bargains abound out of season, when the crowds disappear. Apr to Jun and Sep and Oct are the optimum months for planning a sightseeing trip. For a week's stay, it's less expensive to rent an apartment with a kitchen and balcony. Try Nice Pebbles (www.nicepebbles.com) for options.

Hi Hotel €€€
3 av des Fleurs, T04 9707 2626, www.hi-hotel.net.
Contemporary, industrial-style hotel with a rooftop pool and hammam. The 9 room concepts – open bathrooms in some, movie projectors in others – are a soothing mix of leather, glass and colourful plastics. Boasts its own organic restaurant, Happy Bar and the city's hippest beach club, Hi Beach (www.hi-beach.net).

Hôtel Windsor €€€
11 rue Dalpozzo, T04 9388 5935, www.hotelwindsornice.com.
A tropical garden complete with parrot and a palm-fringed pool makes for perhaps the most memorable stay in Nice. The Windsor's offbeat elegance includes an Ottoman lounger in the foyer, one-off luxury bedrooms designed by local artists, and a low-key cocktail bar.

Le Castel Enchanté €€
61 Route de Saint-Pierre de Féric, T04 9397 0208, www.castel-enchante.com.
Set in the hills just west of Nice, this new bed and breakfast is already a firm favourite. 2 rooms and 2 suites are set over a 19th-century mansion and its palm-fringed swimming pool. Note that it's a 30-min walk into central Nice.

Nice Garden Hotel €€-€
11 rue du Congrès, T04 9387 3562, www.nicegardenhotel.com.
Nine Provençal-style rooms cluster around a sun-dappled Mediterranean garden splashed with orange trees. Superbly located, midway between Nice's main train station and the beach, this welcoming spot is a true gem.

Villa Saint Exupéry Beach €
6 rue Sacha Guitry, T04 9316 1345, www.villahostels.com.
New sister hostel of the award-winning Villa Saint Exupéry Gardens, this budget spot sits just off the super-central place Massena. Complimentary facilities include Wi-Fi, all-you-can-eat breakfast, guided tours and luggage storage. Private en suite rooms are also available.

Restaurants

Nice is blessed with a fine indigenous cuisine. The surrounding hills are filled with olives, fruit and vegetables reared in a sub-tropical climate, while sea bass, urchins, red mullet, bream and rockfish are sourced from local waters. Thanks to several generations of immigration (it's not just artists, royalty and showbiz stars who have emigrated to the sun) visitors will find classic French cuisine alongside Japanese, Moroccan, Turkish, Russian and all manner of Italian. Dining (or indeed taking an alfresco breakfast) in the Old Town is utterly picturesque, although quality and value in this touristy zone are not the best unless you select one of the restaurants listed below. The Port makes for a pretty alternative as many restaurants have seats lined up by the bobbing boats. For more experimental cuisine try the streets just east of avenue Jean-Médecin including rue Gubernatis and place Wilson.

Breakfast
Café Marché €
2 rue Barillerie, T09 8184 9249, www.cafe-marche.fr.
Mon-Sat 0930-1400, Sun 1000-1700.
Tucked away on one of the Old Town's back streets, this cute café makes the most of seasonal, locally sourced ingredients. Don't miss the homemade pancakes, served up as part of their lazy all-day brunch on Sun.

Lunch

Flaveur €€€
25 rue Gubernatis, T04 9362 5395, www.flaveur.net.
Tue-Fri 1200-1400 and 2000-2230, Sat 2000-2230.
In 2009, 2 young brothers – both chefs heralding from Nice's grander establishments – set up this hip restaurant. The result: Provençal dishes modernized with a hint of Far Eastern flavour. Now Michelin-starred, Flaveur's elaborate 2-course lunches are priced at €38.

L'Univers de Christian Plumail €€€
54 bd Jean Jaurès, T04 9362 3222, www.christian-plumail.com.
Tue-Fri 1230-1430, Tue-Sun 1930-2130.
Upmarket, with a summer dining terrace on place Masséna. By night, the single Michelin-starred cuisine is extravagant: dishes based around foie gras, truffles and line-caught sea bass abound. Lunch is lighter and features the excellent value €22 2-course *menu de la semaine*.

L'Ecole de Nice €€
16 rue de la Buffa, T04 9381 3930, www.lecoledenice.com.
Mon 1200-1500, Tue-Fri 1200-2200, Sat 1900-2200.
Dedicated to all things Niçois, this newcomer was launched by local Michelin-starred chef Keisuke Matsushima. Cuisine ranges from fig and ricotta salad drizzled in Provençal honey to Riviera-style *fritto misto* (fried fish), while decor includes works by regional artists Arman, César and Ben.

Bar de la Bourse €
15 place St François, T04 9362 3839.
Mon-Sat 1200-1430.
An Old Town favourite, frequented almost exclusively by locals. The €12 4-course menu is a rollercoaster of regional flavours: a kir aperitif to start, followed by grilled sardines, beef stew or grilled rabbit, topped off with a rich dessert. No nonsense *plat du jour* dishes around €8 each.

Dinner

La Voglia €€€
2 rue Saint Françoise de Paule, T04 9380 9916, www.lavoglia.com.
Daily 1200-1430 and 1900-2300.
There are no reservations at this cours Saleya favourite, so give your name to the young Maitre d' and stand by. It's well worth it. Serving bowls of spaghetti with clams, platters of antipasti and Italian desserts of mammoth proportions that simply blow diners away. Formal service in an atmosphere of noisy bustle.

Café de Turin €€€-€€
5 place Garibaldi, T04 9362 2952, www.cafedeturin.fr.
Daily 0800-2200.
Le Turin is the literal first port of call for most visiting seafood fans. The plastic tables are served by a team of 20 or so waiters, oyster-shuckers, barmen and *fruits de mer* platter platers: the latter being giant *assiettes* of sea snails, urchins, crab, prawns and clams on ice. A Niçois institution for over a century.

La Merenda €€
4 rue Raoul Bosio, www.lamerenda.net.
Mon-Fri 1215-1400 and 1900-2200.
Award-winning chef Dominique Le Stanc left his Michelin stars at the venerable Negresco hotel to take over this hole-in-the-wall eatery. It's tiny, and there's no telephone for reservations or credit cards. Authentic local dishes, from salt cod to chickpea chips, make this a site of foodie pilgrimage.

Chez Pipo €
13 rue Bavastro, T04 9355 8882, www.chezpipo.fr.
Tue-Sat 1130-1430 and 1730-2230, Sun 1730-2230.
The sole 3 items on Chez Pipo's menu are all Niçois classics: *socca* (a chickpea pancake) *pissaladière* (a local onion and olive pizza) and *anchoïade* (an anchovy laden dip). Tables are communal, house wines inexpensive and tasty.

Les Amoureux €
46 bvd Stalingrad, T04 9307 5973.
Tue-Sat 1900-2200.
Arguably the tastiest – and most authentic – Italian pizza outside Naples. Be sure to book well in advance, as this snug eatery is packed out by devoted locals nightly.

Nightlife

Nice does a great job of being a party town for all people. Distractions vary from casinos to comedy and a healthy reggae scene. However, most visitors limit their nighttime activities to lingering over bottles of rosé, strolling along the Promenade and people-watching on the cours Saleya, not that you can blame them.

In summer, the city dances all night long. The Tourist Office website (http://en.nicetourisme.com) features a weekly 'Agenda', detailing every nocturnal event along the coast including firework displays, alfresco opera, open-air cinema screenings, jazz and blues festivals and classical recitals. In Nice, many of the festival-style events are held at the seaside **Théâtre de Verdure**, *Espace Jacques Cotta, T04 9713 3770, www.tdv-nice.org*, and along the adjacent Jardin Albert 1er.

Cultural events occur year-round, with Nice's grand **opera house**, *4 rue Saint-François-de-Paule, T04 9217 4000, www.opera-nice.org*, leading the pack. For theatre, classical, ballet and yet more opera, the **Acropolis**, *Esplanade Kennedy, T04 9392 8300, www.nice-acropolis.com*, has a jam-packed calendar. For original-language art house movies try **Cinéma Mercury**, *16 place Garibaldi, T04 9355 3781, www.mercury-cg06.fr*, and the **Cinémathèque Acropolis**, *3 esplanade Kennedy, T04 9204 0666, www.cinematheque-nice.com*.

Bars are hopping in Nice year-round. For trendy try **Bliss Bar**, *12 rue de l'Abbaye, T04 9316 8238*, for trashy join the legions dancing on the tables at **Wayne's**, *15 rue de la Préfecture, T04 9313 4699, www.waynes.fr*. Predominantly gay club **Le Six**, *6 rue Raoul Bosio, T04 9362 6664, www.le6.fr*, is recommended for an early-hours extravaganza.

Travel essentials

Getting there
Nice Côte d'Azur airport (T08 2042 3333, www.nice.aeroport.fr) is 5 km (3.5 miles) west of the town centre, along the Promenade des Anglais. According to its 10 million yearly passengers, it's a lesson on how to run a transport hub and a symbol of the easy brilliance of the French Riviera. Floor to ceiling windows flood the terminals with natural light, Wi-Fi is gratis, queues are unheard of, the coffee's great and a cycle track links it with the city centre.

In 2016 the airport will be linked to Nice's newish tram system. Until then, the No 98 bus (0550-2340) run by Ligne d'Azur (T08 1006 1006, www.lignedazur.com) departs every 20 mins during business hours for the port, the No 99 (0755-2055) for Nice train

station. Allow 40 mins for the trip. Tickets cost €6, and are valid for the entire day on the city's trams and buses.

Getting around
Once downtown, the city is eminently walkable. It's also served by the Vélo Bleu (www.velobleu.org) bike-sharing scheme. One very useful bus route is the No 15, which runs from the bus station to the museums in Cimiez. Heading further afield, the No 100 bus runs from rue Catherine Ségurane (just off of place Garibaldi) every 15 mins during peak times to every coastal resort east of the city, including Monaco and Menton; No 200 runs every 30 mins at peak times (very slowly) down the coast in the other direction, passing through Cagnes-sur-Mer, Antibes and Cannes. The speedy coastal train service (T3635, www.voyages-sncf.com) stops at every Riviera hotspot from Grasse to the Italian border every half hour or so.

Tourist information
Tourist Information offices reside at Nice Côte d'Azur airport, Nice-Ville train station and by the beach at 5 Promenade des Anglais (all T08 9270 7407, http://en.nicetourisme.com).

Ratings

Art and culture ☆☆☆☆☆
Eating ☆☆☆☆☆
Nightlife ☆☆☆☆
Shopping ☆☆☆☆
Sightseeing ☆☆☆☆
Value for money ☆☆
Overall city rating ☆☆☆☆

Paris

Not a city for the faint-hearted, Paris engulfs the senses with its vibrant culture, architectural marvels, world-class galleries, stylish shopping, pavement cafés and simply fabulous food. With a list like this, it's hardly surprising that the city has a reputation for arrogance; something that could be called merely confidence in itself as both a historical showpiece and a fearless innovator. While it holds tight to its traditions, this modern city continues magically to evolve. Its essence is an effortless balance of old and new, of traditional elegance and creative thinking: it is Notre Dame through cherry blossom from the quai de la Tournelle and rollerblading to the Paris Plage along the banks of the Seine.

More than ever before, Paris of the 21st century is a feisty brew of peoples from around the world. Old-fashioned French flavours have not been lost, or even submerged – men in berets still play *boules* on the quai de la Seine and bourgeois madames still feed tasty titbits to their poodles from the restaurant table, but now there are more ingredients in the city mix, more viewpoints. (It is estimated that 20% of the two million people living in central Paris are immigrants.)

Twirling seductively to her own special tempo, with the rest of Europe gawping from the sidelines, Paris confidently expects to lead the way but is also not afraid to go against the prevailing wind.

The Louvre.

At a glance

Central Paris is divided into 20 numbered districts (*arrondissements*) and is bisected by the River Seine. At its heart are two small islands – Île de la Cité (home to Notre Dame Cathedral) and Île St Louis: both are romantic, timeless and great for a stroll. On the **Left Bank** of the Seine (*Rive Gauche*), **St Germain** still has a high concentration of publishing houses and bookshops but tourist chatter has largely replaced debates on Existentialism and Surrealism. The **Latin Quarter**, to the east, is home to the Sorbonne, while the imposing seventh *arrondissement*, to the west, has a number of key landmarks, including the **Eiffel Tower**, **Les Invalides** and the **Musée d'Orsay**. Southwest is **Montparnasse**, once a place of wild entertainment. North of the Seine on the **Right Bank** (*Rive Droite*), the **Louvre** is a big pull for tourists who buzz around the place du Carrousel snapping the glittering **Pyramide** and the green expanse that is the **Jardin des Tuileries**. From here, the **Champs-Elysées**, long synonymous with wealth, sweeps up to the **Arc de Triomphe**. To the east of the Louvre are three adjoining *quartiers*: **Les Halles**, **Marais** and **Bastille**, while, to the north, **Montmartre** sits prettily on a hill, more like a village than anywhere else in the city and home to the fanciful **Sacré Coeur**. Thanks to some canny facelifts, the working-class districts of **Belleville** and **Ménilmontant**, to the east, are now the hip places to be once the sun goes down.

24 hours in the city

Get up early and head to the Île de la Cité for **Notre Dame** and the **Sainte-Chapelle**. Linger at the flower market, grab a delicious sorbet from the renowned **Berthillon**, then cross the Pont Neuf to the Left Bank. After a caffeine and philosophy fix in *Café de Flore*, eye up the sculptures at the beautiful **Musée Rodin** or browse for books, antiques and fashion around **place St-Germain-des-Prés**. Treat yourself to lunch at *Ze Kitchen Gallerie* or *Le Hide*, in preparation for one of the great museums: the **Louvre** or the **Musée d'Orsay**, perhaps. In the late afternoon, head to the **Marais** for window shopping or **Montmartre** for the view. After dark, *Brasserie Flo* is great for dinner, followed by jazz at *Le Petit Journal*. Alternatively, succumb to the lure of the lit-up **Eiffel Tower**, or join the beautiful people drinking the night away at the off-beat bars along **rue Oberkampf**.

Île de la Cité and Notre Dame

6 pl du Parvis-de-Notre-Dame, 75001. Cathedral T01 4234 5610, www.notredamede paris.fr; Mon-Fri 0800-1845, Sat-Sun 0800-1915, free. Tower T01 5310 0700; Apr-Sep daily 1000-1830 (summer weekends until 2300), Oct-Mar daily 1000-1730; €8.50. Metro Cité. Map E4.

On an island in the Seine, France's most famous place of worship, Notre Dame Cathedral, was built to replace and surpass a crumbling earlier church, on the site where a Roman temple to Jupiter once stood. Pope Alexander III laid the first stone in 1163 and the cathedral took more than 170 years to complete. The building has a spectacular Gothic façade, with a rose window at its western end and magnificent flying buttresses at its eastern end. The nave is at its best when the sun shines through the stained-glass windows, washing it with shafts of light in reds and blues. Place du Parvis de Notre Dame is an epicentre of tourist activity but the gardens at the rear and to the south are comparatively calm. Walk all the way round to appreciate the flying buttresses and the cherry blossoms in spring.

Île de la Cité was once the seat of royal power. Much survives from the original medieval palace complex on the western part of the island, namely the **Conciergerie**, the **Palais de Justice** (still the

Notre Dame.

PARIS

Around the city

city's law courts) and the glittering jewel of **Sainte-Chapelle**, *4 blvd du Palais, 75001, T01 5340 6080, www.sainte-chapelle.monuments-nationaux.fr, Mar-Oct daily 0930-1800, Nov-Feb daily 0900-1700, €8.50*, a chapel built by King Louis IX to house his precious religious relics. Since the early 19th century there has been a colourful and sweet-smelling **Marché aux Fleurs** at place Louis-Lépine, towards the centre of the island (on Sundays the market also sells caged birds and small pets). **Pont Neuf**, the best-loved of all the city's 36 bridges and the oldest (inaugurated in 1607), straddles the Seine at the western end of the island.

Tour Eiffel

Champ de Mars, 75007, T08 9270 1239, www.tour-eiffel.fr.
Mid-Jun to Aug daily 0900-0045; Sep to mid-Jun daily 0930-2345. Lift to Levels 1-2 €8.50, Level 3 €14.50; stairs to Levels 1-2 €5. Metro Bir Hakeim, Trocadéro. Map A4.

Gustav Eiffel won a competition to design a 300 m tower for the Universal Exhibition of 1889. The result was originally reviled by Parisians and was only meant to stand for 20 years; now it's the city's most identifiable landmark. The highest viewing platform is at 274 m and, on a clear day, you can see for more than 65 km. Take the stairs to the first level, with a bistro and the cineiffel museum, which recounts the tower's history on film; on the second level, there are souvenir shops and Alain Ducasse's gourmet restaurant, Jules Verne; the third is home to a recreation of Gustave Eiffel's office and an elegant champagne bar. To avoid long queues (at least an hour), visit early in the morning or late at night, when the tower is lit up like a giant Christmas tree.

Les Invalides

Metro Invalides, Latour Maubourg. Map B4.

The seventh arrondissement exudes extravagance from every pore. Expect 19th-century grandeur rather than quaint backstreets and curiosities. The avenues, mansions and monuments proclaim their importance. Wander rues de Grenelle, St Dominique and Cler, east of the Champ-de-Mars, to see where high society shops and dines.

Sitting splendidly amid the broad avenues is **Musée de l'Armée**, *Hôtel des Invalides, 129 rue de Grenelle, 75007, T08 1011 3399, www.musee-armee.fr, daily 1000-1800 (till 1700 in winter), closed 1st Mon of month, €9.50, Metro Latour Maubourg, Invalides, Varennes*, Louis XIV's hospice for war veterans. This vast Army Museum now charts French military history from prehistoric times to the present. The Église du Dôme is the final resting place of France's vertically challenged Emperor, Napoleon.

Around the corner, **Musée Rodin**, *79 rue de Varenne, 75007, T01 4418 6110, www.musee-rodin.fr, Tue-Sun 1000-1745, €6*, is housed in the light and airy 18th-century Hôtel Biron – the sculptor's last home – which just underwent a two-year

Below left: Eiffel Tower. Below right: Musée d'Orsay clock.

renovation. There are over 500 of Rodin's pieces here, as well as works by Camille Claudel (his model and lover) and Rodin's own collection of paintings, including work by Van Gogh. A wander through the sculpture-filled **gardens**, €1, is equally delightful.

Musée d'Orsay

1 rue de la Légion d'Honneur, 75007, T01 4049 4814, www.musee-orsay.fr.
Tue, Wed, Fri-Sun 0930-1800, Thu 0930-2145 (last entry 45 mins before closing). €9, €12 for temporary exhibitions. Metro Solferino. Map C4.

This 1900 train station-turned-art gallery is worth visiting almost as much for the building as for the great Impressionist treasures it holds. The enormous space is enhanced and illuminated by a vaulted iron-and-glass roof. There are decorative arts and Rodin sculptures on the middle level, with the most popular works, by the likes of Monet, Cézanne, Degas and Signac, on the upper level. Visit during the week to avoid the crowds.

Jardin du Luxembourg

rue de Médicis and rue de Vaugirard, 75006, T01 4264 3399.
Summer daily 0730-1 hr before sunset; winter 0815-1 hr before sunset. Metro Odéon, Notre Dame des Champs. RER Luxembourg. Map D5.

The lovely Luxembourg gardens cover more than 23 ha of the Left Bank. Their centrepiece, in front of the Luxembourg Palace, is the octagonal pool, surrounded by wide paths, formal flowerbeds and terraces. On the eastern side of the garden, accessed by boulevard St Michel, is the Médicis Fountain, an open-air café and ice cream sellers. From April to August there are free daytime musical concerts at the bandstand.

In the western section, towards rue Guynemer, there is an adventure playground and a puppet theatre. Photo exhibitions are often suspended along the garden's iron railings. Bartholdi's Statue of Liberty here is a smaller model of the one given to the United States in 1885.

Musée du Louvre

34 quai du Louvre, 75001, T01 4020 5050, www.louvre.fr.
Mon, Thu, Sat-Sun 0900-1800, Wed, Fri 0900-2145. €12; free Fri after 1800 for under-26s and 1st Sun of month. Ticket-holders can enter via the Pyramid, Porte des Lions or Galerie du Carrousel. Metro Palais Royal. Map D4.

Paris's foremost art gallery is as vast as it is famous. It was constructed as a fortress in the 12th century, lived in as a palace by the late 14th century, rebuilt in the Renaissance style in the 16th century and finally converted into a museum by Napoleon. The wonderful glass pyramid entrance by I M Pei was added in 1989. Today the four floors of the three wings (Sully, Denon and Richelieu) hold some 350,000 paintings, drawings, sculptures and other items, dating from 7000 BC to the mid-19th century. Highlights include *Vénus de Milo* (2nd century BC), Rubens' *Life of Marie de Médici*, the brand-new Department of Islamic Art and, of course, the crowd-pulling *Mona Lisa*.

Champs-Elysées and Arc de Triomphe

pl Charles de Gaulle, 75008, T01 5537 7377, www.arc-de-triomphe.monuments-nationaux.fr.
Apr-Sep daily 1000-2300; Oct-Mar daily 1000-2230. €9.50; free 1st Sun of month Nov-Mar only. Metro Charles de Gaulle-Etoile. Map A2.

The Champs-Elysées has been an international byword for glamorous living since the 19th century. The eponymous avenue is Paris's 'triumphal way', leading from the vast **place de la Concorde** to the **place Charles de Gaulle**, site of the **Arc de Triomphe**. The arch has always been the focus of parades and celebrations: Napoleon's funeral procession was held here in 1840, as were the victory celebrations of 1919 and 1944, and it's the finishing point of the Tour de France cycle race. In recent times Parisians have been snooty about the surrounding tackiness but it seems that the area's fortunes are on the up. Culturally and commercially, the area is undergoing a mini-

Centre Pompidou.

Sacré Coeur.

makeover, with an influx of new restaurants, designer shops and exhibition centres.

Les Halles

With its trendy boutiques, historic squares, hip hang-outs and aristocratic mansions-turned-museums, the Rive Droite is now fashionable and, in parts, smart. It has its low points too – the eyesore of Forum des Halles (currently under massive renovations due to be completed in 2016) and brazenly drunken rue de Lappe in Bastille – but the good far outweighs the questionable. A highlight is the **Centre Pompidou**, *Georges-Pompidou, 75004, T01 4478 1233, www.centrepompidou.fr, Wed, Fri-Mon 1100-2200, Thu 1100-2300, €10-13 permanent exhibitions, €14 temporary exhibitions, permanent exhibitions free on the 1st Sun of the month, Metro Rambuteau*, an architectural masterpiece of the late 1970s that still brings a buzz to the surrounding area.

The multi-coloured fun carries on with the funky fountains in the neighbouring place Igor Stravinsky, and there are plenty of galleries to choose from along rue Beaubourg and rue Quincampoix.

Marais

Metro Rambuteau, St-Paul, Chemin Vert, St Sébastien Froissart. Map F4.

Sandwiched between Les Halles and Bastille is **Marais**, a favourite neighbourhood for aimless wandering, thanks to its winding medieval streets, charming tea rooms and ultra-fashionable shops. The showpiece is **Place des Vosges**, *Metro St Paul*, a beautiful 17th-century square of arcaded buildings. Rue des Rosiers, a long-established Jewish street, has bakeries, kosher restaurants and falafel takeaways, while the city's unabashedly gay centre is around rue Vieille-du-Temple and rue des Lombards.

Bastille

Metro Bastille. Map G5.

The winds of regeneration that the Pompidou Centre blew into Les Halles, brought the **Opéra Bastille** to the Bastille just over a decade later. This gritty, working-class area has emerged as an after-dark hotspot and bastion of designer outlets but it still clings to its revolutionary credentials: raucous protests and demonstrations are a common sight on place de la Bastille. For a glimpse of the grittier side of life, away from trendy rue de la Roquette and rue du Fauboug St Antoine, head to the utterly authentic **Marché Aligre**, *pl d'Aligre, 75012, Tue-Sat 0800-1300, Sun 0800-1400, Metro Ledru Rollin*, and the surrounding streets, where old-style bars full of red-faced locals are still the norm.

Basilique du Sacré Coeur

Parvis du Sacré Coeur, 75018, T01 5341 8900, www.sacre-coeur-montmartre.com.
Daily 0600-2300 (dome and crypt 0900-1900, winter until 1800). Church free, dome and crypt €8. Metro Anvers, Abbesses plus *funiculaire*. Map E1.

It was the Romans who first erected a place of worship on top of this hill to the north of the city. They beheaded Denis, the first bishop of Paris, here in the third century AD. He was canonized as a result and the hill became the 'Mont des Martyrs' for early Christians. The current basilica – a glorious flurry of domes or a fanciful abomination, depending on your point of view – was designed by Paul Abadie and financed largely by national subscription. It took nearly 40 years to build, finally being consecrated in 1919, and now attracts some five million visitors each year. Inside, a golden Byzantine mosaic of Christ by Luc Olivier Merson hovers beatifically over the high altar. The spiral staircase to the dome is worth tackling, if you're partial to a long view, but you can enjoy a similar panorama from the steps of the basilica – along with the crush of tourists, jugglers and pigeons.

Best of the rest

104 Cent Quatre
104 rue d'Aubervilliers, 75019, T01 5335 5000, www.104.fr. Tue-Fri 1200-1900, Sat-Sun 1100-1900. Admission for events and exhibitions varies. Metro Stalingrad, Riquet, Marx Dormoy.
The city's latest contemporary art space housed in a vast old funeral parlour. Cutting-edge installations and new media art abound.

Canal St Martin
75010-75019, 4. Metro République for quai de Valmy, Stalingrad for quai de la Seine.
The canal was built in the 19th century as a shortcut on the Seine. Its most attractive sections have footbridges and barges.

Cimetière du Père Lachaise
16 rue du Repos, 75020, T01 5525 8210, www.pere-lachaise.com, Nov-mid Mar, daily 0800-1730, mid-Mar to Nov, daily 0800-1800. Free. Metro Père Lachaise, Gambetta.
The most celebrated cemetery in France and last resting place for the likes of Jim Morrison, Edith Piaf, Frédéric Chopin, Honoré de Balzac and Oscar Wilde, to name but a very few.

Île St Louis
75001. Metro Pont Marie, Sully Morland.
This island on the Seine is like stepping into a film set for the 17th century.

Musée Galleria
10 av Pierre 1er de Serbie, 75116, T01 5652 8600, www.palaisgalliera.paris.fr. Tue-Sun 1000-1800. €8. Metro Alma-Marceau, Iéna, Boissière.
After four years of renovations, this fashion museum reopened in late 2013.

Musée Jacquemart-André
158 blvd Haussmann, 75008, T01 4562 1159, www.musee-jacquemart-andre.com. Daily 1000-1800. €11. Metro Miromesnil.
In 1872 the portrait artist Nélie Jacquemart painted Edouard André. Nine years later they were married and living in this magnificent mansion on boulevard Haussmann.

Where to stay

Hotels near the big sights are expensive, but there are popular, mid-priced options on rue Saint-Dominique, squeezed between the Eiffel Tower and Les Invalides. The bustling streets of Marais or St Germain also have some good hotels. There are romantic corners on Île St Louis and in Montmartre, while Bastille and Oberkampf are good for night owls.

Hôtel Bourg Tibourg €€€
19 rue Bourg de Tibourg, 75004, T01 4278 4739, www.hotelbourgtibourg.com.
Metro St Paul, Hôtel de Ville.
This wonderful Marais hotel is a Costes/Jacques Garcia masterpiece. The French designer has lived in the Marais for over 20 years. The rooms are exquisitely intimate and deluxe, seamlessly combining French and Oriental influences.

Hotel du Petit Moulin €€€
29/31 rue de Poitou, 75003, T01 4274 1010, www.hotel petitmoulinparis.com.
Metro Saint-Sébastien-Froissard, Filles du Calvaire.
Designed entirely by Christian Lacroix, this quirky yet luxurious bolthole is tucked into the hip northern quarter of the Marais.

The Seven Hotel €€€
20 rue Berthollet, 75005, T01 4331 4752, www.sevenhotelparis.com.
Metro Les Gobelins.

Wow-factor gadget-filled hotel with its own 007 suite (entire Bond DVD catalogue in the drawer). Less expensive rooms with floating baths plus light and sound shows.

Villa Madame €€€
44 rue Madame, 75006, T01 4548 0281, www.hotelvilla madameparis.com.
Metro Saint-Sulpice, Rennes.
Plush St Germain hideaway with board games, iPod docks and international magazines should Paris overwhelm.

Hotel Residence Henri IV €€€-€€
50 rue des Bernardins, 75005, T01 4441 3181, www.residencehenri4.com.
Metro Cluny Sorbonne, Maubert Mutualité.
In a residential area of the Latin Quarter, this superb accommodation – all themed around King Henry IV – is perfect for longer stays, as the 8 rooms and 5 apartments all boast their own kitchenette.

Hôtel Beaumarchais €€
3 rue Oberkampf, 75011, T01 5336 8686, www.hotel beaumarchais.com.
Metro Filles du Calvaire, Oberkampf.
Primary colours and friendly staff are the defining features of this buzzing 33-room hotel.

Hôtel Danemark €€
21 rue Vavin, 75006, Montparnasse, T01 4326 9378, www.hoteldanemark.com.
Metro Vavin.
An elegant and welcoming hotel on a lively street, lined with little cafés and shops. Rooms are smart, cosy and good value.

Hôtel des Deux-Îles €€
59 rue St Louis en l'Île, 75004, T01 4326 1335, www.deuxiles-paris-hotel.com.
Metro Pont Marie.
Lovely, French-style accommodation on Paris's most idyllic island. Specify if you want a bath rather than a shower.

Hôtel Jules €€
49-51 rue La Fayette, 75009, T01 4285 0544, www.hotel-jules.com.
Metro Peletier.
This hip hotel is decked throughout with 50s, 60s and 70s vintage furniture, Bakelite objets d'art and a trippy throwback foyer.

Hotel du Champ de Mars €€-€
7 rue du Champ de Mars, 75007, T01 4551 5230, www.hotelduchampdemars.com.
Metro Ecole Militaire.
A cute budget option, just around the corner from the Eiffel Tower. Rooms are decked out in traditional decor, with some offering a peek of Paris's most famous monument.

Grand Hôtel Lévêque €
29 rue Cler, 75007, T01 4705 4915,
www.hotel-leveque.com.
Metro École Militaire,
La Tour Maubourg.
Located in a market street just a
short stroll from the Eiffel Tower,
offering simple, recently
renovated en suite rooms.
Singles and triples also available.

Restaurants

Breakfast

Le Comptoir du Commerce €€
1 rue des Petits Carreaux, 75002,
T01 4236 3957, www.comptoirdu
commerce.com.
Daily 0700-0200. Metro Sentier.
Pine walls and shutters and
cushioned seating create a
country kitchen ambience.
Good range of breakfasts , plus a
hearty weekend brunch (€22).

Café de Flore €
172 blvd St Germain, 75006, T01
4548 5526, www.cafedeflore.fr.
Daily 0700-0200.
Metro St-Germain-des Prés.
Renowned as an unofficial
philosophical forum, the Café
de Flore retains its intellectual
air, although today's thinkers
need deeper pockets than
their forebears.

Lunch

Le Hide €€
10 rue de General Lanrezac, 75017,
T01 4574 1581, www.lehide.fr.

The art of shopping

Shopping is an essential part of the Paris experience, even if it is only of the window variety. Inventive presentation is an art form here, especially among the city's specialist food retailers. **Place de la Madeleine** is renowned for its gourmet shops, including **Fauchon**, Nos 30, www. fauchon.com, Mon-Sat 0900-2000, a Parisian institution that sells wine, pastries, chocolates and more. There are also treats to be found on **Île St Louis**, such as the famous sorbets and ice cream at **Berthillon**, 31 rue St Louis-en-l'Île, www.berthillon.fr, Wed-Sun 0800-1930, and over 200 varieties of cheese at **La Ferme St-Aubin**, 76 rue St Louis-en-l'Île, Tue-Sun 1000-2000. Don't miss the impressive architecture of the city's department stores and of **Les Galeries**, the 19th-century covered shopping arcades between boulevard Montmartre and rue St Marc. The traditional hotspots for gold-card holders are **rue du Faubourg St Honoré**, **rue de la Paix**, **avenue Montaigne** and **place Vendôme**. More recently, designer names have joined the books and antiques around **place St-Germain-des-Prés**. Smaller, cheaper boutiques are to be found in the **Marais**, the **Bastille** and **Abbesses**. Streets that combine morning food markets (Tue-Sun) and wonderful speciality shops include **rue Cler, rue de Buci, rue Lepic** and **Boulevard Raspail**.

Mon-Fri 1200-1400, 1900-2200,
Sat 1900-2200. Metro Étoile.
Brilliant budget concept based
on French bistro dishes
(*escargots, pot au feu*) but with
a Japanese twist, courtesy of
chef-owner Hide Kobayashi.

Ze Kitchen Gallerie €€
4 rue des Grands Augustins,
75006, T01 4432 0032,
www.zekitchengalerie.fr.
Mon-Fri 1200-1430, 1900-2300,
Sat 1900-2300. Metro St Michel.
Inspirational and inventive, with

an emphasis on the nutritious
as well as the delicious. The
lunchtime menu (€39.60) can
include beef cheeks, Alaskan
crab and wasabi ice cream.

Breizh Cáfe €
109 rue Vieille du Temple,
75003, T01 4272 1377,
www.breizhcafe.com.
Tue-Sun 1130-2200. Metro
Saint-Sébastien – Froissart.
This Marais favourite serves up
superb Breton crêpes, along with
lashings of regional ciders. Low-
key – and highly recommended.

Pause Café €
41 rue de Charonne, 75011,
T01 4806 8033.
Mon-Sat 0800-0200,
Sun 0900-2000.

Nightlife

Metro Bastille, Ledru-Rollin.
The relaxed atmosphere, large terrace and good, reasonably priced food have made this a very popular lunch spot.

Dinner

L'Arpege €€€
84 rue de Varenne, 75007, T01-4705 0906, www.alain-passard.com.
Mon-Fri 1200-1400, 2000-2230. Metro Varenne.
The multi-Michelin-starred offering of Paris's most innovative chef, Alain Passard, who sources ingredients from his own private garden. Brilliant.

La Fermette Marbeuf €€€
5 rue Marbeuf, 75008, T01 5323 0800, www.fermettemarbeuf.com.
Daily 1200-2330.
Metro Franklin D Roosevelt.
An art nouveau extravaganza with ceramic panels featuring animals and flowers. When booking your table, ask to be placed in the back room, under the glass roof with its delicate stained-glass panes.

Miss Kō €€
49/51 av George V, 75008, T01 5367 8460, www.miss-ko.com.
Daily 1200-0100. Metro George V.
The city's latest foodie crush, this Asian fusion eatery was designed by Philippe Starck. The street eats – from gyoza dumplings to bubble tea – are a firm favourite with Paris's fashion set.

For up-to-the-minute info on what's on check the listings magazines *Pariscope* (http://spectacles.premiere.fr) or *L'Officiel des Spectacles* (www.offi.fr).

Bars and clubs

Paris has something to suit every taste, from authentic wine bars with flushed-faced old soaks propping up the zinc counter, to swish venues fit for glamorous celebrities. The **Bastille** is always a popular nightspot, although it can be overrun with tourists. **Oberkampf** is just as lively, but cheaper and more authentic. Nearby **rue St Maur** is getting hotter year by year. A lot of clubs double as live music venues some nights of the week. Many bars also serve food, albeit a limited menu, and there are a growing number of cross-over places. For cocktails hit any of the bars in any upscale hotel listed in this book or try the happy hour at **Le Fumoir**, *6 rue de l'Amiral Coligny, 75001, T01 4292 0024, www.lefumoir.com, Metro Louvre*. More offbeat are **Kitsch**, *10 rue Oberkampf, 75011, Metro Oberkampf*, and the brand new **Le Mary Celeste**, *1 rue Commines, 75003, no tel, www.lemaryceleste.com, Metro Saint-Sébastien–Froissart*. For a Latin-infused blowout dance 'til dawn at **La Java**, *105 rue du Faubourg-du-Temple, T01 4202 2052, www.la-java.fr, Metro Belleville*.

Dance and opera

National and international dance troupes regularly come to Paris to perform. **Opéra Garnier**, *Palais Garnier, rue Scribe and rue Auber, 75009, T08 9289 9090, www.operadeparis.fr, Metro Opéra*, is the principal base of the Ballet de l'Opéra National de Paris, and the best place to see classical ballet and opera favourites. **Opéra Bastille**, *130 rue de Lyon, 75012, T08 9289 9090, www.operadeparis.fr, Metro Bastille*, veers towards more contemporary choices. For ground-breaking shows, with dazzling sets and musical effects, look no further than **Opéra Comique**, *1 pl Boieldieu, 75002, T08 2501 0123, www.opera-comique.com, Metro Richelieu-Drouot*.

Music

If you want a taste of good old-fashioned and newly fashionable *chansons*, head to **Au Lapin Agile**, *22 rue des Saules, 75018, T01 4606 8587, www.au-lapin-agile.com, Tue-Sun 2100-0100, €24, including one drink, Metro Lamarck Caulaincourt*. **L'Olympia**, *28 blvd des Capucines, 75009, T08 9268 3368, www.olympiahall.com, Metro Opéra*, is the home of *chanson*, where Johnny Halliday and Edith Piaf once performed. It still pulls the crowds for a broad range of performers. Jazz lovers, meanwhile, will find blues, strings and brass at **Le Petit Journal Montparnasse**, *13 rue du Commandant Mouchotte, 75014,*

T01 4321 5670, www.petitjournal montparnasse.com, Metro Montparnasse. L'Elysée Montmartre, 72 blvd de Rochechouart, 75018, T01 5507 0600, www.elyseemontmartre. com, Metro Anvers, features acts from all musical backgrounds. Performances start late, so be prepared to sit on the floor and drink beer beforehand. La Maroquinerie, 23 rue Boyer, 75020, T01 4033 3505, www.la maroquinerie.fr, Metro Gambetta, features world acts, from accordion players to flamenco troupes, indie bands to Middle Eastern oud ensembles. For classical music look out for concerts in auditoriums at the Louvre, T01 4020 5555, and the Musée d'Orsay, T01 4049 4814, as well as concerts, mainly chamber music, held in churches, including Sainte-Chapelle (see page 224). For a contemporary classical sound, Cité de la Musique, 221 av Jean-Jaurès, 75019, T01 4484 4484, www.cite-musique.fr, Metro Porte de Pantin, has a varied programme of jazz, ballet, world music and acoustic.

Travel essentials

Getting there

Eurostar (www.eurostar.com) runs up to 20 trains daily from London St Pancras to **Paris Gare du Nord**. (A few services stop in Calais and Lille en route.) **Charles de Gaulle Airport**, aka Roissy, www.aeroportsdeparis.fr, is 23 km northeast of Paris. The best way into the centre is by the RER B train (www.ratp.fr) to Châtelet-Les-Halles (30 mins/€9.50) from Terminals 1 and 2. There is also the **Roissybus**, T32 46 (45 mins/€10) to rue Scribe, near the Opéra Garnier, or regular, albeit more expensive, **Air France** buses (T08 9235 0820, €17) to Porte Maillot, the Arc de Triomphe, the Gare de Lyon and Gare Montparnasse. To reach the city from **Orly Airport**, 14 km south, the best bet is the Orlyval shuttle train (www.orlyval.com, €11.30) to Antony RER station, and on into central Paris. The RATP **Orlybus** runs to Denfert-Rochereau (30 mins/€7.20). Ryanair flies to **Paris Beauvais Airport**, www.aeroportbeauvais.com, to the northwest of the city, from where there's a shuttle bus to Porte Maillot (1 hr/€16). **Paris Airports Service**, T01 5598 1080, www.parisairportservice.com, will pick up from your hotel and charge €27 per person to either CDG or Orly airport (half the cost of a taxi), or less for small groups travelling together.

Getting around

Note that the last two digits of a Paris postcode indicate the *arrondissement*. Central Paris is walkable but you will almost certainly need to use the **metro** system (www.ratp.fr) at some point. There are 16 numbered lines, plus the small cable car (*funiculaire*) up to the Sacré Coeur. Trains run daily 0530-0120. Numbered buses ply the streets daily 0630-2030, with a select few operating a reduced service past midnight. There are fewer **buses** on Sun. Timetables and routes are posted at each bus stop. Always validate your ticket in the machine at the front of the bus when you board. **Tickets** for all of central Paris (Zones 1 and 2) are valid on buses, the metro and RER urban rail. A single costs €1.70; a carnet of 10 tickets is better value at €13.30. Tickets are sold at metro stations and some tobacconists. There are also a number of **passes** available: *Paris Visite* is valid for 1, 2, 3 or 5 days (€10.55, €17.15, €23.40 or €33.70) and can be used throughout Paris and its regions, including Disneyland Paris and Versailles. The pass comes with discount vouchers for certain sights.

Tourist information

Paris Convention and Visitors Bureau, 25 Rue des Pyramides, 75001, T01 4952 4263, www.parisinfo.com, May-Oct daily 0900-1900, Nov-Apr daily 1000-1900. There are other tourist offices at the Gare de Lyon (Mon-Sat 0800-1800), Gare du Nord (daily 0800-1800), Gare de l'Est (Mon-Sat 0800-1900), Anvers (daily 1000-1800) and Paris Expo/Porte de Versailles (during fairs only 1100-1900).

Ratings

Art and culture ☆☆☆
Eating ☆☆☆
Nightlife ☆☆
Shopping ☆☆☆
Sightseeing ☆☆☆
Value for money ☆☆☆
Overall city rating ☆☆☆

Perugia

Capital of the region, and its largest and best-connected city, Perugia is in many ways an anomaly. Its Italian and international universities give it a young, cosmopolitan and lively feel, and its status and size mean that the outskirts, at least, have some of the trappings of modernity. The old centre, however, harbours as impressive a collection of medieval architecture as you will find anywhere, and the views, when they are visible from the tall, arched streets, are stunning. The city lies atop several ridges, and from good vantage points you can see half of Umbria, including Monte Cucco, Assisi and the towns to the south: Trevi, Spello and Montefalco.

Perugia is an intoxicating mix. It's the home of Italy's most famous chocolate, its best jazz festival and one of its best Renaissance painters; it's less pastoral than many of its hill-town neighbours, but often more exciting too. Next to a wine and cheese shop you'll find the latest iPads for sale, and beside a smart wine bar there may be an artisan brewer, where wrinkled Italians mix with bright-eyed international exchange students.

Oratorio di San Bernardino.

Around the city

Corso Vannucci and Palazzo dei Priori

Filled with people taking their evening *passeggiata*, the stunning corso Vannucci is the focus of the Umbria Jazz festival and is an elegant catwalk even in quieter times. From piazza Italia at the southern end, across piazza della Repubblica to piazza IV Novembre, cafés spill out on to the wide pavements, and restaurants set up tables in the middle of the street, which affords a great opportunity for people-watching. For much of the time the street is closed to traffic, which adds to the pleasures of window shopping in the smart boutiques and gazing at the extraordinary Gothic and Renaissance architecture.

At the northern end of the *corso* is the huge and oft-extended **Palazzo dei Priori**, one of Italy's most stunning town halls. From piazza IV Novembre, stone steps curl up to the first floor, where the large and impressive **Sala dei Notari**, *T075 577 2339, Tue-Sun 0900-1300, 1500-1900, free, map C4*, was once used for lawyers' meetings. This was the original palazzo, built in the 13th century, before succeeding centuries expanded the building down corso Vannucci. The assembly hall is richly frescoed and beautifully vaulted.

Piazza IV Novembre

Map C4.

Flanked by the cathedral (see below) and the Palazzo dei Priori (see above), piazza IV Novembre

is the heart of the city. Its centrepiece is the Romanesque **Fontana Maggiore** by the father-and-son team of Nicola and Giovanni Pisano. The fountain was built in the 13th century at the end of a long aqueduct, and it has survived its 730 years remarkably well. It is a beautiful and intriguing piece of work that repays close inspection. Three figures stand in the middle of two large concentric rings of bas-relief, and the whole thing is a mélange of idealism, romance, symbolism, mythology, religion and significant Perugian figures.

Cattedrale di San Lorenzo

piazza IV Novembre, T075-572 3832, www.cattedrale.perugia.it.
Mon-Sat 0730-1230, 1530-1900, Sun 0800-1245, 1600-1900. Free. Map C3/4.

Perugia's 15th-century Gothic cathedral dominates one side of piazza IV Novembre, its showiest and most ornate decoration ostentatiously facing the alternative, secular, power base of the Palazzo dei Priori. Both the front of the cathedral and its interior fail to live up to the expectations raised by the building's flank, though they are certainly not without interest. Note the carefully restored *intarsia* (inlaid woodwork) on the choir stalls and bishop's throne, crafted by Giuliano da Maiano and Domenico del Tasso between 1486 and 1491. There's a 1555 statue of Pope Julius III and a pulpit made especially for San Bernardino of Siena when he addressed the city in 1425. Also here, in the Cappella di San Bernardino, is the 16th-century *Descent from the Cross* by Federico Barocci. In the Cappella di Sant'Anello is the Virgin's supposed wedding ring, said to miraculously change colour depending on who is wearing it.

The **Museo Capitolare della Cattedrale di San Lorenzo**, *T075 572 4853, Apr-Oct daily 1000-1700, Oct to end Mar Tue-Fri 0900-1400, Sat and Sun 1000-1700, €6*, contains 26 rooms of medieval and Renaissance art. Downstairs, recent excavations have uncovered extensive, if not overly spectacular, Roman remains (guided tour at 1100 or 1530, €6).

Fontana Maggiore.

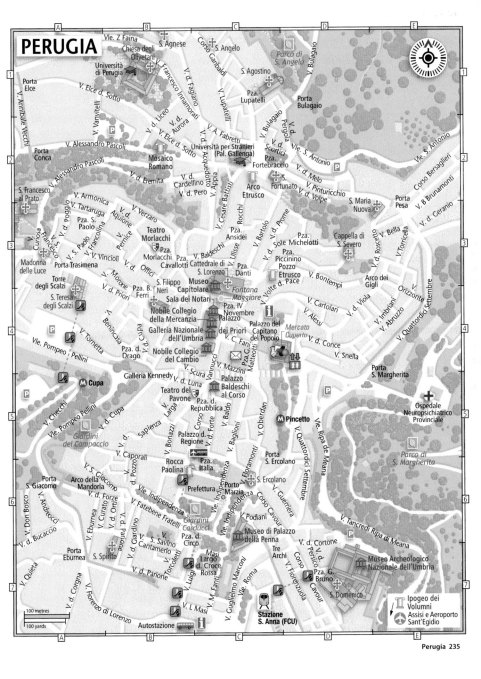

PERUGIA

Vle. Z. Faina
Chiesa degli
Olivetani
S. Agnese
Corso Garibaldi
S. Angelo
Università
di Perugia
V. Francesco Innamorati
V. d. Fagiano
V. Lupatelli
S. Agostino
Pza.
Lupatelli
Parco di
S. Angelo
Porta
Elce
Porta
Bulagaio
Porta
Conca
V. Elce d. Sotto
V. Vanvitelli
V. d. Liceo
V. d. Aurora
V. A. Fabretti
V. Elce d. Sotto
V. Acquedotto
V. Bulagaio
Pergola
Vle. S. Antonio
Porta
Bulagaio
V. Alessandro Pascoli
Università per Stranieri
(Pal. Gallenga)
V. d. Scortici
V. d. Melo
V. S. Antonio
Corso Bersaglieri
Mosaico
Romano
V. d. Eremita
V. d. Cardellino
V. d. Pero
V. d. Appia
Pza.
Fortebraccio
V. Pinturicchio
V. d. Volpe
Porta
Pesa
V. B. Brunamonti
S. Francesco
al Prato
V. Armonica
V. Tartaruga
V. Aquilone
V. d. Verzaro
V. Cesare Battisti
V. Cardellino
Arco
Etrusco
S.
Fortunato
S. Maria
Nuova
V. d. Ceranio
Curosa
Francesco
Pza. S.
Paolo
V. d. Poggio
V. Francolina
Pernice
Rocchi
V. Ansidei
V. Bartolo
V. d. Prome
Pza.
Sole Michelotti
Cappella di
S. Severo
V. d. Roscetto
V. Bella
V. Torricella
Madonna
delle Luce
Porta Trasimena
V. S. Paolo
V. Vincioli
V. Morone
Teatro
Morlacchi
Pza.
Morlacchi
Pza.
Cavallotti
V. Baldeschi
Ulisse
Pza.
Piccinino
Pza.
Etrusco
Pozzo
V. Bontempi
Arco dei
Gigli
V. d. Viola
Orizzonte
V. Quattordici Settembre
Torre
degli Scalzi
S. Teresa
degli Scalzi
Cupa
V. d. Priori
Pza. B.
Ferri
S. Filippo
Neri
Cattedrale di
S. Lorenzo
Museo
Capitolare
Sala dei Notari
Fontana
Maggiore
Pza.
Danti
V. Volte d. Pace
V. Cartolari
V. Alessi
V. Abruzzo
V. Imbriani
Porta
S. Margherita
Vle. Pompeo Pellini
V. Tornetta
Benincasa
Pza. d.
Drago
Nobile Collegio
della Mercanzia
Galleria Nazionale
dell'Umbria
Pza. IV
Novembre
Palazzo
dei Priori
V. C. Fani
Palazzo del
Capitano
del Popolo
Mercato
Coperto
V. d. Conce
V. Snella
Cupa
Vle. Pompeo Pellini
V. Checchi
V. d. Cupa
Galleria Kennedy
Nobile Collegio
del Cambio
V. d. Luna
V. Scura
Vannucci
V. Mazzini
V. G. Matteotti
Palazzo
Baldeschi
al Corso
Pincetto
Ospedale
Neuropsichiatrico
Provinciale
Giardini
del Campaccio
Teatro del
Pavone
Pza. d.
Repubblica
Sapienza
V. Bonazzi
Corso Vannucci
V. d. Forte
V. Baldo
V. Baglioni
V. Oberdan
Porta
S. Ercolano
Vle. Ripa di Meana
V. Quattordici Settembre
Parco di
S. Margherita
Porta
S. Giacomo
Arco della
Mandorla
V. d. Forze
V. Curato
Palazzo
della
Regione
Rocca
Paolina
Pza.
Italia
V. Indipendenza
S. Ercolano
Corso Cavour
V. Guerriera
Porta
Eburnea
V. Andreotti
V. d. Bucaccio
V. S. Giacomo
V. Eburnea
V. d. Ortfis
V. Giardino
Vle. Indipendenza
Prefettura
Porto
Marzia
V. Indipendenza
V. Podiani
V. Tancredi Ripa di Meana
V. Don Bosso
V. d. Corgna
Porta
Eburnea
S. Spirito
V. S. Savino
V. Cantamerlo
V. d. Parione
Giardini
Carducci
Museo di Palazzo
della Penna
Tre
Archi
V. d. Cortone
Corso Cavour
Museo Archeologico
Nazionale dell'Umbria
V. Quieta
V. d. Florenzo di Lorenzo
Pza. d.
Circo
Largo
d. Croce
Rossa
Masi
V. Guglielmo Marconi
Vle. Roma
Pza. G.
Bruno
V. Florenzuola
S. Domenico
100 metres
100 yards
V. Luigi Masi
V. L. Masi
V. M. Fanti
Autostazione
Stazione
S. Anna (FCU)

Ipogeo dei
Volumni
Assisi e Aeroporto
Sant'Egidio

Around the city

Galleria Nazionale dell'Umbria

corso Vannucci 19, T075 586 68410 1410,
www.gallerianazionaleumbria.it.
Tue-Sun 0830-1930. Audio tour available, €6.50.
Map C4.

The region's most important art collection is housed
in 40 rooms on the upper floors of the Palazzo dei
Priori. Good temporary exhibitions are held here;
highlights of the permanent collection include
pieces by Perugino, Pinturricchio and Domenico di
Bartolo, as well as an excellent Piero della Francesca
and a masterly altarpiece by Fra Angelico.

Collegio del Cambio

corso Vannucci 25, T075 572 8599,
www.collegiodelcambio.it.
Mon-Sat 0900-1230, 1430-1730 (closed Mon
afternoon Nov to mid-Mar), Sun 0900-1300,
€4.50. Map C4.

The guild of moneychangers was founded in 1259 and
moved here in 1457, taking on the role of a tribunal in
financial disputes. The guild still exists today, operating
as a charity. The moneychangers clearly weren't
short of a florin or two, hence the expensively
commissioned art that decorates their guildhall. Richly
colourful and remarkably well conserved frescoes
by Perugino and his assistants (perhaps including
the young Raphael) are the highlight, though there is
intricate *intarsia* work too. Don't miss the door through
to the Cappella di San Giovanni Battista, frescoed with
stories of the life of John the Baptist by Perugino's
pupil Giannicola di Paola in the early 16th century.

Pozzo Etrusco

piazza Piccinino 1, T075 573 3669,
www.perugiacittamuseo.it.
Apr and Aug daily 1000-1330, 1430-1800; May-Jul
and Sep-Oct Tue-Sun 1000-1330, 1430-1830;
Nov-Mar Tue-Sun 1100-1330, 1430-1700.
Combined ticket with Cappella di San Severo
and Museo delle Porte e delle Mura Urbiche,
valid for 7 days, €3. Map C3.

Perugia's oldest well is a dank, seeping, dripping
place, an enormous work of engineering but also
somewhat oppressive. Built in the third or fourth
century BC, it held as much as 450,000 litres of
water – enough to supply the whole city. A chain
of buckets on a rope would have been used to
collect the water, suspended from the large stone
beam across the top. These days water is pumped
out electronically to stop the well filling up, and
you can walk down slippery steps to stand in the
middle of it, on a newly constructed bridge.

Cappella di San Severo

piazza Raffaello, T075 573 3864.
For opening times and ticket, see Pozzo Etrusco,
above. Map D3.

Raphael's first documented fresco, painted around
1505 when he was in his early 20s, decorates this
small and starkly plain chapel to the northeast of
piazza IV Novembre. Only the top half is by Raphael,
who was called away to paint the Vatican and left
the fresco unfinished. It was later completed by his
one-time teacher, Perugino. It is fascinating to
compare the styles of student and teacher. At the
back of the chapel, a 19th-century etching shows
what the undamaged fresco once looked like.

Rocca Paolina

Entry from via Marzia, piazza Italia, via Masi or
viale Indipendenza.
Daily 0800-1900. Free. Map B6.

After the papal victory over the city in the Salt War
of 1540, the not-altogether-placatory response by
Pope Paul III was to build an enormous castle right
over the top of the area of the city where the ruling
Baglioni family lived. Hatred of this symbol of
domination simmered for centuries until the
Perugian population finally took their revenge by
pulling the building down in 1859.

By using the existing houses as foundations for
his giant fortress, the pope's project succeeded in
preserving the streets below exactly as they were
in the 16th century. Many can be walked around

now, under the giant vaults built over the area; it's a dim, shadowy, atmospheric place that feels full of the ghosts of the past.

Palazzo della Penna

via Podiani 11, T075-571 6233,
www.sistemamuseo.com.
Tue-Sun 1000-1800, €3. Map C6.

Perugia's 'modern art' museum has works from the 18th and 19th centuries, as well as a collection of six large sketches by Joseph Beuys, which were bought at great expense by the city when the German artist came to visit in 1980. The museum also has a decent collection of Italian Futurist painting. Temporary exhibitions are held on the first floor.

Museo Archeologico Nazionale dell'Umbria

piazza Giordano Bruno 10, T075 572 7141,
www.archeopg.arti.beniculturali.it.
Mon 1000-1930, Tue-Sun 0830-1930. €4. Map D7.

Perugia's excellent archeological museum, in the cloisters of **San Domenico**, is a treasure trove of local finds, most of them pre-Roman. The ground floor, lined with various ancient stone carvings, can be visited without a ticket. For the best bits, however, climb the stairs to the first floor, where some beautiful carved stone funerary urns line the cloister. It is noticeable that many of the grander urns, with statues reclining as if for a banquet on the lids, are for women. In rooms off to the left is a huge collection of amulets from around the world.

Chiesa di San Pietro

via Borgo XX Giugno, T075 35132.
Mon-Fri 0800-1200, 1530-1800. Free.

An extraordinary ensemble of painting, colour and wood wizardry, the Church of St Peter, built in the 10th century is well worth the walk from the centre out to this southeast corner of the city. Among the highlights is a marvellous choir whose *intarsia* work is as good as any in Italy: each armrest is decorated with a different mythological creature. There is a

Best of the rest

Cassero di Porta Sant'Angelo and Museo delle Porte e delle Mura Urbiche
corso Garibaldi, T075 41670. For opening times and ticket, see Pozzo Etrusco, opposite.
Porta Sant'Angelo, the biggest of the city's medieval gates, houses a rather dusty old museum dedicated to the fortification of Perugia, with dilapidated models of the city. Nearby, the round **Chiesa di Sant'Angelo**, *map C1*, built in the fifth and sixth centuries, is the city's oldest church and incorporates 16 ancient Roman columns in its construction.

Collegio della Mercanzia
corso Vannucci 15, T075 573 0366. Mar-Oct Tue-Sat 0900-1300, 1430-1730, Sun 0900-1300; Nov-Feb Tue and Thu-Fri 0800-1400, Wed, Sat 0800-1630, Sun 0900-1300. €5.50. Map C4.
This building became the headquarters of the merchants' guild in 1390 and still oozes wealth and prestige, though it lacks the headlining frescoes of the moneychangers next door.

Orto Medievale
via Borgo XX Giugno, T075 585 6432. Mon-Fri 0800-1700. Free.
This little corner of greenery in the southeast of the city is modelled on medieval thought. It's a slightly strange mix of cosmology, mysticism, numerology and superstition, but is pretty enough to warrant a visit.

Orto Medievale.

Pietà by Perugino on the left wall. The church's bell tower is one of the most distinctive elements of the city's skyline. San Domenico once had a similar spire, but it was demolished in 1540 as it interfered with the view from the Rocca Paolina.

Where to stay

Brufani Palace €€€
piazza Italia 12, T075 573 2541, www.brufanipalace.com.
One of the region's smartest hotels, the 5-star deluxe Brufani is a large, old-fashioned place, with 94 rooms and a swimming pool with a glass bottom, under which there are Etruscan remains. Rooms are furnished with sumptuous fabrics and all the comforts imaginable.

Castello di Monterone €€€
strada Montevile 3, T075-572 4214, www.castellomonterone.it.
Less than 10 mins outside Perugia, on the town's pretty eastern side, this castle has plenty of romance in its 18 rooms. Originally built in the 12th century, the castle was restored in the 1800s. There's a smart restaurant in the ex-dungeon, an outdoor terrace and a swimming pool. The beds and other furniture are all handmade in Umbria.

Hotel Fortuna €€
via Luigi Bonazzi 19, T075 572 2845, www.albergofortuna perugia.com.
This greenery-clad building just off piazza della Repubblica has 52 rooms, the best of which have 18th-century frescoes. Standard rooms are plain but comfortable, with pale fabrics and wooden floors; 'executive' rooms have exercise bikes. There's an antique library and good views from the small roof terrace.

Albergo Morlacchi €
via Leopoldo Tiberi 2, T075 572 0319, www.hotelmorlacchi.it.
Friendly, family-run 2-star hotel in a 17th century building in the heart of Perugia. The neat rooms all have private bathrooms.

Primavera Mini Hotel €
via Vincioli 8, T075 572 1657, www.primaveraminihotel.it.
Friendly little family-run hotel on the 2nd and 3rd floors of a building on a quiet street near piazza Morlacchi. The 9 rooms have TV, free Wi-Fi and minibars; the top one has a private terrace with great views. It's popular, so book ahead.

Restaurants

Nanà €€€
corso Cavour 202, T075 573 3571, www.ristorantenana.it.
Mon-Sat 1300-1430, 2000 till late.
Nanà is a smart and serious restaurant with friendly and very efficient service. There are some tasty starters, such as carpaccio with walnuts and celery; the home-made pasta is delicious, and the meaty seconds are generous. Leave room for one of the exceptional home-made desserts.

Ubu Re €€€
via Baldeschi 8a, T075 573 5461, www.ubure.it.
Closed Mon eve, Sat lunch, all day Sun.
One of Perugia's most sophisticated restaurants, Ube Re is smart but never stuffy and has a personal, human touch. Delicious tasting menus focus on fish or meat and are full of interesting flavours: try black lasagne with mussels and saffron, or duck with pistachios and plum sauce.

Al Mangiar Bene €€
via della Luna 21, T075 573 1047, www.almangiarbene.com.
Mon-Sat 1220-1600, 1930-2300.
Down a steep stepped lane from corso Vannucci, Al Mangiar Bene is a welcoming place with an entirely organic wine list and food to match: wood-fired pizzas as well as excellent traditional Umbrian food.

La Lumera €€
corso Bersaglieri 22, T075 572 6181, www.lalumera.it.
Wed-Mon 1900-0100.
Just outside porta Pesa, La Lumera is a local restaurant with a loyal clientele. Inside are wooden tables and old photos covering the walls, but in summer it moves outside. The menu features a good range of traditional Umbrian classics, such as *umbricelli* (thick spaghetti) with bacon and pecorino cheese.

Travel essentials

Getting there
Perugia airport (T075 592141, www.airport.perugia.it) is 12 km from Perugia and mainly used by low-cost carriers such as Ryanair. Buses run from the airport to Perugia (€3); there is also a shuttle bus operated by ACAP-Sulga; booking in advance is required (T075 500 9641, €8, €14 return). There are also rail connections from Florence to Perugia's **Fontivegge Station** at piazza Vittorio Veneto, 1.5 km southwest of piazza Italia. (Note that Fontivegge station is more commonly known as 'Perugia', not to be confused with Perugia Ponte San Giovanni, or Perugia Università.)

Getting around
There are two train lines that serve the city. From **Stazione Sant'Anna**, south of piazza Italia, Ferrovia Centrale Umbria trains run north to Umbertide and Città di Castello, and south to Todi. The **Minimetrò** is a hi-tech piece of wizardry that slides passengers in space-age pods up the hill from the mainline Fontivegge Station into the centre of town every 2½ mins (Mon-Sat 0700-2105, Sun 0830-2030, €1). It also goes to the Pian di Massiano car park, near the football stadium. Buses depart from the **APM bus terminal** in piazza Partigiani; most city services also stop at piazza Italia, where there's an information and ticket kiosk. However, buses and cars are of little use in the city centre, much of which is closed to traffic, or subject to tortuous one-way routes. There are paid car parks dotted around outside the city walls.

Tourist information
The main tourist information office is at piazza Matteotti 18, Loggia dei Lanari (T075 573 6458, daily 0830-1830). The **Perugia Città Museo Card** (www.perugiacittamuseo.it, €10 for 48 hrs) gives free access for 1 adult and 1 child to 5 of the city's museums as well as discounts at other sights and shops.

Porchetta stand €
piazza Matteotti.
Most mornings, a van sells rolls generously filled with roasted stuffed pig until the food has all gone, usually by about 1400.

Nightlife

Énonè
corso Cavour 61, T075 572 1950, www.enone.it.
Wed-Mon 1900-0100.
With dark wood, chrome and disco beats, Énonè is a funky, modern wine bar, with a long wine list and more than 25 different grappas. The food is also excellent.

Lunabar Ferrari
via Scura 6, T075 572 2966.
Daily 0800-0130.
Despite the corny name, this is a hip cocktail bar, with DJs playing sets after 2300. There are several rooms for chilling with a young Perugian crowd.

Trattoria del Borgo €€
via della Sposa 23a, T075 572 0390, www.trattoriadelborgo.com.
Mon-Sat 1930-2400, closed Aug.
Just off the bottom of via dei Priori, this popular and friendly place, with white walls and wooden beams, is run by a former butcher and his wife. Everything is home made, from the excellent pasta to the tasty desserts. Daily specials make good use of seasonal ingredients. Arrive early or book ahead.

Il Bacio €
via Boncambi 6, T075 572 0909.
Daily 1200-1530, 1900-2430.
You'll need to allow an hour or so to read through all the pizza choices, which include turnip tops. In summer there are tables in the middle of corso Vannucci for the best front row seats in town. Service can be patchy, but the tasty pizzas and the location more than make up for it.

Passeggiata in piazza IV Novembre.

Ratings

Art and culture ☆☆☆
Eating ☆☆☆
Nightlife ☆☆
Shopping ☆☆
Sightseeing ☆☆☆
Value for money ☆☆☆
Overall city rating ☆☆

Pisa

Pisa is now synonymous with just one thing: the Leaning Tower. Yet in medieval times it was a powerful maritime republic. Its decline began with its defeat by the Genoese at Meloria (1284) and continued as the River Arno silted up, thus denying the city its vital access to the sea. In 1406 Pisa was conquered by Florence, and the Medici rulers put their stamp on the city, establishing its university, where the Pisan-born Galileo once taught. Many visitors pause here only briefly, beating a path from Pisa airport to the Leaning Tower, taking a few photos, buying a cheesy souvenir, then making straight for Florence. But do that and you'll miss so much. The Torre Pendente is just one of a cluster of outstanding ecclesiastical buildings in the rightly named 'Field of Miracles', and there are other museums and churches to explore in the centre of the city and along the Arno. What's more, Pisa is the gateway to a fascinating area of Tuscany. Within easy reach are the chestnut-covered hills of the Garfagnana, the prefectly preserved walled city of Lucca and the lively coastal resort of Viareggio. Take your time in this region; you'll be rewarded.

Torre Pendente and Duomo.

Around the city

Piazza dei Miracoli

For details of tickets, see box. Map B1.

The 'Field of Miracles' is the name given to the grassy expanse that is the ecclesiastical heart of Pisa. At one time this was a rather marshy area between two rivers: the (now invisible) Auser and the Arno. It was the site of an early Christian cathedral. It's here that you'll find the famous **Leaning Tower**, as well as the **Duomo**, the **Baptistery**, the **Camposanto** and two museums: the **Museo delle Sinopie** and the **Museo dell'Opera del Duomo**. These snowy marble buildings are dazzling white in the sunshine and may blind you to the stalls around the edge of the piazza selling an extraordinary range of tourist tat.

Duomo

Nov-Feb Mon-Sat 1000-1300, 1400-1700, Sun 1300-1700; Mar Mon-Sat 1000-1800, Sun 1300-1800; Apr-Sep Mon-Sat 1000-2000, Sun 1300-2000; Oct Mon-Sat 1000-1900, Sun 1300-1900. Free.

The building of this magnificent cathedral began in 1063 (1064 in the contemporary Pisan calendar), when victory over the Saracens had brought Pisa enormous wealth. It was a statement to the world that this was a city to be reckoned with. Construction continued until the 13th century.

The cathedral represents the finest Pisan Romanesque style. The first architect, Buscheto, is buried in the wall on the left of the façade – an ornate construction built in the 12th century, which mixes Italian and Moorish influences. The three portals are topped with four tiers of colonnades and there are inlaid mosaics, stones and marble.

Inside, the cathedral is laid out in the shape of a Latin cross. A fire in the 16th century destroyed much of the original interior, so what you see now is a mix of styles. There are Moorish black-and-white striped marble columns, a Byzantine-style gilded mosaic in the apse (which Cimabue completed in 1302), paintings by artists such as Beccafumi, and a 17th-century fresco in the dome.

Piazza dei Miracole tickets

Tickets are available from the **Museo delle Sinopie** or the **central ticket office** near the tower. Admission to the **Leaning Tower** is €18 (pre-book online at www.opapisa.it), and entry is only by guided tours, every 30 minutes or so; cameras are permitted, but no bags. The **Duomo** is free, but you need to collect a coupon from the ticket office which covers two people. Admission to the other sites (Baptistery, Camposanto, Opera del Duomo, Sinopie) costs €5 if purchased individually. For any two attractions, the cost is €7, and for all four, it is €9. Children under 10 go free, but note that children under eight are not allowed to visit the Leaning Tower.

Top: Baptistery of St John detail.
Bottom: Duomo.

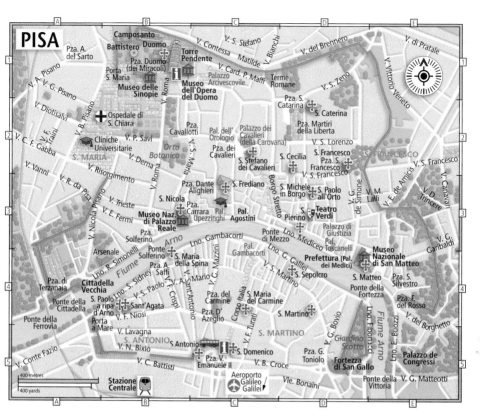

In the centre of the coffered ceiling you can see the Medici coat of arms. To the right-hand side of the altar is the mummified body of the city's patron saint, Ranieri, wearing a silver mask; to the left is the tomb of the Holy Roman Emperor Henry VII.

The most important work is the marble pulpit (1302-1310), which was sculpted by Giovanni Pisano. It is supported by the Virtues, Faith, Hope and Charity, and is covered with reliefs vividly depicting episodes from the New Testament. It is a masterpiece, the last of the great series of Pisano pulpits. After the fire it was dismantled and put into storage; it was eventually re-assembled in the early 20th century, though no-one can be completely certain that everything went back the way it was originally intended.

Torre Pendente

www.opapisa.it.
Entry by guided tour only every 30 mins Nov-Feb daily 1000-1700; Mar daily 0900-1800; Apr to mid-Jun and Sep daily 0830-2030; mid-Jun to Aug daily 0830-2200; Oct daily 0900-1900. No children under 8. Advance booking essential in summer, recommended at other times. €18.

Construction of this, the cathedral's bell tower, started in 1173. Due to the unstable, silty soil on which it was built and its shallow foundations, it began to lean before the third storey was completed, though it originally leaned the opposite way. Attempts were made to counteract this, and building was halted for 100 years. It continued in fits

Around the city

At busy times, on the hour and the half hour, attendants will shut the doors and demonstrate the echo. (Don't try it yourself: they'll tick you off.)

There is a large 13th-century font with inlaid marble panels, designed so that people could be baptised by total immersion. Most striking of all is Nicola Pisano's pulpit, which he completed in 1260. It was the first of the Pisano pulpits and was clearly influenced by Roman art.

Camposanto

For opening hours and admission, see the Baptistery, above.

Enclosed by long marble cloisters, the Camposanto or Holy Field is a walled cemetery, built on the site of an Etruscan burial ground. After the Third Crusade, at the end of the 12th century, the land was reputedly enriched with sacred soil brought from the Holy Land, and it was said that bodies buried here would decompose within 24 hours. Construction of the cloister itself began in 1278, and Roman sarcophagi, which had been re-used as tombs for wealthy Pisans (an early example of recycling), were brought here; you can see them as you walk around the cloisters.

At one time, the walls of the cloisters were covered with frescoes so stunning that they became an important sight on the Grand Tour. But the building was bombed in the Second World War, and the resultant fire melted the lead on the roof, which ran down the walls and destroyed most of the frescoes. You can see the survivors in the **Frescoes Room**: Buonamico Buffalmacco's lurid 14th-century cycles of *The Triumph of Death*, painted after the Black Death had swept through Tuscany, and *The Last Judgment*.

Take a look at the lamp that hangs under an arch in the cloisters. It is known as **Galileo's Lamp**. Legend has it that Galileo observed the lamp as it hung in the cathedral, moving in the breeze. He timed the lamp's swing with his pulse and realized that it took the same number of beats to complete a swing no matter how far it moved. A pendulum, he concluded, could be used to measure time.

and starts until around 1350, with various architects, including Tommaso Pisano, attempting to correct the tilt, which now went the other way. By 1990 the tower had reached a dangerous angle: experts estimated that if nothing were done, it would collapse within 10 years. The tower was closed and a sophisticated programme of adjustment began. Rings of steel were placed around it, lead ingots were used as counterweights and soil was dug out from underneath the northern side. These measures were successful, and the tower now leans only as far as it did in 1838 – decidedly tipsy, but no longer dangerously drunk. It reopened in 2001. The trip to the top involves climbing a narrow spiral staircase with 294 steps.

Battistero

Nov-Feb daily 1000-1700; Mar daily 0900-1800; Apr to mid-Jun and Sep daily 0800-2000; mid-Jun to Aug 0800-2200; Oct daily 0900-1900. €5.

The dazzling marble Baptistery was begun in 1152 and is the largest in Italy. Its shape resembles that of the Church of the Holy Sepulchre in Jerusalem. The first architect was Diotisalvi, but in the 13th century Nicola and Giovanni Pisano modified the building, which was eventually completed in the 14th century. It has a distinctive double dome, with an inner and outer cone, and fine acoustics.

Museo delle Sinopie

For opening hours and admission, see the Baptistery, above.

This museum contains the preliminary sketches, known as *sinopie*, for the frescoes that lined the cloisters of the Camposanto. These were revealed after the paintings were destroyed by bombing in the Second World War and were later detached and displayed here. They take their name from the paint, which was pigmented with red earth from Sinop in Turkey.

Museo dell'Opera del Duomo

For opening hours and admission, see the Baptistery, above.

This museum, housed in an ex-convent near the Leaning Tower, contains statues and treasures from the main buildings in the piazza. There are carved tombstones, richly jewelled reliquaries, engravings and Roman and Etruscan objects. The most important work is a *Madonna and Child* (c1298) carved from ivory by Giovanni Pisano.

Piazza dei Cavalieri

Map C2.

A few streets away from the piazza dei Miracoli is this airy piazza, the historic seat of Pisan government. The most striking building, the *sgraffito*-covered **Palazzo della Carovana** (also known as the Palazzo dei Cavalieri), was remodelled by Giorgio Vasari in the 16th century. It housed an order of knights, the Cavalieri di Santo Stefano, established by the Medici ruler Cosimo I. They acted much like authorized pirates, frequently robbing ships of precious items. It is now a university, founded by Napoleon, specializing in maths and physics. Outside you can see a statue of Cosimo, his foot crushing a dolphin – symbolizing his victory over this maritime city and Medici dominion over the sea.

On the corner of the square, with an archway and clock, is the **Palazzo dell'Orologio**. The tower to the right of the clock is known as the **Torre della Fame** (the Hunger Tower). This was where the Pisan Count Ugolino della Gherardesca was walled up, together with his sons, and left to starve, because the Pisans suspected him of treachery leading to their defeat at the Battle of Meloria. Dante includes the episode in his *Inferno*, describing how the count ate the bodies of his children to stay alive. Not far from here is the **Orto Botanico**, *map B2*, Pisa's botanical garden – a lovely refuge in the heart of the city.

Borgo Stretto and the river

From piazza dei Cavalieri you can walk down via Ulisse Dini and on to via Oberdan and Borgo Stretto: this is Pisa's slickest shopping street, lined with arcades. Look out for **Salza**, the city's historic *pasticceria*, at number 46. Also worth noting is the arresting frontage of the **Church of San Michele in Borgo**. Eventually you'll reach the Arno and the **ponte di Mezzo**. If you cross the river here the road becomes **corso Italia**, a busy but less pricey shopping street. Turn left and you can walk along the Arno to the **Museo Nazionale di San Matteo**, *Tue-Sat 0900-1900, Sun 0900-1330, €8, map D4*, which houses a large collection of Tuscan art; turn right, and you'll come to the **Museo Nazionale di Palazzo Reale**, *Mon-Fri 0900-1400, Sat 0900-1330, €6, map B3*, a 16th-century palace that was the seat of the Medici court during the winter months. (A ticket for both museums costs €12.)

Opposite page: Piazza dei Miracoli.
Below: Piazza dei Cavalieri.

Where to stay

Excursions from Pisa

From Pisa, it is easy to take a train to the coast. **Viareggio** is the liveliest and most famous of Tuscany's seaside resorts, the golden sand almost invisible under the endless rows of sun loungers. Walk around to see the *stile-Liberty* buildings erected during the resort's heyday in the 1920s and 1930s. Just 6 km south of Viareggio is **Torre del Lago**, for many years the home of Giacomo Puccini. **Museo Villa Puccini** (T0584 341445, giacomopuccini.it) is filled with Puccini's original furnishings, musical instruments, rifles and memorabilia. **Lucca**, the birthplace of Puccini, is also within easy reach of Pisa and is a delightful place to visit – the historical centre is immaculately preserved within its city walls. Despite its small size, Lucca was once a significant force in Tuscany and remained essentially independent until Napoleon's era. The city today radiates a confidence born of centuries of power. Don't miss **San Martino Cathedral**, shopping for regional delicacies on **via Fillungo**, a photo-stop in the **piazza dell'Anfiteatro** and a walk (or cycle ride) around the ramparts.

Bagni di Pisa €€€
largo Shelley 18, San Giuliano Terme, T050 88501, www.bagnidipisa.com.
The poet Shelley once stayed at this 18th-century villa, which evokes the grandeur of a more elegant age. Only 20 mins by train from Pisa, it makes a relaxing base for exploring the city and nearby coastline. There's a rooftop swimming pool and spa facilities. The buffet breakfast is excellent.

Hotel Relais dell'Orologio €€€
via della Faggiola 12/14, T050 830361, www.hotelrelaisorologio.com.
This 14th-century fortified house close to the Leaning Tower has been turned into a 5-star hotel with plush rooms. Some feature frescoes, others coffered ceilings, and all are very comfortable though very small. There's a courtyard garden.

Di Stefano €€
via Sant'Apollonia 35, T050 553559, www.hoteldistefano.it.
The best rooms at this hotel are in the recently renovated 11th-century tower house. They have a contemporary Tuscan look, with some original features and fresh, clean bathrooms, some with jacuzzi baths. Facilities include flatscreen TV and a/c.

Top: Lucca.
Bottom: Viareggio.

Royal Victoria Hotel €€
lungarno Pacinotti 12, T050 940111, www.royalvictoria.it.
This riverside hotel seems to have changed little since it first opened in the early 19th century. The rooms have heavy, dark wood furniture and iron bedsteads; some have frescoes. The bathrooms need a facelift. But the public areas are hung with fascinating photos and have plenty of character, and the rooms overlooking the Arno have fabulous views.

Restaurants

Antica Trattoria Il Campano €€€
via Cavalca 19, T050 580585, www.ilcampano.com.
Fri-Tue 1230-1500, 1900-2300, Thu 1900-2300.
This trattoria in the market is in a medieval building with a vaulted ceiling and has some seats outside. Come for home-made pasta, with truffles or wild boar, and a good choice of wines.

Osteria dei Cavalieri €€
via San Frediano 16, T050 580858, www.osteriacavalieri.pisa.it.
Mon-Fri 1230-1400, 1945-2200, Sat 1945-2200.
Fine Tuscan food is served with an imaginative twist at this popular *osteria*. Dishes include courgette pudding, gnocchi with squash flowers and pistachio nuts, and Tuscan tripe. There are some 4-course set menus, including a vegetarian one for €26.

Osteria del Tinti €€
vicolo del Tinti 26, T050 580240.
Tue, Thu-Sat 1900-2400, Sun 1230-1500, 1900-2400.
Good local food, tucked away down a side street. Pasta dishes include *testaroli* with pecorino and olive oil, and there's also gnocchi with monkfish and lemon sauce.

Osteria la Grotta €€
via San Francesco 103, T050 578105, www.osterialagrotta.com.
Mon-Sat 1200-1430, 1945-2230.
Resembling a dark cave inside, with puppets of witches hanging on the walls, this *osteria* offers starters such as toast with *lardo* and figs, filling soups and unusual pasta such as pistachio ravioli.

Cafés and gelaterias
De' Coltelli
Lungarno Pacinotti 23, T050541611.
Daily 1130-0100; closes earlier in winter.
Delicious ices on the Arno.

Dolce Pisa
via Santa Maria 83, T050 563181.
Sat-Thu 0730-2000.
Not far from the Orto Botanico, this is a good place to stop for lovely pastries and espresso.

La Bottega del Gelato
piazza Garibaldi 11, T050 575467.
Summer daily 1100-0100; winter Thu-Tue from 1100.
Many locals rate this as the best *gelateria*. Prepare to queue.

Ratings

Art and culture ☆☆☆☆
Eating ☆☆
Nightlife ☆☆☆
Shopping ☆☆
Sightseeing ☆☆☆☆☆
Value for money ☆☆☆
Overall city rating ☆☆☆☆

Prague

Visitors get rather poetic when they first clap eyes on Prague. The 'Golden City', the 'Belle of Bohemia' and the 'City of a Thousand Spires' certainly has a lot to live up to, but the reality matches the hype. Prague remained blessedly unharmed during the two World Wars, and the Velvet Revolution of 1989 came to pass without a single shot being fired. This translates into a beautiful city with a stunning showpiece centre: winding, medieval lanes flanked by elegant Gothic, baroque and art nouveau façades. As you wander through Europe's largest castle or over famous Charles Bridge, it's hard to imagine that Prague was off-limits to western visitors for several decades. But time moves quickly in this part of the world: the Czech Republic has been a member of the EU since May 2004 and a veneer of sophistication has spread through the capital. Locals aren't surprised: Prague was, after all, at the vanguard of European culture for much of the 19th and early 20th centuries. Vestiges of this past are the main draws today: from the cobbled streets of Staré Město and the haunting atmosphere of the Jewish cemetery to the smoky cellar bars and the graceful concert halls that launched some of Europe's greatest composers. The essence of Prague, however, is something less tangible: getting lost in the medieval Old Town on a foggy evening, or watching the sun set over terracotta roofs and soaring church spires is, quite simply, poetry.

Clock in Old Town Square.

At a glance

The Vltava River, running from south to north through the city centre, neatly splits up the area in which visitors spend most (if not all) of their time. On the right bank is **Staré Město** (Old Town), at the heart of which is **Staroměstské náměstí** (Old Town Square), famous for its astronomical clock. North of here is the old Jewish district of **Josefov**, edged by Parízská boulevard. The winding, narrow streets of the Old Town fan out south of Old Town Square, opening up in the southeast at **Václavské náměstí** (Wenceslas Square), site of the 1989 Velvet Revolution. This is the main hub of **Nové Město** (New Town), Prague's business and commercial district. To the north is the busy square, **Náměstí Republiky**, while, to the south, the wide streets hold many of the biggest hotels, restaurants and department stores. Further east is the residential area of **Vinohrady**, once the royal vineyards.

On the other side of the river is **Malá Strana** (Lesser Quarter). This area of 18th-century town houses and palaces is quieter and even more atmospheric than the Old Town, its streets rolling up towards Hradčany, the castle district. **Hradčany** is completely dominated by the magnificent castle complex, with the central road of **Nerodova** (always full of tour groups trudging to the castle) running back down into Malá Strana. To the south is the green expanse of **Petřín**, a tranquil, leafy hill topped by a little model of the Eiffel Tower.

24 hours in the city

Start early with a coffee in **Old Town Square** to beat the crowds – the astronomical clock begins its daily whirrings at 0900. Look into the brooding hulk of **Our Lady Before Týn** before striking north along Parízská and into the Josefov district. Take a look at the **Old-New Synagogue** and the exhibitions in the **Pinkasova Synagogue** before strolling through the eerily atmospheric **Jewish Cemetery**. For a snack or early lunch, stroll back along Parízská which is lined with cafés and restaurants. Veer west and you'll hit the river and picture-postcard **Charles Bridge**, with its buskers and views of the red-roofed houses of Malá Strana creeping up towards the castle. Once across the bridge, wander along the cobbled lanes centering on **Malostranské náměstí**, the area's busiest square. Lunch here, before the stiff climb up to the castle. You'll need a good few hours to stroll around the complex, after which you'll have earned a Czech beer at one of the little, smoke-filled pubs in Malá Strana. Continue the traditional theme for dinner at **U Medvídků**, back in the Old Town, before checking out the live jazz at **AghaRTA**, or catching the Prague Symphony Orchestra at the **Municipal House**.

Pražský hrad (Prague Castle)

T224 373 368, www.hrad.cz.
Castle grounds daily Apr-Oct 0500-0000; Nov-Mar 0600-2300. Buildings daily Apr-Oct 0900-1700; Nov-Mar 0900-1600. Combined ticket CZK350. Tram 12, 18, 20, 22 or 23, metro Malostranskă. Map, A/B1.

Prague Castle has dominated the city's skyline for over 1000 years and its sprawling complex merits at least half a day's exploration. The first evidence of a castle here dates back to AD 880 and, over the following millennium, the site became the monarchic and spiritual powerhouse of the country. Today it feels like a walled town and is reputedly the world's largest castle, its courtyards linking the palace, cathedral, several churches, museums, galleries and a monastery, all beautifully lit up at night.

St Vitus Cathedral, Prague Castle.

PRAGUE

Around the city

Your first port of call should be **St Vitus' Cathedral** (Chrám sv Vita), the seat of the Archbishop of Prague. The interior of this magnificent Gothic structure is delicately lit by a series of mosaic-style stained-glass windows. Look out for **St Wenceslas's Chapel**, resplendent with over a thousand semi-precious stones.

The **Old Royal Palace** (Starý královský palác) is worth seeing for the soaring, empty expanse of **Vladislav Hall**. It once hosted coronation celebrations; today presidents of the Republic are sworn in here. Wander around the rest of the palace before exiting by **St George's Basilica** (sv Jiří), with its beautifully preserved Romanesque interior, where chamber music recitals are held. Next door is the old monastery, now a gallery.

Behind the monastery is **Golden Lane** (Zlatá Ulička), a cobbled street, lined with 16th-century cottages, today filled with craft shops. (The Prague-born writer, Franz Kafka, briefly stayed at No 22.) At the end of the lane is the **Toy Museum** (Muzeum hraček), *daily 0930-1730, CZK70*, filled with traditional wooden toys and, oddly, hundreds of Barbie dolls. Opposite is **Lobkovicz Palace** (Lobkovický palác), *daily 1000-1800, CZK275*, with its rambling historical collection. Also worth exploring are the castle gardens, particularly the peaceful **Royal Gardens**, which have beautiful views.

Malá Strana

Tram 12, 18, 20, 22 or 23, metro Malostranskă. Map A3.

This wedge of land between the castle and Vltava River, often bypassed by visitors, is a delightful, atmospheric area of cobbled lanes and crumbling baroque façades. At its heart is **Malostranské náměstí**, a busy square fringed with grand neoclassical houses and elegant colonnades. In the centre is the baroque **St Nicholas church** (Sv Mikuláš chrám), *daily 0900-1700, Sun Mass 2030, free, daily tours CZK70*, built in the early 18th century. Its prominent green dome and tower quickly became a major Prague landmark. The inside is quite overwhelming, awash with hectic, multicoloured frescoes.

Petřín

Tram 6, 9, 12 or 20 to Újezd. Map A4.

A steep **funicular railway**, dating from the 1891 Jubilee Exhibition, climbs up green and leafy Petřín hill. At the top of the funicular, pause awhile to soak up the views, then follow the path along the old city wall, which passes a rose garden and observatory, to the **Petřín Observation Tower** (Petřínská rozhledna), *Oct and Mar daily 1000-2000, Apr-Sep daily 1000-2200, Nov-Feb daily 1000-1800, CZK105*. This 60-m high structure is a small-scale version of the Eiffel Tower, also dating from the Exhibition, with a viewing platform offering fabulous views over rooftops, broken by the soaring silhouettes of dozens of spires. Next door is a small neo-Gothic castle with a mirror maze (same times and prices as tower).

Karlův most (Charles Bridge)

Prague's oldest bridge was founded in 1357 by Charles IV and, for many centuries, was the only link between the right and left banks. Today, it is best known for its dozens of statues, although most of these were added in the 18th century. The car-free bridge is thronged with tourists and buskers at all

Above: Charles Bridge and Malá Strana.
Opposite page: Golden Lane.

times of day but, at night, the bridge empties out and takes on a fairytale quality, never more so than in winter, with snowflakes drifting over the water.

Staroměstské náměstí (Old Town Square)

Tram 17 or 18, metro Staroměstská. Map G2.

All roads in Bohemia once led to Staroměstské náměstí, still Prague's most important and jaw-dropping square, a vast cobbled expanse flanked by brightly painted baroque houses. The centrepiece is the **Town Hall**, home to the extraordinary **Astronomical clock** (Orloj) in a tower to the right. Crowds gather on the hour (0900-2100) to watch the figures shuffle out from little doors. They portray various saints, as well as representations of death, vanity, history and greed – the latter is a dodgy depiction of a Jew clutching money bags, albeit minus his beard, which was removed at the end of the war.

Behind the Town Hall is the looming, blackened church of **Our Lady Before Týn** (Panna Marie pred Týnem), its Gothic hulk hiding a surprisingly pretty baroque interior. In winter, a Christmas market selling mulled wine, souvenirs and wooden toys is held on the square.

Josefov

Tram 17 or 18, metro Staroměstská. Map F1.

Prague's old Jewish ghetto is one of the most atmospheric quarters of the city. It's no longer the warren of old streets depicted by Kafka, but the main sights – four synagogues and the cemetery – remain. A good starting point is the **Old-New Synagogue** (Staranová synagoga), *Cervená 2, Summer Sun-Thu 0900-1800, winter Sun-Thu 0900-1700, Fri closes 1 hr before Shabbat, CZK200*, a squat structure dating from 1275. It still functions as a synagogue, making it the oldest still in use in Europe. The other sights in Josefov are visited as part of the **Jewish Museum** (Zidovské Muzeum), *T222 749211, www.jewishmuseum.cz, Sun-Fri Apr-Oct 0900-1800, Nov-Mar 0900-1630, CZK300*. The most striking is the **Old Jewish Cemetery** (Starý zidovský hrbitov). Used from 1439 to 1787, it is the oldest and largest Jewish cemetery in Europe. It is a poignant, mysterious place, with hundreds of ancient headstones bristling from the ground at haphazard angles. The adjoining **Pinkas Synagogue** (Pinkasova

Jewish Prague

Before the Nazi occupation from 1939 to 1945, Prague's Jewish population was a thriving community, numbering some 50,000. Today, the number has dwindled to around 4000. The focal point of the community remains the Josefov district, named after Emperor Josef II, whose 1781 reforms helped bestow civil rights to the Jewish community. The original ghetto actually dated back to the 13th century, although much of it was cleared in a huge late 19th-century development project. This drove out the poorer sections of the community and transformed the winding old alleys into smart boulevards, lined with elegant mansions. With the arrival of the Nazis came forced removals, both to a new ghetto in Trezín, 60 km from the city, and, later, to concentration camps; a staggering two thirds of the population is thought to have died in camps before the end of the war. Ironically, what was left of the old ghetto was spared demolition by Nazi forces thanks to Adolph Hitler's chilling wish to preserve the area as an "exotic museum of an extinct race".

Best of the rest

Church of Our Lady Victorious (Chrám Panny Marie Vítezné)

T257 533 646, www.pragjesu.info. Mon-Sat 0830-1900, Sun 0830-2000. Map B3.

Home of the Infant Jesus of Prague, a 14th-century wax statue measuring 28 cm that was presented to the Carmelites in 1628 and is revered in Catholic countries around the world. Its spangly outfits are changed regularly by the nuns.

Marionette Museum

T380 711 175, www.mozart.cz. May and Oct daily 1000-1600; Jun-Aug daily 1000-1800; Sep daily 1000-1700. Map F2.

Housed in a former church, the exhibition features both antique and modern marionettes alongside a series of puppet theatres. The church's arched ceilings and original beams are ideal for showcasing these incredibly detailed little performers. Check website for productions at the National Marionette Theatre.

Top: Jewish Cemetery.
Bottom: Marionette Museum.

sinagoga) holds a moving Holocaust memorial, with chilling pictures drawn by children from the Trezín ghetto outside Prague, most of whom were later transported to concentration camps.

Náměstí Republiky (Republic Square)

Tram 3, 5, 14, 24 or 26, metro Náměstí Republiky. Off map.

This busy square, in the east of Nové Město, is worth visiting for the **Municipal House** (Obecní dům), *T222 002101, www.obecnidum.cz*, the city's finest art nouveau building. An exuberantly decorated cultural centre, it was opened in 1912 on the site of King's Court. A restaurant, opulent café and Smetana concert hall are on site. Next door is **Powder Tower** (Prasná brána), *daily Apr-Sep 1000-2200, Nov-Feb 1000-1800, Oct and Mar 1000-2000, CZK75*, one of a series of towers that once fortified the Old Town and were used to store gunpowder. The sharply pointed medieval tower is the starting point of the **Royal Mile**, along which Bohemian kings once marched towards their coronation. You can climb to the top for views over Staré Město.

Václavské náměstí (Wenceslas Square)

Tram 3, 9, 14 or 24, metro Muzeum or Můstek. Off map.

Site of the city's most important political protests for the last 150 years, this sloping space is more like a long, divided avenue than a square. Most famously, it was the backdrop to the Velvet Revolution of 1989, when half a million people protested against the government. At the southern end of the square is a statue of St Wenceslas, as well as the vast **National Museum**.

Národní muzeum

T224 497111, www.nm.cz.

The building is currently closed as part of a complete renovation programme. Work began in 2011 and is due to finish in 2015 with the doors scheduled to re-open in June.

Where to stay

Prague is crammed with characterful guesthouses and hotels; those in Staré Město tend to be more expensive, while those in Malá Strana are quieter.

Alchymist Grand Hotel & Spa €€€
Trziste 19, T257 286 011, www.alchymisthotel.com.
This magnificent building, dating back to 16th century, stands proudly at the base of Prague Castle. A great central location, yet manages to remain quiet.

Hotel Aria €€€
Triziste 9, T225 334 111, www.ariahotel.net.
As implied by the name, this is one for music lovers. It's a baroque hotel with a contemporary interior and composer-themed rooms, a comprehensive CD library, a musical director on hand to advise on concert venues in Prague, a music salon and a rooftop café.

Hotel Josef €€€
Rybná 20, Josefov, T221 700 111, www.hoteljosef.com.
Prague's most stylish hotel is a minimalist haven of glass, calm white lighting and the odd splash of colour. Rooms have groovy touches like DVD players and Sony Playstations. Models and rock stars make this their first port of call.

Hotel Archibald €€
Na Kampe 15, T257 531 430, www.archibald.cz.
Atmospheric, old-fashioned house just 50 m from Charles Bridge. Cosy rooms with wooden floors and stencilled walls; the room in the attic has a lovely beamed ceiling.

The Icon €€
V Jame 6, T221 634 100, www.iconhotel.eu.
Urban chic in the heart of the city. A top-notch team of designers created an ultra-modern, slick and stylish environment within a 19th-century building. The hotel's Zen Asian Wellness centre offers up a range of massage treatments to soothe those aching limbs after a busy day of sightseeing.

U Zlatého Jelena €€
Celetná 11/Štuparská 6, T257 531 925, www.goldendeer.cz.
Simple, airy rooms with parquet flooring, brass beds and tall windows, just a few steps from Old Town Square. Ask for a room overlooking the quiet courtyard. The staff are friendly and the breakfasts (included in the price) are substantial.

Czech Inn €
Francouzska 76, T267 267 612, www.czech-inn.com.
A modern and minimalist set-up that offers everything you could possibly want from a hostel. There are 2-bedroom apartments, private rooms and dorms to choose from, with free Wi-Fi throughout and a lively café with regular happy hours, quizzes, live music and an 'all you can eat' breakfast (CZK120).

Restaurants

The restaurant scene in Prague has improved immeasurably in recent years; for one thing, pork is no longer the key ingredient in all dishes. Although a traditional meal in a *pivnice* (pub) remains an essential part of a visit to Prague, there are now also a number of high-quality restaurants serving international cuisine.

Breakfast
Au Gourmand €
Dlouhá 10, T222 329 060, www.augourmand.cz.
Upmarket French boulangerie in the Old Town serving a delicious selection of pastries, cakes, snacks and Italian coffees in a cool, tiled interior.

Café Imperial €
Na Poříčí 15, T246 011 440, www.cafeimperial.cz.
Gorgeous high-ceilinged Hapsburg-era café, with tiled walls, rickety furniture and excellent coffee, which is served with free doughnuts in the morning. Breakfast is a big plate of eggs and sausages, and there are more substantial meals throughout the day.

Lunch
Nebozízek €€
Petrínské sady 411, T257 315 329,
www.nebozizek.cz.
Brilliant views from this traditional restaurant half-way up the funicular to Petřín, with a bright glass-covered terrace. Good salads and Bohemian onion soup, plus fresh fish and hearty game dishes.

Plzenska Beer Hall Restaurant €€
Republic Sq 5, T222 002 770,
www.plzenskarestaurace.cz.
Located inside Municipal House, one of Europe's most impressive art nouveau buildings, the restaurant is an old-fashioned beer hall with plenty of atmosphere. The menu offers a wide choice of traditional local fare, washed down with a large glass of frothy Czech beer.

Dinner
Kampa Park €€€
Na Kampě 8b, T296 826 112,
www.kampagroup.com.
This is Prague's most sophisticated restaurant, with a heated terrace looking over the river. It has a contemporary menu, complemented by a 150-strong wine list. The cooking is sublime: expect dishes like langoustine ravioli, and baby chicken with chanterelles and chorizo.

Lokal €
Dlouha 33, T222 316 265,
www.lokal-dlouha.ambi.cz.

In the heart of the Old Town you can experience authentic Czech dishes at very affordable prices. The restaurant resembles a traditional beer hall, and the atmosphere is relaxed, though usually buzzing with regulars. The food is all home-made, with goulash, pork schnitzel and dumplings making a regular appearance on the menu.

U Medvídků €
a Perštý§ 7, T224 211 916,
www.umedvidku.cz.
This wood-panelled and smoke-filled beer hall attracts a mix of local regulars and tourists. The food is traditional Czech stodge – pork, dumplings and sauerkraut – perfect for soaking up a few jars of the delicious on-tap Budvar, dark and light.

Nightlife

The English-language *Welcome to Prague* publication, produced by the tourist office, has basic seasonal information on up-to-date events. Tickets for the majority of venues can be bought online at www.ticketpro.cz or www.ticketportal.cz.

Bars and clubs
Traditional Prague nightlife revolves around top-notch beer in smoky pubs (*pivnice*), such as **Baráčnická rhychta**, *Tržiště 23*, in Malá Strana or **Kozicka**, *Kozi 1*, in Staré Město. The local beer is the main draw, thanks to famous

Municipal House.

names such as *Pilsner Urquell*, *Staropramen* and *Budvar*. One drawback of these good-value brews is that they attract a profusion of stag parties from the UK. Many bars and pubs now ban such groups from their premises.

Beer aside, many bars offer nightly live music, and a number of stylish cocktail bars have sprung up around the city in recent years, not to mention some dodgy Irish-themed pubs, mostly aimed at tourists. To find some of the best of the former, head to the streets around the north of Old Town Square.

Most of the city's nightclubs are yet to undergo a 21st-century style makeover but they continue to pull in the punters until the wee small hours.

Live music
The jazz scene is thriving, and it suits the vaulted, smoky cellars of the Old Town particularly well. The **Prague Jazz Festival** is held every autumn at **AghaRTA**, *Zelezna 16*, *www.agharta.cz*. Music-lovers also

flock to Prague every May for **Prague Spring**, *T257 312547, www.festival.cz,* one of the world's leading classical music festivals, which begins every year on 12 May with a performance of Smetana's *Má vlast* (My Country) and closes 3 weeks later with Beethoven's *Ninth Symphony.* It has been running since 1946 and attracts scores of symphony, philharmonic and chamber orchestras.

Prague's classical music venues are among the most beautiful buildings in the city. The **Prague Symphony Orchestra** plays at the **Municipal House**, on Náměstí Republiky (see page 254), while the illustrious **Czech Philharmonic** performs at the splendid **Rudolfinum**, *Alsovo nabr 12, T227 059 227, www.ceskafilharmonie.cz.*

Performances of opera and ballet are held amid the neo-Renaissance magnificence of the **National Theatre** (Národní divadlo), *Národní trída, T224 901448, www.narodni-divadlo.cz*; at the opulent **State Opera** (Státní opera), *Legerova 75, T296 117111, www.state-opera.com,* and at the **Estates Theater** (Stavovské divadlo), *Ovocný trh, T224 215 001, www.estatestheatre.cz.* The latter, a beautiful cream and pistachio building, is Prague's oldest theatre and hosted the premieres of Mozart's *Don Giovanni* and *La Clemenza de Tito* in the 18th century. *Don Giovanni* remains one of the most popular operas performed here to this day.

Travel essentials

Getting there
Ruzyně Airport, www.prg.aero, is 20 km northwest of the centre. Buses run every 20 mins to the city centre, taking 20 mins. Take No 119 to Dejvicka metro station, No 100 to Zlicin metro, and No 179 or No 225 to Nove Butovice metro. CZK32 gets you 90 mins on all means of public transport. **CEDAZ**, T220 114 296, www.cedaz.cz, runs a minibus shuttle to Náměstí Republiky (CZK150 per person) every 30 mins daily 0600-2130. Shared group transfers can be booked via www.prague-airport-transfers.co.uk (1-4 people CZK550, 5-8 CZK780). Taxis from outside the airport terminal should cost from CZK500 to the centre. International trains arrive at **Hlavní nádraží**, the city's main railway station. Call T840 112 113, or see www.vlak-bus.cz.

Getting around
The Old Town is easy to walk around, as is Malá Strana, although there's a fairly steep climb to the castle. **Dopravní Podnik** (DP), T296 191 817, www.dp-praha.cz, runs Prague's limited **metro** system, extensive **tram** and **bus** network, as well as a **funicular** train to the top of Petřín hill. The metro system has 3 lines: A (green), B (yellow) and C (red), running daily 0500-2400. Trams operate daily 0430-2400; buses run at similar times. Tram Nos 51-59 and bus Nos 502-514 and 601-603 run at night. The funicular runs daily Apr-Oct 0900-2330 and Nov-Mar 0900-23.20. Tickets need to be bought before boarding and are available from DP Information offices, some metro stations, tourist information centres and news-stands. The single ticket system is complicated, so visitors are better off buying a 24-hr or 72-hr pass (CZK110, CZK310). Tickets must be validated in the machines at stops and in metro stations before travel.

Tourist information
Prague Information Office, T124 44, www.praguewelcome.cz, has several outlets. The newest office is at Rytírská 31 (Mon-Sat 1000-1800). There is also an office in the Old Town Hall (daily 0900-1900) and in the summer a temporary office operates at the Lesser Town Bridge Tower (end of Jun-Oct 1000-1800). The **Prague Card** is available as a 2-, 3- or 4-day option (with or without transport). It gives free access to over 50 monuments and museums and can be purchased with an online discount at www.praguecard.com; 4 days with transport costs CZK1650; 2 days without transport costs CZK850.

Exchange rate Czech Koruna (CZK). £1 = CZK32. €1 = CZK27 (Nov 2013).

Ratings

Art and culture ☆☆☆
Eating ☆☆
Nightlife ☆☆☆☆
Shopping ☆
Sightseeing ☆☆
Value for money ☆
Overall city rating ☆☆☆

Reykjavik

Reykjavik is the coolest of cities. And that's not just because it's the most northerly capital in the world. Set in an expanse of lava fields, close to both the largest desert and biggest glacier in Europe, this remote outpost is so far off the European map it has virtually been granted a licence to be quirky, unconventional and ground-breaking in its music, architecture, sculpture and even lifestyle. With a population of only around 113,000, it is hardly a teeming metropolis but, what it lacks in size, Reykjavik more than makes up for in the brio and creativity of its youthful population. This restless energy is a reflection of the country's powerful, subterranean forces of nature which, with typical ingenuity, have been harnessed to make life more bearable in this harsh, unforgiving environment.

Downtown Reykjavik.

At a glance

The bohemian old town of Reykjavik, known as **101**, is situated between two water features: the harbour and the pond. In between you'll find the heart of the city, **Austurvöllur Square**, with the historic Alþing parliament building and cathedral. Follow the main street, **Austurstraeti**, and you reach Lækjatorg Square, from where the buses leave and the roads radiate. Across the road and up the hill is **Laugavegur**, Reykjavik's busiest street, buzzing with shops, bars and cafés. Down by the harbour, you'll find the flea market at weekends, where you can try specialities such as dried cod or putrefied shark meat (only for those with strong stomachs). Towering above the city is the soaring steeple of **Hallgrímskirkja**, always useful for getting your bearings. The other dominant feature on Reykjavik's skyline is **Perlan** (the Pearl), which sits above the city's hot water tanks. To the east of 101 is **Laugardalur Valley**, where you'll find the city's largest thermal swimming pool, the botanical gardens, zoo and one of the best sculpture museums. Just beyond Reykjavik itself is the vast emptiness of Iceland's weird and wonderful volcanic countryside. Even if you only have a few days, it's worth making the effort to get out of the city.

Solfar sculpture.

Austurvöllur Square

Map B3/4.

Although Lækjatorg Square is the actual centre, Austurvöllur is the real heart of the city. The grassy space was originally six times bigger than it is today and thought to be the site of Ingólfur Arnarson's farm – Reykjavik's first settler. Today it's a popular meeting place, surrounded by cafés and bars. The small church (1787) is actually the modest city **cathedral**; next to it is the **Alþing** (Parliament House), overlooked by a stern-looking statue of Jón Sigurdsson, who led Iceland to independence from Denmark in 1944. In the corner of the square is **Hotel Borg**, a graceful art deco hotel, frequented by the rich and famous. Surprisingly, the Icelandic rock revolution of the 1980s began here and the hotel became a magnet for the city's young punks.

Aðalstræti

Map B3.

This is the oldest street in Reykjavik. Archaeological excavations under the **Hotel Centrum** have revealed the remains of what is thought to be one of the very first settler houses, dating from AD 874 to AD 930. The city's oldest surviving house, dating from 1752, is also on Aðalstræti at No 10; it's now a bar-bistro called Viðalín.

Tjörnin and around

The town pond, Tjörnin, is popular with people out for a stroll or feeding the ducks and greylag geese. It was created at the end of the last Ice Age as a sand and gravel bar, built up by the pounding waves of Faxaflói Bay. The futuristic building that seems to rise right out of the pond is the **City Hall**, *Mon-Fri 0800-1900, Sat and Sun 1200-1800, free*. Inside is a large relief map of Iceland, a café and a small information desk. On the east side of the pond is the **Icelandic National Gallery**, *Fríkirkjuvegur 7, T515 9600, www.listasafn.is, Tue-Sun 1100-1700, ISK1000, free on Wed*, which has exhibitions from around the world and a small sculpture garden.

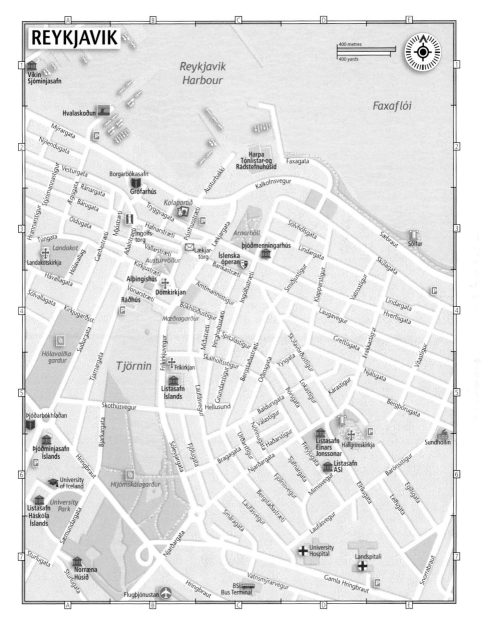

REYKJAVIK

Reykjavik Harbour

Faxaflói

400 metres
400 yards

Víkin Sjóminjasafn

Hvalaskoðun

Mýrargata

Nýlendugata

Vesturgata

Borgarbókasafn

Grófarhús

Harpa Tónlistar-og Ráðstefnuhúsið

Faxagata

Austurbakki

Kalkofnsvegur

Stýrimannastígur

Ránargata

Ægisgata

Bárugata

Túngata

Öldugata

Hrannarstígur

Tryggvagata

Kolaportið

Pósthússtræti

Mjóstræti

Hafnarstræti

Aðalstræti

Ingólfs-torg

Vallarstræti

Austurvöllur

Kirkjustræti

Landakot

Landakotskirkja

Hólavallag

Hávallagata

Garðastræti

Alþingishús

Dómkirkjan

Vonarstræti

Ráðhús

Mæðragarður

Bókhlöðustígur

Lækjargata

Arnarhóll

Lækjar-torg

Íslenska Óperan

Bankastræti

Amtmannsstígur

Ingólfsstræti

Þjóðmenningarhús

Sölvhólsgata

Lindargata

Smiðjustígur

Klapparstígur

Vatnsstígur

Sæbraut

Sólfar

Skúlagata

Lindargata

Hverfisgata

Laugavegur

Skólavörðustígur

Grettisgata

Frakkastígur

Vitastígur

Sölvallagata

Kirkjugarðsst

Suðurgata

Tjarnargata

Hólavalla-garður

Tjörnin

Fríkirkjuvegur

Fríkirkjan

Þingholtsstræti

Spítalastígur

Skálholtsstígur

Grundarstígur

Bergstaðastræti

Óðinsgata

Týsgata

Lokastígur

Njálsgata

Bergþórugata

Listasafn Íslands

Skothúsvegur

Laufásvegur

Hellusund

Baldursgata

Þórsgata

Kárastígur

Þjóðarbókhlaðan

Bjarkargata

Mímisvegur

Þjóðminjasafn Íslands

Hringbraut

Sóleyjargata

Fjölnisvegur

Fjölugata

Bragagata

Njarðargata

Nönnugata

Urðarstígur

Haðarstígur

Freyjugata

Spönngata

Listasafn Einars Jónssonar

Hallgrímskirkja

Listasafn ASÍ

Sundhöllin

Barónsstígur

University of Iceland

Hljómskálagarður

University Park

Listasafn Háskóla Íslands

Sæmundargata

Njarðargata

Bergstaðastræti

Laufásvegur

Smáragata

Laufásvegur

Eiríksgata

Egilsgata

Leifsgata

Sturlugata

Norræna Húsið

Sturlugata

Flugþjónustan

Hringbraut

BSÍ Bus Terminal

Vatnsmýrarvegur

University Hospital

Landspítali

Gamla Hringbraut

Snorrabraut

Þjóðminjasafn

Faxaflói

Around the city

On the opposite side is **Tjarnargata street** with its colourful early 20th-century timber houses.

National Museum of Iceland

Suðurgata 41, T530 2200, www.thjodminjasafn.is.
1 May-15 Sep daily 1000-1700; 16 Sep-30 Apr Tue-Sun 1100- 1700; guided tours daily 1100. ISK 1200; Wed free. Off map.

South of the pond, the National Museum is the best place to get a sense of 1200 years of Icelandic history. Tangible exhibitions and multimedia displays provide a fascinating insight into the Icelandic culture and how the nation has developed from the times of the earliest settlers to the present. The museum covers diverse aspects of the country's history, including mythology, the construction of early Viking buildings, the adoption of Christianity, the Reformation and the Census of 1703. It is well worth a visit.

Old Harbour

Although commercial fishing is now focused around Sundahöfn to the east, the old harbour area to the north of Austurvöllur Square has a certain charm (if you don't mind the lingering smell of fish) and remains busy with an influx of small fishing boats every now and then. The **Kolaportið flea market**, *Geirsgata, T562 5030, Sat and Sun 1100-1700, map B3*, is held in the old customs building by the quay. Locals flock to browse through piles of bric-a-brac and second-hand clothes, and it's a good place to taste some Icelandic delicacies, such as dried cod.

Just behind the customs building, the **Harbour House Museum**, *Tryggvagata 17, T511 5155, www.artmuseum.is, Fri-Wed 1000-1700, Thu 1000-2000, ISK1200*, houses diverse exhibitions by Icelandic and foreign artists. The focus is modern and experimental, with a permanent exhibition by contemporary Icelandic artist, Erró.

Hallgrímskirkja

Skólavörðustígur, T510 1000, www.hallgrimskirkja.is. Daily 0900-1700. Suggested donation ISK100, tower view ISK700. Map D6.

Dominating Reykjavik's skyline is this controversial 74-m-high church, reminiscent of a volcanic eruption. It was designed as part of a competition and took 49 years to build. (It was completed in 1986.) While the interior is quite bare, the views from the top out over the city are wonderful. In front of the church is a statue of Leifur Eríksson, the Viking who is believed to have discovered America around AD 1000.

Perlan and the Saga Museum

Öskjuhlíð Hill, T562 0200, www.perlan.is. Observatory daily 1000-2330. Free. Bus 13 from Lækjatorg Sq. Off map.

Sitting on top of Öskjuhlíð Hill, the **Pearl** is the nearest thing the city has to the Eiffel Tower, with viewpoints out over the city, a café and revolving gourmet restaurant inside. The iconic circular glass building sits atop the city's hot-water storage tanks and hosts regular art exhibitions, expos and concerts. It also houses one of the city's best museums, the **Saga Museum**, *T511 1517, www.saga museum.is, daily 1000-1800, winter 1200-1700, ISK2000*, which charts the early history of the country through the medieval stories of the sagas.

Down at the foot of the hill you'll find **Nauthólsvík Beach**, a quirky man-made beach with imported yellow sand and geothermal pools. A dip here is a must, come rain or shine.

Perlan.

Laugardalur Valley

Bus 14 from Lækjatorg Sq.

The name Reykjavik literally translates as 'smoky bay', the first settlers having mistaken the steam from the hot springs in the Laugardalur Valley for smoke. The springs are now used to feed **Laugardalslaug Thermal Pool**, *Sundlaugavegur 30a, T411 5100, Mon-Fri 0630-2200, Sat and Sun 0800-2200, ISK550*, the city's biggest swimming pool.

Across from the Laugardalslaug pool complex is the white-domed **Ásmunder Sveinsson Sculpture Museum**, *Sigtún, T553 2155, www.listasafnreykjavikur. is, May-Sep daily 1000-1700, Oct-Apr 1300-1700, ISK1200*. Ásmunder Sveinsson was one of the pioneers of Icelandic sculpture and many of his abstract pieces draw on Icelandic literature, fairytales and nature.

Blue Lagoon

240 Grindavík, Reykjanes Peninsula, T420 8800, www.bluelagoon.com.
Sep-May daily 1000-2000; Jun daily 0900-2100; Jul-Aug 0900-0000. From ISK5,500. Buses Jun-Sep from BSÍ terminal and Keflavík airport.

One of Iceland's most popular tourist attractions, the Blue Lagoon is best visited en route to the airport and is the perfect way to relax at the end of your trip. The lagoon is a steaming pool of milky turquoise water that leaches minerals from the lava

Outdoors

Being so close to nature is a major appeal when visiting Reykjavik and it's easy to get out of the city for a half or full day. One of the most popular day trips is the Golden Circle, which takes in three of Iceland's finest natural and historic features within a day's journey of Reykjavik. It is a good way to get a taste of the country's bizarre scenery. **Þingvellir National Park**, 49 km northwest of the city, www.thingvellir.is, was the site of the ancient Viking parliament. In the centre of the park you can see a dramatic rift in the earth where the Eurasian and American continental plates are pulling apart by 2 cm a year. To the northeast, **Geysir**, www.geysircenter.is, is the site of the original spouting hot spring that gave its name to all such natural features. Although it's no longer very active, another hot spring, **Strokkur**, spurts up to around 30 m, every four minutes. Some 10 km further on, **Gulfoss** is a huge two-step waterfall that partially freezes in winter. It's best to hire a car to reach these sights, but there are plenty of tours available. **Iceland Excursions**, www.grayline.is, and the **Activity Group**, www.activity.is, offer tours and a variety of activities, including dog sledding, horse riding across lava fields, white-water rafting and snowmobiling – an exhilarating way to see the ice fields and glaciers. Whale-watching trips provide the chance to see minke, humpback and orca whales, as well as dolphins and seals.

bed, filling it with healing properties. Lie back, put on a mud pack and try not to let that whiff of sulphur put you off.

The Blue Lagoon.

Where to stay

Reykjavik has a great range of accommodation from extravagant hotels to quality guesthouses. Many hotels shut down Oct-May.

Hotel 101 €€€
Hverfisgata 10, T580 0101, www.101hotel.is.
An ultra-fashionable boutique outfit with sculptures, murals, Icelandic art and an airy bar and restaurant. It's all very minimalist chic, and the spa and gym downstairs will help you keep as glam as the surroundings. A futuristic, luxury experience in the heart of the city.

Hotel Borg €€€
Pósthússtræti 11, T551 1440, www.hotelborg.is.
Reykjavik's finest is an art deco hotel in Austurvöllur Sq with lovingly preserved rooms and modern art. It's a movie-star haunt: Catherine Deneuve shacked up here when she came to visit Björk, and Marlene Dietrich stayed in 1944.

4th Floor Hotel €€
Laugavegur 101, T511 3030, www.4thfloorhotel.is.
A sleek, modern and intimate hotel in a prime spot for exploring the city's museums and art galleries. Laugavegur is also the city's main shopping street and home to some of Reykjavik's best nightlife. Location, location, location.

Guesthouse 101 €€
Laugavegur 101, T562 6101, www.iceland101.com.
Modern and spacious guesthouse in a large concrete building just off the main street, with moderate-sized rooms. Ideal location in the centre of the city for shopping, drinking and dining.

Kex Hostel €
Skulagata 28, T561 6061, www.kexhostel.is.
A quirky hostel housed in an old biscuit factory and furnished with re-cycled and vintage furniture and bric-a-brac. The factory is also home to the Living Art Museum, which adds to the hostel's bohemian air. A perfect location with a range of sleeping options available, from shared dorms to family rooms and hotel-standard doubles with en suite.

Restaurants

There is plenty of Icelandic and international cuisine. Standards are high – and so are the prices.

3 Frakkar €€€
Baldursgata 14, T552 3939, www.3frakkar.com.
Mon-Fri 1130-1430 and 1800-2200, Sat and Sun 1800-2300.
Meaning the 'three Frenchmen', this seafood restaurant specializes in Icelandic classics such as puffin and whale meat. Small and traditional. Free wine if you have to wait for a table.

Dill Restaurant €€€
Sturlugotu 5, T552 1522, www.dillrestaurant.is.
Mon-Tue 1130-1700, Wed-Sat 1130-2200, Sun 1300-1700.
Push the boat out at this cosy restaurant (seats 30) and order the 7-course menu, complete with carefully selected wines to accompany each course: New Nordic Kitchen at its best. This place opened its doors in 2009 and is still a hot ticket, making it essential to book ahead.

Fiskfelagid (Fish Company) €€€
Vesturgotu 2a, T552 5300, www.fiskfelagid.is
The name suggests fish, but there are plenty of other dishes on offer. Groups may like to choose the 'Round the World' menu or the 'Round Iceland' menu for some tantalizing taste sensations. One of the city's more expensive dining options, but worth splashing out on.

Baejarins Beztu €
corner of Tryggvagata and Pósthússtræti, www.bbp.is.
Reykjavik's original hot dog kiosk has become something of an institution. The hot dogs (*pylsur*) come with mustard, ketchup and raw or fried onions and are very tasty.

Sægreifinn €
Verbúð 8, T553 1500, www.saegreifinn.is.
May-Aug daily 1130-2300; Sep-Apr daily 1130-2200.

Run by 3 local fishermen including the 'sea baron' himself, this is actually a fish shop with a couple of wooden benches outside. The charming harbour setting and truly rustic feel make it a good, cheap spot for lunch. Try the delicious lobster soup or a barbecued fish kebab.

Nightlife

Bars and clubs
For many people, Reykjavik's nightlife is the main reason for coming to this cold and windswept spot. It's different to clubbing in other European destination, partly due to the size of the city, but, just as the country is geologically young and dynamic, so is its nightlife. The long summer days and yawning winter nights give a whole new twist to the concept of partying till dawn. Fri and Sat are the wildest nights, with clubbing till 0800. Bars and clubs don't really fill up until 2400 as the high alcohol prices – ISK800 for a pint of beer – force many locals to drink at home before heading into town. There are plenty of bars around Laugavegur such as bohemian **Kaffibarinn**, *Bergstadastræti 1*, rocking **Dillon**, *Laugavegur 30*, cool **Astro**, *Austurstraeti*, and lively **Vegamót**, *Vegamótastígur 4*. Later on, music fans often head to **Bakkus**, *Laugavegur 22*, with its nightly live music gigs or DJ sets,

accompanied by an impressive array of vodkas. A smaller version is the popular **Café Solon**, *Bankastraeti 7A*, which turns from a daytime bistro into a night-time club with guest DJs. Austurvollur Sq seems to be the in place for clubbers to congregate after closing time.

Live music
It's possible to find live music being performed every night of the week. Try **Gaukur á Stong**, *Tryggvagata 22*, and **Faktory**, *Smidjustig 6*, for anything from techno to latino.

Travel essentials

Getting around
Keflavík International Airport, T425 6000, www.kefairport.is, is 48 km from Reykjavik. The reliable Flybus (www.re.is/flybus) meets all incoming flights and drops you at your hotel or guesthouse, ISK1950, 45 mins. If you're determined not to fly, it is also possible to get to Iceland by boat with **Smyril Line**, T+298 345 900, www.smyrilline.com, from Denmark and Norway via the Shetland and Faroe Islands. (**NorthLink Ferries**, T+44 (0)845 600 0449, www.northlinkferries.co.uk, link Lerwick in Shetland with Aberdeen.) The ferry lands at Seyðisfjörður on the east coast, 682 km from Reykjavik.

Getting around
101 Reykjavik is small enough to walk around on foot. A stroll around town takes 20 mins; to walk to Laugavegur Valley or Öskjuhlíð Hill takes 30 mins. The yellow **Straeto** city buses operate Mon-Fri 0700-2400, Sat and Sun 1000-2400. They are reliable and efficient, running every 20 mins, less frequently at weekends. A single fare is ISK350. Lækjatorg Sq is the main bus terminal for local travel, where you can pick up route maps and timetables. Reykjavik is well suited to cycling as it is mainly flat. Bike rental is available from guesthouses and other places for around ISK2500 a day. To get out of the city, it's best to hire a car (**ALP Car Rental**, T562 6060, www.alp.is) or take a tour. Otherwise, buses run from the BSÍ terminal, Vatnsmyrarvegur, T552 2300.

Tourist information
The main tourist office is **The Centre**, Aðalstræti 2, T590 1500, www.visitreykjavik.is, Jun- mid Sep daily 0830-1900, mid Sep-May Mon-Fri 0900-1800, Sat 0900-1600, Sun 0900-1400. It provides all the information you could possibly need and can arrange tours, car hire and concert tickets. There's a bureau de change, internet access and tax refund centre here. Also useful is **This is Iceland**, Laugavegur 20, T561 6010, www.visiticeland.com, which offers free internet and a tour booking service. A **Reykjavik Welcome Card** (ISK2900 for 24 hrs, ISK3600 for 48 hrs and ISK4200 for 72 hrs) is available from the tourist office and offers free entry to the major museums and swimming pools as well as being a free bus pass.
  Exchange rate Icelandic Kronur (ISK). £1 = ISK192. €1 = ISK163 (Nov 2013).

Ratings

Art and culture ☆☆☆☆☆
Eating ☆☆☆☆
Nightlife ☆☆☆☆
Shopping ☆☆☆☆
Sightseeing ☆☆☆☆☆
Value for money ☆☆☆
Overall city rating ☆☆☆☆

Rome

All roads lead here; it wasn't built in a day, and, while in the city, you should do as the locals do, which might at first glance appear to be a lot of suicidal driving, sitting in piazzas drinking *aperitivi* and shopping in expensive boutiques. The Eternal City is so layered with history, sights and legend that it's unwise to aim to do more than scratch the surface. Much of Italy's best ancient Roman remains and Renaissance art and architecture are here, sometimes alongside (or even underneath) pared-down Futurist minimalism. The city's baroque fountains, despite being continually draped in camera-toting tourists, are spectacularly grand. And you should leave time for markets and museums, designer shops and *pizzerie* serving the thinnest, crispest pizzas. The Vatican – the world's smallest sovereign state – has more of interest than many large countries, from the gasp-inducing Sistine Chapel and Raphael masterpieces to the cathedral of St Peter.

Unlike some other Italian cities, Rome retains a sense of being intensely and vividly relevant; it is, after all, the capital of a major European country and the centre of a world religion. Surrounded by over 2000 years of history, contemporary Rome continues blithely to go about its business.

Foot of Emperor Constantine.

At a glance

Trains, and most of Rome's many visitors, arrive at **Stazione Termini**, to the east of the city centre. From the chaotic front of the station, via Nazionale heads from **piazza della Repubblica** southwest towards **piazza Venezia** and the main area of sights. The grandiose ugliness of the white marble **Il Vittoriano** (Victor Emmanuel II monument), sits to the south of piazza Venezia, with the hill of the **Campidoglio** (one of Rome's famous seven hills, complete with great museums and a beautiful piazza) behind it. The biggest area of ancient ruins stretches east and south from the Campidoglio: the vast **Colosseo** (Colosseum), the **Foro Romano** (Forum) and the hill of the **Palatino** effectively form a single archaeological zone of temples, arches, political and civic remains. The central areas of the city are enclosed on the eastern side of a large bend in the **River Tevere** (Tiber), which winds through the city. **Piazza Navona**, with its grand fountains and buildings, is usually considered to be the central point of the city, though the earthier marketplace of **campo de' Fiori**, just to the south, has more reason to be thought of as Rome's heart. Also here are many of Rome's main sights; the **Pantheon** is the city's most complete Roman building, and there are also many good shopping streets. On the northeastern edge of this central area, **via del Corso** is a long straight road lined with many of the city's smartest shops, leading north to **piazza del Popolo** and the green hill of **Pincio**. On the eastern side of via del Corso are two of the prime tourist hotspots: the **Fontana di Trevi** (Trevi Fountain) and the **Scalinata Trinità dei Monti** (Spanish Steps). On the other side of the river, **Trastevere** is boho and arty and has laid-back streets filled with bars and restaurants, though there's less in the way of conventional sights. To the north, also on the western side of the river, the **Castel Sant' Angelo** stands guard over a statue-lined bridge. From here, Mussolini's grand **via della Conciliazione** is the best approach to the **San Pietro** (St Peter's) and the **Vatican**.

24 hours in the city

Get up early to wander around **piazza Navona** and the fruit and vegetable market in **campo de' Fiori**. Dedicate the rest of the morning to the **Forum** and the **Palatine**, ending up in the **Colosseum**. Then head northwest through the atmospheric streets near the river for lunch. In the afternoon hit St Peter's, leaving enough time to queue and to climb up into the dome and onto the roof for spectacular views. (Even longer queues mean that trying to see the **Sistine Chapel** and the rest of the Vatican in one day is probably an inefficient use of your time. If you must see them, get here as early as possible and be prepared to wait.) In the evening return to the **campo de' Fiori**, by this time transformed into a chic *aperitivi* spot. After a prosecco here, head across the river for food in **Trastevere**, and, if you want to party, head further south to the increasingly fashionable area of **Testaccio**.

Musei Capitolini

piazza del Campidoglio, T06 6710 2475,
www.museicapitolini.org.
Tue-Sun 0930-2000. €13. Map E4.

Designed in the 16th century by Michelangelo, the piazza del Campidoglio and museums on the Capitoline hill are a brilliantly conceived ensemble.

Michelangelo's regal Cordonata staircase leads up to the piazza from the via del Teatro di Marcello, just south of piazza Venezia. In placing the stairs on the western side of the piazza, Michelangelo changed its orientation: instead of facing the Forum, it faces contemporary Rome.

The museums themselves are in the **Palazzo dei Conservatori** and **Palazzo Nuovo**: two

Foro Romano.

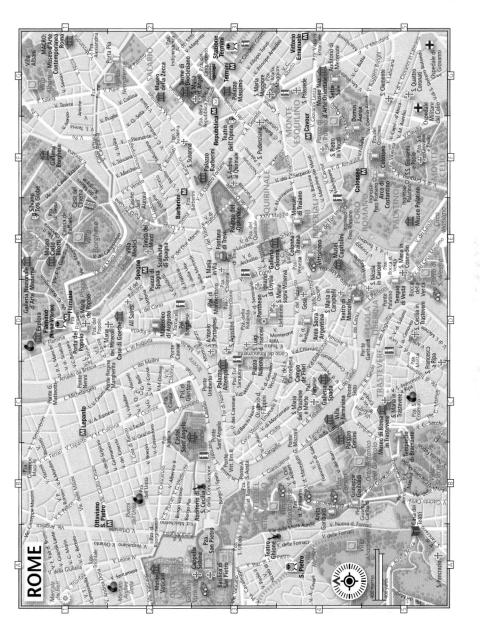

ROME

buildings facing the piazza and connected by the **Galleria Congiunzione**, an underground passage opened as a part of the Millennium celebrations and also allowing access to the Roman **Tabularium**, the archive of ancient Rome. There are good views from here over the Roman Forum.

The **Capitoline Museum** in the Palazzo dei Conservatori contains statues, bronzes and other artefacts. In its courtyard are the remnants of the enormous statue of Constantine that once stood in the Forum, including his gigantic hand. The rest of the statue was made of wood and has not survived. The second floor has works of art, including a Caravaggio and a Titian.

The **Palazzo Nuovo** contains an impressive collection of ancient marble statuary.

Romulus and Remus

In Roman mythology, Romulus and Remus were twins who founded the city of Rome. Their mother, Rhea Silvia, despite being a Vestal Virgin, was raped by Mars, the god of war and conceived the twins. Their uncle, Amulius, ordered a servant to kill the twins but instead they were cast adrift in a boat on the river Tiber. They were found by Tiberinus, the river god, and suckled by a she-wolf on the Palatine Hill, before being discovered by a shepherd who raised the children as his own. Once they became adults, Romulus and Remus returned home, killed their uncle and then built a settlement on the Palatine Hill in 753 BC. Remus killed Romulus, but then, feeling remorse, named the city after his brother. The historical background to the myth is unclear; it is likely that there was a settlement on the Palatine Hill before 753 BC. However, these details haven't stopped the she-wolf becoming a symbol of the city – a bronze of her suckling the twins can be seen in the Capitoline Museums.

Foro Romano and Palatine

via de Fori Imperiali, T06 3996 7700.
Daily 0830-1 hr before sunset. €12, combined with the Colosseum and valid for 2 days. Map E5.

Rome was almost certainly first settled on the Palatine hill, overlooking a crossing of the river Tiber. According to legend, it was here that Romulus and Remus, the founders of the city, were brought up by a she-wolf. Roman emperors built their palaces on the hill, while commerce, worship and justice took place in the Forum below.

Visitors are largely free to wander among the broken columns, and it's not hard to imagine the centre of the Roman Empire as it would have been 2000 years ago. There's little or no information, however, and a map of the ruins is useful in order to make out what is what. Highlights include the **Temple of Castor and Pollux**, the **Arch of Septimus Severus** and the **Arch of Titus**. The **Casa delle Vestali** was home to the Vestal Virgins for a minimum of 30 years of chastity.

The Palatine hill has remains of grand palaces including recently opened rooms in the **Casa di Augusto**, *end Mar-end Oct Sat-Mon, Wed and Thu 0830-1330*, as well as the 16th-century Hortus Farnese, Europe's oldest botanical gardens.

Colosseo

piazza del Colosseo, T06 3996 7700.
Daily 0830-1 hr before sunset. €12 including Forum and Palatine, valid for 2 days. To avoid the queues, buy the joint ticket at the Forum. Map F5.

Rome's most iconic building, sold in plaster miniature by souvenir sellers all over the city, the Colosseum is an impressive structure. Built from AD 72 to 80 by Emperor Vespasian and his son Titus, the city's ancient amphitheatre once seated as many as 70,000 people and was used for gladiatorial combat. Nine thousand animals are reported to have been killed during its 100-day opening celebrations.

It occupies the site of one of Nero's palaces, the Domus Aurea. A floor has been constructed at the

Colosseo.

level where the original would have been, but you can still see into the underground section where animals and combatants were kept.

The marble with which it was once clad was removed during the Renaissance and baroque periods to build houses and to construct St Peter's.

Musei Vaticani

viale Vaticano 100, T06 6988 4676, www.museivaticani.va.
Mon-Sat 0900-1800, last entry 1600, €15. Last Sun of month 0900-1400, last entry 1230, free. Map A2.

The Vatican Museums have an extraordinary wealth of art, including the masterpieces of Michelangelo in the **Capella Sistina** (Sistine Chapel), and those of Raphael in the **Stanze di Raffaello**. Michelangelo famously lay on his back for four years, between 1508 and 1512, to create his astonishing *Creation* on the ceiling. (Goethe said of it: "Without having seen the Sistine Chapel one can form no appreciable idea of what one man is capable of achieving.") He returned 23 years later to spend another six years painting the darker *Last Judgement* on the end wall above the altar. There is a self-portrait in it – Michelangelo paints himself

as a flayed skin in the hand of St Bartholomew. Both paintings were subject to a controversial restoration in the 1980s and 1990s which some claim now makes the frescoes too colourful.

The Raphael Rooms are only slightly less astounding: four rooms are frescoed with themes of truth and beauty as well as the achievements of popes. The most famous image includes depictions of Leonardo as Plato, Michelangelo as Heraclitus and Raphael as himself.

Start early and, especially in high season, be prepared for a long wait to get in. Once inside, colour-coded routes help find a way through the Papal treasure troves. Most visitors head straight for the Sistine Chapel but there is plenty more to see.

Basilica di San Pietro

piazza San Pietro, T06 6988 1662.
Apr-Oct daily 0700-1900; Nov-Mar Thu-Tue 0700-1830, Wed 1300-1830. Free. Cupola: Apr-Oct daily 0800-1800; Nov-Mar daily 0800-1700. €5 (or €7 if you take the lift to the 1st stage). Bare shoulders and knees not allowed in the basilica. Map A3.

The biggest church in Christendom, St Peter's can hold 60,000 people. The basilica's current incarnation was started in 1506. The original plans were drawn up by Bramante but then changed by Raphael, who took over after the original architect's death. Michelangelo then took charge and changed the plans again, and it was largely his Greek cross design with its enormous dome that was finally consecrated in 1626.

Inside, the enormity of the Vatican's church is emphasized by a line in the floor displaying the lengths of other big churches around the world. Of the many highlights, Michelangelo's *Pieta*, sculpted from marble when he was only 24 years old, is the most affecting. Regrettably now behind glass, the sculpture loses some, but not all, of its disarmingly human qualities. Another highlight not to be missed is the climb up into the dome and out onto the terrace. From here there are great views down into the Vatican gardens in one direction and, in the other, over the 140 statues of saints on the colonnade to the piazza below. Note that there are 551 steps to climb, or 320 if you opt to take the lift up the first stage.

If you're here on a Wednesday morning, you can get a glimpse of the Pope in the distance addressing enthusiastic crowds in piazza San Pietro.

Il Vittoriano

piazza Venezia.
Monument and museum summer daily 0930-1730; winter daily 0930-1630. Free; lift €7. Map E4.

The Monumento a Vittorio Emanuele II, more often called simply il Vittoriano, or, with less deference, the wedding cake or the typewriter, is one of Rome's most memorable monuments, if not its most beautiful. Built at the turn of the 20th century in honour of King Victor Emmanuel, it has always been controversial: its construction involved the demolition of an old part of the city, and many Romans consider it out of proportion and out of style with its surroundings.

It now serves various purposes – the tomb of the unknown soldier is here, with an eternal flame, as are various exhibition spaces and the **Museo del Risorgimento**, with information about the unification of Italy. The upper levels are a good point from which to look across at the **Mercati di Traiano** (Trajan's Markets), and a glass lift ascends right to the top for an expensive but impressive view over the city.

Fontana di Trevi

piazza di Trevi. Map E3.

Made especially famous by Anita Ekberg, who took the plunge in *La Dolce Vita*, the Trevi Fountain sits at the end of the Aqua Virgo, one of the aqueducts that supplied ancient Rome with crucial fresh water from outside the city (these days the water is treated with chlorine). Designed by Nicola Salvi in 1730 using elements of an earlier design by Bernini, the baroque fountain is Rome's grandest and is semi-permanently surrounded by a sea of coin-throwing tourists and by security guards who stop anyone wading in.

Scalinata di Spagna

Map E2.

In some ways an unlikely candidate for tourist must-see status, the 18th-century Spanish Steps consist of 138 stairs originally built into the hill to connect the Spanish embassy with the Holy See.

At the top of the monumental stairs is the church of **Trinità dei Monti** from where the views across the city's rooftops are spectacular. Shoppers gather for a rest in the **piazza di Spagna** at the bottom. John Keats lived in a house at the bottom of the steps and died there in 1821. It is now a museum dedicated to the poet and his contemporaries: **Keats-Shelley House**, *piazza di Spagna 26, T06 678 4235, www.keats-shelley-house. org, Mon-Sat 1000-1300, 1400-1800, €5.*

Pantheon

piazza della Rotunda, T06 6830 0230.
Mon-Sat 0830-1930, Sun 0900-1800. Free. Map D3.

Built in AD 125 by Emperor Hadrian to replace an earlier building that had been destroyed by fire, the Pantheon is ancient Rome's most complete monument. A perfectly circular rotunda, the building is 43 m wide and 43 m high. A central oculus in the dome is open to the sky and lets through striking shafts of sunlight into the shadows. The dome was the largest in Western Europe until Brunelleschi's dome in Florence's Duomo was built in 1436.

The building was consecrated in AD 609 as a Christian church. Partly for this reason the Pantheon was spared the damage inflicted on other Roman structures. The reason for the dome's survival may also have something to do with the composition of Roman concrete.

Since the Renaissance the building has been used as a tomb for the famous. Those buried here include Raphael and two Italian kings.

Piazza Navona

Map C3.

The central piazza of Rome, piazza Navona was built on top of the first-century Stadium of Domitian, which explains its rectangular shape. Surrounded by baroque architecture, the main points of interest in the piazza are its fountains, notably Bernini's central **Fontana dei Quattro Fiume** (Fountain of the Four Rivers), representing the Danube, the Ganges, the Nile and the Río de la Plata. The **Fontana Nettuno**

Opposite page: Michelangelo's *Pieta*.
Above: Pantheon.

(Fountain of Neptune), at the northern end of the piazza, is by Giacomo della Porta.

Campo de' Fiori

Map C4.

A more proletarian counterpoint to piazza Navona's aristocracy, the campo de' Fiori (commonly referred to simply as Il Campo) has a lively and high-quality fruit and vegetable market and plenty of equally lively bars and restaurants. In recent years Il Campo has been increasingly gentrified, but it retains some of its down-to-earth feel. It really comes into its own in the evenings, once the stalls are cleared away and locals descend to drink *aperitivi* at the outdoor tables and watch the world go by. The central statue is of Giordano Bruno, a philosopher burned at the stake here in 1600 for suggesting that philosophy was superior to religion. Julius Caesar also died nearby.

Best of the rest

Castel Sant'Angelo
lungotevere Castello 50, T06 681 9111.
Tue-Sun 0900-1930. €7. Map C3.
Hadrian's final resting place was built in AD 135
and has great views as well as a chapel designed by
Michelangelo. Over the centuries it has served as
both a refuge and a prison for popes, and it was the
setting for Puccini's opera *Tosca*.

Museo dell'Ara Pacis
lungotevere in Augusta, www.arapacis.it.
Tue-Sun 0900-1900. €8. Map D2.
Richard Meier's boldly contemporary space holds
Emperor Augustus's altar, one of the great works of
Ancient Rome.

Museo e Galleria Borghese
piazzale del Museo Borghese 5, T06 32810,
www.galleriaborghese.beniculturali.it.
Tue-Sun 0900-1900, booking essential. €11. Map F1.
Some of the city's best Renaissance art and statuary
is to be found in Rome's elegant park. Includes
masterpieces by Bernini and Titian.

San Clemente
via di San Giovanni in Laterano, www.basilicasan
clemente.com. Mon-Sat 0900-1230, 1500-1800. Map G5.
This 12th-century church has fourth-century origins
and a Roman street beneath it.

The Ghetto

Map D4.

Jews have lived in Rome for over 2000 years, meaning
that the Roman Jewish community is the oldest in
Europe. The relative security of Roman Jews through
the ages came at the cost of a tax imposed by the
Catholic church from the 14th century onwards.

Shops in this area west of the Capitoline hill offer
kosher pizza and there is an attractive synagogue in
which the **Museo Ebraico di Roma**, *Lungotevere de'*
Cenci, T06 6840 0661, www.museoebraico.roma.it,
Jun-Sep Sun-Thu 1000-1900, Oct-May Sun-Thu 1000-1700,
€11, details centuries of maltreatment by the Vatican
as well as the rounding up of 2000 Jews in 1943.

Trastevere

Map C5.

The name Trastevere (the stress is on the first 'e')
comes from the Latin *trans Tiberim*, meaning over
the Tiber. This area on the west bank retains some
of its centuries-old otherness and a somewhat
bohemian identity. It is at its best in the evenings,
when many Romans come and visit its lively bars
and relatively cheap restaurants. It is also worth a
wander during the day, however.

The church of **Santa Maria in Trastevere**, *piazza*
Santa Maria in Trastevere, T06 581 9443, daily 0730-2100,
is the area's most obvious sight and has some
glittering 13th-century mosaics. It is one of the oldest
churches in Rome and is set in a cobbled piazza.

To the north is a green area of parks around
the Gianicolo hill, including the **Orto Botanico**
(Botanical Garden), *largo Cristina de Svezia 24*.
Originally established in 1833, it hosts over 3500
species and includes a 'scent and touch' garden.

Trastevere mosaic.

Where to stay

Many of Rome's cheaper sleeping options are near the station, though few can be wholeheartedly recommended. Trastevere and the southern part of the *centro storico* offer many of the best mid-range options, while further north, around the Spanish Steps, prices and standards of service rise still further. In general, the city's hotels are expensive compared to the rest of southern Europe.

Hotel Art by the Spanish Steps €€€
via Margutta 56, T06 328711, www.hotelartrome.com.
Sleekly modern and self-consciously hip, Hotel Art sometimes tries too hard, but generally its efforts pay off. It has micro-lighting, wooden floors and colour schemes in place of floor numbers.

Hotel Eden €€€
via Ludovisi 49, T06 478121, www.edenroma.com.
This hotel has refined old-fashioned elegance, a stylish bar and restaurant and great views from the terrace garden. If money is no object you may want to consider booking the penthouse – a snip at over €5000 a night.

Astoria Garden €€€-€€
via Bachelet 8, T06 446 9908, www.hotelastoriagarden.it.
One of the best options near the station, the Astoria Garden has smart if rather generic rooms and, as the name suggests, a garden. Good value out of season.

Campo de Fiori €€€-€€
via del Biscione 6, T06 6880 6865, www.hotelcampodefiori.com.
Ivy-clad and antique-filled, with great views from the roof terrace; the hotel also has apartments for rent nearby.

Casa Howard €€€-€€
via di Capo Le Case 18 and via Sistina 149, T06 6992 4555, www.casahoward.com.
The name is the Italian title of EM Forster's novel, *Howard's End*, from which you might imagine a staid attempt at Englishness – you'd be wrong. This excellent-value designer B&B has 2 locations. The design is bright and colourful and the attention to detail commendable, from the slippers and the fresh breakfasts to the carefully sourced soap.

Donna Camilla Savelli €€€-€€
via Garibaldi 27, T06 588 861, www.hoteldonnacamillasavelli.com.
This ex-convent in Trastevere has plush rooms arranged around an attractive garden courtyard. There are excellent views of the city from the imperial suite.

Hotel Santa Maria €€€-€€
vicolo del Piede 2, T06 589 4626, www.htlsantamaria.com.
A friendly place in the middle of Trastevere, Santa Maria has an attractive central courtyard with orange trees, where a good breakfast is served. Free Wi-Fi as well as bicycles to borrow for sightseeing.

Arco dei Tolomei Guesthouse €€
via Arco dell'Arco dei Tolomei 27, T06 5832 0819, www.bbarcodeitolomei.com.
A homely little Trastevere B&B with lots of faded floral wallpaper, books and plenty of antique charm.

Hotel Navona €€
via dei Sediari 8, T06 6830 1252, www.hotelnavona.com.
Very central and good value, Navona has some antique style, and you'd be hard pushed to find anything else as reasonable within a stone's throw of piazza Navona itself. The same owners also run the more upmarket **Residenza Zanardelli**.

Restaurants

Many of the best restaurants are in the area around campo de' Fiori or across the river in Trastevere, where eating out is traditionally a little cheaper. Spaghetti carbonara is the archetypal traditional Roman dish, which you'll find nearly everywhere. Be sure to try a thin, crispy Roman pizza, too.

Lunch

Òbikà €€
*via dei Prefetti 26a, T06 683 2630,
www.obika.com.*
A restaurant based entirely
around 1 ingredient: mozzarella.
The real buffalo-milk stuff arrives
fresh daily from Naples, Salerno
and Caserta. The design mixes
steely minimalism with ancient
Roman touches.

Da Lucia €
*vicolo del Mattonato 2, T06 580
3601, www.trattoriadalucia.com.*
Popular and steadfastly
old-fashioned, this Trastevere
back-street eatery is one of the
best places to get a simple bowl
of spaghetti.

Il Bocconcino €
*via Ostilia 23, T06 7707 9175,
www.ilbocconcino.com.*
A traditional *osteria* that's popular
with locals despite being close
to the Colosseum. Tasty dishes
are made with fresh local
ingredients; look for tripe on Sat,
or traditional dumplings on Thu.

Il Forno di Campo de' Fiori €
*campo de' Fiori 22, T06 6880 6662,
www.fornocampodefiori.com.*
Simple but notoriously delicious
white or red pizza by the slice
attracts lots of local workers
at lunchtimes. Closes for the
afternoon at 1430, so don't turn
up too late.

Dinner

Al Bric €€€
*via del Pellegrino 51-52,
T06 687 9533, www.albric.it.*
A well-informed wine list is the
centrepiece of this *enoteca*, which
also serves imaginative food,
combining the traditional and the
modern. Dishes include swordfish
stroganoff and duck pappardelle.

Da Felice €€
*via Mastro Giorgio 29, T06 574
6800 , www.feliceatestaccio.it.*
A smart place in the increasingly
fashionable district of Testaccio,
offering contemporary tweaks
on Roman classics.

Il Margutta €€-€
via Margutta 118, T06 326 50577.
A Roman institution, this
vegetarian restaurant offers an
extensive buffet at lunchtime,
as well as inventive à la carte
dishes in the evening.

Dar Poeta €
*vicolo del Bologna 46, T06 588
0516, www.darpoeta.com.*

One of Rome's most popular
pizzerias, Dar Poeta also
packs in customers for its
calzone filled with Nutella.

Trattoria da Augusto €
piazza de' Renzi 15, T06 580 3798.
Trattoria da Augusto can be
chaotic but is never less than
good-natured. The food is
excellent traditional fare served
outside on communal tables in a
less smart piazza than the nearby
Santa Maria. You'll do better if
you speak some Italian, since
menus are mostly of the spoken
variety. Be prepared to hang
around to get a table.

Cafés and gelaterias

Il Gelato di San Crispino
*via della Panetteria 42,
T06 679 3924.*
Some have suggested that the
exceedingly good ice cream
served here might be the best in
the world. Try the trademark
gelato di San Crispino, flavoured
with honey, and you may never
be able to eat a *Cornetto* again.

Nightlife

Bars and clubs

Trastevere and the area around campo de' Fiori are often considered the liveliest for nocturnal Roman activities; campo de' Fiori is especially good for an early evening *aperitivo*. The best nightclubs, however, are to be found in **Testaccio**, a previously working-class area to the south. Many of the city's nightclubs are smart and pricey, and the live music scene is limited, but the number of alternative venues is increasing, and interesting events often happen at the city's *centri sociali*. Nights start (and finish) late – don't expect much action before midnight – and note that during the summer months some clubs move out to the coast. Listings magazines like *Roma Cè* give up-to-date details of what's on.

Live music

Classical music and opera tends to fare better than other music, especially in summer, when events sometimes take place in great outdoor settings, from Testaccio's ex-slaughterhouse to the Baths of Caracalla and the Botanical Gardens. The Renzo Piano-designed **Auditorium Parco della Musica**, *via P de Coubertin 15, www.auditorium.com*, has injected new life into Rome's music scene.

Travel essentials

Getting there

Fiumicino Airport, T06 65951, www.adr.it, 25 km southwest of the city centre, is the city's main airport. The **Leonardo Express** rail service connects the airport to Rome's main train station every half an hour 0630-2330. It's a 35-min journey and costs €14. A taxi to or from the centre of the city costs €45. **Ciampino Airport**, T06 65951, www.adr.it, 15 km southeast of the centre, is the smaller airport and serves budget airlines. There are various ways of getting to Ciampino, some of which are not quite as simple or cheap as they should be. A **Terravision** bus service runs to coincide with flights, €6 single, €11 return. A taxi costs €35. Alternatively you can catch a bus (every 20 mins) to make the short hop to Ciampino station from where trains connect to **Roma Termini** every 10 mins. International trains, including the Palatino sleeper service from Paris, arrive at the Termini station, www.trenitalia.com.

Getting around

The same ticket system covers bus, metro and tram systems. Standard tickets cost €1.50 and are valid for 100 mins from the time of being stamped on all forms of transport. Confusingly, however, they can only be used once on trains and metros. For €6 you can buy a *giornaliero* ticket which lasts all day. The bus system is relatively efficient, though routes from the station to the Vatican have a reputation for pick-pockets. The metro is also efficient, but less useful to visitors since it mostly links the suburbs to the city centre. Licensed taxis are white and have meters. Don't use anything else purporting to be a taxi.

Tourist information

There are useful **Punti Informativi Turistici** around the city centre at locations such as: piazza delle Cinque Lune (nr piazza Navona), T06 6880 9240, daily 0930-1900; via Leopardi 24, Mon-Fri 0930-1900; Fiumicino airport and Termini railway station. A useful website is www.060608.it.

Shopping

Rome still has plenty of small shops run by local families rather than big chains: Trastevere and the streets around campo de' Fiori are great areas for discovering bookshops, delicatessens, antique dealers and craft shops.

Rome's most famous products are shoes and other fashion accessories, such as bags and gloves. For fashion, **via del Corso** and the roads that run off it make up Rome's main shopping area where you'll find the headquarters of brands such as *Gucci* and *Bulgari*. Via Frattina, via Condotti and via del Babuino are especially good for burning holes in wallets.

Ratings

Art and culture ☆☆☆☆
Eating ☆☆☆☆
Nightlife ☆☆☆
Shopping ☆☆
Sightseeing ☆☆☆☆
Value for money ☆☆☆☆
Overall city rating ☆☆☆☆

Seville

Even within Spain the name of this one-time mercantile powerhouse is spoken like a mantra; Sevilla is a word laden with sensuality and promise. Delving beyond the famous icons: the horse carriages, the oranges, the flamenco, the haunting Semana Santa celebrations, you'll find a place where being seen is nothing unless you're seen to be having fun; a place where the ghosts of Spain walk the streets, be they fictional, like Don Juan and Carmen, or historical, like Cervantes and Columbus.

Seville has an astonishing architectural heritage within its enormous old town, still girt by sections of what was once Europe's longest city wall; you could spend weeks here and not get to see all the sights. But don't spend all your time sightseeing, for chief among the city's delights is its tapas culture. The Sevillanos claim to have invented tapas; many of your most pleasurable moments in this hot, hedonistic city will come with glass and fork in hand.

Courtyard in Alcázar.

At a glance

The historic hub of Seville is dominated by two awesome symbols of power and wealth, the **Real Alcázar palace**, and the **cathedral** with its emblematic **Giralda** – a sublime tower in beautiful brick. Nearby, Seville's Moorish and Jewish heritage is still elusively alive among the narrow streets of **Barrio Santa Cruz**, just east of the cathedral, and home to some fine tapas bars. South of the cathedral, the optimistic buildings erected for the 1929 Exhibition have been put to good use; students bustle about and city folk stroll in the blessed shade of the **Parque María Luisa**, with its improbably grand **Plaza de España** and two museums. **El Arenal**, west of the cathedral and once the sandy, seedy, flood plain of the Guadalquivir river, was built up around Seville's bullring and is now a riverside area with a theatre, good tapas and the fine art of the Hospital de la Caridad. To the south, **Triana**'s trendified riverbank is a mass of bars and restaurants; its backstreets full of tradition and beautiful tiles. A cluster of plazas, shopping streets, hidden baroque churches and the fabulous Metropol Parasol fill Seville's old town (**Centro**). Nearby, quiet **San Vicente** offers the fine Museo de Bellas Artes. **La Macarena**, to the north, has friendly local bars, lively markets and quiet lanes brimming with Gothic- Mudéjar convents and churches. The river island of **Isla de la Cartuja** was the site of World Expo 1992.

Below top: Bull Ring.
Below bottom: Tobacco Factory tiles.

Cathedral and La Giralda

Pl del Triunfo s/n, T954 563 150,
www.catedraldesevilla.es.
Sep-Jun Mon-Sat 1100-1730, Sun 1430-1830;
Jul-Aug Mon-Sat 0930-1630, Sun 1430-1830.
Last entry half an hour before. Mon afternoon
pre-reserved visits only. Admission €8. Map D3.

At the beginning of the 15th century, 150 years after the fall of Seville to the Christians, a cathedral was erected over the site of a mosque. **Santa María de la Sede** is the result: a Gothic edifice of staggering proportions and with a spectacularly ornate exterior. Inside, the immense, solemn interior is made up of nearly 50 chapels and a massive five-naved central structure, all crammed full of artistic treasures. The mosque's minaret, the

superb **Giralda** tower (and the city's symbol), was retained as the bell tower, and can be climbed via a series of ramps, while pretty **Patio de los Naranjos**, the Moorish ablutions area, has also survived.

Real Alcázar

Pl del Triunfo s/n, T954 502 323,
www.alcazarsevilla.org.
Oct-Mar 0930-1700 (daily), Apr-Sep 0930-1900,
last entry 1 hr earlier, €8.75. Map D4.

The present Alcázar owes its Islamic look (horseshoe arches, stucco, Arabic calligraphy and coffered ceilings) not to the Moorish rulers (little remains from that period) but to the Castillian kings Alfonso X and his son Pedro I. As well as being a sumptuous palace and a popular residence for visiting Spanish royalty, the Alcázar was once a considerable fortress, as you can see when you pass through the chunky walls of the red **Puerta del León**. From here you emerge into a large courtyard dominated by the impressive façade of the main palace of the Castillian kings (inscriptions about the glory of Allah – Pedro I was a pretty enlightened man – adjoin more conventional Latin ones proclaiming royal greatness). To the left is the **Patio del Yeso**, one of the few remaining Moorish structures. Across the courtyard are chambers built by Fernando and Isabel to control New World affairs. Magellan planned his trip here and there's an important *retablo* from this period of the Virgen de los Navegantes. There's also the vast, fantastic garden to stroll in; take a peaceful break from the sometimes frenetic centre. Atmospheric night visits are available at weekends (€12).

Museo de Bellas Artes

Plaza del Museo 9, T954 786 500, www.museodebellasartesdesevilla.es.
Mid-Sep to May Tue-Sat 1000-2030, Sun 1000-1700; Jun to mid-Sep Tue-Sat 0900-1530, Sun 1000-1700. Free for EU citizens. €1.50 for others. Map B2.

Seville's major art gallery is a must-see, housed in a picturesque 17th- to 18th-century convent. Thoughtfully laid out and thankfully uncluttered, it's a treasure trove of Spanish art from the 15th-20th centuries including El Greco, Velásquez, Murillo, Zurbarán – and a late portrait by Goya.

Espacio Metropol Parasol

Pl de la Encarnación, www.setasdesevilla.com.
Viewing platform Mon-Fri 1030-2400, Sat, Sun 1030-0100, €1.35. Map D1.

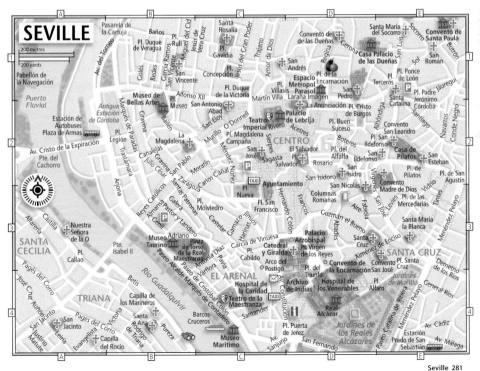

Semana Santa and Feria de Abril

Seville's Holy Week processions are an unforgettable sight. Mesmeric candlelit lines of hooded figures and cross-carrying penitents make their way through the streets accompanied by the mournful notes of a brass band and two large *pasos* (floats), one with a scene from the Passion, one with a statue of Mary. This isn't unique to Seville but what makes it so special is the Sevillans' extraordinary respect for, and interest in, the event. Members of nearly 60 *cofradías* (brotherhoods) practise intensively for the big moment when they leave their home church and walk many hours through the streets to the cathedral and then home again. Some of the brotherhoods have well over a thousand in the parade; these consist of *nazarenos*, who wear pointed hoods (adopted by the KKK, but designed to hide the face of a man repentant before God), *penitentes*, who carry crosses, and *costaleros*, who carry the *pasos*. The first brotherhoods walk on Palm Sunday and the processions continue up until Easter Sunday, when a single *cofradía* celebrates the Resurrection.

Feria de Abril (usually in April, depending on Easter), originally a livestock market but now a major event in the Seville calendar, provides a lively antidote to the solemnity of Semana Santa. Line upon line of colourful marquees (*casetas*) reverberate to the slurping of manzanilla and the gyrations of pairs dancing *sevillanas*.

Consisting of six giant interlinked wooden structures (nicknamed Las Setas, or 'the mushrooms'), this striking addition to the cityscape was designed by Jürgen Mayer and opened in 2011. A spectacular series of walkways puts you up among the city's rooftops, giving great views in all directions. It's a magical place to be at sunset. Downstairs is a food market and Roman remains.

Barrio Santa Cruz

Once home to much of Seville's Jewish population, atmospheric Santa Cruz is the most charming of the city's barrios: a web of narrow, pedestrian lanes linking attractive small plazas with orange trees and shady terraces aplenty. There is a fairly standard tourist beat but you can easily get away from it. It's also a good place for hotels, restaurants and shopping. While there are a few sights of interest, such as the excellent baroque church of **Santa María la Blanca** and the **Hospital de los Venerables**, *T954 562 696, www.focus.abengoa.es, daily 1000-1400, 1600-2000, €5.50*, the main enjoyment to be had is wandering around and trying to guess where you'll end up.

South of the cathedral

Much of the area south of the cathedral is taken up with the large green space of **Parque María Luisa**. It was used as the site for the grandiose 1929 Ibero-American Exhibition that the Primo de Rivera dictatorship hoped would return Seville and Spain to the world spotlight. The legacy is a public park and a beautiful series of buildings. The **Hotel Alfonso XIII**, just south of the Alcázar, is one of the most sumptuous in Spain. Next door, the **Antigua Fábrica de Tabacos**, *C San Fernando 4, T954 551 000, Mon-Fri 0800-1500, free*, is the cigarette factory made famous in the late 19th century by Carmen; it's now used by the university. In the park beyond, the Plaza de España is an impressive colonnaded space. Two of the pavilions from the 1929 exhibition have been converted into outstanding museums: the colourful **Museo de Artes y Costumbres Populares de Sevilla**, *Pl de América 3, T954 712 391, mid-Sep to May Tue-Sat 1000-2030, Sun 0900-1700; Jun to mid-Sep Tue-Sat 0900-1530, Sun 1000-1700, free to EU residents, €1.50 for others*; and the rich **Museo Arqueológico**, *Pabellón de Bellas Artes, Pl de América s/n, T954 786 474, same opening details*. A walk through this part of town provides a fascinating view of an architectural ensemble built just years before the Civil War that plunged the city and country into decades of poverty and monoculturalism.

El Arenal

Built up in the 19th century, El Arenal has some of Seville's major landmarks. The **Torre del Oro**, *Paseo de Colón s/n, T954 222 419, Mon-Fri 0930-1845, Sat-Sun 1030-1845, €3*, is a beautiful Moorish tower. The exhibition is mediocre but worth seeing for the prints of Seville in the late 16th century. **La Maestranza**, *Paseo de Colón 12, T954 224 577, www.realmaestranza.com, Nov-Apr 0930-1900, May and Oct 0930-2000, 0930-2300 Jun-Sep except fight days when it's open 0930-1500, €7*, is one of Spain's most important temples of bullfighting.

The **Hospital de la Caridad**, *C Temprado 3, T954 223 232, Mon-Sat 0900-1300, 1530-1900, Sun 0900-1230, €5*, is a nursing home with a remarkable collection of 17th-century Sevillan art including haunting masterpieces by Juan de Valdés Leal. The **Río Guadalquivir** itself is also a major attraction here; although there are no longer galleons bound for the Spanish Main, there are several outdoor bars, river cruises, and a place to hire canoes.

Triana

Triana is many people's favourite part of Seville It has a picturesque riverfront lined with bars and restaurants, and was for a long time the gypsy barrio and home of flamenco in Seville (its backstreet bars are still the best place to catch impromptu performances). Triana is also famous for ceramics; most of the *azulejo* tiles that so beautifully decorate Seville's houses come from here, and there are still many workshops in the area. It's got a different feel to the rest of the city, and *trianeros* are still a tight-knit social group. While the riverfront and surrounds are fairly trendy these days, venture into some of the smaller backstreets and you'll find that Triana preserves more of its history and associations than any other part of Seville.

Best of the rest

Archivo de las Indias
Pl del Triunfo s/n, T954 500 528, www.mcu.es. Mon-Sat 0930-1700, Sun 1000-1400. Free.
In the 18th century this square and sober Renaissance building was converted into the state archive. It's a fascinating record of the discovery and administration of empire; from the excited jottings of Columbus to mundane book-keeping of remote jungle outposts.

Casa de Pilatos
Plaza de Pilatos s/n, T954 225 298, www.fundacion medinaceli.org. Nov-Mar 0900-1800, to 1900 Apr-Oct, €6 lower floor, €8 both, free Tue from 1300.
A stunning 15th-century blend of Renaissance classicism and Mudéjar styles.

Torre del Oro.

Where to stay

With dozens of hotels in renovated old Seville mansions, there's a wealth of attractive, intimate lodgings to choose from.

Alfonso XIII €€€
C San Fernando 2, T954 917 000, www.hotel-alfonsoxiii.com.
One of Spain's most luxurious hotels, this huge neo-Moorish building is beautifully decorated with opulent patios. The hotel is 5-star in every sense of the word, with prices around €300-500 per room.

Corral del Rey €€€
Corral del Rey 12, T954 227 116, www.corraldelrey.com.
This boutique hotel is a faultlessly realized restoration of an historic palacio, with an irresistible romantic ambience.

Las Casas del Rey de Baeza €€
Pl Jesús de la Redención 2, off C Santiago, T954 561 496, www.hospes.es.
An enchanting old building surrounding a communal courtyard near Casa Pilatos, superbly restored. Rooftop pool and terrace as well as a beautifully decorated library and lounges.

Hotel Alminar €€
C Álvarez Quintero 52, T954 293 913, www.hotelalminar.com
This solid three-star hotel trades in warm personal service; with only a dozen rooms, it feels like they've got time for all their guests.

Hotel Amadeus €€-€
C Farnesio 6, T954 501 443, www.hotelamadeussevilla.com.
A lovely small hotel with a classical music theme. Some rooms are fabulous, some merely excellent. Roof terrace with views of the centre and the Giralda. Highly recommended.

El Rey Moro €
C Lope de Rueda 14, T954 563 468, www.elreymoro.com.
Sitting between 2 central Santa Cruz streets, this excellent hotel is built around a large 3-storey patio with wooden columns.

YH Giralda €
C Abades 30, T954 228 324, www.yh-hoteles.com.
This is a minimalist marble-decorated hotel in a great but quiet location. Good service and elegant, comfortable rooms are value at any time but real bargains off-season.

Restaurants

Your best moments in Seville are likely to be spent eating. Tapas were invented here, and it's one of the places in Spain where they're done best. There's little distinction between tapas bars and restaurants, so we've listed them all together. A standard tapa will cost €2-3. The menú del día, a filling, set price 3-course lunch (1330-1530 roughly) normally costs €8-14.

Abades Triana €€€
C Betis 69, T954 286 459, www.abadestriana.com.
This Triana riverbank restaurant occupies a hard-to-miss modern building that's all glass and light, offering wonderful views over the Guadalquivir and across to the old town. You pay for the view but quality is good, with very tasty fish dishes and an inventive tapas degustation menu. The location is especially seductive at night.

Taberna del Alabardero €€€
C Zaragoza 20, T954 502 721.
Hospitality school and one of the city's best restaurants, with a delicious seasonal menu. House specials include *corvina* (sea bass). Downstairs is an atrium bar serving snacks and *raciones*.

Bar Pepe Hillo €
C Adriano 24, T954 215 390. 1200-0100.
A legend in its own tapas time, especially for stews and croquettes. High-ceilinged and buzzing.

Bodega Santa Cruz €
C Rodrigo Caro 2, T954 213 246. 1200-2400.
A busy and cheerful bar serving some of Seville's choicest tapas and *montaditos* (delicious little toasted sandwiches).

Casa Morales €
C García Vinuesa 11, T954 221 242.
Great old traditional place with big sherry jars, *montaditos*

served on wooden trays, and the tab chalked up on the bar in front of you.

La Blanca Paloma €
C San Jacinto 49, T605 816 187.
This cheerful Triana venue is a fantastic place for tapas and meals, with a philosophy of originality combined with good humour and high-quality ingredients.

La Goleta €
C Mateos Gago, Barrio Santa Cruz, T954 218 966.
Tue-Sun 0900-1500, 2000-2300. Tiny bar with loads of character. Limited but excellent tapas, particularly the 'candid' tortilla.

Nightlife

Seville's nightlife can't compete with Barcelona or Madrid but around Plaza Alfalfa and Calle Betis in Triana it's usually lively into the wee small hours. While much of the flamenco is geared to tourists, the quality of these performances is usually high, even if the atmosphere's a bit sterile. It's also possible to track down a more authentic experience; many bars have dedicated flamenco nights. The quality varies but the cost is minimal and occasionally you'll see something very special. At weekends things liven up in other parts of the city: the Viapol zone in the new town, Nervión, has a vibrant local scene, with heaps of bars and discotecas, and the character-packed Alameda de Hércules buzzes with a fairly alternative set.

Shopping

Seville's main shopping area is the Centro around **Calles Sierpes**, **Tetuán**, **Velásquez**, **Cuna** and **Plaza del Duque**. This busy area is the place to come for clothes, be it modern Spanish or essential Seville Feria fashion: shawls, flamenco dresses, mantillas, ornamental combs, fans and castanets. Head to the **Alameda de Hércules** area for more offbeat stuff. If it's ceramics you're after, **Triana** is the place to go; there are dozens of attractively decorated shops. Most can arrange reasonably priced secure international delivery.

Ratings

Art and culture ☆☆☆
Eating ☆☆☆
Nightlife ☆☆☆
Shopping ☆☆☆
Sightseeing ☆☆
Value for money ☆☆
Overall city rating ☆☆☆

Stockholm

Elegantly built over several small islands, Stockholm can lay a fair claim to having one of the world's most beautiful city locations. In recent years it has shed its reputation as a provincial backwater and transformed itself into a far more cosmopolitan and dynamic place. No longer blond or bland, the city now pulsates with a creative energy that has helped form an urban culture with its sights firmly set on the world stage. Synonymous with both high design and hi-tech, it remains an eminently manageable and civilized place whose laid-back charm is reflected in its friendly, confident inhabitants, around a quarter of whom were born outside Sweden. Predominately young, these "new Swedes" are changing the way Stockholm thinks about itself.

Streets of old town.

At a glance

The most important of Stockholm's 14 islands are those on which the city centre is built, only a few metres from the mainland. Stadsholmen, better known as **Gamla Stan**, is a mixture of narrow lanes and grand buildings, while adjacent **Riddarholmen** is also rich in historical associations. **Skeppsholmen**, to the east, has the ultra-cool modern art museum, while **Kungsholmen** to the west, houses the iconic City Hall. To the south, **Södermalm** is the biggest island and one of the city's main entertainment districts. Here, around the central **Medborgarplatsen**, you'll find bars and restaurants that reflect the cosmopolitan, design-led influences of 'new' Sweden. This is also the centre of Stockholm's relaxed gay scene.

The modernist-inspired **city centre** is on the mainland to the north, 10 minutes from **Södermalm**. The streets around **Stureplan** offer exclusive clubbing and shopping, while **Vasastaden** is a busy commercial hub centred around T-Centralen train station.

Heading east from the city centre along the waterfront to the island of **Djurgården** is one of the most beautiful walks in any European city. Boasting three of Sweden's biggest attractions (Gröna Lund amusement park, Skansen and the Vasa museums), Djurgården is also a great place to relax in rural tranquillity.

Gamla Stan

Metro Gamla Stan. Map C5.

This island is the site of the majority of Stockholm's historic buildings and has been the stage on which much of Swedish history has been played out. Gamla Stan combines a residential area with a selection of government and royal buildings, not to mention plenty of cafés in its narrow streets with gabled roofs.

Just behind the main square, **Stortorget**, is Stockholm's impressive Cathedral and Royal Church, **Storkyrkan**, *Trångsund 1, Sep-May daily 0900-1600, Jun-Aug Mon-Fri 0900-1700, Sat-Sun 0900-1600, SEK40, guided tours Wed 1015 and Thu 0915, at no extra cost.* It is ornately decorated and has a number of important baroque artworks including the outstanding *St George and the Dragon* (Berndt Notke) from 1489.

Royal Palace (Kungliga Slott)

www.kungahuset.se.
Times vary; some sections closed during state visits. SEK150. Metro Gamla Stan. Map C4.

The massive bulk of Nicodemus Tessin's building dominates central Stockholm and is a powerful statement of the ambitions of the Swedish monarchy in the 18th century. Replacing an earlier palace that burnt down, it was completed in several stages and finally occupied in 1754. The austere façade is guarded by several stone lions. Its sumptuous interior is undeniably impressive and about as far as you can get from modern Swedish minimalism.

During state visits the Royal Apartments are closed but the three museums within the palace stay open and contain some interesting collections associated with the monarchy. The changing of the guard, which takes place at 1215 every day (1315 on Sunday), is a well-drilled reminder that the Swedish monarchy is still solidly in place.

Vasa Museum (Vasamuseet)

Galärvarvsvägen 14, Djurgården,
T08 5195 4800, www.vasamuseet.se.
Sep-May daily 1000-1700, Wed 1000-2000;
Jun-Aug daily 0830-1800. SEK130.
Bus 47 or 69 from Central Station. Map E3.

In 1628, at the height of Sweden's military power, the warship *Vasa*, which was to be the flagship of

Below: Vasa Museum.
Opposite page: Royal Palace.

the Swedish navy, made its maiden voyage. It sank barely one mile out to sea. The story of the building of the *Vasa*, its demise and rescue from the seabed is well told in this purpose-built museum. There is plenty of historical background and multimedia displays but the main draw is the ship itself. It is huge and its stern has an impressive number of warlike figures and martial symbols.

Skansen

Djurgården, T08 442 8000, www.skansen.se.
May-Jun daily 1000-1900; Jul-Aug daily 1000-2200; Sep daily 1000-1800; Oct-Apr daily 1000-1500. From SEK100. Bus 47 from Central Station or 44. Off map.

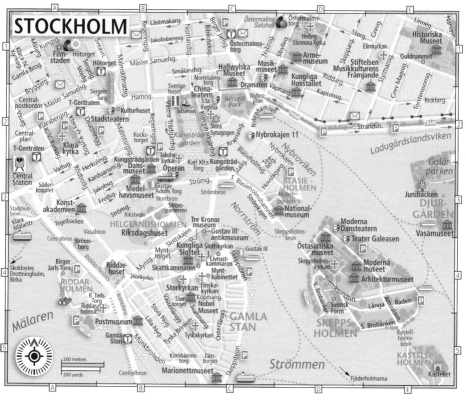

STOCKHOLM

Above: City Hall.
Below: Stockholm panorama.

Best of the rest

Hallwylska Museum
Hamngatan 4, T08 519555, www.hallwylskamuseet.se.
Tue, Thu-Sun 1200-1600, Wed 1200-1900. SEK70. Map C1.
A remarkably opulent house standing as a monument to the various collections built up over a lifetime by its magpie-like owners.

National Historical Museum
Narvavägen 13-17, T08 5195 5600, www.historiska.se.
Sep-Apr Tue-Sun 1100-1700, Wed 1100-2000; May-Aug daily 1000-1700. SEK80.
Ancient gold, art from the Romanesque and Gothic periods plus the world's oldest carpet and a unique Viking collection out in Östermalm.

Stadshuset (City Hall
Hantverkargartan 1, T08 5082 9058, www.international. stockholm.se/cityhall. Tours every 30 mins in summer (0930-1600) and every hr in winter (1000-1500). SEK100 with Metro T-Centralen.
The Blue Room, modelled on an Italian Piazza, and the Byzantine-inspired mosaics are the highlights of this iconic building which hosts the Nobel Prize dinner; you can try the menu in the Stadshuskälleren cellar restaurant.

The prototype of all open-air museums, Skansen holds a sentimental place in every Swede's heart. A kind of Noah's Ark for Swedish rural buildings and industry, it first opened its doors in 1892. All the buildings were moved here from other parts of Sweden in an attempt to preserve a rural heritage that was rapidly disappearing with industrialization. There are displays of traditional crafts and a collection of Scandinavian animals including bears and elks. The summer-only open-air theatre hosts sing-a-long concerts which are an unmissable celebration of all things Swedish.

Nationalmuseum

Södra Blasieholmshamnen, T08 5195 4300, www.nationalmuseum.se.
Mon, Wed, Fri-Sun 1000-1800, Tue and Thu 1000-2000. SEK 100. Metro Kungsträdgården. Map D3.

The paintings housed in this elegant building reflect all periods of art history. Highlights include Lucas Cranach's portrait of Martin Luther from 1526 and some fine Rembrandts. Swedish painters such as Larsson and Zorn are also well represented. The other permanent collection focuses on Swedish design and is a must-see for anyone who has ever bought IKEA furniture or marvelled at a cleverly designed household appliance.

**Museum of Modern Art and
Swedish Museum of Architecture**

*Exercisplan, Skeppsholmen, T08 5195 5200,
www.arkdes.se, www.modernamuseet.se.*
Wed-Sun 1000-1800, Tue 1000-2000. SEK50-
SEK120. Metro Kungsträdgården. Off map.

Located on the city centre island of Skeppsholmen
and housed in the same converted military
building, these museums are rapidly becoming
Swedish design icons. The Modern Art museum's
permanent collection includes Magritte's *The Red
Model* and paintings by Picasso, Dali and Matisse.

The outstanding Museum of Architecture has
a permanent display illustrating the history of

Swedish urbanism as well as temporary exhibitions.
There is an excellent restaurant and café.

Östermalms Saluhall

Östermalmstorg, www.ostermalmshallen.com.
Mon-Thu 0930-1800, Fri 0930-1900, Sat
0930-1600. Metro Östermalmstorg (take the
Östermalmstorg/Nybrogatan exit). Map D1.

This superb indoor market, in a late 19th-century
characterful building, is the place to visit for
good food, either in the form of ingredients or
handmade meals, including takeaways that are perfect
for a picnic. Choose anything from sushi to Swedish
specialities at over 20 stalls, delis, cafés and restaurants.

Travel essentials

Getting there
Stockholm is served by four international airports,
www.swedavia.com. The main one, **Arlanda**, T08 797
600, is 45 km from the city. **Arlanda Express** trains,
www.arlandaexpress.com, depart from underneath
the terminal to T-Centralen (20 mins; SEK490 return).
Buses run by **Flygbussarna**, www.flygbussarna.se,
leave every 15 mins for the 40-min journey to the
centre and cost SEK99 single, SEK198 return. A taxi will
cost SEK500 and takes around 45 mins (**Stockholm
Taxi**, T08 150 000, www.taxistockholm.se).

Skavsta airport, T01 552 804, is 100 km from the
city and is the base for budget airlines. Buses to and
from Stockholm take 80 mins and cost SEK139 single,
SEK268 return. A taxi will cost around SEK1450; contact
Nyköping Taxi, T01 5521 7500.

Västerås airport, T021 805 600, is 85 km from the
city. **Flyggbussarna** takes 75 mins and charges SEK268
return. A taxi will cost about SEK1700 and take an hour
(**Västerås Taxi**, T021 185 000).

From **Bromma Airport**, T08 797 6874, the 20-min
journey with **Flyggbussarna** costs SEK150 return. A taxi
(**Stockholm Taxi**, T08 150 000) will take 15 mins and
cost about SEK300.

Mainline **train services** all run from **T-Centralen**
and are operated by either Swedish Rail (www.sj.se)
or Connex (www.veolia-transport.se). The high-speed
X2000 tilting train links Stockholm with Copenhagen
in around 5½ hrs.

Getting around
Central Stockholm is compact and easily walkable.
Stockholm Transport, www.sl.se, operates the
efficient metro system as well as local buses and
commuter trains. Tickets valid for 24 or 72 hrs
(SEK115 or SEK230) allow unlimited access to the
whole network. **Ferries** to the archipelago (see
box on page 293) are run by **Waxholmsbolaget**,
T08 679 5830, www.waxholmsbolaget.se, and
Strömma Kanalbolaget, T08 587 140, www.
stromma.se, and depart from Nybroplan on the
mainland. **Rentabike**, T08 660 7959, www.rentabike.se,
is well established and reliable. Canoe hire is available
from **Djurgårdsbrons Sjöcafé**, T08 660 5757.

Tourist information
The **Stockholm Tourist Centre** is the first port of call
for the city's visitors, Vasagatan 14, T08 5082 8508,
www.visitstockholm.com, Jan-Apr and mid-Sep to Dec
Mon-Fri 0900-1800, Sat 0900-1600, Sun 1000-1600;
May to mid-Sep Mon-Fri 0900-1900, Sat 0900-1600,
Sun 1000-1600. It books hotels and city tours, offers
free Wi-Fi and sells Stockholm Cards.

Exchange rate
Swedish Krona (SEK). £1 = SEK10.6. €1 = SEK8.9 (Nov
2013).

Where to stay

Finding reasonably priced accommodation in Stockholm can be a challenge, and you are advised at all times to book well in advance. Most places to stay in the centre have discounted weekend rates or other special offers. Try the tourist office website, www.stockholmtown.com, for bed and breakfast accommodation.

Grand Hotel €€€
Södra Blasieholmshamnen, T08 679 3500, www.grandhotel.se.
Metro Kungsträdgården.
Stockholm's most famous hotel has an unrivalled position on the waterfront and is unsurpassed for class and service. Its exquisite bar is a good place to spot a famous face.

Rival Hotel €€€
Mariatorget 3, T08 5457 8900, www.rival.se.
Metro Mariatorget.
Stylish and classy hotel in central Södermalm with individually designed rooms. The hotel is owned by Benny (from Abba) and if one of his musicals is in town there are good-value packages on offer.

Hotel Stureplan €€
Birger Jarlsgatan 24, T08 440 6600, www.hotelstureplan.se.
Beautiful boutique hotel that seamlessly blends modern and traditional when it comes to design. It offers a fantastic base for exploring the city, located in the best neighbourhood. The mammoth buffet breakfast allows you to fuel up for the day ahead.

Victory Hotel €€
Lilla Nygatan 5, T08 506 400 00, www.thecollectorshotels.se.
Named after Lord Nelson's *HMS Victory*, the hotel oozes charm and is located in the city's historical Old Town. In honour of its name, the Victory is jammed to the gills with an extensive collection of marine antiques lovingly collected by its owner. The collection itself attracts visitors to the hotel.

STF Hostel af Chapman €
Flagmansvägen 8, Skeppsholmen, T08 463 2266, www.svenskaturistforeningen.se.
Deservedly famous central hostel. Most of the rooms are land-based but some are aboard an old clipper moored to Skeppsholmen. Book well in advance if you want one of these. There is also a bar.

Restaurants

Swedish food has undergone something of a revolution in the past few years with the opening of a wave of international restaurants. Södermalm is the best place to find these, while Gamla Stan has traditional Swedish food of a high quality and price.

Den Gyldene Freden €€€
Österlånggatan 51, T08 249 760, www.gyldenefreden.se.
Mon-Thu 1130-1430, 1700-2200, Fri 1700-2300, Sat 1300-2300. Metro Gamla Stan.
Sweden's oldest restaurant has been around for over 200 years. The fish-heavy menu always has some Nordic influences. Romantic and classy.

Gondolen på Södermalm €€€
Katarinahissen, Stadsgården 6, T08 641 7090, www.eriks.se.
Mon-Fri 1130-1430, 1700-2300, Sat 1600-2300 (cocktail bar open until 0100 Mon-Sat). Metro Slussen.
Sitting on top of the KF Huset at Slussen (take the lift from the waterfront), this is one of Stockholm's best restaurants. The modern menu competes with the decor for sophistication,

and the view from the restaurant is spectacular.

Restaurang Prinsen €€
Master Samuelsgatan 4,
T08 611 1331,
www.restaurangprinsen.eu.
Mon-Fri 1130-2330, Sat 1200-2330, Sun 1300-2230.
Having first opened its doors over a century ago, Prinsen is well and truly established as the city's top bohemian eatery. Artists and writers rub shoulders with tourists, all there to soak up the special atmosphere and enjoy the excellent Swedish and Continental dishes on offer.

Le Bar Rouge €
Brunnsgrand 2-4, T08 505 244 33,
www.lerouge.se.
Le Bar and its sister restaurant downstairs, Brasserie Le Rouge, shouldn't be confused as being the same place. For affordable lunches and a selection of small dishes stay upstairs and chill in the French Boudoir. For something more substantial you can head to the Brasserie in the evening but be prepared to dig a little deeper into your pockets.

€ Ortagarden
Nybrogatan 31, T08 662 1728,
www.ortagarden-gastrogate.com.
This is the city's oldest vegetarian restaurant. It offers a never-ending buffet, crammed full of fresh vegetarian dishes. The interior has an old-fashioned feel, with its high ceilings and stylish

decor, making it a relaxing place to pull up a chair and while away an afternoon.

Nightlife

Going out in central Stockholm is an expensive, flashy affair that involves a lot of queuing. The pubs around Medborgarplatsen and Frihemsplan are more relaxed. The best option is to pick a place with live music and spend the evening there.

For clubs, **Berns**, *Berzelii Park, T08 5663 2222, Metro Östermalmstorget*, is an impressive complex tucked away at the back of Berzelii Park, with a relaxed atmosphere and a young crowd. Book in advance to get to the **Absolut Ice Bar**, *Nordic Sea Hotel, T08 5056 3520, SEK180 entrance including drink*. You're only likely to go here once, but it's an unforgettable experience: after donning your silver parka you will be served a drink in a bar where everything is made of ice. **The White Room**, *Jakobsbergsgatan 29, T08 5450 7600, www.whiteroom.se*, is an incredibly trendy club that attracts an über-cool crowd. For live music, check out one of **Debaser**'s 2 venues at *Karl Johans Torg 1*, or *Medborgarplatsen 8, www.debaser.se*; both host Swedish and international bands.

Stockholm's islands

With picturesque red houses, perfect beaches and beautiful scenery, the thousands of islands which make up Stockholm's archipelago make an excellent place for an excursion from the city. No matter how short your time in Stockholm a day trip should be a priority. Stockholmers are very proud of having the islands on their doorstep and the lucky ones try to commute by boat during the summer.

The islands vary in size and character. Some, like **Vaxholm**, are lived on all the time, while others have no permanent population. Geographically they are divided into the Northern, Middle or Southern archipelago depending on their position in the Baltic. The closest are the **Fjärderholmarna islets**, about 25 minutes by boat. Vaxholm is a year-round option and a good introduction to the archipelago.

Some of the islands can be reached by ferry throughout the year from Nybroplan on the mainland. The main companies operating ferries to the archipelago have detailed information on their websites. Waxholmsbolaget and Strömma Kanalbolaget are the biggest operators (see Travel essentials box). The tourist office website, www.visitstockholm.com, has details of individual islands and accommodation options. For details of how to book longer stays in wooden cottages on the archipelago, refer to www.visitsweden.com.

Ratings

Art and culture ☆☆☆
Eating ☆☆☆
Nightlife ☆☆☆☆
Shopping ☆☆
Sightseeing ☆☆☆
Value for money ☆☆☆
Overall city rating ☆☆☆

Valencia

Valencia once languished in the shadow of flashy Madrid and trendy Barcelona but its days as a wallflower are long over. The word is out: Valencia, with its vibrant medieval core, its fantastic nightlife, shopping and restaurants, its sandy beaches and some of the most spectacular contemporary architecture in Europe, is the hottest destination on the Mediterranean. The city has twice hosted the America's Cup, and the Formula 1 Grand Prix takes place here every other year. The new marina and entertainment zone, an extended metro and a slew of slick amenities have cemented the city's position as one of the most forward-looking destinations in Spain. But its traditional charms – the palm-lined boulevards, baroque belltowers, Modernista markets and golden beaches – still assert their pull. It's a city in which old and new, shabby and sleek, co-exist peacefully.

Lights in the streets of Valencia for Las Fallas.

La Seu and El Micalet (Catedral and El Miguelete)

*Pl de la Reina 1, T963 918 127,
www.catedraldevalencia.es.*
Cathedral and museum: summer Mon-Sat
1000-1830, Sun 1400-1830; winter Mon-Sat
1000-1730. Micalet 1000-1300, 1630-1900, Sun
1000-1300, 1700-1930. Cathedral €4/€3, museum
€1.20/€0.80, Micalet €2/€1.50. Bus 6, 16, 28. Map B2.

Plaça de la Reina, a long, elegant space surrounded
by cafés and palm trees, is one of the city's most
important squares. (It's also the most touristy: you
can't miss the horse-drawn carriages clattering
around the narrow streets for a fat fee.) It's
dominated by Valencia's vast and imposing
cathedral, topped with the city's much-loved
symbol, the octagonal bell tower known as the
Micalet. It was largely completed by the end of the
15th century but, in the late 1700s, baroque
craftsmen added the florid façade, with its thickly
encrusted sculptural decoration and swooping lines.
The cathedral's greatest treasure is kept in the
Capilla del Santo Cáliz, where a jewel-encrusted

Cathedral in Reina Square.

chalice carved from agate is set into a pale alabaster
altarpiece that fills an entire wall. (Drop a euro in the
machine to light up the altarpiece for full operatic
effect.) The chapel sits next to the Sala Capitular, which
houses the cathedral **museum** with a fascinating
collection of religious art, statuary and sculpture.
A separate entrance leads to the **Micalet**, the
slim bell tower with lacy Gothic tracery. Huff and
puff up the 207 steps for staggering views across
the blue-tiled cupolas, baroque towers and
higgledy-piggledy maze of the Old City.

At a glance

Valencia divides neatly into three general areas,
each with a distinctive atmosphere. The **Old City**,
4 km inland, is still the heart of Valencia, home to
most of the sights and the best selection of nightlife
and shopping. It's the perfect neighbourhood for a
wander – you won't need public transport. Spreading
out from the Old City eastwards to the sea is the **New
City**, a largely anonymous area of bland offices and
apartments, but also the site of the glittering **Ciutat
de les Arts i les Ciències** (City of Arts and Sciences).
It's quite a walk (around 3 km) from the Old City, but
a pleasant stroll along the gardens which line the
former riverbed of the Riu Túria. The New City links
the Old City with Valencia's vast working **port** (El
Grau), its glossy new marina and the main city beach
of **Malvarrosa**. This long, golden stretch is lined
with a modern promenade, behind which are the
scruffy, cheerful neighbourhoods of **Malvarrosa** and
Cabanyal which once belonged to the dock workers
and fishermen.

Mercat Central (Mercado Central)

*Pl del Mercat, T963 829 100,
www.mercadocentralvalencia.es.*
Mon-Sat 0730-1430. No fish market on Mon.
Bus 26, 27. Map A2.

Southwest of the cathedral in the other main square
of the old city, Valencia's central market
is one of the most beautiful in the country, a vast
Modernista concoction of wrought iron and stained
glass surmounted with cupolas and whimsical
weathervanes. The Comunitat Valenciana isn't
known as 'Spain's orchard' for nothing: inside you'll
find a breathtaking array of colourful, fresh produce
displayed on around 400 stalls. The market is always
busy, but get there early to catch it in full swing –
breakfast at one of the dozens of stalls inside the
market or tucked around the edges is an institution.

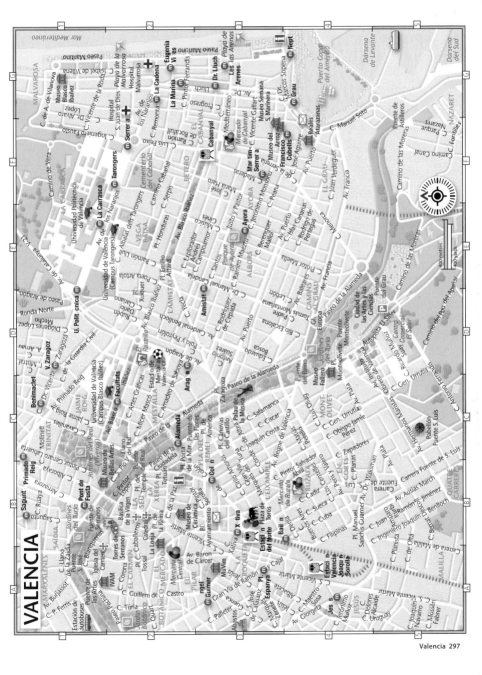

VALENCIA

Around the city

La Llotja (La Lonja)

C/Lonja 2, T962 084 153.
Winter Mon 1000-1400, Tue-Sat 1000-1900,
Sun 1000-1500; summer Tue-Sat 1000-1800,
Sun 1000-1500. €2/€1, free Sun (for stamp
and coin market) and public hols.

The silk exchange is quite simply the most
beautiful building in Valencia. Sitting squarely
opposite the main entrance to the central market,
it is one of the finest examples of civic Gothic
architecture in Europe and was declared a World
Heritage Monument by UNESCO in 1996.
Construction began in 1483 under the direction
of the brilliant Pere Compte, a master stonemason,
engineer and architect. The project was completed
in just 15 years. The splendid main hall, the **Sala de
Contratación**, is vast, with a lofty, vaulted ceiling
which reaches almost 18 m at its highest point.
To feel an echo of the buzz that would have
animated the Llotja 500 years ago, visit it on a
Sunday morning when a popular stamp and coin
market is held in the Sala de Contratación.

Bioparc

*Avda Pío Barjoa 3, 46015 Valencia, T902 250 340,
www.bioparkvalencia.es.*
Bus 7, 17, 29, 61, 81 and 95. Metro to Nou
d'Octubre, then 10-min walk. Open daily from
1000; hours change regularly, so check the
website. €23.80, €18 children 4-12, under 4s free.
Off map.

Take a stroll through the gardens which line the
former Turó riverbed to find one of the city's
biggest attractions: the Bioparc. This 'new-
generation' zoo employs clever landscaping to
recreate the natural habitats of its animal residents,
and has hidden the enclosure fences so that
visitors feel as though they are strolling with
wildebeest or hanging out with the lions.
Unsurprisingly, it's a huge hit with kids.

Ciudad de las Artes y las Cièncias (Ciudad de las Artes y las Ciencias)

Av Autopista al Saler 1-7, T902 100 031, www.cac.es.
Museu de les Ciències mid-Oct to Mar Mon-Thu
1000-1800, Fri-Sun 1000-1900; Apr-Jun and Sep
to mid-Oct daily 1000-1900; Jul-Aug daily
1000-2100. €8/€6.20. L'Hemisfèric: check website
for times and prices. L'Oceanogràfic: Oct to
mid-Jun Sun-Fri 1000-1800, Sat 1000-1900;
mid-Jun to end Jun and mid-Sep to end Sep
Sun-Fri 1000-1900, Sat 1000-2000; early Jul and
early Sep daily 1000-2000; mid Jul-Aug daily
1000-2400. €27.90/€21. Combined tickets also
available from €36.25. Bus 35, 95. Map D4.

Having seen how new architecture revitalized
the fortunes of Barcelona up the coast, Valencia
commissioned the glossy La Ciutat de les Arts i les
Ciències in order to raise its international profile.
The futuristic complex designed by local celebrity
architect Santiago Calatrava has been an
overwhelming success and you may need to book
in advance to get into some of its attractions in the
high season. There are five main sections: **Museu
de les Ciències** (a science museum that looks more
like a 23rd-century airport), l'**Hemisfèric** (laser
shows, IMAX and planetarium), L'**Umbracle** (a
palm-lined walkway), L'**Oceanogràfic** (an aquarium
in a series of beautifully sculpted pale pavilions, the
biggest in Europe), and the **Palau de les Arts** (a
venue for the performing arts). The buildings –
although that seems too tame a term for these
bold, graphic shapes – seem to emerge from the
cool, blue pools that surround them.

Oceanogràfic.

Travel essentials

Getting there
Valencia's International Airport, T902 404 704, www.aena-aeropuertos.es, is in Manises, 8 km west of the centre of town. The metro (lines 3 and 5) runs between the airport and the city centre (journey time 25 mins, single ticket €3.90, free with Valencia Card, see below). There is also a local bus service (line 150, €1.40, journey time 40 mins). Local, regional and some high-speed trains arrive into the Modernista Estació del Nord, near the Old City, while AVE trains arrive at the new Valencia Joaquim Sorolla train station, C San Vicente Martir 171, T902 320 320, www.renfe.com.

Getting around
The Old City is best explored on foot; most of the main sights are within walking distance of each other. An excellent **bus** network will take you to places further afield like La Ciutat de les Arts i Ciències, the port and beaches, and the Llac Albufera. The N1 night bus connects the seaside neighbourhoods with the centre. A single ticket (available on the bus) costs €1.50. Bus Turístic runs a hop-on/hop-off city tour; there are 2 routes and fares are €17 for 24 hrs with discounts for children (under-7s are free). The **metro**

system is largely aimed at commuters, but Line 4 (a tram-line above ground) is handy for the beach at Malvarrosa. Single metro or tram tickets (€1.10) are available from machines in stations. Useful **travel passes** include: BonoBus (10 single rides for €8) and T1/2/3 (1-, 2- or 3-day tickets valid for unlimited transport on bus, tram and metro for €4, €6.70 and €9.70 each). The **Valencia Card** is valid for 1, 2 or 3 days (€15/ €20/ €25) and offers unlimited public transport (including the metro fare to/from the airport), plus discounts in museums, shops and restaurants. It is available from tourist offices, metro stations, some tobacconists and hotels.

Tourist information
Offices at: Pl de la Reina, T963 153 931, Mon-Sat 0900-1900, Sun and hols 1000-1400; Pl de l'Ajuntament, T963 524 908, Mon-Sat 0900-1900 and Sun 1000-1400; C de la Paz 48, T963 986 422, Mon-Fri 1000-1800, Sat 1000-1400; and Estació del Nord, C Jàtiva 24, T963 528 573, Mar-Oct Mon-Fri 0830-2030, Sat, Sun and hols 0930-1730; Nov-Feb Mon-Fri 0830-2030, Sat 0930-1730, Sun and hols 0930-1430, closed 1-6 Jan, 25 Dec, www.turisvalencia.es, www.valencia.es.

Platjes (Beaches)

North: bus 1, 2, 19, 31, 32 and summer-only services 20, 21, 22. South: to El Palmar with Autocares Herca approximately every hr in winter, every half hr in summer. Buses are yellow; take buses 'El Perellò' or 'El Palmar', fares from €2, approx. 30 mins.

Heading north of the port is a long sandy beach which runs for several miles. Valencianos usually just call the whole stretch Platja de Malvarrosa, but in fact it is divided into sections: nearest the port is **Platja de Levante** or **Platja Las Arenas**, with a string of restaurants, hotels and bars squeezed next to each other on the Passeig Neptuno. It quickly becomes the **Platja de Cabanyal**, before turning into the **Platja de Malvarrosa**, and finally the **Platja de Alboraia**. The water is a tad murky, owing to the proximity of the port (the beaches south of the city are

cleaner), but it is still fine for swimming. There are rows of stripy beach huts, loungers for rent, snack bars and showers, and the whole length of the beach is backed by a modern promenade lined with palms and an outdoor market in summer. The further north you trek, the fewer people you'll find, but this is still a city beach and you won't find a quiet corner in the height of summer.

The beaches south of the port are quieter, cleaner and wilder than the main city beach of Malvarrosa. They are also harder to get to, unless you have your own transport, and have fewer amenities, so bring a packed lunch and lots of bottled water. The beach of **El Saler** becomes the beach of **La Devesa**, with a small nudist section at its most southerly end. These beaches are backed by beautiful sand dunes and a dense, gnarled pine forest. There are walks through the forest and opportunities to see the birds which make their home around **Llac Albufera**.

Where to stay

Las Arenas €€€

C Eugenia Viñes 22–24,
T963 120 600, www.h-santos.es.
A long neglected 19th-century
spa hotel on the beachfront has
been magnificently transformed
into the city's grandest 5-star
resort hotel. It features
contemporary rooms, most
with sea views, a spa and beauty
centre, and an outdoor pool
set amid extensive gardens.
The service is outstanding.

Caro Hotel €€

C Almirante 14, T963 059 000,
www.carohotel.com.
Chic and central, this boutique
hotel is set in a stylishly restored
former palace. The coolly
elegant guest rooms are
spacious, the fashionable
restaurant a delight, and the
staff are efficient and friendly.

Parador El Saler €€

Platja del Saler, T961 611 186,
www.parador.es.
Yellow metrobus services 190a,
190b, 191, 290 to El Perelló. Ask
to be dropped off at the parador.
A modern hotel overlooking
sand dunes and surrounded by
pine forest. There's an 18-hole
golf course, swimming pool
and good restaurant and the
beaches are empty (well,
sometimes) and golden. It often
has special deals, so check the
website before you go.

7 Moons B&B €€-€

Av Navarro Reverter 13-1,
www.7moons.es.
This friendly B&B offers airy and
elegantly decorated guest rooms
(including one with a private
terrace), which all have flatscreen
TVs and Wi-Fi. A delicious
breakfast featuring home-made
preserves and other treats is
served every morning. The
charming owners are full of
helpful tips and can organize
tickets and excursions if required.

Antigua Morellana €

C En Bou 2, T963 915 773,
www.hostalam.com.
Excellent *hostal* in an 18th-
century mansion just a step
from the Llotja and the Mercat
Central, with charming owners
and clean, well-equipped rooms,
all with bathrooms.

Restaurants

Ricard Camarena Restaurant €€€

C Sumsi 2,
www.ricardcamarena.com.
Tue-Sat 1330-1600 and
2000-2200.
Award-winning creative cuisine by
Ricard Camarena, an exceptional
wine list and exquisite, designer
surroundings make this ideal for a
special meal. Dishes might include
bream with lemon and capers, or
roast kid with an aubergine and
anchovy tartare, all beautifully
presented. Camarena also has a

more affordable bistro, Canalla (C
Maestro José Serrano 5, T963 74 05
09, www.canallabistro.com) and a
tapas bar in the Mercado Central.

Appetite €€

C Pintor Salvador Abril 7,
T961 105 660.
Daily 1400-1600 and 2030-2400
A deservedly popular address
in the fashionable Ruzafa
neighbourhood, this serves
fantastic cuisine from southeast
Asia. Watch your food being
prepared in the open kitchen as
you enjoy one of the excellent
house cocktails.

El Refugio €€

C d'Alt, T963 917 754,
www.refugiorestaurante.com.
Daily 1400-1600 and 2100-2330.
Charming and intimate, this serves
delicious Mediterranean cuisine
with a creative touch in a simple
dining room with changing art
exhibitions on the exposed brick
walls. There are great-value set
meals at lunch time.

El Tap i Altres Terres €€

C Roteros 9, T963 912 627.
Daily 1900-2400.
Simply decorated with
whitewashed walls and wooden
tables, this serves a range of
Mediterranean sharing plates.
There are imaginative salads
and platters of local cheeses
and charcuterie, as well as more
elaborate fare such as langoustine
carpaccio and lasagne with
confit of duck. The wine list is

particularly good, and they often arrange special tasting evenings.

La Pitanza €€
C Quart 5, T963 910 927,
www.lapitanza.com.
Daily 1330-1600 and 2030-2400.
Perfectly located in the fashionable Carme district, this stylish but relaxed spot offers delicious local fare, including rice dishes and seafood, prepared with a modern twist. The food is accompanied by a good selection of local wines – choose from the set menus or go a la carte.

Tapas bars and cafés
Bar El Kiosko
C Derechos 38.
Mon-Sat 0700-2400,
Sun 0700-1600.
This traditional bar doesn't ooze charm, but it has a terrace on the delightful Plaza Dr Collado and serves great-value tapas and simple meals. The staff are cheerful and friendly, too.

Bar Pilar
C Moro Zeit 13, T963 910 497.
Daily 1200-2400.
A timeless old bar just off the Plaça del Tossal, where people order up a portion of mussels and toss the shells in the orange buckets underneath the bar. Give your name to the waiter if you want to get a seat.

Bodega Casa Montaña
C Josep Benlliure 69, T963 672 314.
Mon-Fri 1300-1530 and
2000-2330, Sat 1230-1530 and 2000-2330, Sun and public hols 1230-1530.
Traditional, buzzy tavern still going strong thanks to its excellent wines and tapas.

Bodeguilla del Gato
C Catalans, T963 918 235.
Daily 2000-0200.
Charming and old-fashioned tavern, serving a wide range of classic tapas at reasonable prices. It's always full, so get there early, especially if you want a seat on the terrace.

Café Sant Jaume
C Cavallers 51, T963 912 401.
Daily 1200-0200.
Beautiful little café set in a former pharmacy, with swirling Modernista woodwork. It's in the centre of the city's main nightlife street so it's perfect for people-watching.

Nightlife

Valencia's nightlife is concentrated in different areas. Currently, the trendiest addresses are in the Ruzafa area, just outside the historic centre. The Carmen neighbourhood, within the old city walls, is also packed with restaurants, bars and clubs, and the heart of the gay scene is here on C Quart. There are also bars and clubs near the **university** in the new part of town: check out the streets around the Pl Honduras, near Avinguda Blasco Ibáñez and look out for the following favourites: **Radio City** (Old City), **The Music Box** (club and live music venue), **Akuarela** (by the beach), **Jimmy Glass** (for jazz), **Roxy Club** (New City club). In summer, everyone heads to big outdoor clubs (*terrazas*) in the suburbs. There's plenty going on around the port and along the bar-lined seafront promenade.

Infernal affairs

Les Falles is one of the most important fiestas in Spain. It dates back to the Middle Ages, when carpenters used to light a bonfire in honour of Sant Josep, their patron saint. Gradually, effigies were thrown into the fire, often depicting rival organizations. Now, the vast creations take all year to build and are paraded through the streets from 13 to 19 March. They can be of anything – cartoon characters, politicians, buxom ladies, animals – and each neighbourhood vies to create the best. They are accompanied by mini-versions known as 'Ninots', the winning Ninot being the only one to escape the flames. Each day, firecrackers blast out over Plaça del Ajuntament, bullfights are held and the evenings culminate with a massive firework display. The fiesta finishes with a bang on 19 March when the Falles are thrown into an enormous pyre, the Cremà. You can find out more about the event at **Museu Faller (Museo Fallero)**, *Pl Monteolivete 4, T963-525478, Tue-Sat 1000-1800, until 1900 in summer, Sun and hols 1000-1500. €2/€1, free on Sun and public hols.*

Ratings

Art and culture ☆☆☆☆☆
Eating ☆☆☆
Nightlife ☆
Shopping ☆☆☆
Sightseeing ☆☆☆☆☆
Value for money ☆☆
Overall city rating ☆☆☆☆

Venice

Peerlessly photogenic, Venice can seem like a beautiful relic or a vulnerable novelty without much of a contemporary purpose. A one-time global sea power, the city may or may not actually be sinking but its precarious hold on dry land is increasingly at risk from rising sea levels, and high tides in winter regularly flood its piazzas and streets. It is a gorgeously unlikely city, built on shifting sands, filled with great art, churches and palaces, and wonderfully free from road traffic. And if you can get away from the massed tourists in piazza San Marco to one of the city's less popular corners, you'll find that, despite the *acque alte*, there is life in Venice and no small amount of pride.

Sunrise at San Marco.

At a glance

Most visitors to Venice arrive in the city's far west, from where, once you leave the train or car, all transport is by water or on foot. From here, the **Canal Grande** snakes in a reverse 'S' through the city, crossed only by the Ponte della Costituzione (designed by Santiago Calatrava) between the station and the road terminus at piazza Roma, the Ponte degli Scalzi (by the station), the arcaded Ponte Rialto and the Ponte Accademia. To the north of the canal is the generally quieter district of **Cannaregio**, with **Castello** to the east. South of Cannaregio, **Santa Croce** and **San Polo** are nestled into the first bend of the Grand Canal, with another, more residential area, the Dorsoduro, on Venice's southern edge. In the second bend of the canal is the busy central area of **San Marco** and many of the city's main sights. Orientation in the narrow winding streets is famously hard, though you can get an excellent overview of the city from the top of the Campanile in **piazza San Marco**. Many visitors converge here, having followed a series of signposts that mark out a circuitous route to and from the station, via the Rialto. Around the Venetian lagoon, a ferry ride away, are the islands of **Giudecca**, **Murano**, with its glass-blowing industry, colourful **Burano** and the packed but fashionable beaches of **Lido**.

24 hours in the city

Venice is at its best early in the morning, so get up with the sun, when only locals and workers will be around. Have a *caffè* and *cornetti* in a café (the touristy ones won't open until the trains start arriving a bit later) and check out the fruit and vegetable markets and, especially, the *pescaria* (fish market) in the **Rialto**. Starting early will also enable you to get to **San Marco** before the tour groups and hordes of pigeon feeders. Have a look in the **basilica** and, perhaps, the **Palazzo Ducale** and then climb to the top of the **Campanile** before the crowds get too big. For lunch, pick one of the cafés and restaurants on or around the busy **campo Santa Margherita** in the Dorsoduro, such as *Il Caffe*. From here you are well placed for a wander along the waterside **Zattere** and to take in some art at either the **L'Accademia** or the **Peggy Guggenheim Collection**. Next, head slowly across the city to reach atmospheric **Cannaregio** by supper time, perhaps looking in on a church, such as **Santa Maria dei Frari** in San Polo, and having an ice cream or an *aperitivo* along the way. A boat ride is probably best left until the evening; avoid the twee temptation of a gondola and opt instead for a *vaporetto* up the Grand Canal.

San Marco

Piazza San Marco, www.basilicasanmarco.it.
Apr-Sep Mon-Sat 0945-1700, Sun 1400-1700;
Oct-Mar Mon-Sat 0945-1700, Sun 1400-1600.
Museum €5, Treasury €3, Pala d'Oro €2. Map F4.

Originally built in the ninth century to house the body of St Mark (stolen from Alexandria), the ornate and spectacular basilica of San Marco is the city's cathedral and centrepiece. John Ruskin called San Marco a 'treasure-heap', and its exterior is indeed a bewildering collection of styles and ornamentation, including Gothic spires, medieval mosaics and a group of porphyry figures (the Tetrarchs) in the southwestern corner made from fourth-century Egyptian marble. Built on the Greek cross plan, the Basilica has a large central cupola, with a smaller dome on each arm of the cross. Despite having been rebuilt and redecorated over the years, as the wealth of the empire grew, its

Piazza San Marco.

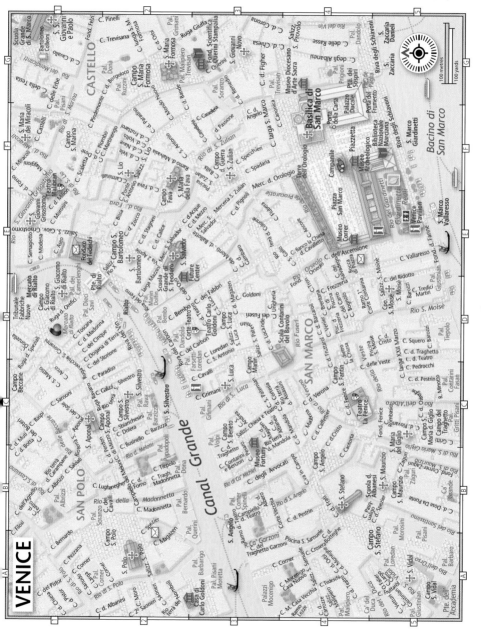

VENICE

Around the city

form has changed little since its consecration at the end of the 11th century.

Highlights of the interior include the 13th-century Rose Window, the dazzling golden mosaics depicting stories from the Bible, and the **Pala d'Oro** – an extravagantly rich golden altarpiece. The basilica **museum** is on the first floor and contains religious treasures and the original bronze horses (probably second-century Roman) that were stolen from Constantinople in 1204. Life-size replicas grace the external balcony (**Loggia dei Cavalli**), from where there are fabulous views over the expansive piazza below, a magnetic gathering point for Venice's pigeons and tourists.

Palazzo Ducale

Piazza San Marco, T041 271 5911.
Apr-Oct daily 0830-1830; Nov-Mar daily 0830-1730. Musei di Piazza San Marco ticket (€16.50) also allows entrance to other museums around the city: Museo Correr, Museo Archeologico and the Sale Monumentali della Biblioteca Marciana. Map G4.

Adjacent to the basilica, the Doge's Palace – largely a result of 14th- and 15th-century construction – combines Verona pink marble with ornate Gothic porticos to great effect. The main courtyard is dominated by the so-called Giants' Staircase, at the top of which each new Doge was crowned. Inside, Domenico and Jacopo Tintoretto's *Paradiso* covers the end wall of the Great Council Hall.

The **Ponte dei Sospiri** (Bridge of Sighs) is an enclosed passageway through which prisoners once walked between their cells and the interrogation rooms in the palace. The best view of it is from Ponte della Paglia, at the palace's southeastern corner.

Campanile di San Marco

Piazza San Marco, T041 522 4064, www.basilicasanmarco.it.
Easter-Jun and Nov daily 0930-1900; Jul-Oct daily 0900-2000; Dec-Mar 0930-1545. €8. Map F4.

The smaller **Torre dell'Orologio**, *on the north side of the piazza, T041 522 4951*, may be more ornate, but the 99-m-high Campanile is easily Venice's most iconic tower. Originally built in the ninth-century, the present incarnation of San Marco's bell tower dates from 1514, although it collapsed in 1902 and was subsequently rebuilt. Views from the top are fantastic: big vistas are rare in the city and here is nearly the whole island laid out in one broad sweep.

Canal Grande

Venice's most famous canal is a 4-km watery highway that snakes through the heart of the city and is currently crossed by just four bridges. A *vaporetto* trip along the canal is a must. Apart from being the quickest way to travel, it's also the best way to see some of Venice's greatest buildings: baroque **Ca' Rezzonico** (see page 308); decorative **Ca d'Oro**, *www.cadoro.org*; Michele Sanmicheli's frescoed **Palazzo Grimani**, *www.palazzogrimani.org, map C3*; Gothic **Ca' Foscari** (now a university) and **Palazzo Barbarigo**, *map A3*, with its Murano glass mosaics.

Ponte Rialto

Map D1.

The city's oldest bridge, originally made of wood, collapsed in 1444 and again in 1524. Antonio da Ponte's stone design was completed in 1591 and has stood ever since, becoming one of Venice's icons. However, the jewellery shops that line the

Top: Rialto Bridge.
Above: Ca d'Oro.
Opposite page: Palazzo Ducale.

That sinking feeling?

Everyone knows that Venice is sinking. However, most recent studies have suggested that the subsidence of the city from 1920 to 1970 has all but stopped and, now, Venice is probably sinking by only 0.5 mm a year – roughly in line with the rest of the Adriatic coast.

That may not be much consolation to local residents as they wade through their city or move their valuables upstairs. The *acque alte* (high waters) are an increasingly frequent problem in winter. High tides combined with wind from the wrong direction brings the sea sweeping across Venice's *campos* and streets and into its buildings. Sirens and a network of raised walkways mean that life goes on, but it's far from a happy situation in which to live. (For information on *acqua alte*, call T04 124 11996 or visit www.comune.venezia.it/maree.)

In part the flooding can be blamed on rising sea levels. The loss of 10 cm of height during the 20th century also contributed. (Most now accept that this was due to the industrial extraction of water from rocks below the surface – a practice that was outlawed in the 1960s.) There is much less agreement about the solution, however. In 2003 the Italian government under Silvio Berlusconi gave their approval to MOSE (nominally the Modulo Sperimentale Elettromeccanico, but with a biblical nod to the holding back of the Red Sea), a grand plan to block the high water with a series of pontoons at the entrances to the lagoon. Costing around €3 billion and due to be completed around 2014, environmentalists think the pontoons will destroy the important ecosystem of the Venetian lagoon. Others point out that a project originally designed in the 1980s may be ineffective to cope with sea levels predicted to rise with global warming.

Dorsoduro

Across the Canal Grande from San Marco is the *sestiere* of Dorsoduro. The wooden **ponte dell' Accademia** leads to Venice's art school, **L'Accademia,** *T041 522 2247, www.gallerieaccademia.org, Mon 0815-1400, Tue-Sun 0815-1915, €9 or more for exhibitions.* It occupies an ex-convent and houses one of Italy's great art collections, including works by Titian, Canaletto, Giovanni Bellini, Tintoretto, Andrea Mantegna and Paolo Veronese. East of here along

arcades of the bridge are expensive and best avoided. Venice's market moved to the Rialto area in 1097. For a glimpse of Venice as it might be without tourists, head to the **Pescaria** (fish market) early in the morning. Next door in the **Erberie** market abundant fruit and vegetables from the Veneto are sold with equal panache.

Cannaregio.

the canal is the **Peggy Guggenheim Collection**, *Palazzo Venier dei Leoni, www.guggenheim-venice.it, Wed-Mon 1000-1800, €14*. Once the collector's home, it now has works by Picasso, Kandinsky, Pollock and a notoriously erect horse rider on view. At the eastern tip of Dorsoduro are the 17th-century custom house and the church of **Santa Maria della Salute**, built to mark the end of a plague epidemic in 1630. On the south side of Dorsoduro, the 2-km **Zattere** quayside is one of the city's best spots for the evening *passegiata*, with great views across to Giudecca island.

Cannaregio

With fewer sights than most other *sestieri*, Cannaregio in the north of the city is perhaps the least touristy Venetian neighbourhood, except along its southern edge. Long parallel canals retain some of their working-class feel and it can be one of the most rewarding parts of the city in which to wander. It also has some of the best restaurants. The **Canale di Cannaregio** was once the main way into the city and has some suitably grand buildings. East of here, three parallel canals have less ostentatious charms. Just south, off Rio di San Girolamo, the **Ghetto Nuovo** was the Venetian Jewish ghetto, created in the 16th century and the origin of the word 'ghetto'. The **Museo Ebraico**, *www.museoebraico.it, Jun-Sep Sun-Fri 1000-1900, Oct-May Sun-Fri 1000-1730, €4*, tells the story of Venetian Jews. In the far east of the district, **Santa Maria dei Miracoli**, *map F1*, is an exquisite early Renaissance church built in the 1480s.

Best of the rest

Burano
vaporetto 12 from Fondamente Nuove.
The colourful houses of Burano are its biggest selling point, but evidence of the island's lace-making heritage can still be experienced in its museum and shops, though genuine hand-woven Burano lace is hard to find.

Ca' Rezzonico
Fondamenta Rezzonico 3136, T041 241 0100, carezzonico.visitmuve.it, €8.50.
Housing the Museum of 18th-century Venice, this is perhaps your best chance to experience the interior of one of Venice's baroque palaces. Giorgio Massari's enormously grand ballroom and paintings by Canaletto and Tiepolo are some of the highlights.

Frari
campo dei Frari, San Polo, T041 275 0462, €3.
An enormous church filled with art by Titian, Giovani Bellini and others, Santa Maria Gloriosa dei Frari is almost always referred to by its shorter name.

Lido
vaporetti from San Zaccaria.
Venice's famously fashionable beach sits on the far side of this long, thin island that serves as the city's barrier to the Adriatic. Just about every grain of sand is occupied in summer and you have to pay (or be staying at smart hotels) for access to many parts.

Murano
vaporetti from Fondamente Nuove.
On this island, a near neighbour of Venice, there is a museum dedicated to Venetian glass and glass-blowing factories that can be visited. There are also some interesting churches.

Museo Diocesano di Arte Sacra
Castello 4312, T041 296 0630, www.veneziaupt.org, €5. Map G4.
The beautiful Romanesque **Chiostro di Sant' Apollonia**, inside the Museum of Sacred Art, is one of Venice's lesser-known architectural beauties and dates from the early 14th century. The museum itself is less impressive, but it does contain some remnants of an earlier version of the Basilica of San Marco that are nearly 1000 years old.

Where to stay

Venice's hotels are, by reputation, expensive and over-booked. It's certainly worth reserving ahead at busy times, especially during the Biennale or the Film Festival. Most of Venice's visitors are day trippers and the advantages of being able to wander around the relatively unfrequented city in the evenings or early mornings far outweigh the price of a room.

Ca' Pisani €€€
Dorsoduro 979/a, T041 240 1411, www.capisanihotel.it.
A Venetian rarity, Ca' Pisani is a chic modern hotel in a 16th-century building. Sharp lines and hip colour schemes contrast effectively with the Dorsoduro surroundings.

Gritti Palace €€€
Campo Santa Maria del Giglio 2467, T041 794611, www.grittipalace.com.
Set on the Grand Canal in a 15th-century palace, this must be this city's most sumptuous hotel. It re-opened in 2013 after extensive restoration and now boasts atmospheric interiors, fine artworks and antiques.

Palazzo Abadessa €€€
Calle Priuli, Cannareggio, T041 241 3784, www.abadessa.com.
This small palace – just 13 rooms – is a little further from the main sights but has a lovely private garden to compensate. Each room is individually decorated.

Hotel Flora €€€-€€
San Marco 2283/a, T041 520 5844, www.hotelflora.it.
Venetian opulence abounds in this building where Titian may have painted. There are lots of antiques and a vine-covered courtyard.

Locanda ai Santi Apostoli €€€-€€
campo Santi Apostoli, Cannaregio 4391/a, T041 099 6916, www.locandasantiapostoli.com.
Some of the city's most reasonably priced views over the Grand Canal, from wooden-beamed rooms.

Pensione Seguso €€-€
Zattere 779, T041 528 6858, www.pensionesegusovenice.com.
On the corner of a canal and the Zattere waterfront in the Dorsoduro, the 2-star Seguso has an English colonial air, decent rooms and some excellent views.

Villa Rosa €€-€
C della Misericordia 389, T041 716569, www.villarosahotel.com.
Very convenient for the station, yet far enough back from the tourist traps of Rio Terrá Lista di Spagna to be quiet, the flower-clad Villa Rosa is an attractive option on the edge of Cannaregio.

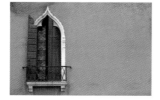

Restaurants

Venice's cuisine is not the city's strong point, but if you find a table outside in a piazza on a warm summer's evening or beside a canal watching the boats go by, then the food will almost certainly taste good. Risotto is a Venice staple, as is seafood, but there are plenty of restaurants specializing in other Italian delights. It's worth bearing in mind that most places close much earlier in the evening (at around 2100) than in the rest of Italy. Eating out is also expensive here. The Dorsoduro and the northwest parts of Cannaregio are the best places to get away from the trilingual menus to experience something cheaper and more traditionally Venetian.

Harry's Bar €€€
San Marco 1323, T041 528 5777.
Closed Mon.
Famous (and wealthy) enough to threaten legal action against places around the world who copy the name, Harry's is a Venetian institution on the Canal Grande. Frequented by film and opera stars, those who can afford the high prices for both food and drink, and those who come just to gawp.

Osteria Enoteca San Marco €€€-€€
Calle Frezzeria, San Marco 1 610, T041 528 5242, www.osteriasanmarco.it.
This former inn is now a popular restaurant serving plenty of

seafood, including crab gnocchi, as well as meaty Venetian classics. Good wine list.

Ae Oche Pizzerie €€
Zattere, Dorsoduro 1414, T041 520 6601, www.aeoche.com.
This trendy newcomer occupies a warehouse on the waterfront with outside tables (weather permitting). It serves some of the city's best pizzas in a lively atmosphere.

Aqua Pazza €€
Campo Sant'Angelo, San Marco 3808/10, T041 277 0688, www.veniceacquapazza.com.
Open late, Aqua Pazza serves truly excellent southern Italian pizzas out in the campo for extortionate prices and with an authentic air of slightly surly chaos. Other good southern Italian options, such as deep-fried vegetables and a mixed fish grill, make the poor service bearable.

Osteria Alla Zucca €€
Ponte del Megio, Santa Croce 1762, T041 524 1570, www.lazucca.it.
Near San Giacomo dell'Orio, this friendly little trattoria is good for vegetarians. The handful of tables outside on the street fill up quickly.

Osteria Anice Stellato €€
Fondamenta de la Sensa, Cannaregio 3272, T041 720744, www.osterianicestellato.com.
Closed Mon, Tue.
A reminder of Venice's one-time status as an important port linking east and west, Anice Stellato uses more spices than are usual in Italian cooking, combining them with Venetian cuisine to good effect. Out of the way on one of Cannaregio's long, quiet canals, this colourful little place usually has more locals than visitors.

Osteria Bea Vita €€
Fondamenta degli Ormesini, Cannareggio 3082, T041 275 9347.
A rarity in Venice: you can sit outside beside a canal and share tables with locals rather than tourists. The good-value lunch menu is pasta- and risotto-based.

El Refolo €
Via Garibaldi, Castello 1580. From 1730 Tue-Sun.
Popular wine bar serving simple snacks and sandwiches, accompanied by a good choice of wines. A great place to soak up some local atmosphere.

La Perla €
Rio Terrà dei Franceschi, Cannaregio 4615, T041 528 5175, www.laperlavenezia.com.
Tue-Sun; closed Aug.
Busy little pizza restaurant: cosy, friendly and always crowded.

Nightlife

Bars
Venice's nightlife is infamously somnolent – wander around the city at an hour when most Mediterranean cities would be sparking into life and you will probably find dark empty streets.

The Dorsoduro is the area that bucks this trend somewhat; **campo Santa Margherita** is the best area for a *giro de ombre* (bar crawl). If you're Venetian, this usually involves the over-consumption of glasses of *spritz*, a misleadingly cheap and quaffable combination of wine, soda water and a bitter, usually Campari, Aperol or Cynar.

Live music
Nightclubs are practically non-existent, though some bars (such as **Il Caffe**, campo Santa Margherita) have live music. The jazz scene is perhaps the least moribund of the Venetian performing arts; try **Paradiso Perduto**, *Fondamenta della Misericordia*, in Cannaregio, for jazz and blues. **La Fenice**, *campo San Fantin, San Marco 1965, T041 2424, www.teatrolafenice.it*, is one of the country's top opera venues, and classical music, especially by Vivaldi, is regularly performed in the city's churches.

Festivals

Venice comes into its own during its many festivals. The most important of these are the **Venice Biennale**, *www.labiennale.org* (Jun-Oct every other year), the world's largest non-commercial contemporary art exhibition; the prestigious **Venice Film Festival** (late Aug, early Sep) and **Carnevale** (Feb), when the city

Travel essentials

Getting there
Venice Marco Polo, T041 260 9240, www.veniceairport.it, is the city's main airport, 19 km by road and 8 km by sea from the city, to the north of the lagoon. It is connected by boat to San Marco and the Zattere regularly (www.alilaguna.it, 1 hr, €15). Water taxis are much more expensive (up to €100 for 4 people) but will take you right to your hotel. Or travel by bus to piazzale Roma, every 30 mins (40 mins, €10).

About 32 km from the city, **Venice Treviso**, T042 231 5131, www.trevisoairport.it, is a small airport used by *Ryanair*. Buses run to and from piazzale Roma to coincide with flights (45 mins; €10 single, €18 return). Alternatively, bus 6 (10-15 mins; €1) runs to Treviso train station every 30 mins for frequent train connections to Venice.

Special day and night rail services connect **Venice Santa Lucia train station** with Paris, Nice, Vienna and Salzburg (www.trenitalia.it). The **Venice Simplon-Orient Express** (www.orient-express.com) luxury train service runs to the city from London or Paris.

Getting around
Despite the canals, the best way to get around is on foot. *Vaporetti* are fairly large passenger boats which ply several routes around and through the city, primarily up and down the **Canal Grande** and the **Canale di Cannaregio** and to other islands in the lagoon. *Traghetti* are gondolas without the silly hats, which cross the Canal Grande at places where there are no bridges. *Vaporetti* tickets cost €7 single, €20 for 24 hrs or €35 for 72 hrs and are available from booths at the stops. *Traghetti* cost €0.50 per crossing; pay the boatman and stay standing, if you can. Gondolas cost €80 for 40 mins for a maximum of 6 people per gondola; the price rises to €100 after 1900.

Tourist information
Azienda di Promozione Turistica, www.turismovenezia.it, has 2 central offices: in piazza San Marco, S Marco 71/f, T041 529 8711, daily 0900-1900, and in the Ex Giardini Reali, T041 529 8711, daily 0900-1900. The **Venice Card** (www.hellovenezia.com) is available as a Senior card (€39.90 for over 30s) and Junior card (€29.90 for under 30s; under-6s free). Valid for 7 days from first use, the card provides free entrance to 11 museums and 15 churches, plus reduced admission to exhibitions and cultural events. There is also a **San Marco Venice Card** (€24.90), which gives free access to 4 museums on St Mark's Square, as well as 3 churches.

heaves with masked revellers and thicker-than-ever throngs of tourists. Look out too for lesser known festivals, such as **Festa di Liberazione**, the Communist Party's annual knees-up in late summer, and the **Festa del Redentore** (Jul), which celebrates the end of the plague of 1576 with a procession from San Marco to Il Redentore, followed by a firework display.

Ratings

Art and culture ★★★★☆
Eating ★★★★☆
Nightlife ★★★☆☆
Shopping ★★★☆☆
Sightseeing ★★★☆☆
Value for money ★★☆☆☆
Overall city rating ★★★☆☆

Vienna

For centuries the most powerful city in continental Europe, Vienna oozes with the memories, traditions, riches and ambitions of Europe's most calculatingly expansionist dynasty: the Habsburgs. Imposing yet florid palatial architecture defines the city, whether lining grand boulevards or set among landscaped parks. The opera house, myriad concert halls and art collections bear testimony to a taste for high culture in a city that harboured Beethoven, Mozart, Brahms, Klimt and Schiele. Traditionally straight-laced and uptight, this one-time outpost of the Cold War now finds itself again at the heart of an expanded Europe that it once would have ruled. Blowing off its cobwebs and newly alive with the influences of its position at a cultural crossroads, it is hard to have a bad time in Vienna.

Detail of the roof of St Stephen's Cathedral.

At a glance

The cultural core of Vienna lies within the city's old town (Altstadt), defined by the **Ringstrasse**, formerly the medieval walls. A tram ride will cast you back to fin de siècle Habsburg times and past the famous **Opera** that echoes with Mozart, Brahms and Beethoven. The **Museums Quarter** (MQ) lies in the southwest of the Ring and consists of the Imperial Palace (now the Kunsthistoriches Museum – one of the most important fine arts museums in the world), the former Imperial Stables with their unique balletic Lippizaner white stallions, and also the MUMOK and Leopold museums of contemporary and modern art. Between your Brueghels and Klimts, you'll be able to enjoy a host of atmospheric, relaxed and even hip bars, restaurants and shops in the ultimate meeting of high art and high life. For film aficionados (and kids) the **Prater funfair** and Ferris wheel of *Third Man* fame lie to the northeast across the Danube. If you'd rather just recline and be Austrian for the weekend, the elegant, tightly packed streets of the Altstadt are home to Vienna's unsurpassable cafés. By day you can follow in the footsteps of Trotsky and Freud with some cake and a whipped-cream coffee, and by night enjoy the studied melange of new-imperial and ultra-modern. Vienna is a long way from the waltzes of Johann Strauss and that famous 1980s pop video by Ultravox.

Der Wiener Ring

In 1857 the Habsburgs razed the city's medieval wall to create a monument to their vanity. This took the form of a grand boulevard circling the centre, lined with extravagant and imposing royal buildings, private residences, vast squares and parks, puffed up monuments and elegant cafés. One hundred and 50 years on it acts as a walk-by window on the Habsburg dynasty and is best viewed by hopping on either the No 1 or No 2 tram; in doing so you will be able to take in, at least from the outside, Otto Wagner's **Post Office** building, the **Vienna Opera House**, the **Imperial Palace**, **Museum of Fine Arts**, the **Burgtheater** and the **University**.

Vienna Opera House.

St Stephen's Cathedral

T01 515 52 3054, www.stephanskirche.at.
Mon-Sat 0600-2200, Sun 0700-220. €1.
U-bahn Stephansplatz, bus 1A, 2A, 3A. Map E2.

Austria's most important Gothic building, Vienna's cathedral was begun in the 12th century although the oldest remaining parts are the Romanesque **Great Gate** and the **Towers of the Heathens**, dating from the 13th century. If you have a head for heights, climb the 343 steps to the top of the 137-m-high **South Tower** (*Steffl* to locals). Gothic was out of vogue by 1579 when the **North Tower** was capped by a cobbled-together Renaissance spire. Inside are a number of treasures, notably the red marble sepulchre of Emperor Frederick III, sculpted from 1467 to 1513 by Niclas Gerhaert van Leyden.

Imperial Palace and Museums Quarter (MQ)

MQ, T01 523 5881 1730, www.mqw.at.
Daily 1000-1900, individual museum times vary.
U-bahn Museums Quartier, Volkstheater, bus 2A, 48A, tram 49. Map A4/A5.

Until the end of the First World War, the Imperial Palace was the centre of the Austro-Hungarian empire. Since then it has been transformed into a veritable empire of the arts. The Museums Quarter ranks as one of the 10 largest cultural complexes in the world, complete with bars and restaurants in which to digest it all. The following are just some of the highlights the area encompasses.

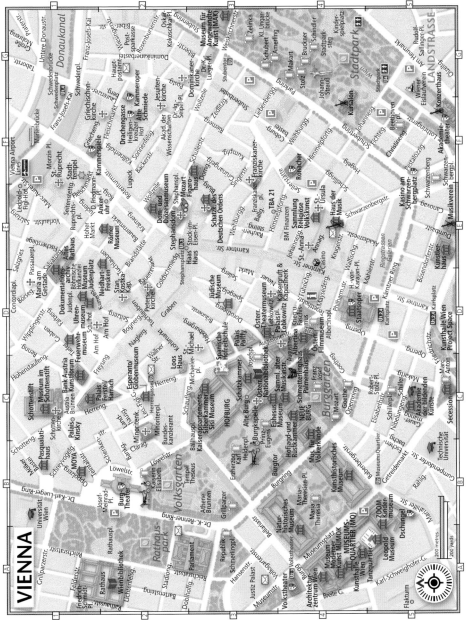

VIENNA

Around the city

Spanish Riding School (Spanische Hofreitschule)

1 Michaelerplatz, T01 533 9031, www.srs.at.
Tue-Sun 0900-1600 (until 1900 on Fri performance days). Guided tours daily 1400, 1500 and 1600, €16. U-bahn Herrengasse, bus 2A. Map C3.

Even if you are not of an equine inclination it is impossible not to be moved by the beauty of the famous Yugoslavian Lippizaner white stallions on display. The art of classical riding taught by the school dates back to the Renaissance. (The stables are some of the few Renaissance buildings in Vienna.) Here you can live the history of these horses and admire gala balletic exhibitions of incredible precision. The impressive riding hall was furnished in baroque style by Joseph Emanuel Fischer von Erlach between 1729 and 1735 and was supposed to provide children of the aristocracy with the chance to take riding instruction. You can watch the morning training sessions and visit the stables.

Kunsthistorisches Museum

1 Maria-Theresien-Platz, T01 525 240, www.khm.at.
Tue, Wed, Fri-Sun 1000-1800, Thu 1000-2100. €13 (€12). U-bahn Volkstheater, Museums Quartier, bus 2A, 57A. Map B4.

Vienna's Museum of Fine Arts was built in 1891 next to the Imperial Palace in order to house the Habsburgs' extensive art collections. During their reign they managed to amass the largest collection of Brueghel paintings in the world, including his *Farm Wedding*, plus Raphael's *Madonna in the Meadow*, Vermeer's *Allegory of Painting*, Velazquez's Infanta paintings and masterpieces by Rubens, Rembrandt, Dürer, van Dyk, Holbein, Titian and Tintoretto. As such, it must surely rank among the most important fine art museums in the world.

Leopold Museum

7 Museumsplatz, T01 52570, www.leopoldmuseum.org.
Wed, Fri-Mon 1000-1800, Thu 1000-2100. €12 (€10.80). U-bahn Museums Quartier. Map A5.

The passionate art lover Dr Rudolf Leopold amassed hundreds of masterpieces and has his own museum to showcase, among other things, the world's largest collection of works by Egon Schiele. Other major artists featured here are Gustav Klimt and Oskar Kokoschka, and furniture and other pieces by Otto Wagner. Combined, they give an insight into early 19th-century Vienna.

MUMOK

T01 52500, www.mumok.at.
Mon 1400-1900, Tue, Wed, Fri-Sun 1000-1800, Thu 1000-2100. €10 (€8). U-bahn Volkstheater. Map A4.

Left: Spanish Riding School.
Right: Schönbrunn Palace.

The Museum of Modern Art traces the path of Vienna's avant garde through Pop Art, Nouveau Réalisme and Vienna Actionism. Warhol, Jasper Johns, Marcel Duchamp, George Brecht and Otto Muehl are all here. MUMOK also presents art history from classic modern works up to the present, ranging from Kupka to Kandinsky.

Schloss Schönbrunn

Schönbrunnner Schlosssstrasse 13, T01 8111 3239, www.schoenbrunn.at.
Apr-Jun and Sep-Oct daily 0830-1730; Jul-Aug 0830-1830; Nov-Mar 0830-1700. From €11.50. U-bahn Schönbrunn, bus 10A, trams 10, 58.

This mouthwatering baroque palace was built around 1700 and is now a UNESCO World Heritage Site. It includes 2000 rooms of wall-to-wall imperial splendour (only 40 can be visited), all set in a symmetrical, classically landscaped garden complete with maze and the world's oldest zoo. Emperor Franz Joseph (1848-1916) was born here in 1830, later marrying the Empress Sisi and keeping her in unsustainable style; he spent the last two years of his reign here.

Sigmund Freud Museum

Berggasse 19, T01 319 1596, www.freud-museum.at.
Daily 0900-1800. €9 (€7.50). U-bahn Schwarzspanierstrasse, bus 40A, trams D, 37, 38, 40, 41, 42. Off map.

Psychology students or anyone who rails against the therapy culture should visit the apartments where it arguably all started. Freud lived and worked here from 1891 to 1938 and all his furniture, possessions, letters, documents, photographs and even an oedipal home movie by his daughter are here.

Travel essentials

Getting there
Schwechat Airport, T01 70 070, www.viennaairport.com, is 19 km southeast of the city centre. The **City Airport Train** (CAT), www.cityairporttrain.com, takes you non-stop to the City Air Terminal at Wien-Mitte junction near Vienna Hilton and St Stephen's Cathedral. Journey time is around 16 mins, daily 0538-2335 (online €11, €17 return). On the way back you can check in at the City Air Terminal. **Vienna Airport Lines** buses link the city to the airport from Schwedenplatz, Südtiroler Platz, the City Air Terminal at Hotel Hilton and Westbahnhof (€8). Journey time is around 20 mins, daily 0500-2400. The S-bahn is the cheapest option. Take line S7 (every 30 mins; journey time 35 mins). Get an Aussenzonen (outer zone) ticket for €4.40 (€2.20 if you have a Vienna Card, see below) and have it punched before entering the train. A taxi costs around €15. Bratislava's **MR Štefánika Airport** in Slovakia is only 60 km east of Vienna and close enough to be an alternative to Schwechat. There are various options for shuttling to and from this airport, as well as car rental desks.

As Central Europe's main rail hub, Vienna has good connections to most other major European destinations. **Eurostar**'s London–Vienna service via Paris takes around 14 hrs. Vienna has several train stations; check whether you're arriving at Westbahnhof, Südbahnhof or Franz Josefs Bahnhof.

Getting around
Vienna is very pleasant for exploring on foot. The city's network of efficient and picturesque trams (especially Nos 1 and 2 which go clockwise and anti-clockwise around the famous Ring), buses or the art nouveau underground system, is easy to use. A single trip costs €2.10, a 24-hr card costs €7.10 and a 72-hr card costs €15.40.

Tourist information
Over 200 discounts are available in the city with the **Vienna Card** (€19.90), available at hotels and the **Tourist Information Centre**, 1 Albertinaplatz, T01 24555, www.wien.info, daily 0900-1900. The card is also available at all sales offices or information booths of the Vienna transport system. It allows unlimited travel by underground, bus and tram, discounts on airport transfer services, reductions (see prices in brackets in Sights section) at museums, theatres, concerts, shops, restaurants, cafés and bars. There's another tourist office in the Arrivals hall at the airport, 0600-2200. **Wien-Hotels & Info**, T01 24555, 0900- 1900, has a hotel booking service.

Where to stay

Vienna is rich in stylish, sometimes overblown, hotels recalling its imperial past, as well as a new breed of design hotels more conscious of the city's contribution to modernism. However, there is not as much choice at the bottom end.

Grand Hotel Wien €€€
Karntner Ring 9, T01 515 800, www.grandhotelwien.com.
Located just a few steps from the Vienna State Opera, this Viennese institution (est.1870) is right in the heart of the city. The 5-star luxury accommodation is matched by the international gourmet cuisine on offer at the hotel's 4 restaurants.

Hotel Sacher €€€
Philharmonikerstrasse 4, T01 514 560, www.sacher.com.
Deliberately and eccentrically old fashioned, this family-run hotel likes to live in a 19th-century time warp. Romantic, at times camp, but never dull, this is the best address for a taste of Habsburg decadence.

Style Hotel €€€
Herrengasse 12, T01 22780, www.stylehotel.at.
Housed in an art nouveau building opposite the city's famous Café Central, the 78 well-appointed, art deco rooms offer every luxury, while delicious Italian cuisine is served in the Sapor restaurant. The bar is increasingly attracting a stylish post-prandial clientele.

Alstadt Vienna Hotel €€
Kirchengasse 41, T01 522 6666, www.altstadt.at.
Old-world pretentions at half the price. This historic patrician's house in the centre of the old city is family-run and comfortably furnished with Italian furniture and striking decor. There are 25 rooms, some with lovely views and plenty of atmosphere.

The Guest House €€
Fuhrichgasse 10, T01 512 1320, www.theguesthouse.at.
The latest addition to the city's thriving boutique hotel scene opened its doors in Oct 2013. Sleek interiors with an über-stylish brasserie and bakery on site should ensure its popularity.

Hostel Ruthensteiner €
Robert Hamerlinggasse 24, T01 893 4202, www.hostel ruthensteiner.com.
The city's 1st independent hostel was founded in 1968 and is still going strong. Clean, bright and very friendly, with a great location only a few mins walk from Westbahnhof train station. Dorms and private rooms available, all with free Wi-Fi.

Restaurants and nightlife

The line between food and fun has been blurred in Vienna, as in many European cities. There are classic Viennese restaurants but as an alternative, or even after your *Wienerschnitzel*, the main focus is on a wide variety of hybrid bar-restaurants and restaurant-clubs. A visit to at least one of Vienna's famous cafés should not be missed.

Steirereck im Stadtpark €€€
Am Heumarkt 2A, Landstrasse1030, T01 713 3168, www.steireck.at.
Mon-Fri 1130-1430 and 1830-2300.
An old gourmet favourite of Vienna foodies. Choose your room for a formal or relaxed ambience. Always grand but refreshingly laid-back.

Café Central €€
Herrengasse 14, T01 533 3764, www.palaisevents.at.
Mon-Sat 0730-2200, Sun 1000-2200.
With its gaudy Gothic vaulted ceiling, this was a favourite of Trotsky and also, allegedly, where Hitler thought up *Mein Kampf*. A piece of the city's heritage as much as any museum.

Chill Out Lounge €€
Salvatorgasse 6, T01525 1213, www.chillout-lounge.at.
Mon-Sat 1700-0200, Sun 1800-0200; food served daily 1800-2330.

Unlike some cocktail bars, this place has a distinct lack of neon signs and chrome bar stools. Instead you'll find cosy rattan chairs and a very relaxed atmosphere. Chill over cocktails without the pretension.

Glacis-Beisl €€

Breite Gasse 4, T01 526 5660, www.glacisbeisl.at.
Daily 1100-0200.
This is affordable and authentic Austrian food at its very best. A very popular haunt for locals, serving up a traditional menu of beef goulash, pork dumplings and some of the city's finest Viennese Schnitzel.

Palmenhaus €€

Burggarten, T01 533 1033, www.palmenhaus.at.
Mon-Thu 1000-0000, Fri-Sat 1000-0100, Sun 1000-2300.
A beautifully renovated palmhouse in the heart of the museum district. Summer seating outside and good quality nibbles year round. On Fri night, the sophisticated air is replaced by a groovy club scene.

Kaffee Alt Wien €

Bäckerstrasse 9, T01 512 5222.
Daily 1000-0200.
A studenty vibe ensures that the intellectual traditions of this café continue over illuminating drinks and a renowned goulash.

The Third Man

In his 1949 story of drug racketeering in war-torn Vienna, film director Carol Reed masterfully turned the city into a towering and brooding character to rival the film's central figure – Orson Welles' Harry Lime. With his sense of Impressionism coupled with stark chiaroscuro, he produced some of the most iconic and memorable scenes in world cinema, the locations of which are easily visited to this day. Harry Lime first appears, or rather a white cat appears at his shiny feet, in the doorway of **No 8 Schreyvogelgasse** before the two set off in a nocturnal chase around the city. The famous Ferris wheel scene, which closes with Lime's immortal (but factually inaccurate) put-down about the Swiss and cuckoo clocks, takes places on the 19th-century **Riesenrad** (Prater 90, T01 729 5430, www.wienerriesenrad.com, check website for times,, €9/8). The 65 m Ferris wheel with its wooden cabins sits within the city's Prater funfair park where there are still many original and traditional carousel rides. The windblown cemetery where Lime is twice buried (alongside Beethoven and Brahms) is the **Zentral Friedhof** on Simmerigen Hauptstrasse. Joseph Cotton stays at the Sacher Hotel, famous for its eponymous cake. If you can stomach it, parts of the sewers, where the film reaches its climax, can be visited by joining a guided **Third Man tour of the city**, www.viennawalks.tix.at.

Point of Sale €

Schleifmühlgasse 12-14, T01 941 6397, www.thepointofsale.at.
Sun-Thu 1000-0100, Fri-Sat 1000-0200.
Late breakfast is the principal attraction here, served into the afternoon as you watch life go by on the lively Schleifmuehlgasse.

Porgy & Bess

Riemengasse 11, T01 512 8811, www.porgy.at.
Originally a porn cinema, a complete refurbishment now sees this building play home to one of Vienna's best jazz clubs from 2030 till late. An eclectic mix of music from around the globe sits alongside traditional jazz. A great place to while away an evening.

Credits

Footprint
Editor: Sophie Blacksell Jones
Editorial assistant: Katrina Rose
Production and layout:
Emma Bryers
Picture editor: Kassia Gawronski
Maps: Gail Townsley, Kevin Feeny
Cover design: Pepi Bluck
Publisher: Patrick Dawson
Managing Editor: Felicity Laughton
Advertising: Elizabeth Taylor
Sales and marketing: Kirsty Holmes

Contributors
Dana Facaros: Carcassonne & Narbonne. Rebecca Ford: Florence, Naples, Perugia, Pisa, Rome, Venice. Jane Foster: Athens, Dubrovnik. Mary-Ann Gallagher: Barcelona, Bruges, Madrid, Valencia. Alan Murphy: Edinburgh. Alex Robinson: London. Rutherford/Tomaseti: Istanbul, Marseille, Milan, Nice, Paris. Andy Symington: Bilbao, Seville. Ally Thomson: Amsterdam, Belfast, Berlin, Brussels, Budapest, Copenhagen, Dublin, Lisbon, Prague, Reykjavik, Stockholm, Vienna.

Print
Printed in Spain by GraphyCem.

Pulp from sustainable forests

Contains Ordnance Survey data © Crown copyright and database right 2013. Licence no 100027877.

Publishing information

Footprint European City Breaks
© Footprint Handbooks Ltd
January 2014

ISBN 978-1-907263-85-9
CIP DATA: A catalogue record for this book is available from the British Library

® Footprint Handbooks and the Footprint mark are a registered trademark of Footprint Handbooks Ltd

Published by Footprint
6 Riverside Court
Lower Bristol Road
Bath BA2 3DZ, UK
T +44 (0)1225 469141
F +44 (0)1225 469461
www.footprinttravelguides.com

Distributed in North America by
Globe Pequot Press, Guilford, Connecticut

Footprint feedback
We try as hard as we can to make each Footprint guide as up to date as possible but, of course, things always change. If you want to let us know about your experiences – good, bad or ugly – then don't delay, go to footprintbooks.com and send us your comments.